Urban Health

Readings in the Social, Built, and Physical Environments of U.S. Cities

Edited by

H. Patricia Hynes and Russ Lopez

Boston University School of Public Health
Boston, MA

JONES AND BARTLETT PUBLISHERS
Sudbury, Massachusetts
BOSTON TORONTO LONDON SINGAPORE

World Headquarters

Jones and Bartlett Publishers
40 Tall Pine Drive
Sudbury, MA 01776
978-443-5000
info@www.jbpub.com
www.jbpub.com

Jones and Bartlett Publishers
Canada
6339 Ormindale Way
Mississauga, Ontario L5V 1J2
Canada

Jones and Bartlett
Publishers International
Barb House, Barb Mews
London W6 7PA
United Kingdom

Jones and Bartlett's books and products are available through most bookstores and online booksellers. To contact Jones and Bartlett Publishers directly, call 800-832-0034, fax 978-443-8000, or visit our website www.jbpub.com.

Substantial discounts on bulk quantities of Jones and Bartlett's publications are available to corporations, professional associations, and other qualified organizations. For details and specific discount information, contact the special sales department at Jones and Bartlett via the above contact information or send an email to specialsales@jbpub.com.

This publication is designed to provide accurate and authoritative information in regard to the Subject Matter covered. It is sold with the understanding that the publisher is not engaged in rendering legal, accounting, or other professional service. If legal advice or other expert assistance is required, the service of a competent professional person should be sought.

Production Credits

Publisher: Michael Brown
Production Director: Amy Rose
Associate Editor: Katey Birtcher
Editorial Assistant: Catie Heverling
Production Editor: Tracey Chapman
Production Assistant: Roya Millard
Marketing Manager: Sophie Fleck

Manufacturing and Inventory Control
   Supervisor: Amy Bacus
Composition: Cape Cod Compositors, Inc.
Cover Design: Kristin E. Ohlin
Cover Image: © Photos.com
Printing and Binding: Malloy, Inc.
Cover Printing: Malloy, Inc.

Library of Congress Cataloging-in-Publication Data
Urban health : readings in the social, built, and physical environments of U.S. cities / [edited by] H. Patricia Hynes and Russ Lopez.
      p. ; cm.
      Includes bibliographical references and index.
      ISBN-13: 978-0-7637-5245-3 (pbk.)
      ISBN-10: 0-7637-5245-2 (pbk.)
   1. Urban health—United States.   2. Public health—United States.   3. Urbanization—Health aspects—United States.   I. Hynes, H. Patricia.   II. Lopez, Russ.
      [DNLM: 1. Urban Health—United States.   2. Environment Design—United States.   3. Health Status Disparities—United States.   4. Public Health—United States.   5. Socioeconomic Factors—United States.   6. Urbanization—United States. WA 380 U7175 2009]
      RA566.3.U73 2009
      362.1'0420973—dc22

                                                          2008014880
6048

Printed in the United States of America
12 11 10 09 08   10 9 8 7 6 5 4 3 2 1

For those who enlightened my life

Pat Hynes

To my late father,
Joe G. Lopez,
who understood the power
of people working together to improve our world

Russ Lopez

Table of Contents

              21st Century   129
              Jonathan M. Samet and John D. Spengler

ARTICLE 7:   Urban Sprawl and Public Health   141
              Howard Frumkin

ARTICLE 8:   Obesity, Physical Activity, and the Urban Environment:
              Public Health Research Needs   169
              Russ Lopez and H. Patricia Hynes

Section III: The Physical Environment   187

ARTICLE 9:   Health, Wealth, and Air Pollution: Advancing Theory
              and Methods   191
              *Marie S. O'Neill, Michael Jerrett, Ichiro Kawachi, Jonathan I. Levy,
              Aaron J. Cohen, Nelson Gouveia, Paul Wilkinson, Tony Fletcher,
              Luis Cifuentes, and Joel Schwartz*

ARTICLE 10:   Examining Urban Brownfields through the
              Public Health "Macroscope"   217
              Jill S. Litt, Nga L. Tran, and Thomas A. Burke

ARTICLE 11:   A Current Appraisal of Toxic Wastes and Race in the
              United States—2007   237
              Robin Saha

ARTICLE 12:   Urban Horticulture in the Contemporary United
              States: Personal and Community Benefits   261
              H. Patricia Hynes and Genevieve Howe

ARTICLE 13:   Cities: The Vital Core   277
              Joel Rogers

              Article Credit Lines   283
              Index   287

List of Figures

List of Tables and Textboxes

About the Article Authors

Douglas S. Massey   Henry G. Bryant Professor of Sociology and Public Affairs, Princeton University

Dennis Raphael   Associate Professor & Undergraduate Program Director, York University

Arline T. Geronimus   Professor in the Department of Health Behavior and Health Education and a Research Professor in the Population Studies Center at the Institute for Social Research at the University of Michigan

Robert J. Sampson   Henry Ford II Professor of the Social Sciences, Department Chair, Sociology Department, Harvard University

Stephen W. Raudenbush   Lewis–Sebring Professor of Sociology and Chairman of the Committee on Education at the University of Chicago

James Krieger   Clinical Associate Professor of Medicine and Health Sciences, School of Public Health and Community Medicine, University of Washington; Chief of Epidemiology Planning and Evaluation, Seattle–King County Department of Public Health

Donna L. Higgins   Centers for Disease Control and Prevention, Atlanta, Georgia

Jonathan M. Samet   Jacob I. and Irene B. Fabrikant Professor in Health, Risk and Society, and Chair, Department of Epidemiology, Johns Hopkins Bloomberg School of Public Health

John D. Spengler   Akira Yamaguchi Professor of Environmental Health and Human Habitation, Department of Environmental Health, Harvard University School of Public Health

Howard Frumkin   Director, National Center for Environmental Health, Agency for Toxic Substances and Disease Registry, Centers for Disease Control and Prevention, Atlanta, Georgia

Marie S. O'Neill   Assistant Professor of Epidemiology, University of Michigan School of Public Health

Michael Jerrett   Associate Professor, Environmental Health
                            Sciences, School of Public Health, University of
                            California, Berkeley

Jill S. Litt   Assistant Professor, Department of Preventive
                            Medicine and Biostatistics and the Environmental
                            Studies Program, School of Arts and Sciences,
                            University of Colorado at Boulder

Nga L. Tran   Department of Health Policy and Management,
                            Johns Hopkins Bloomberg School of Public Health

Robin Saha   Assistant Professor, Environmental Sciences,
                            University of Montana

Genevieve Howe   Director, Environmental Health Campaign,
                            Ecology Center, Ann Arbor

Joel Rogers   Professor of Law, Political Science and Sociology,
                            University of Wisconsin Law School; Contributing
                            Editor, *The Nation*

About the Editors

H. Patricia Hynes is an environmental engineer turned Professor of Environmental Health who works on issues of the urban environment (including lead poisoning, asthma and the indoor environment, safe housing, and urban agriculture); environmental justice; and feminism. She has won numerous awards for her writing, teaching, and applied research, including the 2003 National Delta Omega Award for Innovative Curriculum in Public Health for her course, taught with Russ Lopez, "Urban Environmental Health"; the U.S. EPA Environmental Merit Award for the Lead-Safe Yard Project (2000) and the Healthy Public Housing Initiative (2004); and the 1996 National Arbor Day Foundation Book Award for her book, *A Patch of Eden: America's Inner-City Gardeners*. Professor Hynes was Co-Principal Investigator of the Healthy Public Housing Initiative, an asthma and integrated pest management intervention project in Boston public housing, and co-director of the Lead-Safe Yard Project. She is currently working on a soil-contamination study in Boston's urban gardens and co-directing a regional training center for public health and housing professionals, the Center for Healthy Homes and Neighborhoods.

Russ Lopez, a native of California, received his Bachelor of Science degree in Applied Earth Sciences from Stanford University and his Master of City and Regional Planning degree from the Kennedy School of Government at Harvard University. He has a doctorate in Environmental Health from the Boston University School of Public Health. Past employment includes working on urban and environmental issues for then Lt. Governor John Kerry of Massachusetts. He also worked for 10 years in various positions for the City of Boston on housing, community development, and environmental concerns. Dr. Lopez was the first Executive Director of the Environmental Diversity Forum, a coalition of environmentalists and community activists advocating for environmental justice issues throughout New England. His interests include urban environmental health and the role of the cities, neighborhoods, and the structure of the built environment in public health outcomes. Dr. Lopez has published articles on the health effects of racial segregation, income inequality, and urban sprawl. He is an Assistant Professor at the Boston University School of Public Health.

Introduction

The idea of urban health casts a wide and generous net over people and places, over the health of people living in cities, and over the dignity of their lived environment. Health care and food security, safe housing and neighborhoods, economic opportunity and equality of opportunity for all, environmental protection and nearby green space—each and all of these *social, built, and physical goods* are essential for living well in cities. The plight of working people and immigrants in the newly industrializing, heavily polluted, filthy cities of the nineteenth and early twentieth centuries gripped reformers and unified them to confront the hazardous living and working conditions. After some structural successes, however, interest in urban health waxed and waned throughout the twentieth century in the professional and political imagination, being driven by episodic epidemics, waves of immigrants, war, social activism, and ideological shifts in U.S. politics.[1]

Attention to people living in cities and urban health is on the rise again from many corners of public consciousness. This is spurred, in part, by the fact that we have become a world of cities: More than 50 percent of people now live in cities; and up to three-quarters of the world's population will dwell in cities within a few decades. People and governments on all continents are taking the development path of urbanization, some willingly and some desperately. Another driving factor in the renaissance of urban health is the Healthy Cities movement launched by the World Health Organization in 1986[2] and the more recent New Cities and Cities for Progress (www.citiesforprogress.org) movements in the United States. The confounding social reality—namely that the majority of poor people, people of color, single women with children, immigrants, and the wealthy live in cities such that racial segregation and income inequality are greatest in cities—is another compelling cause for focusing on cities. A fourth dynamic may well be the resurgence of alliances among activists, public professionals, and engaged researchers who share a core goal—healthy people and communities in healthy cities. Here we think of the innovative work of some municipal health departments (www.bphc.org) and hospitals (www.bmc .org/pediatrics/special) to address gender, racial, and ethnic health disparities by both improving health services for women and children, minority residents, and immigrants and also by addressing their housing conditions and nutrition with community-based initiatives. The reemergence of farmers' markets, community gardens, and farms in cities has been catalyzed by urban-centered nonprofit and grassroots organizations that are largely supported by foundations, municipal grants, and federal funds. This recent advance combines the goal of affordable, nutritious food in inner cities with neighborhood rebuilding, engaging urban youth in organic food and ecology, and creating local markets for peri-urban farmers (www.foodsecurity.org).

And finally, the environmental justice movement has recast the paradigm of environment as *nature remote from people* by redefining environment as the *place where we live, work, play*, and *pray*. Environmental justice has linked environmental protection indissolubly with social justice by demanding equal protection from pollution for all communities, irrespective of economic status, race, and ethnicity and by affirming that all people have an equal right to a clean environment (www.ejrc.cau.edu). This paradigm of environment has brought environmental protection from the countryside to the city and generated urban environmental health initiatives and landmark studies, including *Toxic Wastes and Race* (1986) and *Toxic Wastes and Race at Twenty* (2007).*

Our book is intended for those who care deeply about cities—their people and their social, built, and natural environments—and for those who grasp the inevitability of urbanization and wrestle with its complexities. Many voices from many fields speak with a mix of authority and deep moral and social concern about the fate of those most exploited and vulnerable in cities. We have chosen to bring together in this book research on the reality of extreme social inequality in U.S. cities and its impact on people's health[3,4,5]; the multiple adverse health effects of urban sprawl[6]; the role of poor housing conditions, indoor air, and neighborhood quality on the health and well-being of urban people[7,8]; and the cumulative and unjust burden of environmental pollution in the neighborhoods of lower income and people of color in U.S. cities and metropolitan areas.[9,10,11] In each section of the book, we include studies of solutions that promote community resilience and community health[12,13,14] and studies that propose agendas for action research and public policy to improve the lived environment and health of people, particularly those most vulnerable living in cities.[4,15]

Our introduction provides a retrospective on the allied fields of public health, urban planning, and environmental protection that have separately and collectively, in the distant past and in recent times, worked on behalf of the poor and marginalized in cities. In between that distant past and the near present, each of these fields lost—in whole or in part—their social compass. A unified and socially committed mission of urban health in the twenty-first century might be able to change that.

Public Health and Urban Health

Modern public health grew in response to the acute health crises caused by the hazardous living and working conditions in fast growing, newly industrializing

---

*Both studies were commissioned and published by the United Church of Christ Justice and Witness Ministries. jwm@ucc.org.

cities of nineteenth-century England and the United States. Human, animal, factory, and slaughterhouse waste; contaminated local wells, rivers, and harbors; dangerous factory conditions and overcrowded slum housing—all outpaced local solutions and government regulation of industry.[16] Health officers documented excessive death rates in urban slums, which showed that cities were much less healthful than rural areas, especially for the poor and working class.[17] Public health prescriptions mirrored those of the early urban planning profession; waste removal and off-site disposal, closed sewers, protected drinking water sources and supplies, ventilation in factories and housing, rodent control, housing code and zoning, child labor laws, and access to urban greenspace. These reforms helped precipitate the emerging fields of sanitary engineering and occupational health. Public health measures together with housing code and zoning reform, sanitary engineering and urban planning largely solved the epidemics of infectious and waterborne diseases in nineteenth-century cities.[17]

As these responses to the pathologies of rapid industrialization and laissez faire capitalism began to systematize and professionalize, however, their social and ecological dimensions were generally eclipsed by more physical and mechanistic paradigms. The germ theory of disease added a scientific basis and prestige to public health and contributed to its professionalization. It also gave ascendancy to a biomedical model of health that eclipsed community-oriented public health.[1] Mortality and morbidity indices emerged as the primary measures of health; and treating the diseased individual replaced preventing disease and promoting health at the community level as the primary focus of health care.[18]

Urban Planning and Urban Health

A parallel trend in urban planning shifted public perception from the city as a living organism, whose unit of life is the local neighborhood, to the city as a constructed environment where old brick and mortar were interchangeable with new concrete and steel. Subsequently, city planners and governments bifurcated and often eliminated older, well-loved working-class neighborhoods and replaced them with sterile high rises, high-end housing, institutional buildings, civic centers, and multilane highways for commuter traffic, in the heyday of urban renewal and suburban development. Of the estimated 2500 neighborhoods razed by urban renewal (more truthfully described as "Negro removal"), nearly 65 percent were African American.[19] The dire consequences for urban African Americans, in particular, of this massive government program instigated by the 1949 Housing Act, included the loss of neighborhood assets and business base; erosion of social and civic organizations, culture, and neighborhood networks; overcrowding in remaining Black neighborhoods; and profound psychic trauma—a toxic compound that has caused lasting personal and community crisis.[19]

Early twentieth-century cities were composites of dense and heterogeneous housing located near workplaces, in which working classes and ethnic groups often rubbed shoulders with the well-to-do,[20] who, nonetheless, carried their biases of elitism, racism, and ethnic prejudice. Urban redevelopment and suburban development in the 1950s and 1960s were mainly commandeered by planning professionals in city government, the private sector housing market, and federal housing and highway policy. It ultimately segregated the poor in cities from the middle class in suburbs and rendered poverty invisible.[21] By 1990, with the fait accompli urbanization and isolation of the poor, more than two-thirds of all central city poor people lived in poor or very poor neighborhoods.[3] Concurrently, the racial and ethnic composition of many major U.S. cities shifted as whites left cities for suburbs and migrated from older industrial regions of the country to newer, whiter regions. Of the 100 largest U.S. cities, almost one-half now have a majority of people of color; and nearly three-quarters of them have a declining white population and an increasing Hispanic population.[22]

Impact on Health

Health is, foremost, a social fact, and it follows a social gradient.[23] Neighborhoods with higher percentages of the poor have higher levels of infant mortality, increased risk of avoidable deaths associated with crime and violence, and a greater chance that they will bear a disproportionate burden of the environmental costs of contemporary society.[24,25] Thus, a dire consequence of urban planning disconnected from neighborhood health is that poor people in cities suffer excessive illness and death, not only because of poverty, but also because of poorer social, built, and physical environment conditions. In addition, medical care, divorced from public health, treats clinical symptoms, while overlooking social and neighborhood causes of ill health.*

Environmental Protection and Urban Health

The natural environment was significantly sacrificed in nineteenth-century industrial cities for economic growth, with the exception of grand central parks. Banishing nature was "not the inevitable way to build cities," observes a prominent urban historian, "but instead a bad mutation brought on by nineteenth- and twentieth-century land greed."[26] Early nature preservation efforts focused on national parks, with their idea of nature as wilderness apart from cities and uncontaminated by urban social pathologies, machines, noise, and pollution. (A strong strain of anti-urbanism, pitting city against idyllic countryside, has coursed through American history from Jefferson, Thoreau, and Muir to early boosters of suburbs.) With the post–World War II industrial growth and spiral-

---

*[Exceptions include the Department of Pediatrics at the Boston Medical Center (www.bmc.org/pediatrics/special), which provides social, economic, and legal advocacy for families; but such facilities are exceptions and not the rule.]

ing automobile use, widespread pollution spurred some of the most influential environmental analysis, activism, and government action in U.S. history.

Rachel Carson's *Silent Spring* was published in 1962 with the searing message that saturating nature with chemical pesticides is a "peacetime" war on the environment, a war that dooms and silences life along the ecological pathways of air, water, soil, plants, and all organisms from minute biota up the food chain to humans. Earth Day—April 22, 1970—mobilized some 20 million people who participated in river clean ups, recycling campaigns, and environmental teach-ins.* That same year the federal government created its first environmental agency, due in great part to the heated national debates provoked by *Silent Spring*.

With the creation of the U.S. Environmental Protection Agency (EPA) in 1970 and the passage of nearly a score of environmental laws and amendments over the next decade, the natural environment became partitioned into inert elements whose physical and chemical properties could be measured and remediated with a growing set of new environmental technologies. The EPA's mission did not sustain the marriage of ecosystem health and human health that was so fully expressed in *Silent Spring*, and its enforcement programs subsequently ignored for decades communities multiply burdened by waste, race, poverty, and no political power.[28,29]

These early versions of nature and environment—remote wilderness; grand central parks in cities; and air, soil, and water divorced from community health—need to be reexamined in the light of urbanization. For as the world inexorably urbanizes, neither the environment as the distinct media of air, water, and soil nor nature as wilderness separate from cities can capture the complex living environment of the now primary human habitat and migration point—the city.

Cities and their metropolitan areas constitute the dominant locus of the human ecological footprint on the planet. In the United States, cities and their adjacent suburbs ("metro cores") generate two-thirds of the national economy, and metropolitan statistical areas (metro cores plus more regional suburbs and towns connected to them) account for nearly 90 percent of the national economy.[14] The economic power of cities, with its potential to impact global warming, was concretized by Patrick McCrory, the mayor of Charlotte, North Carolina, while attending a meeting of mayors to discuss climate change initiatives: "We are the ones building roads, designing mass transit, buying police cars and dump trucks and earthmovers. We are the ones lighting up the earth when you look at those maps from space."[30]

---

*Senator Gaylord Nelson, a prodigious environmental advocate and activist and progenitor of Earth Day, defined the environment concretely and with more social prescience than the movement of the day: "[It] . . . is rats in the ghetto. It is a hungry child in a land of influence. It is 'public housing' that isn't worthy of the name. It is a problem whose existence is perpetuated by the expenditure of $25 billion a year on the war in Vietnam, instead of our decaying, crowded, congested, polluted urban areas that are inhuman traps for millions of people."[27]

But even as U.S. city mayors move in advance of a regressive and recalcitrant federal government on local climate change and many other environmental initiatives, this lacuna—the absence of urban environment in most writing, deliberating, and policy making on the crises of the global environment—remains.

Signs of Change

There is a growing ferment of activity from within cities—in urban universities and research institutes, in local government, and within community-based organizations that work for environmental justice, safe and affordable housing, public transit, and nearby green space—that portends well for the urban (and global) environment. The U.S. Conference of Mayors agreed unanimously in June 2005 to implement aspects of the Kyoto Protocol, an international treaty to reduce greenhouse gas emissions that the U.S. government has refused to ratify. A coalition of 145 mayors of cities has formed to take climate change-related action, such as slowing urban sprawl, restoring urban forests, promoting and using alternative technologies, and educating their citizens. Returning to their roots, many in public health and community-minded medicine have rediscovered urban housing and neighborhoods as environmental factors in health disparities. This has spurred an important evolution in journals, such as the *Journal of Urban Health*, formerly *The Bulletin of the New York Academy of Medicine*, and new public health programs of study and research with a focus on urban communities.

Asthma prevalence has increased dramatically over the past 25 years, with rates as high as 30 percent in inner city neighborhoods. Parent and community advocacy have pushed for engaged research and advocacy on three fronts—the built, physical, and sociomedical—with initiatives to enhance medical services for the urban poor; to decrease local sources of air pollution; and to achieve clean, dry, and pest-free indoor housing condition (www.buac.org; www.lungusa .org). Urban sprawl and the epidemic of obesity have generated a surge of studies on built environment and its influence on exercise, diet, and trends in overweight and obesity among U.S. citizens. The wave of research on built environment and health culminated in a series of articles in joint editions of the *American Journal of Public Health* (Issue 93) and the *American Journal of Health Promotion* (Issue 18) in 2003. Urban greening, specifically community gardens and urban agriculture on vacant lands in inner and center city neighborhoods of hundreds of municipalities, including all of the large U.S. cities, is hailed as instrumental in eco-literacy, youth development, community health, nutrition, social cohesion, and beneficial reuse of abandoned and vacant land (www.community garden.org).

In the collection we have assembled, our intention is to unify the *social, built*, and *natural* or *physical* environments of cities, and to do so within the integrative framework of environmental justice. We have selected noteworthy and pioneering articles that present the state of knowledge on emerging and reemerging urban health topics, such as housing and health, indoor air and urban horticulture; and innovative and integrative research studies on more established urban environmental health topics, such as air quality and brownfields. Many of the articles are grounded in social justice and environmental justice and offer a continuum of perspectives on contemporary urban health. Two, in particular, pose substantially different perspectives on the fate of U.S. cities. The opening chapter documents the historical trend in segregation and economic isolation of poor and minority people in cities, most egregiously African Americans, yielding a hardening divide between Black and White in America. The closing chapter provides a hopeful prognosis for the civic health of cities (in counterpoint to current regressive federal policies), citing the substantial economy of metropolitan areas, the dynamic cultural and educational life of cities, and progressive trends in social and environmental policies in "high-road" cities.

For Those Who Care About Urban Health

The audience we have in mind for this urban health reader includes people like ourselves and our students in higher education institutions whose focus of teaching, learning, research, and community collaboration is urban health, society, and habitat. We also hope this reader speaks to nonprofit organizations and foundations that have healthy people and healthy cities as their mission and work; urban policy institutes and organizations; and people working in municipal, state, and federal government programs with a focus on environmental justice and urban environment. Finally, we created this collection for readers who love cities and are challenged by their complex mix of federal and private sector disinvestment, social and economic inequality, diversity, community-organizing, innovation, and energy—in other words, their plight, their assets, and their potential—and who are committed to their just and healthful future.

References

1. Fee E, Brown TM. The unfulfilled promise of public health: déja vu all over again. *Health Affairs.* http://content.healthaffairs.org/cgi/content/abstract/ 21/6/31. Accessed February 2, 2008.
2. Hancock T. The evolution, impact and significance of the healthy cities/ healthy communities movement. *Journal of Public Health Policy* 1993; 14(1):5–18.
3. Massey DS. The age of extremes: concentrated affluence and poverty in the twenty-first century. *Demography* 1996; 33(4):395–412.
4. Raphael D. Health inequities in the United States: prospects and solutions. *Journal of Public Health Policy* 2000; 21(4):394–427.
5. Geronimus A. To mitigate, resist, or undo: addressing structural influences on the health of urban populations. *American Journal of Public Health* 2000; 90(6):867–872.

6. Frumkin H. Urban sprawl and public health. *Public Health Reports* 2002; 117:201–217.
7. Krieger J, Higgins D. Housing and health: time again for public health action. *American Journal of Public Health* 2002; 92(5):758–768.
8. Samet JM, Spengler JD. Indoor environments and health: moving into the twenty-first century. *American Journal of Public Health* 2003;93(9): 1489–1493.
9. O'Neill MS, Jerrett M, Kawachi I, et al. Health, wealth, and air pollution: advancing theory and methods. *Environmental Health Perspectives* 2003; 111(16):1861–1870.
10. Litt JS, Tran NL, Burke T. Examining urban brownfields through the public health "macroscope." *Environmental Health Perspectives* 2002; 110(Supplement 2):183–193.
11. A current appraisal of toxic wastes and race at twenty in the United States— 2007. *Toxic Wastes and Race at Twenty—1987–2007: A Report Prepared for the United Church of Christ Justice and Witness Ministries.* 2007. jwm@ucc.org.
12. Sampson RJ, Raudenbush SW, Earls F. Neighborhoods and violent crime: a multilevel study of collective efficacy. *Science* 1997; 277(5328):918–924.
13. Hynes HP, Howe G. Urban horticulture in the contemporary United States: personal and community benefits. *Acta Horticulturae* ISHS 2004; 643:171–181.
14. Rogers J. Cities: The vital core. *The Nation* (2005, June 20);20–22.
15. Lopez R, Hynes HP. Obesity, physical activity, and the urban environment: public health research needs. *Environmental Health: A Global Access Science Source* 2006; 5(25).
16. Frumkin H, Frank L, Jackson R. *Urban Sprawl and Public Health: Designing, Planning and Building for Healthy Communities.* Washington, DC: Island Press; 2004.
17. Rosen G. *A History of Public Health.* Baltimore: The Johns Hopkins University Press; 1993.
18. Dubos R. *Mirage of Health.* New York: Harper & Row; 1959.
19. Fullilove MT. *Root Shock: How Tearing Up City Neighborhoods Hurts America, and What We Can Do About It.* New York: Ballantine Books; 2004.
20. Rae DW. *City: Urbanism and Its End.* New Haven, CT: Yale University Press; 2004.
21. Harrington M. *The Other America: Poverty in the United States.* New York: MacMillan Books; 1962.
22. Vlahov D, Galea S. Urbanization, Urbanicity, and Health. *Journal of Urban Health* 2002; 79(4, Supplement 1):S1–S12.
23. Marmot M, Wilkinson R, Eds. *Social Determinants of Health.* New York: Oxford University Press; 1999.
24. Diez-Roux A. Invited Commentary: Places, people, and health. *American Journal of Epidemiology* 2002; 155(6):516–519.

25. Acevedo-Garcia D, Lochner KA, Osypuk TL. Future directions in residential segregation and health research. *American Journal of Public Health* 2003; 93(2):215–221.
26. Warner SB. *To Dwell Is to Garden: A History of Boston's Community Gardens.* Boston: Northeastern University Press; 1987, p. xii.
27. Sullivan P. Gaylord Nelson: His Earth Day sparked environmental activism. *The Boston Globe* (2005, July 4):B11.
28. Hynes HP. *The Recurring Silent Spring.* New York: Teachers College Press; 1987.
29. Gottlieb R. *Forcing the Spring: The Transformation of the American Environmental Movement.* Washington, DC: Island Press; 1993.
30. Kyriakou N. Blue Skies, Green Cities. http://www.commondreams.org/headlines05/0720-04.htm. Accessed July 20, 2005.

SECTION I

Introduction to the Social Environment

Since World War II, the field of public health has not substantively challenged inequities of employment, housing, and health care in the United States.[1] Its primary focus has been on lifestyle behaviors, such as smoking, drinking, drug use, unsafe sex, nutrition, and, more recently, obesity and exercise. This may be because structural causes of inequality—which underlie poor housing, persistent poverty, lack of health insurance, and many damaging lifestyle behaviors—require social mobilizing and political will and are generally resistant to change. This is particularly true in the United States, where extremes of wealth and poverty, the dismantling of welfare programs, and a growing hard-heartedness toward government services for those in need result in a cautious public health community and an underdeveloped grasp of the social determinants of health.[2]

Health is a social fact that is experienced by individuals, by neighborhoods, and by societies as a whole. The chapters in this section look deeply into the structural roots of inequality that affect all of these levels of health. The authors share a bias for action and argue for moving beyond research on social determinants of health to social policy and action.

Within the domain of Social Environment, we include structures of poverty, income inequality, economic isolation, racism, segregation by race and ethnicity, discrimination by sex and lack of neighborhood services, all of which are firmly linked with worse health. Studies show, for example, that poor and racially segregated neighborhoods have fewer supermarkets and pharmacies and more liquor stores and fast food outlets, a recipe for poor nutrition, obesity, and related chronic diseases of diabetes and cardiovascular disease.[3] This section considers many negative social conditions of urbanization that are precursors of poor health, such as concentrated poverty, abandoned housing, and greater crime in central cities. It also offers a positive example of neighborhood social involvement that counters the negative ecology of poverty and racial segregation.

Chapter 1 presents late-twentieth century trends in growing income inequality in cities and metropolitan areas that are shaping social structures in the twenty-first century. In Chapters 2 and 3, authors Raphael and Geronimus argue for the need to address the roots of inequality, including racism, disdain for the poor, and public policy on housing, education, and minimum wage, if we are to achieve the goal of eliminating health disparities. Geronimus adds the caveat that "autonomous institutions within minority communities"—a source of mutual aid and cultural affirmation—must not be undermined by social policy and can be partners in eliminating health disparities. In the final chapter, Sampson and colleagues add an original insight and ingredients regarding social change within highly segregated and deeply poor neighborhoods. This is the personal and social strength of neighbors joined with their readiness to intervene—what they call "collective efficacy"—as a force for change and an antidote to the inevitable defeat of persistent and isolated inequality.

The years since Massey wrote his seminal piece, "The Age of Extremes," have seen his bleak prognosis of future trends come true. If anything, he underestimated the extent to which inequality would increase and the impacts this increase in inequality would have on health and well being in the United States and elsewhere. Perhaps no one could have predicted the extent to which inequality would dominate the first decade of the new millennium.

Income inequality growth moderated or slightly declined in the United States during the late 1990s, and it then increased at the beginning of the twenty-first century to levels not seen in this country since the 1920s. For example, the Gini index measure of inequality reached .470 in the United States in 2006, up from .397 in 1967.[4] Racial segregation in the United States has fared little better. In 1997, the Harvard Project on School Desegregation found that Black and Latino school children were as segregated in public schools as they were in 1954, the year of the landmark ruling in *Brown v. Topeka* that *de jure* outlawed racial discrimination in public schools.[5] The June 2007 Supreme Court ruling against modest desegregation programs in Louisville and Seattle was an immense setback both for those school systems and also for the public commitment to strive for an integrated, pluralistic society and away from social apartheid. Nor is social inequality a uniquely U.S. phenomenon; it is increasing in Europe and rapidly increasing in the developing world, including China and India.

For those of us concerned about urban populations and environmental quality, there are important environmental consequences of inequality. For example, in their comparative study of the 50 U.S. states, Boyce and colleagues[6] found that environmental regulation decreased as inequality increased, with the implication that an increasingly unequal world will lead to an increasingly polluted world. This is especially grave, given that global ecosystems are nearing a tipping point with the accelerating loss of biodiversity and habitat, the increase in global pollution and greenhouse gases, and the growing impacts of climate change.

So what is to be done? Perhaps the first necessary response is an acknowledgment that inequality is increasing. Massey sounded a warning in 1996. In the winter of 2007, even President Bush and Federal Reserve Chairman Bernanke acknowledged that income inequality in the United States was an issue. But recognition must be followed by action. The large and profound social implications of inequality must be addressed. For sure, the root causes of poor health must be kept uppermost and must be *mitigated, resisted,* and *undone* if the more proximate effects—health disparities, unemployment, homeless, food insecurity, and so on—are to be resolved.

References

1. Freudenberg N, Galea S, Vlahov D, eds. *Cities and the Health of the Public.* Nashville, Tennessee: Vanderbilt University Press, 2006.
2. Raphael D. Public policies and the problematic USA population profile. *Health Policy.* 2007; 84:101–111.
3. Morland K, Wing S, Roux AD, Poole C. Neighborhood characteristics associated with the location of food stores and food service places. *Am J Prev Med.* 2002; 22(1):29.
4. U.S. Bureau of the Census. Historical Income Tables. (Online). http://www.census.gov/hhes/www/income/histinc/h04.html. Accessed November 13, 2007.
5. Orfield G, Bachmeier M, James D, and Eitle T. Deepening segregation in American public schools: A special report from the Harvard Project on School Desegregation. *Equity Excellence Educ.* 1997; 30(2):5–24.
6. Boyce J, Klemer A, Templet P, Willis C. Power distribution, the environment and public health: A state-level analysis. *Ecol Econ.* 1997; 29:127–140.

The Age of Extremes: Concentrated Affluence and Poverty in the Twenty-First Century

Douglas S. Massey

Urbanization, rising income inequality, and increasing class segregation have produced a geographic concentration of affluence and poverty throughout the world, creating a radical change in the geographic basis of human society. As the density of poverty rises in the environment of the world's poor, so will their exposure to crime, disease, violence, and family disruption. Meanwhile the spatial concentration of affluence will enhance the benefits and privileges of the rich. In the twenty-first century the advantages and disadvantages of one's class position will be compounded and reinforced through ecological mechanisms made possible by the geographic concentration of affluence and poverty, creating a deeply divided and increasingly violent social world.

Poverty is old news. For thousands of years the great majority of human beings have lived and labored at a low material standard of living. In the first hunter-gatherer societies that emerged on the savannahs of Africa, in the agrarian villages that later appeared in the highlands of the fertile crescent, in the great agricultural empires that arose in Mesopotamia, the Mediterranean area, India, and China, most people were very poor. This iron fact of life prevailed in all human societies until quite recently.

Despite universal material deprivation, human societies evolved cultures and social structures that permitted people to live and reproduce in relative peace. Social order was possible in conditions of pervasive poverty because of one fundamental condition: The deprivation existed at low geographic densities. Under this circumstance, the socially disruptive correlates of poverty occurred infrequently and could be managed, more or less, through informal means; and because the poverty-stricken masses rarely came into contact with the tiny elite, they did not perceive the full extent of their relative deprivation.

The one place where rich and poor families came into direct contact was in cities, but preindustrial urban centers were few in number and never contained more than a tiny fraction of the human population. In premodern cities, moreover, the wealthy were constantly exposed to the poor and their privations, because preindustrial technologies permitted neither the separation of work from residence nor the segregation of the elite from the masses. Class integrity was maintained largely through social means, not physical separation. Indeed, the coexistence of poverty and wealth at high densities created problems of social order, as any student of ancient Rome can attest.

The industrial revolution of the nineteenth century upset the apple cart by creating and distributing wealth on a grand scale, enabling affluence and poverty to become geographically concentrated for the first time. Through urbanization, the rich and the poor both came to inhabit large urban areas. Within cities new transportation and communication technologies allowed the affluent to distance themselves spatially as well as socially from the poor, causing a rise in the levels of class segregation and a new concentration of affluence and poverty.

For a short time after World War II, mass social mobility temporarily halted the relentless geographic concentration of affluence and poverty in developed countries. The postwar economic boom that swept Europe, Japan, and the United States created a numerically dominant middle class that mixed residentially with both the upper and the lower classes. After 1970, however, the promise of mass social mobility evaporated and inequality returned with a vengeance, ushering in a new era in which the privileges of the rich and the disadvantages of the poor were compounded increasingly through geographic means.

In the coming century, the fundamental condition that enabled social order to be maintained in the past—the occurrence of affluence and poverty at low geographic densities will no longer hold. In the future, most of the world's impoverished people will live in urban areas, and within these places they will inhabit neighborhoods characterized by extreme poverty. A small stratum of rich families meanwhile will cluster in enclaves of affluence, creating an unprecedented spatial intensification of both privilege and poverty.

As a result of this fundamental change in the geographic structure of inequality, the means by which the undesirable correlates of poverty were managed in the past will break down. The juxtaposition of geographically concentrated wealth and poverty will cause an acute sense of relative deprivation among the poor and heightened fears among the rich, resulting in a rising social tension and a growing conflict between the haves and the have-nots. As I demonstrate below, we have entered a new age of inequality in which class lines will grow more rigid as they are amplified and reinforced by a powerful process of geographic concentration.

The Spatial Concentration of Poverty

Poverty is notoriously difficult to define; statistics on its incidence are unreliable and difficult to acquire, especially in the developing world. Tabatabai and Fouad conducted a survey of poverty estimates in developing countries for the International Labour Office and found that most regions lacked statistics dating back more than a few years.[1] In Latin America, however, they were able to assemble reasonably accurate estimates of poverty rates beginning in 1970. To illustrate trends in the geographic concentration of poverty in developing countries, I apply rates of rural and urban poverty estimated by Tabatabai and Fouad for Latin America to rural and urban populations estimated for this region by the United Nations.[2] The resulting distribution of poverty by rural–urban status is shown in Figure 1-1 for 1970, 1980, and 1990.

In 1970 most of Latin America's poor—nearly two-thirds—lived in the countryside, typically in isolated farming communities, small agrarian villages, and tiny rural hamlets. In the ensuing two decades, however, the poor urbanized rapidly. By 1980 the balance of rural and urban poverty was approaching parity, and by 1990 a substantial majority (60%) of Latin America's poor lived in urban areas. This transformation of the geographic structure of human deprivation was so quick that the ratio of rural-to-urban poverty in 1990 was almost precisely opposite the ratio that had prevailed only 20 years earlier.

Therefore, in this hemisphere, poverty is already well on the way to complete urbanization. The typical poor Latin American of the twenty-first century will not live in a village or town but in a city, and most likely a very large one. Although data limitations prevent me from demonstrating this fact for other regions of the developing world, projected trends in urbanization suggest that a majority of the world's poor will soon live in cities.

The urban concentration of poverty is already well advanced in developed countries. Figure 1-2 shows the metropolitan distribution of poor people in the

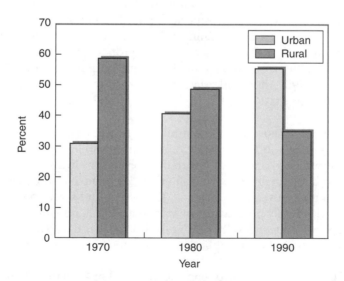

Figure 1-1. Distribution of the Poor by Rural–Urban Status: Latin America, 1970–1990

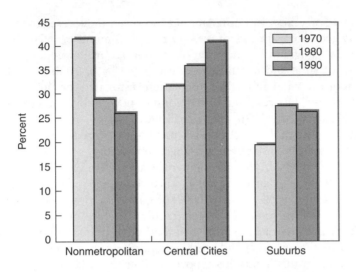

Figure 1-2. Distribution of the Poor by Metropolitan Status: United States, 1970–1990

United States in 1970, 1980, and 1990.[3,4,5] By 1970 U.S. poverty was already predominantly urban; 56% of all poor persons lived either in central cities or in suburbs. Nonetheless, a large plurality of the poor (44%) lived in nonmetropolitan areas only two decades ago.

Over the next 20 years, however, the percentage of poor people living in nonmetropolitan areas dropped steadily, to 31% in 1980 and to 28% in 1990; thus by the early 1990s, 72% of America's poor lived in urban areas. Not only was poverty becoming more urbanized, however; it was also becoming more highly concentrated in the urban core. The proportion of poor people who lived in central cities stood at 34% in 1970, but the figure rose to 39% in 1980 and to 43% in 1990. Meanwhile the percentage of the poor living in suburbs, after rising during the 1970s, fell slightly during the 1980s and reached 29% in 1990.

While American poverty was becoming more concentrated in central cities, it was also concentrating in already poor urban neighborhoods. John Kasarda (1993:265) recently computed the share of poor persons living in poor and very poor neighborhoods at different points in time. He defined a poor neighborhood as one with a tract poverty rate from 20% to 40%, and a very poor neighborhood as one with a tract poverty rate of more than 40%; nonpoor neighborhoods had a tract poverty rate below 20%.[6] Figure 1-3 displays the distribution of poor persons among these three neighborhood types in 1970, 1980, and 1990 for the 100 largest central cities of the United States.

In 1970, 45% of central-city poor people lived in a neighborhood that was not poor, whereas 55% lived in a poor or very poor neighborhood (38% in the former and 17% in the latter). Over the next two decades, however, the concen-

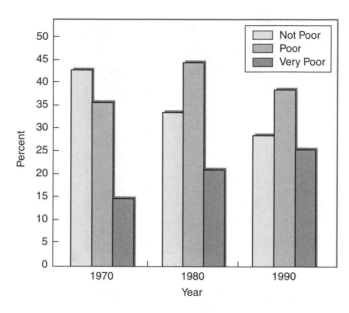

Figure 1-3. Distribution of Central City Poor by Neighborhood Type: United States, 1970–1990

tration of poor people in poor places increased sharply. From 1970 to 1990, the percentage of central-city poor people living in nonpoor areas declined from 45% to 31%, while the percentage living in poor neighborhoods increased from 38% to 41%. Meanwhile the share living in very poor neighborhoods grew markedly, from 17% to 28%. As of 1990, more than two-thirds of all central-city poor people lived in poor or very poor neighborhoods.

Elsewhere Mitchell Eggers and I argue that the P* isolation index popularized by Stanley Lieberson[7,8] provides a reliable and accurate summary measure of poverty concentration.[9] This index gives the rate of poverty in the neighborhood of the average poor person. The left-hand side of Figure 1-4 presents isolation indices for poor inhabitants of the nation's 10 largest metropolitan areas in 1970, 1980, and 1990, using data recently published by Abramson, Tobin, and VanderGoot.[10]

Over the past two decades, class isolation among the poor has risen steadily, growing by 21% between 1970 and 1990. As of 1990, the average poor resident of the nation's largest metropolitan areas lived in a neighborhood where roughly one-quarter of his or her neighbors were also poor. Analyses performed by Abramson and colleagues show that this geographic concentration of human poverty was remarkably widespread, and in some metropolitan areas reached extreme levels. By 1990 the average poor person in New York, Chicago, and Detroit lived in a neighborhood where 29% of the people were poor; the typical

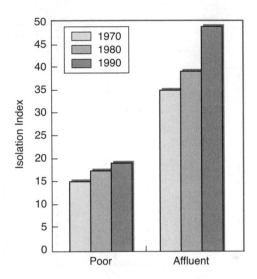

Figure 1-4.   Concentration of Affluence and Poverty in the 10 Largest Metropolitan
Areas: United States, the New World Order

poor resident of New Orleans lived in a neighborhood where the poverty rate
was a remarkable 35%. Over the past two decades, the social environment of the
poor shifted to higher and higher densities of poverty.

The Spatial Concentration of Affluence

Despite a substantial and growing effort to study concentrated poverty, remarkably little attention has been given to the concentration of affluence. Since the
dawn of urbanism, however, the elite have always clustered in cities for purposes
of command and control. Indeed, in preindustrial times they tended to settle in
and around the city center.[11] Because communications were rudimentary, effective administration required face-to-face interaction that could be achieved only
through physical propinquity. Moreover, because transportation technologies
were limited, goods and services required by the elite had to be produced, distributed, and sold near their places of residence.

The core of preindustrial cities thus tended to house a variety of social classes,
generating considerable face-to-face interaction across class lines. Although the
rich may have been centralized, they were not separated physically from the
masses, and although a wide social gulf separated them from the poor, affluence
itself was not spatially concentrated.[12,13]

This residential status quo was terminated in the nineteenth century by improvements in technology. Advances in transportation, communication, and
construction led to an increase in density at the urban core, a separation of work

from residence, and new possibilities for physical separation between the classes. Especially in the United States, the middle and upper classes began to leave central cities for affluent suburbs on the urban periphery early in the twentieth century, first axially along rail lines and then, as the automobile became more widely available, concentrically throughout a wide hinterland. The working classes meanwhile clustered in factory zones adjacent to the central business district, creating the spatial structure made so famous by my predecessor at the University of Chicago, Ernest Burgess.[14]

Although we have no direct measure of income segregation before 1940, we know that ethnic segregation increased substantially during the late nineteenth and early twentieth centuries in response to the changed ecological structure of the city.[12,15,16] It is reasonable to surmise that class segregation also increased. After World War II, however, both class and ethnic segregation clearly declined,[15] fueled by an ongoing process of generational succession, social assimilation, and mass economic mobility unleashed by the postwar boom.[17]

As shown in seminal work by Blau and Duncan[18] and Featherman and Hauser,[19] a remarkably fluid and open stratification system emerged in the United States during the years after World War II. Socioeconomic status came to depend less on one's social origins than on one's achievements; the result was a sustained decline in income inequality and an unprecedented rise in living standards. From 1947 to 1973, U.S. families doubled their incomes, while inequality declined by 5%.[20] According to James Smith,[21] the share of families with middle-class incomes grew from a minority of 40% of the population in 1940 to two-thirds of the population in 1970, while the poverty rate fell from 34% to 11%. In only 25 years the United States became a middle-class society structured meritocratically.

This broader trend toward socioeconomic equality was expressed spatially, as the degree of residential segregation between the upper and the lower classes was reduced sharply. According to calculations by Albert Simkus,[22] residential dissimilarity between high- and low-status workers declined markedly between 1960 and 1970. In the metropolitan areas he studied, the average dissimilarity index between professionals and laborers decreased by 19% from 1960 to 1970, while that between managers and service workers decreased by 117%. At the same time, residential dissimilarity between managers and laborers dropped by 23%, and that between managers and service workers by 17%. Therefore, during the 1960s, people located at the extremes of the American occupational structure were moving rapidly together in residential terms, and observers at the time thought class segregation was on the wane.

Sometime during the mid-1970s, however, this pattern was reversed, and the classes once again began to pull apart socially and spatially. Just as we observe an increase in the concentration of poverty between 1970 and 1990, we also encounter a remarkable increase in the concentration of affluence. The right-hand side of Figure 1-4 shows P* isolation indices for affluent persons in the 10 largest metropolitan areas of the United States. This index gives the proportion affluent in the neighborhood of the average affluent person. The figures for 1970 and 1980 come from work I published earlier with Mitchell Eggers;[23] the figure for 1990 was computed especially for this address by Nancy Denton. Following James Smith,[21] I define the affluent as persons living in families whose incomes are at least four times the poverty level for a family of four—about $54,000 in 1990 dollars.

As Figure 1-4 clearly shows, affluence is even more highly concentrated spatially than poverty. Whereas the average poor person lived in a neighborhood that was 19% poor in 1970, the typical affluent person lived in a neighborhood that was 39% affluent. In the ensuing years, this already high concentration of affluence became even more intense: The isolation index increased to 43 in 1980 and to 52 in 1990. By the beginning of the present decade, in other words, the typical affluent person lived in a neighborhood where more than half the residents were also rich; the outcome was a social environment that was far more homogeneously privileged than at any time in the previous 20 years. In their daily lives, affluent residents of U.S. urban areas were increasingly likely to interact only with other affluent people, and progressively less likely to interact with other classes, especially the poor.

The hallmark of the emerging spatial order of the twenty-first century will be a geographic concentration of affluence and of poverty. Throughout the world, poverty will shift from a rural to an urban base; within urban areas poor people will be confined increasingly to poor neighborhoods, yielding a density of material deprivation that is historically unique and unprecedented. As poverty grows more geographically concentrated over time, its harmful by-products also will become more highly concentrated, intensifying social problems that the affluent will naturally seek to escape. Class segregation will increase, ratcheting up the concentration of affluence and poverty in self-reinforcing fashion.

This new ecological structure stems from deep and powerful forces operating in the world today. Simply put, concentrated poverty follows from any process that gathers poor people together in space and then impedes their socioeconomic and residential mobility. At the end of the twentieth century, poor people are being assembled geographically through an ongoing process of urbanization that is already well advanced. Their social mobility is blocked by the emergence of a global economic structure characterized by stagnant mean incomes, rising inequality, and growing class rigidity; and their spatial mobility is stymied by a rising tide of class segregation that is exacerbated, in many places, by an ongoing pattern of deliberate racial and ethnic exclusion. Welcome to the new world order.

The Urbanization of Poverty

In a world where the great majority of people live in cities, poverty perforce will be urbanized. Figure 1-5 shows projected trends in the level of urbanization

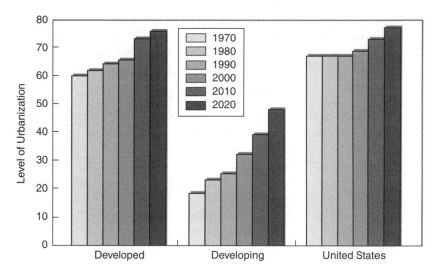

Figure 1-5. Level of Urbanization in Developed and Developing Countries, 1970–2020

from 1970 to 2020 in developed regions, developing nations, and the United States.[2] Obviously most inhabitants of developed countries already live in urban areas: The proportion urban in the developed world was 74% in 1990 and is projected to reach 82% by 2020; in the United States the respective figures are 75% and 84%. Therefore, among developed nations, poverty already is highly urbanized, and this concentration will increase slowly but steadily in the coming decades.

The potential for change is considerably greater in the developing world. As late as 1970, only one-quarter of its population was urban; in 1990 the figure was only 35%. The path of urbanization, however, generally follows a logistic curve, beginning slowly and then accelerating rapidly for a time before leveling off and gradually approaching an upper asymptote.[2,24] Developing countries are now in that segment of the logistic curve characterized by rapid growth; the percentage urban is projected to rise rapidly in the next two decades, reaching 41% by the turn of the century and 47% in 2010.

Sometime between 2010 and 2020 the developing world as a whole will cross a significant dividing line: For the first time, a majority of its population will live in cities. Because the great majority of these new urbanites will be impoverished by any standard, this event implies that poverty also will become concentrated in urban areas. Therefore, early in the next century, the typical poor citizen of Planet Earth will cease to inhabit a small town or rural village, and instead will live in a large city. Because there is no precedent for a reversal of urbanization once it has begun, the future of human poverty almost certainly lies in cities. Barring a catastrophe that wipes out much of the world's urban population, poverty will become progressively urbanized during the next century, and nobody can do much to change this fundamental fact.

The Return of Inequality

Urbanization stems entirely from rural–urban migration rather than from natural increase within cities.[2,24] Historically, much of this urbanizing population movement was internal, with peasants leaving rural areas for cities in their own countries, but a substantial part has always been directed to urban destinations overseas. Such was the case in Europe as it underwent development in the nineteenth century;[25,26] much the same is occurring in developing nations today.[27]

When they arrived in cities, rural in-migrants of the past took advantage of numerous ladders of mobility to climb out of poverty and into the working, middle, and even upper classes.[7,17] Through the mid-1970s a pattern of widespread social mobility prevailed for in-migrants to cities, not only in developed countries such as the United States[18,19,28] but also in developing societies such as Mexico.[29,30]

In the future, however, poor migrants who arrive in the world's burgeoning metropolises will be more likely to stay poor. Industrial growth and development from 1870 to 1970 produced a wholesale upgrading of the occupational structure to create a diamond-shaped status distribution that supported mass upward mobility, rising income, and declining inequality; in contrast, the postindustrial transformation since 1973 has produced an hourglass economic structure of high-paying jobs for the well-educated, a dwindling number of middle-income jobs for the modestly schooled, and many, many poorly paid jobs for those with little schooling. Such a structure creates few opportunities for mobility and carries great potential for inequality.

We are thus in an era of high and rising inequality.[20,31,32,33] Figure 1-6 presents Gini indices measuring income inequality in selected developed nations in 1980 and 1990.[34] During the 1980s, inequality increased most sharply in Anglophone countries such as Australia, Ireland, Britain, and the United States, where the Gini rose from 33 to 36. The index also rose in Scandinavia (Finland, Norway, and Sweden) and western Europe (Austria, Belgium, Germany, and the Netherlands). Only the relatively poor countries of southern Europe—Italy, Spain, and Portugal, where incomes were lower and inequality was greater to begin with—opposed the trend toward greater inequality. The shifts in Gini coefficients may appear modest, but they conceal a rather profound transformation in underlying economic structure.

The nature of this transformation may be discerned by a closer look at trends in the United States during two contrasting eras: 1949–1969 and 1973–1991. During the earlier period, median family income doubled in real terms; this increase was shared by families throughout the income distribution. When Sheldon Danziger and Peter Gottschalk[35] divided family incomes by the

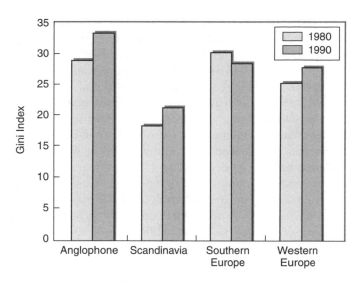

Figure 1-6.   Gini Indices for Income Inequality in Developed Countries: 1980–1990

poverty line and observed changes between 1949 and 1969, they found that relative incomes in the bottom quintile increased by 457%, while those in the next lowest quintile increased by 169%. In the two highest quintiles, meanwhile, relative incomes grew respectively by 102% and 93%. Therefore, in the postwar economy that prevailed through the early 1970s, everyone did better—the poor as well as the rich. A rising tide lifted all boats, and the poverty rate dropped from 40% to 14% while the Gini index fell from 38 to 35.[20]

After 1973, however, the median family income stagnated in real terms, ending only 6% higher in 1991. This stagnation in average income was produced by divergent trends at the extremes of the distribution. From 1973 to 1991, relative incomes for families in the two bottom quintiles declined by 19% and 8% respectively, whereas those for families in the two top quintiles increased by 21% and 22%.[35] Rather than a rising tide that lifted all boats, after 1973 Danziger and Gottschalk found uneven tides that elevated the yachts of the rich but beached the dinghies of the poor.

As a result of these contrasting trends, the shape of the income distribution changed gradually. As Martina Morris and her colleagues have shown, the middle categories shrank while the extremes expanded.[36] After 1973 the poverty rate stopped falling in the United States, and the Gini index for family income rose from 35 to 40 by 1991.[20] This 14% increase in inequality over the course of 18 years wiped out the entire postwar decline, and by 1991 had produced a more skewed distribution of income than existed in 1947! Similar trends were occurring elsewhere in the developed world. Except for Australia and the United Kingdom, however, they were less dramatic than in the United States.[34] In continental Europe, the new economic order was expressed more strongly as stagnating employment than as a decline in real wages. Income inequality rose slightly in European countries during the 1970s and 1980s, but unemployment increased fivefold between 1973 and 1985.[55] Despite population growth, European employment fell in absolute terms between 1973 and 1985, yielding a jobless rate whose degree and permanence were unprecedented in the postwar era.

It is much more difficult to make factual statements about trends in inequality in developing countries. Certainly in Mexico, the one developing country I know well, prospects for socioeconomic mobility seem bleak. From 1980 to 1989, the real minimum wage declined by 47%, GDP per capita declined by 9%, and the percentage of families earning less than twice the minimum wage, a rough indicator of poverty, rose to include 60% of the population.[96] According to conservative estimates, 48% of all Mexicans lived in poverty by 1989;[37] by 1996 Mexican wages had lost 68% of their 1982 value.[38] Over the course of the 1980s, Mexico's standard of living fell to levels last seen in the 1960s. In just five years, from 1984 to 1989, income inequality increased enough to cancel out half of the decline achieved over the two previous decades;[39] it would have increased even more if not for the massive entry of additional household workers into the informal workforce.[40,41] Rates of occupational mobility increased during the 1980s, but most of the movement was downward.[42]

Therefore, whether they stay in Mexico or come to the United States, poor Mexicans migrating from rural communities will face dim prospects for social mobility wherever they go, be it Los Angeles or Guadalajara. On both sides of the border, rural–urban migrants will confront a socioeconomic structure that offers few ladders of mobility, little access to high-wage employment, and, for those without education, the strong possibility of an enduring place at the bottom of the income distribution.

These trends are not likely to moderate soon. Although the causes of the new inequality are under debate, my own reading of the literature suggests that the transformation stems from three broad, interrelated trends that are rooted deeply in the postindustrial economic order: the computerization of production, the globalization of capital and labor markets, and the fragmentation of consumer markets.

The cybernetic revolution has profoundly altered the nature and the social organization of human production. During the 1970s and early 1980s, computerization swept through manufacturing. Older manufacturing plants that employed thousands of well-paid, unionized workers were replaced by new, capital-intensive facilities where a few workers operated mechanized, continuous-flow production lines controlled by computers and staffed by robots. Manufacturing productivity soared, and those plants that could not compete either closed their doors or relocated to low-wage areas overseas. Employment in manufacturing plummeted, especially in older urban areas;[43] as manufacturing employment dwindled, so did union membership. Between 1969 and 1989 the share of nonagricultural workers in unions dropped from

29% to 16%; in the private sector the level of unionization reached 12%, a figure last seen in the 1920s.[44]

While manufacturing bore the brunt of the cybernetics revolution during the 1970s and early 1980s, the moment of truth came for the service sector during the late 1980s and early 1990s. Large bureaucratic organizations loaded with mid-level white-collar workers gave way to reengineered, downsized, and flattened organizations that were "lean and mean."[45]

Making use of new, ultrafast computer chips and fiber optics, programmers wrote software that routinized human expertise within canned algorithms that had user-friendly interfaces. Armed with these new cybernetic tools, one modestly trained operative could perform all of the tasks formerly carried out by scores of expensive white-collar workers, often in a fraction of the time. During the 1990s, the gray flannel suit gave way to the pink slip as corporations shed mid-level bureaucrats by the thousands.[45,46]

While computers were transforming productivity in manufacturing and services, they were also facilitating a revolution in the geographic reach of factor markets. Over the past two decades markets for capital and labor have globalized, causing a worldwide competition for funds and workers. Capital now roams the world incessantly, seeking companies and countries that offer high returns and low risks, while labor finds itself in a global hiring hall where high-wage workers in developed nations compete directly with millions of desperately poor workers throughout the developing world.

This globalization of factor markets was facilitated by the rising speed of communications, the declining costs of transportation, the increasing ease of international movement, the growing prevalence of smaller and lighter consumer products, and the rising importance of knowledge in the productive process. If the owners of capital find more attractive prospects in one venue, or dislike developments in another, they can shift billions of dollars across international borders in a nanosecond, as Mexico learned to its dismay in December 1994. Likewise, if producers based in developed nations need to reduce their labor costs, they can easily relocate factories to low-wage areas overseas, or they can simply wait for immigrants from these areas to appear at their factory gates.

The third development of the postindustrial era has been the fragmentation of consumer markets. From 1870 to 1970, nations in general and the United States in particular prospered because companies were able to manufacture standardized goods and sell them to a growing mass market of middle-class consumers who exhibited similar needs and tastes. Products became more affordable because economies of scale reduced their price; consumer markets grew because mass production required armies of well-paid, unionized workers to staff the manufacturing apparatus and legions of salaried white-collar workers to administer it.[46,47]

Since 1970, international competition, technological innovation, and demographic shifts have fragmented these mass markets. In response, firms have developed new strategies to cater to small, specialized market niches that rely on new techniques of flexible production, just-in-time delivery, outsourcing, and continuous-flow production. Under the old industrial regime, companies were large, hierarchies were deep, authority was rigid, markets were massive and homogeneous, and firms were slow to respond to shifts in consumer demand. In the new postindustrial order, companies are lean, hierarchies are flattened, authority is flexible, markets are fragmented and diverse, and successful firms move quickly to anticipate shifting demand. The end result is a further segmentation of labor markets in developed countries and additional downward pressure on salaries and wages.[45]

The forces of computerization, globalization, and fragmentation have operated simultaneously over the past two decades in mutually reinforcing fashion; it is fruitless to ask which came first or which is most important. Rather, the three processes have fed off one another to cause a marked and seemingly permanent change in the economic structure of nations and the world.

The abruptness of the discontinuity is suggested by the disappearance of numerous well-established empirical regularities that characterized economic life in the United States through 1970. In contrast to the industrial regime of the past, wages in the new postindustrial economy are not related to trends in productivity; poverty is not correlated with the business cycle; corporate pay is not tied to the company's profitability; and there is no longer an association between workers' wages and managers' salaries.[35,47]

That something profound has happened is obvious from a simple recitation of the titles of books that I read in preparing this address: *The End of Affluence*,[47] *The End of Equality*,[48] *The End of Work*,[46] *The Jobless Future*,[49] *The Age of Diminished Expectations*,[55] *Understanding American Economic Decline*,[50] *America Unequal*,[35] *The Winner-Take-All Society*,[51] *Revolt of the Elites*,[52] and *The Next American Nation*.[53]

Clearly we are in a new era, and there is no going back. Computers cannot be disinvented; instantaneous telecommunications cannot be undone; transportation cannot become slower and more expensive; the globalization of factor markets will not be reversed; and the homogeneous mass consumer markets of the postwar era will not return soon. If anything, the pace of technological change will quicken to reinforce the structural changes that have already occurred. The age of economic inequality is upon us.

Class Segregation

Not only have the rich and the poor been pulling apart economically through a transformation of the income distribution; since 1970 they have also been separating spatially through a resurgence of class segregation. In the United States, the geographic barriers between rich and poor have increased steadily, resulting in a significant rise in residential segregation by income, as shown in Figure 1-7. The left-hand bars show the degree of residential dissimilarity between poor and nonpoor persons in 1970, 1980, and 1990 in the 10 largest metropolitan

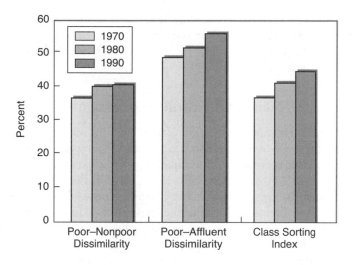

Figure 1-7. Measures of Income Segregation in the 10 Largest Metropolitan Areas: United States, 1970–1990

areas of the United States.[10] The middle bars show the extent of residential dissimilarity between affluent and poor families; figures for 1970 and 1980 come from Massey and Eggers, and those for 1990 from Nancy Denton.[9,54] Both series reveal a steady rise in the degree of segregation between the haves and the have-nots in U.S. society. The poor–nonpoor index rose from 37 in 1970 to 40 in 1980 to 41 in 1990, while the poor–affluent index rose from 49 to 52 to 56 over the same period.

In a forthcoming paper, Paul Jargowsky shows that the use of dissimilarity indices to measure class segregation confounds changes in the spatial distribution of income groups with changes in the shape of the income distribution itself, thereby understating the degree of class segregation. To control for this bias, he proposes an alternative "class sorting index" based on the correlation ratio, which I present on the right-hand side of Figure 1-7. This index increases from 37 to 45 between 1970 and 1990, a confirmation that earlier trends based on the index of dissimilarity were not merely methodological artifacts. Detailed analyses conducted by Jargowsky and by Abramson et al. show that increasing class segregation was remarkably widespread among regions and population groups. Whether one looks south, north, east, or west, or at whites, blacks, Hispanics, or Asians, America became a more class-segregated society during the 1970s and 1980s.[10,63]

Because of an absence of data, once again it is difficult to assess whether comparable trends are occurring elsewhere in the developed world, or whether U.S. trends can be generalized to developing regions. I suspect that I would detect similar trends elsewhere if I had the requisite ecological data, although perhaps the trends would be less striking than in the United States. Certainly in Mexico, the evidence suggests a long-standing pattern of residential segregation between high- and low-income groups in metropolitan areas, an ecological gulf that widened significantly during the 1980s.[56–59]

Racial and Ethnic Segregation

Given a high and rising level of urbanization, growing income inequality, and rising class segregation, an increase in the geographic concentration of affluence and poverty is all but inevitable. These spatial processes are magnified, however, when they occur in a group that is also segregated on the basis of an ascribed characteristic such as race; and no feature of our national life has proved to be as enduring as the residential color line separating black from white America.[60] Because of a history of discrimination in the real estate and banking industries, the persistence of white racial prejudice, and a legacy of racially biased public policies, blacks continue to be the most residentially segregated group in the United States.[61,62]

As a result, when black poverty rates rose during the 1970s and 1980s, the increased poverty was absorbed by a small set of racially homogeneous, geographically isolated, densely settled neighborhoods packed tightly around the urban core; and because class segregation was increasing as well,[63] a disproportionate share of the economic pain was absorbed by neighborhoods that were not only black but also poor. As a result, broader trends toward income inequality and class segregation in the United States isolated poor blacks far more severely than poor whites.

By 1990, according to John Kasarda,[6] 41% of poor blacks in U.S. central cities lived in poor neighborhoods, and 42% lived in very poor neighborhoods, figures well above the comparable levels for whites (32% and 11% respectively). Computations performed by Lauren Krivo and colleagues[64] show that the extent of poverty concentration was 50% higher among central-city blacks in 1990 than among central-city whites (with an isolation index of 32 for the former and 21 for the latter).

Focusing on central cities, however, understates the black–white contrast. When Mitchell Eggers, Andrew Gross, and I examined the 50 largest metropolitan areas in 1980, we found that 64% of poor blacks lived in neighborhoods with a poverty rate over 20%, compared with just 13% of poor whites.[65] The isolation indices we computed revealed that the level of poverty concentration for poor blacks was four times that of poor whites.

To a great extent, then, increases in the concentration of poverty observed during the 1970s and 1980s in U.S. urban areas reflect rising inequality caused by racial rather than class segregation. At any given level of income segregation, poverty is concentrated most strongly in cities that are also racially segregated; and when for the degree of class segregation is controlled, racial segregation exerts a powerful independent effect on the extent of poverty concentration.[23]

Were black–white segregation to be eliminated, a principal force behind the spatial concentration of poverty in the United States would disappear.

Unfortunately, although Reynolds Farley and William Frey have detected "small steps toward an integrated society," we are not yet able to debate whether the glass is half empty or half full. At this point the glass is about 80% empty and 20% full. Figure 1-8 presents black isolation indices and black-white dissimilarity indices for 1970, 1980, and 1990 in the 30 U.S. metropolitan areas with the largest black populations. Although black–white dissimilarity declined by 10% in the two decades after 1970, it still stood at a remarkable 73% in 1990. This figure is higher than even the most extreme scores observed for other groups, such as Hispanics and Asians.[61]

A glance at the isolation indices yields an even more pessimistic picture: During the 1980s the small declines of the 1970s were arrested and reversed. Over the 20-year period, average black isolation decreased from 69% to 65% and then rose again to 67%. The sad fact is that African Americans were virtually as isolated in 1990 as on the day when Congress passed the Fair Housing Act in 1968.

As if these patterns were not enough, the numbers are even more disturbing in one set of metropolitan areas. On the basis of an analysis of 1980 data, Nancy Denton and I coined the term hypersegregation to describe places where blacks were highly segregated on multiple geographic dimensions simultaneously.[62] Nancy has reexamined the issue using 1990 data and has found that black hypersegregation not only continues, but in many ways it has grown worse.[54] Of the 16 metropolitan areas defined as hypersegregated in 1980, 14 met the technical

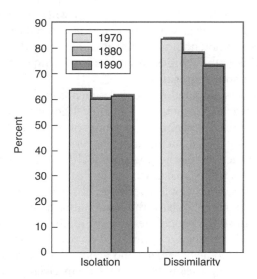

Figure 1-8.   Black Segregation in the 30 U.S. Metropolitan Areas with the Largest Black Populations: 1970–1990

criteria again in 1990. The two areas that missed the threshold did so by a trivial amount, and all areas that were hypersegregated in 1980 showed an increase on at least one dimension of segregation by 1990.

Thus, metropolitan areas that were hypersegregated in 1980 generally remained so in 1990, and we found little trend away from this extreme pattern of racial isolation. On the contrary, hypersegregation spread to new urban areas during the 1980s. Of the 44 nonhypersegregated metropolitan areas that Nancy and I examined in 1980, six met the criteria in 1990, bringing the total number to 20. Taken together, these areas contain 11 million African Americans, who together constitute 36% of the black population of the United States.

Thus it is quite clear that racial segregation will not disappear from U.S. urban areas soon, and that its poverty-concentrating effects will be with us for the foreseeable future. Although trends in racial and ethnic segregation are documented less clearly in other countries, we know that racial and ethnic minorities are rapidly growing throughout Europe, Australia, and Japan as a result of international migration,[66] and that these growing populations have aroused racist sentiments in many countries. Insofar as these sentiments are translated into residential segregation, broader trends toward concentrated affluence and poverty will be exacerbated.

The Political Ecology of Inequality

Unless there is a radical departure from recent trends, poverty and affluence are almost certain to become geographically concentrated at high levels throughout the world early in the next century. Increasingly the poor and the rich will inhabit large urban areas, and within these places they will concentrate in separate neighborhoods. This ecological structure constitutes a radical departure from the past, and creates the potential for a new geopolitical order capable of compounding the benefits and liabilities of class by superimposing administrative segmentation on economic segregation.

Whether or not this potential is realized depends on how political districts are constructed. Insofar as the boundaries of local governmental units can be arranged to approximate the geographic contours of concentrated affluence and poverty, and insofar as the financing and delivery of public services can be shifted down the political hierarchy, the potential for reinforcing class advantages and disadvantages will be maximized.

In a society where most people live in small towns and villages, rich and poor families must mix socially, share the same public services, and inhabit the same political units. In such a geopolitical structure, the poor benefit from public institutions to which the rich are committed by reason of self-interest. When poverty and affluence become urbanized and geographically concentrated, however, the affluent acquire a means to separate themselves politically from the poor through the judicious drawing of political lines in space. If they can create separate governmental and administrative districts that encompass concentrations of poverty, and if they can force these poor districts to supply and pay for their own services, then the affluent will be able to insulate themselves from the economic costs imposed on society by the poor.

In the United States, the poor are isolated politically by the segmentation of metropolitan regions into a patchwork of separate municipalities. The concentration of affluence in certain suburbs generates high real estate values that allow the affluent to tax themselves at low rates while offering generous, even lavish municipal services. The concentration of poverty in central cities and some inner suburbs generates a high demand for services but yields low property values; thus, higher tax rates are required to support generally inferior services. The end result is a vicious cycle whereby city taxes are raised to maintain deficient services; consequently families with means are driven out; property values then decline further; the result is more tax increases and additional middle-class flight, which further exacerbate the concentration of poverty.

Under an ecological regime of concentrated affluence and poverty, efforts to decentralize government and shift the financing and provision of services to local government represent a means of enhancing the social and economic well-being of the rich at the expense of the poor. Political decentralization is progressive and democratic only in a world where all classes live together in small communities; this antiquated model of society no longer prevails, however, although it appears frequently in the writings of conservative thinkers (see Herrnstein and Murray, 1994).[67] In today's world of dense, urban agglomerations characterized by pronounced income inequality and increasing class segregation, political decentralization is punitive and regressive, forcing the poor to bear most of the cost of their own disadvantage. In a world of small towns and modest communities, political decentralization yields the social world of Andy Hardy; in a class-segregated world of large urban areas it produces the bleak vision of the Blade Runner.

Many mechanisms compound class advantages and disadvantages in the new ecology of inequality, but perhaps the most significant occurs through schools. Education is the most important single resource presently traded on global labor markets: In recent years workers with college and post-graduate degrees have seen their earnings rise, while high school graduates' and dropouts' wages have fallen. Access to high-quality education thus has become the crucial factor determining one's position in the postindustrial pecking order.

Because the emerging ecological structure concentrates the best-prepared students in areas of resource abundance while gathering the least well-prepared students in areas of resource scarcity, it necessarily exacerbates class inequities and promotes a more rigid stratification of society. Students from low-income families with poorly educated parents, little experience with books or reading, and multiple social problems attend schools with the fewest resources to help them learn, while students from affluent families with well-educated parents, extensive experience with books and reading, and few social problems attend well-funded schools that are most able to promote learning. The spatial concentration of affluence

and poverty thus raises the odds that affluent children will receive a superior education while poor children will get inferior schooling.

The Cultural Ecology of Inequality

Until recently, poverty, though endemic, was spread uniformly in space and
rarely occurred at high densities. Most impoverished families lived in small rural
communities where the range of material well-being was limited. The few affluent families that were present locally were not especially affluent, and they
tended to be closely related to others in the community. Truly wealthy families
in the governing elite lived far away; the prevalent atmosphere in most places
was one of collective poverty and shared deprivation.

In such settings, proclivities toward violence, crime, and other maladies exacerbated by material deprivation could be held in check by informal means. In
small rural communities, as generations of cultural anthropologists have shown,
everyone knows everyone else, either directly through personal experience or
indirectly through ties of kinship or friendship. Through social networks, re-
wards and punishments are meted out to reinforce and maintain accepted standards of behavior. Age-old devices such as gossip, ridicule, shame, and ostracism,
backed occasionally by physical discipline, are employed to punish public depar-
tures from accepted behavior, whereas praise, esteem, and prestige are accorded
to those who conform (see Foster, 1967).[97]

As observed by theorists from Emile Durkheim[68] to Edward Banfield,[69]
these informal mechanisms of social control, which prevail in small towns and
villages produce a repressive moral code that preserves public order and main-
tains social stability at the cost of individuality, innovation, and change. Louis
Wirth, however, noted in his classic 1938 essay that these informal mechanisms
break down in large, densely settled, and diverse urban populations. Great size
confers anonymity and a certain immunity from social interference by friends
and relatives. In a city, rural migrants are freed from the constraints of tradition
to pursue their own individual interests and tastes, conducting activities that
might have been discouraged or even punished in their communities of origin.

Wirth was disturbed by the implications of urbanism; he viewed it as breed-
ing impersonality, isolation, alienation, anomie, and a proliferation of vice and
deviance, a collection of maladies he generically labeled *urban malaise*. Certainly
there was plenty of malaise in his own time and place, Chicago in the 1930s,
which by any standard exhibited high rates of violence, alcoholism, prostitution,
drug abuse, and intergroup conflict. All of this was documented extensively by
Wirth's students and colleagues at the University of Chicago.

In subsequent years, however, key postulates of Wirth's theory were not
sustained by research, and his ideas fell into disrepute. Although correlations
between urbanism and various forms of social deviance endured over time,
urban sociologists such as Claude Fischer[70] did not find that urban-dwellers
were isolated, alienated, or anomic. Indeed, inhabitants of large cities were con-

nected to other people just as fully as inhabitants of small towns. Although the networks they built were composed more of friends than of family, their social circles were about the same size and they were just as satisfied with their lives.

It is clear that Wirth failed because he looked at the social world of Chicago in the 1930s and made the wrong inference. He saw high rates of unconventional and antisocial behavior, and attributed these outcomes to urbanism. I believe that what he actually saw in Depression–era Chicago were the consequences of concentrated poverty. Louis Wirth was the first social scientist to note a connection between the geographic concentration of poverty and the proliferation of socially destructive behavior, although he didn't quite recognize it at the time.

The social malaise observed by Wirth did not stem from urbanism per se, but from the concentration of poverty during the Great Depression. A few years after Wirth wrote his essay, St. Clair Drake and Horace Cayton[71] published a map showing the percentage of families on relief in various Chicago neighborhoods in 1934. This map is almost identical to a map published 40 years later by William Julius Wilson.[72] In the 1980s, as in the 1930s, the spatial concentration of material deprivation stemmed from the same underlying causes: rising income inequality and growing class segregation amplified by racial segregation.

Drake and Cayton's maps clearly revealed the close connection between high concentrations of poverty and various social problems such as unwed childbearing, delinquency, and disease. The importance of these empirical connections was soon forgotten, however, as mass socioeconomic and residential mobility during the 1950s and 1960s weakened the ecological correlations underlying Wirth's theory and discredited his ideas. A series of detailed ethnographic studies also showed that poor urbanites were anything but socially disengaged and alienated.[73–76]

In 1975 Claude Fischer proposed a theory to account for the connection between urbanism and unconventionality without resorting to concepts such as alienation, anomie, and malaise. His analysis provides a way of understanding the cultural consequences of concentrated affluence and poverty. In essence, Fischer argued that cities create fertile conditions for the emergence and perpetuation of urban subcultures. Under conditions of geographic concentration, subcultures emerge and intensify to produce high rates of unconventional behavior. Apparent deviance within cities occurs not because urbanites are alienated or anomic, but because they are deeply embedded in intense, socially cohesive subcultures that sustain and reinforce attitudes and behaviors which the wider public finds exotic, foreign, or deviant.

According to Fischer, "subcultural theory seems really to be a theory of *group concentration* . . . [and] subcultural processes are revealed to be fundamentally about *intragroup accessibility*. Spatial agglomeration is . . . one way group members gain access to one another [and] in the end, [it] . . . is largely about the ability of subcultural members to communicate, to create 'moral density' . . . it is not necessarily about *cities* per se" (emphasis in original).[77] The geographic agglomeration, through urbanization, of people with similar traits gives rise to distinct subcultures that reflect the characteristics of the people who are concentrated in space.

In this sense, the advent of geographically concentrated affluence and poverty as the dominant spatial structure of the twenty-first century has profound implications for the nature of social life. Not only will the informal means by which past societies preserved public order break down and ultimately disappear under the onslaught of urbanization; they will be replaced by new cultural forms rooted in the ecological order of concentrated affluence and poverty.

Just as poverty is concentrated spatially, anything correlated with poverty is also concentrated. Therefore, as the density of poverty increases in cities throughout the world, so will the density of joblessness, crime, family dissolution, drug abuse, alcoholism, disease, and violence. Not only will the poor have to grapple with the manifold problems due to their own lack of income; increasingly they also will have to confront the social effects of living in an environment where most of their neighbors are also poor. At the same time, the concentration of affluence will create a social environment for the rich that is opposite in every respect from that of the poor. The affluent will experience the personal benefits of high income; in addition, they will profit increasingly from the fact that most of their neighbors possess these advantages as well.

Therefore, in the emerging ecology of inequality, the social worlds of the poor and the rich will diverge to yield distinct, opposing subcultures. Among those at the low end of the income distribution, the spatial concentration of poverty will create a harsh and destructive environment perpetuating values, attitudes, and behaviors that are adaptive within a geographic niche of intense poverty but harmful to society at large and destructive of the poor themselves. At the other end of the hierarchy, a contrasting subculture of privilege will emerge from the spatial niche of concentrated affluence to confer additional advantages on the rich, thereby consolidating their social and economic dominance.

Perhaps no consequence of concentrated poverty is as destructive as the proliferation of crime and violence. Criminal behavior is associated strongly with income deprivation; thus the geographic concentration of poverty will cause a concentration of criminal violence in poor neighborhoods.[78] According to estimates I developed for Philadelphia, every one-point increase in the neighborhood poverty rate raises the major crime rate by 0.8 point.[79,80] Krivo and Peterson use data from Columbus, Ohio, to show that moving from a neighborhood where the poverty rate is under 20% to a neighborhood where it is over 40% increases the rate of violent crime more than threefold, from around 7 per thousand to about 23 per thousand.[81]

How will the poor adapt to an environment where violence is endemic and the risk of victimization great? At the individual level, a logical adaptation is to become violent oneself. As my colleague Elijah Anderson has discovered through his ethnographic fieldwork, one can deter potential criminals and increase the odds of survival by adopting a threatening demeanor, cultivating a reputation for the use of force, and backing that reputation with selective violence.[82] In a social world characterized by endemic violence, an obsessive concern with respect becomes a viable adaptive strategy.[83]

Therefore, given the progressive concentration of violence, some poor people certainly will adopt violent attitudes and behavior as survival strategies. As more people adopt more violent strategies for self-preservation, the average level of violence in poor neighborhoods will rise, leading others to adopt still more violent behavior. As the average level of violence rises over time, more people will adopt increasingly violent strategies to protect themselves from the growing threat of victimization, and ultimately will produce a self-perpetuating upward spiral of violence.

The fundamental need to adapt to structurally embedded conditions of endemic violence leads to the emergence of a "code of the streets" that encourages and promotes the use of force. Asking residents of poor neighborhoods to choose a less violent path or to "just say no" to the temptation of violence is absurd in view of the threatening character of the ecological niche they inhabit. To survive in such areas, one must learn and (to a significant extent) internalize the code of violence described by Anderson. In this way, aggression is passed from person to person in a self-feeding, escalating fashion.

Recent brain research suggests that this internalization of violence is more than a socially learned reaction that one can set aside whenever the situation warrants. Repeated exposure to high levels of danger and physical violence wire emotional predispositions to rage and violence directly into the brain and make them an organic part of a person's makeup. Research has shown that perceptions of danger are channeled directly to a small mass of neural cells known as the amygdala, which sits above the brain stem near the bottom of the limbic ring.[84] The amygdala is capable of generating an emotional response that triggers aggressive, violent behavior without passing through the neocortex, the center of rational thought.[85] Emotional responses developed through the limbic system are learned, but they are unconscious and automatic. Perceptions of danger may be signaled not only by physical threats but also by symbolic injuries to self-esteem or dignity.[84] The threat triggers the amygdala to produce a limbic surge, which releases catecholamines to generate a quick rush of energy lasting minutes. At the same time, the amygdala activates the adrenocortical system to produce a general state of readiness that lasts for hours or even days. Adrenocortical arousal, in turn, lowers the subsequent threshold for anger and increases the intensity of emotions, raising the odds that the rational centers of the brain will be overwhelmed by powerful emotions beyond the control of the neocortex.

By dramatically increasing the exposure of the poor to violence from a very early age,[86] the new ecological order will maximize the number of people with hair-trigger tempers and elevated predispositions to violence. These emotional reactions, moreover, will not be turned on and off easily and rationally in response to shifting social contexts. People who grow up in areas of concentrated poverty and violence will experience profound spillover effects in other areas of life: Disagreements with bosses, spouses, and children will be more likely to turn violent, and thus the odds of successful employment, marriage, and childrearing will be diminished. Concentrated poverty is a stronger predictor of violent crime than of property crime, and of violence between people known to one another than between strangers.[81,87]

The contrasting ecologies of affluence and poverty will also breed opposing peer subcultures among rich and poor youths. As affluence grows more concentrated, the children of the privileged will socialize increasingly with other children of well-educated and successful parents. Knowledge of what one does to prepare for college and an appreciation of the connection between schooling and socioeconomic success will be widespread in the schools of the affluent. Students will arrive in the classroom well prepared and ready to learn. School officials need only build on this base of knowledge and motivation by using their ample resources to hire well-informed guidance counselors and enthusiastic, talented teachers.

Meanwhile, the children of the poor increasingly will attend schools with children from other poor families, who themselves are beset by multiple difficulties stemming from a lack of income. Parents will be poorly educated and will lack adequate knowledge about how to prepare for college. Children will not fully appreciate the connection between education and later success. Supervision and monitoring of students will be difficult because so many come from single-parent families, and the schools will be unable to offset this deficit because of funding limitations. Students will arrive in the classroom poorly prepared, and neither the dispirited guidance counselors nor the overworked, underpaid teachers will expect much from the students.

In such settings an alternative status system is almost certain to develop. Under circumstances where it is difficult to succeed according to conventional standards, the usual criteria for success typically are inverted to create an oppositional identity.[88,89] Children formulate oppositional identities to preserve self-esteem when expectations are low and when failure by conventional standards is likely. Thus, in areas of concentrated poverty, students from poor families will legitimize their educational failures by attaching positive value and meaning to outcomes that affluent children label deviant and unworthy. In adapting to the environment created by concentrated poverty, success in school will be devalued, hard work will be regarded as selling out, and any display of learning will be viewed as uncool.

Oppositional subcultures already have become entrenched in many black inner-city areas of the United States, where high levels of racial segregation have produced unusually high concentrations of poverty and educational distress.[90] Once such a subculture becomes established, it acquires a life of its own that contributes independently to the perpetuation of educational failure, the reproduction of poverty, and the cultural transmission of low socioeconomic status from person to person, family to family, and group to group.[91,92]

Into the "Age Of Extremes"

Thus a new age of extremes is upon us. In the social ecology now being created around the globe, affluent people increasingly will live and interact with other affluent people, while the poor increasingly will live and interact with other poor people. The social worlds of the rich and the poor will diverge, creating the potential for radical differences in thought, action, values, tastes, and feelings, and for the construction of a new political geography that divorces the interests of the rich from the welfare of the poor. For the first time in human history, the advantages and disadvantages of one's class position in society will be compounded and reinforced by a systematic process of geographic concentration.

I have tried to present my arguments at a general level, describing the forces that produce geographically concentrated affluence and poverty and outlining the consequences of these trends without reference to a specific racial or ethnic group. I believe that social scientists in the United States have focused too narrowly on the problems of African Americans in urban ghettos, and thus have mistakenly racialized processes that are much broader and more general than most observers realize.

The effects of ongoing urbanization, rising income inequality, and growing class segregation are exacerbated by racial segregation so that the effects are most salient and most visible among African Americans, but the basic processes are sweeping the world and concentrating poverty everywhere. In presenting the arguments at a general level, I seek to create a theoretical link between violence in Harlem and disorder in the slums of Rio and Mexico City, between social breakdown on the South Side of Chicago and the collapse of authority in rapidly urbanizing societies of Africa. In my view, the spatial concentration of poverty is implicated in the escalation of crime, disease, family breakdown, and the proliferation of various social pathologies throughout the world.

I also believe that social scientists' attention has concentrated too narrowly on the poor and their neighborhoods. Our obsessive interest in the generation and reproduction of class is rarely focused on the affluent. Scores of ethnographers descend on the homes, bars, and street corners of the poor to chronicle their attitudes and behavior; few attempt to infiltrate the mansions, clubs, and boutiques of the wealthy to document the means by which they maintain and reproduce their affluence. The concentration of affluence and poverty means that the social lives of the rich and the poor increasingly will transpire in different venues; we must study both in order to fully comprehend the newly emerged system of stratification.

Although I have sketched a few of the ecological mechanisms by which inequality will be created and reproduced in the postindustrial society of the twenty-first century, my list is not exhaustive. A great deal remains to be said, written, and researched. Although limitations of time and space do not permit me to go into detail, I believe that the concentration of poverty is a primary force behind the spread of new diseases such as AIDS and the resurgence of old ones such as tuberculosis;[93-94] it also stands behind the creation and perpetuation of joblessness and the decline of marriage among the poor.[64,95,72] It is implicated as well in the increase in unwed childbearing,[95] and I believe it contributes to the spread of homelessness around the United States and the world. No doubt concentrated poverty also can be implicated in a variety of other social and economic phenomena in ways that have yet to be discovered.

I have attempted to explain how our social world has been transformed by the forces of spatial redistribution, it is more difficult to describe how the harmful social consequences of this transformation might be avoided. Confronting the new ecology of inequality is particularly difficult because concentrated poverty creates an unstable and unattractive social environment that is at once a cause and a consequence of class segregation. The social chaos stemming from concentrated poverty propels the affluent further into geographic and social withdrawal, and their departure further isolates the poor and stokes the fires of social disorder. Insofar as racial and ethnic segregation perpetuate concentrated poverty and its consequences in minority communities, the proliferation of antisocial behaviors will fuel pejorative stereotypes and intensify prejudice, making political solutions so much more difficult.

How does the future look to me? Bleak, because I know that it is in the elite's narrow self-interest to perpetuate the status quo. Addressing serious issues such as increasing income inequality, growing class segregation, racial prejudice, and the geographic concentration of poverty will inevitably require sacrifice, and the immediate course of least resistance for affluent people will always be to raise the walls of social, economic, and geographic segregation higher in order to protect themselves from the rising tide of social pathology and violence.

If the status quo indeed is the most likely outcome, inequality will continue to increase and racial divisions will grow, creating a volatile and unstable political economy. As class tensions rise, urban areas will experience escalating crime and violence punctuated by sporadic riots and increased terrorism as class tensions rise. The poor will become disenfranchised and alienated from mainstream political and economic institutions, while the middle classes will grow more angry, more frustrated, and more politically mobilized. The affluent will continue to withdraw socially and spatially from the rest of society, and will seek to placate the middle classes' anger with quick fixes and demagogic excesses that do not change the underlying structure responsible for their problems.

This scenario is by no means inevitable, and I sincerely hope it will not come to pass. Yet we are headed in this direction unless self-conscious actions are taken to change course. A principal motivation for my pessimistic candor and perhaps overly brutal frankness is to galvanize colleagues, students, politicians, and reporters into action. Until now, neither the nature of the new ecological order nor its social implications have been fully realized; my purpose here is not to offer facile solutions to difficult problems, but to begin a process of serious thought, reflection, and debate on the new ecology of inequality, from which solutions ultimately may emerge. Until we begin to face up to the reality of rising inequality and its geographic expression, no solution will be possible.

References

1. Tabatabai H, Fouad M. *The Incidence of Poverty in Developing Countries: An ILO Compendium of Data*. Geneva: International Labour Office, 1993.
2. United Nations. *World Urbanization Prospects: 1994 Revision*. New York: United Nations, 1995.
3. U.S. Bureau of the Census. *1970 Census of Population Subject Reports: Low-Income Population*. PC(2)-9A. Washington, DC: U.S. Government Printing Office, 1973.
4. U.S. Bureau of the Census. *1980 Census of Population, General Social and Economic Characteristics, Part I: U.S. Summary*. PC80-1-Cl. Washington, DC: U.S. Government Printing Office, 1983.
5. U.S. Bureau of the Census. *1990 Census of Population, Social and Economic Characteristics: Metropolitan Areas*. CP-2-1B. Washington, DC: U.S. Government Printing Office, 1993.
6. Kasarda JD. Inner-City Concentrated Poverty and Neighborhood Distress: 1970–1990. *Housing Policy Debate* 1993; 4: 253–302.
7. Lieberson S. *A Piece of the Pie: Blacks and White Immigrants since 1880*. Berkeley: University of California Press, 1980.
8. Lieberson S. An Asymmetrical Approach to Segregation. In: Peach C, Robinson V, Smith S, eds. *Ethnic Segregation in Cities*. London: Croom Helm, 1981: 61–82.
9. Massey DS, Eggers ML. The Ecology of Inequality: Minorities and the Concentration of Poverty, 1970–1980. *AJS* 1990; 95: 1153–1189.
10. Abramson AJ, Tobin MS, VanderGoot MR. The Changing Geography of Metropolitan Opportunity: The Segregation of the Poor in U.S. Metropolitan Areas, 1970–1990. *Housing Policy Debate* 1995; 6: 45–72.
11. Sjoberg G. *The Preindustrial City: Past and Present*. New York: Free Press, 1960.
12. Hershberg T. *Philadelphia: Work, Space, Family, and Group Experience in the 19th Century*. New York: Oxford University Press, 1981.
13. Zunz O. *The Changing Face of Inequality: Urbanization, Industrial Development, and Immigrants in Detroit, 1880–1920*. Chicago: University of Chicago Press, 1982.
14. Burgess EW. The Growth of the City: An Introduction to a Research Project. In: Park RE, Burgess EW, eds. *The City*. Chicago: University of Chicago Press, 1925: 47–62.
15. Massey DS. Ethnic Residential Segregation: A Theoretical Synthesis and Empirical Review. *Sociol Soc Res* 1985; 69: 315–350.

16. Massey DS, Denton NA. *American Apartheid: Segregation and the Making of the Underclass*. Cambridge, MA: Harvard University Press, 1993.
17. Alba RD. The Twilight of Ethnicity among American Catholics of European Ancestry. *Ann Am Acad Pol Soc Sci* 1981; 454: 86–97.
18. Blau PM, Duncan OD. *The American Occupational Structure*. New York: Free Press, 1967.
19. Featherman D, Hauser RM. *Opportunity and Change*. New York: Academic Press, 1978.
20. Levy F. *Dollars and Dreams: The Changing Distribution of American Income*. New York: Russell Sage Foundation, 1987.
21. Smith JP. Poverty and the Family. In: Sandefur GD, Tienda M, eds. *Divided Opportunities: Minorities, Poverty, and Social Policy*. New York: Plenum, 1988: 141–172.
22. Simkus A. Residential Segregation by Occupation and Race in Ten Urban Areas, 1950–1970. *Am Sociol Rev*. 1978; 43: 81–93.
23. Massey DS, Eggers ML. The Spatial Concentration of Affluence and Poverty during the 1970s. *Urban Aff Q*. 1993; 29: 299–315.
24. Preston SH. Urban Growth in Developing Countries: A Demographic Reappraisal. *Popul Dev Rev*. 1979; 5: 195–216.
25. Hatton TJ, Williamson JG. What Drove the Mass Migrations from Europe? *Popul Dev Rev*. 1994; 20: 533–561.
26. Nugent W. *Crossings: The Great Transatlantic Migration, 1870–1914*. Bloomington: Indiana University Press, 1992.
27. Massey DS. International Migration and Economic Development in Comparative Perspective. *Popul Dev Rev*. 1998; 14: 383–414.
28. Hauser RM, Featherman DL. *The Process of Stratification: Trends and Analysis*. New York: Academic Press, 1977.
29. Balan J, Browning HL, Jelin E. *Men in a Developing Society: Geographic and Social Mobility in Monterrey, Mexico*. Austin: University of Texas Press, 1973.
30. Munoz H, de Oliveira O, Stern C. *Migracion y Desigualdad Social en la Ciudad de Mexico*. Mexico, DF: Universidad Nacional de Mexico y Colegio de Mexico, 1977.
31. Braun D. *The Rich Get Richer: The Rise of Income Inequality in the United States and the World*. Chicago: Nelson-Hall, 1991.
32. Oliver ML, Shapiro TM. *Black Wealth/White Wealth: A New Perspective on Racial Inequality*. New York: Routledge, 1995.
33. Wolff EN. 1995. The Rich Get Increasingly Richer: Latest Data on Household Wealth during the 1980s. In: Ratcliff RE, Oliver ML, Shapiro TM, eds. *Research in Politics and Society, Vol. 5*. Greenwich, CT: JAI, 1995: 33–68.
34. Atkinson AB, Rainwater L, Smeeding TM. *Income Distribution in OECD Countries: Evidence from the Luxembourg Income Study*. Paris: Organisation for Economic Cooperation and Development, 1995.
35. Danziger S, Gottschalk P. *America Unequal*. Cambridge, MA: Harvard University Press, 1995.

36. Morris M, Bernhardt AD, Handcock MS. Economic Inequality: New Methods for New Trends. *Am Sociol Rev.* 1994; 59: 205–219.
37. Escobar Latapi A. Mexico: Poverty as Politics and Academic Disciplines. In: Oyen E, Miller SM, Samad SA, eds. *Poverty: A Global Review.* Oslo: Scandinavian University Press, 1996: 539–566.
38. Equipo Pueblo. Salaries Continue to Plummet. *Mexico Update 69.* 1996; April 23: 1.
39. Cortes F, Rubalcava, RM. El Ingreso Familiar: Su Distribución y Desigualdad 1984–1989. *Demos: Carta Demográfica sobre Mexico.* 1992; 5: 28–30.
40. Cortes F. La Evolución de la Desigualdad del Ingreso Familiar Durante la DCcada de 10s Ochenta. Unpublished manuscript, Centro de Estudios Sociológicos, El Colegio de Mexico, 1994.
41. Gonzalez de la Rocha M. *Los Recursos de la Probeza: Familias de Bajos Ingresos de Guadalajara.* Guadalajara: El Colegio de Jalisco, 1986
42. Escobar Latapi A. Movilidad, Restructuración, y Clase Social en Mexico: El Caso de Guadalajara. *Estud Sociol.* 1995; 13: 231–260.
43. Kasarda JD. 1995. Industrial Restructuring and the Changing Location of Jobs. In: Farley R, ed. *State of the Union: America in the 1990s.* New York: Russell Sage Foundation, 1995: 215–268.
44. Freeman RB. How Much Has De-Unionization Contributed to the Rise in Male Earnings Inequality? In: Danziger S, Gottschalk P, eds. *Uneven Tides: Rising Inequality in America.* New York: Russell Sage Foundation, 1993: 133–163.
45. Harrison B. *Lean and Mean: The Changing Landscape of Corporate Power in the Age of Flexibility.* New York: Basic Books, 1995.
46. Rifkin J. *The End of Work: The Decline of the Global Labor Force and the Dawn of the Post-Market Era.* New York: Putnam, 1995.
47. Maddrick J. *The End of Affluence: The Causes and Consequences of America's Economic Dilemma.* New York: Random House, 1995.
48. Kaus M. *The End of Equality.* New York: Basic Books, 1992.
49. Aronowitz S, DiFazio W. *The Jobless Future: Sci-Tech and the Dogma of Work.* Minneapolis: University of Minnesota Press, 1994.
50. Bernstein MA, Adler DE. *Understanding American Economic Decline.* Cambridge, UK: Cambridge University Press, 1994.
51. Frank RH, Cook PJ. *The Winner-Take-All Society.* New York: Free Press, 1995.
52. Lasch C. *The Revolt of the Elites and the Betrayal of Democracy.* New York: Norton, 1995.
53. Lind M. *The Next American Nation: The New Nationalism and the Fourth American Revolution.* New York: Free Press, 1995.
54. Denton NA. Are African Americans Still Hypersegregated? In: Bullard RD, Grigsby JE III, Lee C, eds. *Residential Apartheid: The American Legacy.* Los Angeles: CAAS Publications, University of California, 1994: 49–81.
55. Krugman P. *The Age of Diminished Expectations.* Cambridge, MA: MIT Press, 1994.

56. Alegria T. Segregación Socioespacial Urbana: El Ejelnplo de Tijuana. *Estud Demogr Urbanos Col Mex.* 1994; 9: 411–428.
57. Delgado J. De 10s Anillos de la Segregación: La Ciudad de Mexico 1950–1987. *Estud Demogr Urbanos Col Mex.* 1990; 5: 237–274.
58. Rubalcava RM, Schteingart M. Diferenciación Socioespacial Intraurbana en el Area Metropolitana de la Ciudad de Mexico. *Estud Sociol.* 1985; 3: 21–85.
59. Walton J. Guadalajara: Creating the Divided City. In: Cornelius WA, Kemper RV, eds. *Metropolitan Latin America: The Challenge and the Response.* Beverly Hills: Sage, 1978: 25–50.
60. Massey DS. The Residential Segregation of Blacks, Hispanics, and Asians: 1970 to 1990. In Jaynes GD, ed. *Immigration and Race Relations.* New Haven: Yale University Press, 2000.
61. Farley R, Frey WH. Changes in the Segregation of Whites from Blacks during the 1980s: Small Steps toward a More Integrated Society. *Am Sociol Rev.* 1994; 59: 23–45.
62. Masse DS. Denton NA. Hypersegregation in U.S. Metropolitan Areas: Black and Hispanic Segregation along Five Dimensions. *Demography.* 1989; 26: 373–393.
63. Jargowsky PA. Take the Money and Run: Economic Segregation in U.S. Metropolitan Areas. *Am Sociol Rev.* 1996 Dec; 61(6): 984–98.
64. Krivo L, Peterson RD, Rizzo H, Reynolds JR. *Race, Segregation, and the Concentration of Disadvantage: 1980–1990.* Presented at the annual meetings of the Population Association of America, New Orleans, 1996.
65. Massey DS, Gross AB, Eggers ML. Segregation, the Concentration of Poverty, and the Life Chances of Individuals. *Soc Sci Res.* 1991; 20: 397–420.
66. Stalker P. *The Work of Strangers: A Survey of International Labour Migration.* Geneva: International Labour Office, 1994.
67. Herrnstein RJ, Murray C. *The Bell Curve: Intelligence and Class Structure in American Life.* New York: Free Press, 1994.
68. Durkheim E. *The Division of Labor in Society.* Simpson G, translator. Glencoe, IL: Free Press, [1893] 1933.
69. Banfield EC. *The Moral Basis of a Backward Society.* New York: Free Press, 1967.
70. Fischer CS. *To Dwell among Friends: Personal Networks in Town and City.* Chicago: University of Chicago Press, 1982.
71. Drake SC, Cayton HR. *Black Metropolis: A Study of Life in a Northern City.* New York: Harcourt, Brace, 1945.
72. Wilson J. *The Truly Disadvantaged: The Inner City, the Underclass, and Public Policy.* Chicago: University of Chicago Press, 1987.
73. Gans HC. *The Urban Villagers: Group and Class in the Life of Italian Americans.* New York: Free Press, 1962.
74. Stack C. *All Our Kin: Strategies of Survival in a Black Community.* New York: Harper and Row, 1974.

75. Suttles GD. *The Social Order of the Slum: Ethnicity and Territory in the Inner City*. Chicago: University of Chicago Press, 1968.
76. Whyte WF. *Street Corner Society*. Chicago: University of Chicago Press, 1955.
77. Fischer CS. Toward a Subcultural Theory of Urbanism. *Am J Sociol*. 1975; 80: 1319–1341.
78. Massey DS, Condran GA, Denton NA. The Effect of Residential Segregation on Black Social and Economic Well-Being. *Soc Forces*. 1987; 66: 29–57.
79. Massey DS. American Apartheid: Segregation and the Making of the Underclass. *Am J Sociol*. 1990; 96: 329–358.
80. Massey DS. Getting Away with Murder: Segregation and Violent Crime in Urban America. *Univ PA Law Rev*. 1995; 143: 1203–1232.
81. Krivo L, Peterson RD. Extremely Disadvantaged Neighborhoods and Urban Crime. *Soc Forces*. 1996; 75: 619–650.
82. Anderson E. The Code of the Streets. *Atl Mon*. 1994; 273(3): 80–94.
83. Bourgois P. *In Search of Respect: Selling Crack in El Barrio*. Cambridge, UK: Cambridge University Press, 1995.
84. Goleman D. *Emotional Intelligence: Why It Can Matter More Than IQ*. New York: Bantam Books, 1995.
85. LeDoux J. Sensory Systems and Emotion. *Integr Psychiatry*. 1986; 4: 237–243.
86. Ousseimi M. *Caught in the Crossfire: Growing Up in a War Zone*. New York: Walker, 1995.
87. Miles-Doan R, Kelly S. Neighborhood Contexts of Assaultive Violence: A Tract-Level Study of Disaggregated Rates in Duval County, Florida—1992. Presented at the annual meetings of the Population Association of America, New Orleans, 1996.
88. Ogbu JU. *Minority Education and Caste: The American System in Cross-Cultural Perspective*. New York: Academic Press, 1978.
89. Ogbu JU. Minority Status and Schooling in Plural Societies. *Comp Educ Rev*. 1983; 27: 168–190.
90. Fordham S, Ogbu JU. Black Students' School Success: Coping with the "Burden of Acting White." *Urban Rev*. 1986; 18: 176–206.
91. Anderson E. *Streetwise: Race, Class, and Change in an Urban Community*. Chicago: University of Chicago Press, 1990.
92. Portes A. Children of Immigrants: Segmented Assimilation and Its Determinants. In: Portes A, ed. *The Economic Sociology of Immigration: Essays on Networks, Ethnicity, and Entrepreneurship*. New York: Russell Sage Foundation. 1995: 248–280.
93. Garrett L. *The Coming Plague: Newly Emerging Diseases in a World out of Balance*. New York: Farrar, Straus, and Giroux, 1994.
94. Wallace R, Wallace D. U.S. Apartheid and the Spread of AIDS to the Suburbs: A Multi-City Analysis of the Political Economy of a Spatial Epidemic. *Soc Sci Med*. 1995; 36: 1–13.

95. Massey DS, Shibuya K. Unraveling the Tangle of Pathology: The Effect of Spatially Concentrated Joblessness on the Well-Being of African Americans. *Soc Sci Res.* 1995; 24: 352–366.
96. Sheahan J. *Conflict and Change in Mexican Economic Strategy: Implications for Mexico and Latin America.* La Jolla: Center for U.S.-Mexican Studies, University of California, San Diego, 1991.
97. Foster GM. *Tzintzuntzan: Mexican Peasants in a Changing World.* Boston: Little, Brown, 1967.

Health Inequities in the United States: Prospects and Solutions

Dennis Raphael

The purpose of this paper is to consider the issue of health inequities in the USA with particular emphasis on public health responses to such inequities. Much of its content will focus upon the emerging literature on what are termed the social determinants of health.[1,2] This literature links health outcomes to how societies are organized and structured. And one of the most important societal factors related to health appears to be the degree of economic inequality within a nation, state, province, or municipality.[3,4] Economic inequality affects health directly by creating greater poverty and indirectly by weakening social structures that support health. Recognition of the important role played by the social determinants of health will require public health workers to reconsider and expand their concepts of health and how to work for health. It will also require health workers to consider the economic and political forces that create inequality. To date, such reconsideration of the role of public health in reducing health inequities by considering the social determinants of health has been—with some notable exceptions—uncommon in the USA.

Defining Health, Health Promotion, Social Determinants of Health, and Economic Inequality

There is a difference between a health inequality and a health inequity. A health inequality is simply the existence of health status differences among the population. In contrast, Dahlgren and Whitehead[5] argue that a health inequality becomes an inequity when it is avoidable, unnecessary, and unfair—a clear statement of a values position. Values held by a society and its citizens become especially important as consideration is given to the source of health inequities and the willingness or unwillingness of a society to address these inequities.

The ideas that shape this consideration of health inequities in the USA are rooted in concepts of health and health promotion as outlined by the World Health Organization (WHO) in the *Ottawa Charter for Health Promotion*.[6,7]

These concepts have strongly influenced thinking about health in Canada and Europe; less so in the USA. *Health* refers to both the health status of individuals and to the health of communities. Among individuals, health refers to the incidence of illness and premature death as well as the presence of physical, social and personal resources that allow for the achievement of personal goals. Considering communities, health refers to the presence of economic, social and environmental structures that support the physical, psychological, and social well-being of community members.[8,9]

Health promotion is the process of enabling people to increase control over, and improve their health.[7] It occurs through processes of enabling people, advocacy, and mediating among health and other sectors. Specific actions are developing personal skills, creating supportive environments, strengthening communities, influencing governments to enact healthy public policies, and re-orienting and improving health services. Health promotion has a strong values emphasis, an emphasis that is frequently lacking in various conceptions of population health.[10]

Social determinants of health are the social and economic conditions within a society that influence whether people are healthy or ill. There is an emerging consensus concerning what these social determinants might be. There is less consensus on how these determinants can be influenced to improve health. *Economic inequality* refers to the unequal distribution in income and wealth of residents within a nation, state, province, or locality. Increasing economic inequality is becoming a focus of the public policy community in the USA, Canada, and the UK.[11-23]

Why Be Concerned About the Social Determinants of Health?

While there have been significant improvements in health status among the populations of western industrialized nations as a whole, there continue to be wide disparities in population health between nations as well as within them.[24,25] Access to medical care has been hypothesized as being responsible in part for such differences, and clearly such access is important.[26] Nevertheless, to illustrate the limits of considering access to health care as a key determinant of health, in the late 1970s Canadian researchers—in a nation with a universal health care system—found the difference in life expectancy between the lowest and highest quintiles of Canadian income earners to be 4.4 years; for disability-free life expectancy, the difference was 11 years.[27]

Differences in heart disease have been shown to be due to elevated serum cholesterol resulting from diets rich in saturated fats, cigarette smoking, hypertension, and lack of physical activity. But studies carried out in the United Kingdom and the United States found that most of the differences in heart disease mortality among occupational and educational classes cannot be accounted for by these factors.[28,29] More recently Lantz et al.'s analyses of data from a nationally representative prospective study of US adults revealed that lifestyle factors of alcohol and tobacco use, body mass index, and activity accounted for a rather small proportion of variance in total mortality rates as compared to income.[30] These and other studies indicate that there are additional factors that predict illness and death. What might these other factors be?

Non-medical factors that affect health go by a variety of titles such as prerequisites for health, determinants of health, and social determinants of health, among others. The *Ottawa Charter for Health Promotion*[7] identified the prerequisites for health as being peace, shelter, education, food, income, a stable ecosystem, sustainable resources, social justice and equity. Clearly, these prerequisites represent a concern with structural issues. From another direction, Health Canada[31] accepted direction from the Canadian Institute for Advanced Research[32] in outlining determinants of health—only some of which are social determinants—of income and social status, social support networks, education, employment and working conditions, physical and social environments, biology and genetic endowment, personal health practices and coping skills, healthy child development, and health services. A British working group specifically identified "social determinants of health" as being the social gradient, stress, early life, social exclusion, work, unemployment, social support, addiction, food, and transport.[1,2] The broadest application of a social determinants of health approach involves analysis of the role political ideology plays in promoting economic inequality and weakening communal social structures.[33] In these analyses, social determinants of health involve the overall structure of an economic system and how it allocates economic resources across the population.

In this paper the focus is upon social determinants of health associated with the distribution of economic resources within a jurisdiction.[34] Such a focus leads to initial consideration of poverty and its effects upon individuals and communities. But the distribution of economic resources within a society is also associated with whether social supports and health services—also contributors to health—are available to the population. Finally, how a society distributes economic resources may also contribute to overall social cohesion, an additional contributor to the health of the population. After providing an overview of recent work on economic inequality and health inequities, the focus is upon issues related to the USA scene. An analysis of the current situation in Canada is also available.[35]

Poverty and Its Effects on Health

Poverty is the most obvious manifestation of inequality in distribution of economic resources and potentially the strongest determinant of health.[36] The effects of poverty on health have been known since the 19th century,[37] but recent interest in its effects on health was spurred by the publication in the United Kingdom of the *Black* and the *Health Divide* reports.[38] These reports documented how those in the lowest employment-level groups showed a greater likelihood of suffering from a wide range of diseases and having a greater likelihood of death from illness or injury at every stage of the life cycle. Differences in health were seen across the socioeconomic range from professional status to manual labor.

Interest in poverty and its health effects have continued unabated in the UK, and updates on health inequities within Britain and means of addressing such inequities are available.[39-42] Indeed, British work in the health inequities area is the most advanced among industrialized nations and an excellent source of research ideas and potential courses of action. Canadian work on the social determinants of health and means of addressing health inequities resulting from these determinants are provided by Raphael[35,43,44] and Townsend.[20]

A recent USA Department of Health and Human Services report[26] documented the wide range of income-related health differences that exist between poor and not poor children, adults, and seniors. In addition to mortality and many morbidity differences, disparities are also seen for activity limitation among children and adults as well as cigarette smoking and being overweight. To illustrate the magnitude of these health differences, heart disease death rates reported for Americans between the ages of 25–64 earning <$10,000 was 318 per 100,000; for those earning $10,000–14,999, 251 per 100,000; for those earning $15,000–$24,900,142 per 100,000, and those earning $25,000 or more, 126 per 100,000. Similar findings were obtained for deaths from lung cancer and diabetes. Additionally, poverty has consequences in terms of performance in school, use of the health care system, and quality of attained employment.

No examination of the health effects of poverty can ignore the relationship between economic inequality and poverty. Societies that are economically unequal have higher levels of poverty. Recent re-analysis of data from the *Luxembourg Income Study*[45] found the relationship between degree of income inequality within a nation (as measured by the Gini index) with child poverty for 16 industrialized Western nations was strong, positive, and reliable ($r = .77$). The USA has both the highest levels of economic inequality and the greatest level of child poverty. The Gini index is a measure of economic inequality and considers how economic resources are distributed across the population. If all the wealth within a population was owned by one person, the index would be 1.00. If there was complete equality the index would be 0.00. A number of economic inequality indices have been developed and are described in Kawachi and Kennedy.[46]

Economically Unequal Societies Provide Fewer Social Safety Nets

A second approach, moving the level of analysis from the individual to the societal, discloses that economic inequality directly affects poor people as more of a society's resources get shifted to the well-off. This occurs through the organization of the income tax system by which the well-off have—as compared to other nations—lower tax rates. Additionally, benefits to the poor in the form of social assistance benefits and social services may also be reduced.[45] Nations, states/provinces, and municipalities with greater economic inequality have weaker social safety nets,[47] an important determinant of health for all individuals, but especially for the poor.[48,49] The USA has the lowest percentage of tax revenues as a percentage of gross domestic product of all Organization for Economic Cooperation and Development (OECD) nations, and it provides less services and supports than most OECD nations.[50]

The importance of social infrastructure to health is recognized as a basic principle of the *Healthy Cities Movement*.[51] *Healthy Cities* projects emphasize developing healthy municipal public policy by recognizing health as involving the interaction of physical, mental, social, and spiritual dimensions. There is also a commitment to the view that "Since housing, environment, education, social services, and other city programs have a major effect on health in cities, strengthening these are important."[51,p.8]

Consistent with this analysis, two intensive community-based ethnographic studies recently carried out in Toronto showed the profound importance of community agencies and resources for low-income people.[52] When provided with simple open-ended questions about factors that influenced community members' health and well-being, not only service providers, but community members and elected representatives saw reductions in funding to these agencies and to other supports for citizens as threatening the health of community members.[53]

Economically Unequal Societies Have Higher Mortality Rates

The third way economic inequality affects health is through weakening overall population health through mechanisms that are just beginning to be investigated. Wilkinson[25] brought together much of the research showing that societies with greater economic inequality have higher mortality rates. For example, after decades of rapidly increasing economic inequality—itself correlated with increasing disparity in mortality rates—the most well-off in Britain now have higher death rates among infants and adult males than the least well-off in Sweden.[54,55]

There are also findings that the well-off in economically unequal American communities have greater mortality rates than the well-off in relatively equal communities.[56] To illustrate the magnitude of these effects, the differences in death rates from all causes between cities with high income inequality and low per capita income (926 per 100,000), and those with low income inequality and high per capita income (786 per 100,000), is 140 per 100,000, a figure that exceeds the overall rate of USA deaths from heart disease, 130.5 per 100,000.[57] Similarly, homicide rates in the 50 USA states are correlated with degree of economic inequality even after controls for absolute level of income, poverty, and race are applied.[58] Additionally, a just-published analysis by Wolfson et al. confirms that differences in mortality between American states are best predicted from the degree of overall economic inequality rather than absolute income levels of individuals within the state.[59] Findings like these led the *British Medical Journal* to editorialize: "What matters in determining mortality and health in a society is less the overall wealth of that society and more how evenly wealth is distributed. The more equally wealth is distributed the better the health of that society."[60] Why should this be the case?

Economically Unequal Societies Have Weaker Social Cohesion

In *Unhealthy Societies: the Afflictions of Inequality*, Wilkinson argues that societies with greater economic inequality begin to "disintegrate"—that is, they show evidence of decreased social cohesion and increased individual malaise.[25] These are hypothesized to be precursors of increased illness and death. Kawachi and Kennedy[61] make the case that economic inequality contributes to the deteriorating of what has been termed social capital, or the degree of social cohesion or citizen commitment to society.[62,63] When the level of analysis is shifted to the societal level from the individual, the economic inequality and health relationship can be considered in terms of societal structures and public policy rather than as problems of individual health status and coping. As one example, these kinds of analysis can perhaps illuminate how differences between the USA and Canada in economic inequality may help explain mortality differences between the two nations.[64] Canadian mortality rates are strikingly lower than those in the USA, as is the degree of economic inequality.

Two main schools of thought have emerged concerning the mechanisms by which economic inequality contributes to poor health. Kawachi, Kennedy, and Wilkinson in the recently published collection of readings, *Income Inequality and Health*, emphasize the "Wilkinson hypothesis" of psychosocial and social cohesion explanations for health inequities.[4] An emphasis is placed upon how perceptions of relative deprivation among citizens in unequal societies foster poor health and well-being. They pay rather less attention to the material deprivation issues and the role social policy decisions play in supporting health. While the hypothesis is compelling, it has been severely critiqued for its lack of emphasis on the material conditions of societies.[36,65] It should also be noted that there has been little empirical research that specifically tests the relative deprivation hypothesis.

The British authors of the *Widening Gap*, however, explain socioeconomic differences in health in terms of how ". . . the social structure is characterized by a finely graded scale of advantage and disadvantage, with individuals differing in terms of the length and level of their exposure to a particular factor and in terms of the number of factors to which they are exposed."[42,p.102] They bring together empirical research that links material deprivation during childhood and adulthood with the incidence of illness and death. The British workers emphasize 13 key critical periods of the life course during which people are especially vulnerable to social disadvantage. These include fetal development, nutritional growth and health in childhood, entering the labor market, job loss or insecurity, and episodes of illness, among others. Material disadvantage and the absence of societal supports during these key periods work against health. Recent work by Lynch et al. provide longitudinal support for the impact of material deprivation during childhood on adult health status.[66]

Should Public Health Consider Economic Inequality as a Health Issue?

Considering the clear evidence that poverty and economic inequality lead to health problems, what is the role for public health in addressing these issues? Public health responses will be determined by the frame of reference through which these findings are considered.[43] Labonte outlines three approaches toward considering and promoting health: the biomedical, lifestyle, and socio-environmental.[67] In the biomedical approach, emphasis is on high-risk groups, screening of one sort or another, and health care delivery. The behavioral approach focuses on high risk attitudes and behaviours and developing programs that educate and support individuals to change behaviours. The socio-environmental approach focuses on high-risk conditions and considers how individuals adjust to these conditions or move to change them. Another way of thinking about focus is whether interest is on the individual (including biomedical and lifestyle aspects), community (including social supports and connections), or structural (including community resources, policy decisions, and distribution of economic resources).[44]

How does an individual or organization adopt a frame of reference? Sylvia Tesh argues that the approach one takes may be based more on ideology and values than the objective evidence associated with each theory.[68] In current debates about the determinants of health, ideology plays itself out in debates about the relative importance of personal and structural factors in determining health.[69, 70]

One striking example of the role that ideology can play in public health action is the contrast between the ten tips for better health provided by the British Medical Officer Liam Donaldson[71] and by Professor David Gordon of Bristol University[72] (Table 2-1).

The former sees the determinants of health as primarily involving lifestyle choices and individual control; the latter conceptualizes health determinants as primarily structural and beyond individual control. Actually, both approaches should be used. In the case of tobacco, for example, societal policies with regard

TABLE 2-1   Ideology and Public Health

Ten Tips For Better Health (Donaldson, 1999)
1. Don't smoke. If you can, stop. If you can't, cut down.
2. Follow a balanced diet with plenty of fruit and vegetables.
3. Keep physically active.
4. Manage stress by, for example, talking things through and making time to relax.
5. If you drink alcohol, do so in moderation.
6. Cover up in the sun, and protect children from sunburn.
7. Practise safer sex.
8. Take up cancer screening opportunities.
9. Be safe on the roads: follow the Highway Code.
10. Learn the First Aid ABC—airways, breathing, circulation.

An Alternative Ten Tips for Better Health (Gordon, 1999)
1. Don't be poor. If you can, stop. If you can't, try not to be poor for long.
2. Don't have poor parents.
3. Own a car.
4. Don't work in a stressful, low paid manual job.
5. Don't live in damp, low quality housing.
6. Be able to afford to go on a foreign holiday and sunbathe.
7. Practice not losing your job and don't become unemployed.
8. Take up all benefits you are entitled to, if you are unemployed, retired or sick or disabled.
9. Don't live next to a busy major road or near a polluting factory.
10. Learn how to fill in the complex housing benefit asylum application forms before you become homeless and destitute.

to the funding and character of educational programs are important, and structural policies such as clean air acts and taxation of tobacco products are crucial. Generally, however, the public health emphasis in the USA has been so focused on lifestyle aspects of health as to virtually ignore structural issues such as those raised by Gordon.

It is possible to accept the importance of income as a determinant of health but decide to focus on interventions for people with low incomes without addressing the income issue. An illustrative example is an editorial in the *Journal of the American Medical Association* that called for limited public health action towards improving the parenting skills of low income parents and working to communicate high expectations to poor children.[73] It is also possible to focus on improving social networks among low income people without addressing the income issue.[74]

This paper advances the position that public health should deal with poverty and low income as a major risk factor, just as it deals with all other important risk factors such as tobacco, alcohol, and saturated fats. Indeed, economic inequality is an important constraint on educational campaigns to reduce the prevalence of these risk factors. In the case of tobacco, Terris[75] has pointed out that in 1993 the gradient for age-adjusted prevalence of cigarette smoking ranged from 36% in the least educated to 14% in the most educated. He commented that:

> More attention must be paid to the great majority of the people of the United States who are not in the social class which has 16 or more years of education. Only 14% of that social class are current cigarette smokers. Among the rest of the American people, 25% to 36% are still current smokers. It is essential that we make every effort to close this inequality gap, that we pay special attention to the working class population, that we involve labor unions in our campaigns rather than continue to work solely with corporate elites, that we enlist the assistance of the numerous labor and minority publications, that we devise educational approaches and materials that are geared to the interests and concerns of low-income blue-collar and white-collar workers, and that we speak the language of the people instead of the jargon of academia.[75,pp.43,3–34]

What Evidence Is Available Concerning Economic Inequality and Health in the USA?

The hypotheses outlined suggest that greater economic inequality will be associated with greater incidence of poverty, greater evidence of poor health, and greater likelihood of signs of societal disintegration. What USA evidence is available concerning these hypotheses?

Despite spending a greater percentage of GDP (13.5%) on health care than any other industrialized nation, the USA performs poorly in international health status comparisons: "For nearly all available outcome measures, the United States ranked near the bottom of the OECD countries in 1996, and the rate of improvement for most of the indicators has been slower than the median OECD country."[76,p.6] Among the 29 Organization for Economic Cooperation and Development nations, USA life expectancy ranked 19th for females and 22nd for males.[77] A recent report from the WHO calculated "Healthy Life Expectancy" among 139 nations, and the USA placed 24th in these rankings.[78] The reasons given for this low ranking included the very poor health status of Native Americans, rural African-Americans, and the inner city poor. The USA also has very high levels of cancers related to tobacco use, a high coronary heart disease rate, and high levels of violence, especially homicide, when compared to other industrialized nations.

The Fordham Institute for Innovation in Social Policy has for the past 12 years reported overall USA and state scores on an Index of Social Health.[79] The index consists of 16 indicators of health and well-being. Overall scores on the Index have been declining in the USA since the mid-1970s even as GDP has increased. Using the period of 1970–1996, four indicators improved: infant mortality, high school dropouts, poverty for those 65+ years, and life expectancy for those aged 65+. However, there are seven indicators for which performance worsened: child abuse, child poverty, teenage suicide, number of health care uninsured, average weekly wages, income inequality, and violent crime. Six indicators

TABLE 2-2   USA Rankings on Various Social Indicators as
                    Compared to Other Industrialized Nations

Measure	USA Ranking (1 is best)
Child Poverty (1990)	17 of 17
Elderly Poverty (1990)	15 of 17
High School Dropouts (1996)	17 of 17
Income Inequality (1990)	18 of 18
Infant Mortality (1995–1996)	21 of 25
Life Expectancy (1990)	17 of 23
Teenage Births (1991–1995)	5 of 5
Unemployment (1996)	2 of 10
Wages (1996)	13 of 23
Youth Homicide (1992–1995)	22 of 22
Youth Suicide (1992–1995)	15 of 22

show variable performance for the period: teenage drug use, teenage births, alcohol-related traffic fatalities, affordable housing, and unemployment.

What is particularly illuminating are comparisons of USA indicators with those of other nations. Table 2-2 shows rankings of the USA as compared to selected industrial nations culled from various international sources.[79] Outside of unemployment rates, the USA compares unfavorably to other industrialized nations (Table 2-2). The USA has the highest level of child poverty among western industrialized nations. These issues are complicated by the USA spending less than most other industrialized nations on social services and other program spending.

Economic Inequality Is Increasing in the United States

The USA has witnessed an unprecedented increase in income and wealth inequality in the past two decades.[80,81] Former Secretary of Labor, Robert Reich, observes: "Almost two decades ago, inequality of income, wealth, and opportunity in the United States began to widen, and today the gap is greater than at any time in living memory. All the rungs on the economic ladder are farther apart than they were a generation ago and the space between them continues to spread."[82,p.1]

In international comparisons, "Measures of social distance and overall inequality indicate that the United States has the most unequal distribution of adjusted household income among all 22 countries covered in the [Luxembourg Income] study."[50,p.201] In an analysis of OECD countries' degree of inequality, Smeeding notes that "Thus the United States, which had the most unequal income distribution in 1979, also had the most unequal distribution in 1994, with inequality growing rapidly through the mid 1990s."[50,p.212] Most of the inequality is due to the lower living standards and wages of the least well-off in American

TABLE 2-3   Changes in American Family Income
for Periods 1947–1979 and 1979–1998
by Income Quintile and Top 5%

	1947–1979	1979–1998
Bottom 20%	+116%	–5%
Next 20%	+100%	+3%
Middle 20%	+111%	+8%
Next 20%	+114%	+15%
Top 20%	+99%	+38%
Top 5%	+86%	+64%

society. "American low income families are at a distinct disadvantage compared with similarly situated families in other nations."[50,p.201] The poor living conditions of low-income Americans are seen as resulting from low wages and low social spending by the USA.

In the volume within which Reich's and Smeeding's chapters are contained, editors Auerbach and Belous identify three main factors contributing to the increase of income disparity: (a) labor market forces including shifts due to globalization and in relative demands of different types of labor and the decline of unionization; (b) growing diversity in the composition of households such as the rise of single-parent families and families with dual earners; and (c) political policy changes including changes in the tax structure and in social welfare programs.

Documentation is widely available of the growing gaps in income and wealth among American.[12,13,80,81] The recent report, *Divided Decade: Economic Disparity at the Century's Turn*,[12] presents a striking contrast in the distribution of income growth between two recent periods of USA history (Table 2-3).

Further, changes in after-tax family income from 1977–1999 were bottom 20% (–9%); second 20% (+1 %); middle 20% (+8%), fourth 20% (+14%); top 20% (+43%); top 1% (+115%). Wealth differences among Americans are even greater. By 1997, the top 1% of the USA population controlled 40% of American wealth. The top 5% controlled 62% of wealth.[13] The trends caused even the *US News and World Report* and the *New York Times Magazine* to take notice and consider the implications of such concentration of wealth for the well-being of society.[83,84]

Health Differences in the USA Related to Race

It was noted earlier that health differences are strongly related to income differences. Issues of economic resource allocation and health inequities in the USA are complicated by increasing racial segregation within American communities. In 1985 the USA Department of Health and Human Services identified six causes of death that collectively accounted for more than 80% of excess mortality among non-white populations: cancer, cardiovascular disease and stroke, chemical dependency, diabetes, homicides, suicides and unintentional injuries.[85] Indeed, health difference among blacks and whites in the USA have been known for over 150 years.[86] Table 2-4 shows USA mortality rates by income class and race for 1986 as calculated by Pappas et al.[87] Terris[24] noted that "very large difference by income class occur in each of the four groups studied, and that these differences are much greater than the differences by race. Indeed the authors report that 'the differences in overall mortality rates according to race were eliminated after adjustment for income, marital status, and household size.'"

More recent data contained in *Health, United States, 1998: Socio-economic Status and Health Chartbook* reinforce the continuing role race plays in both health status and the determinants of health status.[26] Median family income for white families for 1996 was $38,800; for black families $23,500, and for Hispanic families $25,000. Similar racial patterns were seen for percent of persons poor and not poor (p. 144), educational attainment of persons 25–64 (p. 145), heart disease death rates among adults 25–64 (p. 152), health insurance coverage among adults 18–64 (p. 158), and unmet needs for health care during the past year among adults 18–64 (p. 159).

The racial wealth gap in the USA is striking. Recent statistics indicate that in 1995 the median household net worth of white families was $61,000, that of black families $7,400, and Hispanic families $5,000. Financial worth, excluding ownership of a residence, was $18,100 for white families, $200 for black families, and $0 for Hispanic families.[13]

To put the income, race, and health issues into some perspective, Williams, Yu, and Jackson recently studied the relationship of income, race, education level, and perceived discrimination to self-reported health, bed-days, well-being, and psychological distress among 520 Detroit area whites, 586 blacks, and 33 other minority group members.[88] Not surprisingly, there

TABLE 2-4   Age-adjusted Death Rates by Income Class, Black and White Men and Women Age 25–64, U.S.A., 1986

	Men		Women	
Income	White	Black	White	Black
Under $9,000	16.0	19.5	6.5	7.6
$9,000–14,999	10.2	10.8	3.4	4.5
$15,000–18,999	5.7	9.8	3.3	3.7
$19,000–24,999	4.6	4.7	3.0	2.8
$25,000 or more	2.4	3.6	1.6	2.3

were profound differences in education, household income, class, and race-related stress between black and whites. Blacks reported significantly more health-related problems than whites. Many of these differences could be accounted for statistically by differences in income. Indeed, racial differences for self-reported ill health and for bed-days were reduced to trend levels (p. 10) once income was considered, and became non-significant for well-being and psychological distress. The role of discrimination in producing differences in levels of the social determinants of health for differing racial groups is not considered in this research.

Up-to-date discussions of the role racism and discrimination plays in population health are available.[89–91] But it appears that race, as well as gender and social class, influences health through four principal pathways: The new research holds that these social relations [social class, race, gender] are determinants of population health and disease through four principle pathways: (1) by shaping exposure and susceptibility to risk factors, events, and processes; (2) by shaping exposure and susceptibility to protective factors, events, and processes; (3) by shaping access to, and type of, health care received; and (4) by shaping health research and health pathways.[92,p.100]

Signs of Disintegration

It has been argued that societies with high levels of economic inequality show symptoms of societal disintegration. The form that societal disintegration takes in each society may be unique. In Britain, increasing economic inequality has been associated with increased alcoholism, crime rates, and deaths by road accidents and infectious diseases, poorer reading scores, increased drug offenses, decaying family functioning, and decreased voter turnout, among others.[25] In the United States economic inequality among the 50 states has been related to a mixed bag of indicators that may be seen as involving indicators of disintegration. Degree of inequality was related to levels of unemployment, proportion of the population incarcerated, use of income vouchers, food stamps, and proportion of the population with no health insurance. Similar findings were reported for having no high school education, high school leaving, reading and math proficiency, education spending, and library books per capita.[58]

As noted, scores on the *Fordham Social Health Index* have been declining in the USA since the mid-1970s even as Gross Domestic Product has increased. Glyn and Millibrant consider the social and economic costs of economic inequality to society; as noted the USA has the greatest degree of economic inequality among industrialized nations.[93] One area that can be recognized as a sign of disintegration is increasing economic and racial segregation of American communities. Orfield describes how polarization in income contributes to decaying inner cities and suburbs in American cities.[94]

Economic and Racial Segregation and Potential Health Effects

Another complicating situation in the USA is the degree of economic and racial segregation in American cities and the potential adverse health effects associated with such segregation.[95-96] In *Metropolitics: A Regional Agenda for Community and Stability*, Orfield lays bare the dilemmas faced by major American cities in general and Minneapolis in particular: "It couldn't happen here . . . The Twin Cities were immune to urban decline, inner suburban decay, urban sprawl—and the polarization that has devastated and divided older, larger regions. After all, we were not Chicago, Detroit, or Milwaukee . . . If it could happen here, no American region is immune. Once polarization occurs, the concentration of poverty, disinvestment, middle class flight and urban sprawl grow more and more severe."[94,p.1]

Orfield documents how poverty and racial composition have become concentrated within specific areas of the Twin Cities region. He also describes how competing interests that arise among central cities, surrounding suburban rings, and developing suburbs both reflect these changes and serve to accentuate them. Confirming Orfield's observations, the *New York Times* recently reported that the overall probability of a black American student having white classmates was reduced from 34.7% in 1989–1990 to 32.4% in 1997–1998.[97] Minnesota, however, showed the second greatest increase in rates of racial segregation in the nation, with the probability of a black student having white classmates decreasing almost 25%, from 61.2% in 1989–1990 to 46% in 1997–1998.

The validity of Orfield's observations concerning economic and racial segregation were confirmed by a survey by the Fannie Mae Foundation of 149 leading USA urban historians, planners and architects who were asked to identify the top 10 influences on American cities over the next 50 years.[98] Ranked first and second were "growing disparities of wealth" and "suburban political majority." Ranked fourth was "perpetual underclass in central cities and inner-ring suburbs." Ranked seventh was "deterioration of the 'first-ring' post-1945 suburbs." Health workers cannot ignore how these developments have the potential to influence the health and well-being of individuals and the communities within which people live and work.

Finally, recent work, drawing on data from the National Longitudinal Mortality Study, found that the degree of minority residential segregation predicted mortality rates among black men aged 25–44 years, non-black men and women aged 45–64 years, and black women 65 years and older.[99] Once controls for family income were introduced, black men aged 25–44 who lived in the most segregated areas had almost three times higher risk, and among black women in this age group the risk of death was almost twice the rate for those in less segregated areas.

Clearly, the literature concerned with urban issues has much to offer health workers concerned with the social determinants of health. Such work directs attention to structural issues associated with public policy and the conflicts between differing communities that may increasingly arise as a result of increasing economic and racial segregation. Identifying sources of resistance to necessary policy changes helps to illuminate the forces maintaining inequality and suggests avenues for action.[100,101]

The recently published volume, *Developmental Health and the Wealth of Nations*, outlines biological, psychological and social mechanisms by which income differences influence health.[102] Of most relevance for the present discussion is the statement by Brooks-Gunn et al.:

> Comparing across chapters in this volume suggests that income gradients during childhood are steeper in the United States than in Canada or the United Kingdom . . . First, as we just stated, more U.S. children are in deep poverty than in the two comparison nations. Second, the income disparities between the rich and poor and near poor are much larger in the United States than in Canada or the United Kingdom. Unless policies address these inequities . . . it is likely that the SES gradient will remain steeper for US children than for Canadian or British children, with the consequent risks for the developmental health of the American population that we have identified.[103,p.122]

Public Health Responses to Health Inequities: The Canadian Scene

In the USA population health researchers have documented the strong association between degree of economic inequality and a number of indicators of population health. There are also a number of organizations that have raised the issue of economic inequality such as United for a Fair Economy.[12,13] A particularly interesting USA response has been the development of the Living Wage Movement—a movement that has scored a number of victories.[104]

However, considering the magnitude of increasing economic inequality in the USA and the rather limited public health response to the issue, it seems valuable to consider—in addition to USA responses—how Canadian health workers have responded to increasing economic inequality.

A recent review considered the current state of Canadian public health responses to health inequities.[44] Concern about increasing economic inequality in Canada has been raised primarily by the social development rather than the public health sector. This is surprising since Canada has been a world leader in the development of theory related to health promotion and the "new public health."[105,106] Studies indicate that while the health-related effects of economic inequality and poverty are known to many public health professionals, public health responses—with few notable exceptions—are limited to the delivery of ameliorative programs to those living in poverty. While federal, provincial, and public health association documents include economic inequality as a determinant of health,[6,31,107–109] discussions of the role that economic inequality plays in creating poverty, its impact upon community structures that support health, and the causes of increasing inequality, have been, for the most part, isolated from public health discourse and practice.

One exception to this tendency was the City of Montreal's report, *Social Inequalities in Health*, in which the director of public health presented an extensive discussion of the role that social inequalities, specifically economic resources, played in determining the health of Montrealers.[110] In the report's final chapter, Counteracting Poverty and its Consequences, avenues of action open to the Department of Public Health were outlined. These actions included monitoring, research and evaluation, transmission of knowledge, regional programming, and strategic action. Concerning strategic action, this includes keeping decision-makers and public opinion informed of the department's concerns about social issues important to the health and well-being of residents.

A number of developments are cause for optimism in Canada. Economic inequality is a continuing focus of many social development and anti-poverty organizations. Statistics Canada provides ongoing reports of the degree of economic inequality, and The Federation of Canadian Municipalities[111] has instituted a Quality of Life Index project that uses measures that should be sensitive to increasing economic inequality such as income, affordability of housing, and presence of social infrastructure. In this analysis of the Canadian situation, a number of action areas were suggested to move the economic inequality, poverty, and health agenda forward. These were: (a) develop communication between various sectors concerned with economic inequality; (b) contribute papers to academic and professional journals on income-related developments and their potential for affecting the health of Canadians; (c) use the media to educate citizens about the consequences of increasing economic inequality and poverty upon health; (d) lobby local health departments to begin taking seriously a determinants of health approach, which includes consideration of the importance of economic inequality and poverty; (e) lobby governments to maintain the community and service structures that help to maintain health and well-being; and (f) begin to understand the forces that create economic inequality and poverty.

Policy Options

If USA public health workers were to highlight policy options to reduce economic inequality, what would some of these look like? One of the few policy programs outlined by a USA public health professional is also one of the most complete. In 1994, Milton Terris, the editor of the *Journal of Public Health Policy*,[24] presented 12 recommendations that if implemented would totally alter the social environment in the USA. These recommendations are presented in the Appendix. The centerpiece of this program is a massive government effort to assure that all Americans are provided with the health prerequisites outlined in the *Ottawa Charter for Health Promotion*.

Terris also noted that profound changes in USA public policy are responsible for much of the increase in economic inequality. While the maximum income tax rate as of 1989 for 86 countries averaged 47%, in the USA the maximum had been reduced to 28%. He comments:

> Inequities in income in the United States have been deliberately widened by federal, state, and local tax policy. The maximum federal income tax rates stayed at 91% during the fifties, fell to 70% during the sixties and seventies, and were reduced to 28% in the eighties. This sharp decline in the progressive character of the income tax was accompanied by a sharp increase in the regressive social security tax rates from 3% in 1955 to 15% in 1989 . . . Furthermore, state and local taxes need to be drastically revised. Currently only 26% of their tax revenues come from income taxes, as compared with 72% for the federal government. Regressive taxes—sales, excise and property taxes—account for 74% of local and state taxes. The situation needs to be reversed in order to achieve a more equitable tax policy and to further narrow the incredibly wide income disparities in our population.[24,p.14]

The *New York Times* also noted that "States are cutting taxes, but taxes that fall most heavily on the poor, like those on sales and gasoline, are being cut the least.[112]

In Canada, the *Growing Gap* report outlined a number of "Ways to Close the Gap." Yalnizyan[22] recommended closing the five gaps that exist between rich and poor as follows:

- *Employment Gap:* create a better distribution of working time; provide publicly needed goods and services; adopt procurement policies; improve access to capital; ensure high quality, low cost education and child care; enforce employment equity legislation; undo the bias in the tax system; and enact a review investment mechanism with teeth.
- *Value Gap:* join a union, support a union, form a union; raise minimum wage to a living wage; call for 'maximum salaries'; improve pay equity, and demand better corporate behavior.
- *Income Gap:* supplement low wages; restore and improve income supports; and provide a guaranteed minimum income.
- *Common Goods Gap:* make housing more affordable; create a system of universally accessible, high quality child care; restore the health of the health system; expand universal health provisions; improve public education and access to higher education; enhance parks, libraries and community services.
- *Wealth Gap:* reinstate the inheritance tax; review family trust provisions; and prevent increased concentration of ownership.

British researchers have recommended strong government action to close the widening health gap. In the volume, *The Widening Gap*, Shaw et al. make three main points in their discussion of how to narrow the health gap:[42]

- The key policy that will reduce inequalities in health is the alleviation of poverty through the reduction of inequalities in income and wealth.

- There is widespread public support for poverty reduction in Britain and the government has pledged to eliminate child poverty by 2020.
- Poverty can be reduced by raising the standards of living of poor people through increasing their incomes in cash or "in kind." The costs would be borne by the rich and would reduce inequalities overall—simultaneously reducing inequalities in health.

In a follow-up volume, *Tackling Inequalities*, Pantazis and Gordon provide detailed policy prescriptions for addressing health inequities in Britain.[41] Also in Britain, the Acheson Independent Inquiry into Inequalities in Health outlined 39 sets of recommendation that provide a rich source of ideas for reducing health inequities.[39] Thirteen of these sets of recommendation are presented under the following headings with one example of each type of action presented:

- *General Recommendations:* We recommend that as part of health impact assessment, all policies likely to have a direct or indirect impact on health should be evaluated in terms of their impact on health inequalities, and should be formulated in such a way that by favouring the less well off they will, wherever possible, reduce such inequalities.
- *Poverty, Tax and Benefits:* We recommend that further reductions in poverty of women of childbearing age, expectant mothers, young children and older people should be made by increasing benefits in cash or in kind to them.
- *Education:* We recommend the provision of additional resources for schools serving children from less well off groups to enhance their educational achievement. The Revenue Support Grant formula and other funding mechanisms should be more strongly weighted to reflect need and socioeconomic disadvantage.
- *Employment:* We recommend further investment in high quality training for young and long-term unemployed people.
- *Housing and Environment:* We recommend policies which improve housing provision and access to health care for both officially and unofficially homeless people.
- *Mobility, Transport, and Pollution:* We recommend the further development of a high quality public transport system which is integrated with other forms of transport and is affordable to the user.
- *Nutrition and the Common Agricultural Policy:* We recommend strengthening the CAP Surplus Food Scheme to improve the nutritional position of the less well off.
- *Mothers, Children, and Families:* We recommend an integrated policy for the provision of affordable, high quality day care and preschool education with extra resources for disadvantaged communities.
- *Young People and Adults of Working Ages:* We recommend measures to prevent suicide among young people, especially among young men and seriously mentally ill people.

- *Older People:* We recommend policies which will further reduce income inequalities, and improve the living standards of households in receipt of social security benefits.
- *Ethnicity:* We recommend that the needs of minority ethnic groups be specifically considered in the development and implementation of policies aimed at reducing socioeconomic inequalities.
- *Gender:* We recommend policies which reduce the excess mortality from accidents and suicide in young men. Specifically, improve the opportunities for work which will ameliorate the health consequences of unemployment.
- *The National Health System:* We recommend that providing equitable access to effective care in relation to need should be a governing principle of all policies in the NHS. Priority should be given to the achievement of equity in the planning, implementation, and delivery of services at every level of the NHS.

The policy recommendations which have been proposed in Canada, the United Kingdom, and the United States indicate the need to move from epidemiologic research to public health action, from demonstrating the major impact of economic inequality on community health, to the development and implementation of specific policies and programs to reverse the continuing increase in economic inequality. In the USA, which has the most unequal income distribution among the industrial nations, the public health movement has been willing to make general statements on the social determinants of health, but there has been little or no attempt to concretize these general statements through advocacy and action on the specific policies and programs identified in this paper. It is time to move forward.

APPENDIX

Determinants of Health:
A Progressive Political Platform

Excerpted from Terris, M., *Journal of Public Health Policy* 15 (1994): 5–17.

Recommendation 1: That the United States adopt the policy of Free Public Education for All the People, including all levels of education; that it correct the current methods of financing public education to guarantee equity in the annual spending per pupil in all school districts of the nation, whether rich or poor, urban or rural; and that it achieve such equity, as well as major improvement in the quality of public education, through a large scale program of federal grants-in-aid to the states, based on state plans that guarantee equity in spending per pupil in all school districts and that meet national standards of educational quality.

Recommendation 2: That the federal, state and local governments provide funds for a massive housing program which will not only eliminate homelessness but will provide decent, affordable housing for everyone in the United States. This will not only resurrect the construction industry from its current desperate situation, but will provide large numbers of construction workers with increased purchasing power that will help other American industries to recover from depression. Such a program must include full protection of labor's right to organize, effective affirmative action to employ blacks and other minorities as well as women, and close monitoring of expenditures and quality.

Recommendation 3: That a similar large scale program be instituted for the renewal and expansion of the nation's neglected and decaying public infrastructure: public buildings, schools, hospitals, health centers, water supply and sewage disposal systems, roads, bridges, railways, subways and other necessary public facilities.

Recommendation 4: That it be made national policy to move from the current norm of the 8-hour day to a 6-hour day with full protection of wage and salary levels, in all branches of industry, and that the federal, state and local governments take the initiative by instituting the 6-hour day for all government employees and for those employed in private industries where the funding for their wages and salaries comes from governmental grants and contracts.

Recommendation 5: That obstacles to employment of women be removed by the development of a large-scale program of child care centers of good quality, financed by federal, state, and local governments; by national legislation mandating paid maternity leave for all women, which has long been established throughout Europe; by enforcement of the principle of equal pay for equal work by men and women; and by affirmative action to overcome all other forms of gender discrimination.

Recommendation 6: That education and training programs be developed in all communities to enlarge the knowledge and skills of unemployed persons and to provide counseling and assistance in obtaining employment; such programs should be funded with federal financial support and meet national educational standards.

Recommendation 7: Raise the current totally inadequate minimum wage so that full-time workers who receive that wage have incomes above the poverty level.

Recommendation 8: Revise the Social Security program to guarantee a level of benefits for low-income retirees which is above the poverty level.

Recommendation 9: Persons unable to work because of physical or mental impairments should receive government subsidy adequate to keep them from falling below the poverty level.

Recommendation 10: Initiatives to strengthen the development of third world countries and their achievement of higher living standards are essential to full employment and higher living standards in the United States. One such initiative is the Pan American Health Organization's environmental health plan.

Recommendation 11: That the federal maximum income tax rate be set at 70%, and that the share of local and state revenues raised by progressive, graduated income taxes be increased to 75%, in order to provide equity in taxation policy, help narrow the very wide income disparities, and provide the funds needed to implement a progressive political program.

Recommendation 12: That the military budget be cut by 50% now, with further cuts to follow, and that funds so released be used exclusively to provide jobs, housing, and health for all Americans.

Acknowledgment: Portions of this paper were first presented at the session *Social Inequities in Public Health* during the *Public Health Partnership 2000 Conference: Celebrating a Century of Success*, April 7, 2000, at the Earl Brown Heritage Center in Brooklyn Center, Minnesota.

References

1. Marmot MG, Wilkinson RG, editors. *Social Determinants of Health.* Oxford: Oxford University Press, 1999.
2. Wilkinson RG, Marmot M. *Social Determinants of Health: The Solid Facts.* Copenhagen: World Health Organization, 1998. On-line at http://www.who.dk/healthy-cities/.
3. Daniels N, Kennedy B, Kawachi I. Justice is Good for Our Health: How Greater Economic Equality Would Promote Public Health. *Boston Rev,* 25 (1), (2000) pp. 4–21. On-line at http://bostonreview.mit.edu/BR2~.~/daniels.html.
4. Kawachi I, Kennedy BO, Wilkinson RG, editors. *The Society and Population Health Reader. Volume I: Income Inequality and Health.* New York: The New Press, 1999.
5. Dahlgren G, Whitehead M. *Policies and Strategies to Promote Social Equality in Health.* Stockholm: Institute of Future Studies, 1991.
6. Canadian Public Health Association. *Action Statement on Health Promotion.* Ottawa, 1996. On-line at http://www.cpha.ca.
7. World Health Organization. *Ottawa Charter on Health Promotion.* Geneva, 1986. On-line at http://www.who.dk/policy/ottawa.htm.
8. Ashton J, editor. *Healthy Cities.* Philadelphia: Open University Press, 1992.
9. Davies JK, Kelly MP, editors. *Healthy Cities: Research and Practice.* New York: Routledge, 1993.
10. Raphael D, Bryant T. Putting the population into population health. *Can J. Pub Health.* 2000. 91: 9–12.

11. Auerbach J, Belous R, editors. *The Inequality Paradox: Growth of Income Disparity.* Washington, DC: National Policy Association, 1998.
12. Collins C, Hartman C, Sklar H. *Divided Decade: Economic Disparity at the Century's Turn.* Boston: United for a Fair Economy, 1999. On-line at http://www.stw.org.
13. Collins C, Leondar-Wright B, Sklar H. *Shifting Fortunes: The Perils of the Growing American Wealth Gap.* Boston: United for a Fair Economy, 1999.
14. Galbraith J. *Created Unequal: The Crisis in American Pay.* New York: The Free Press, 1998.
15. Laxer J. *The Undeclared War: Class Conflict in the Age of Cyber-capitalism.* Toronto: Viking, 1998.
16. McQuaig L. *The Wealthy Banker's Wife: The Assault on Equality in Canada.* Toronto: Penguin, 1993.
17. Montague P. Economic inequality and health. *Rachel's Environment & Health Weekly #497.* Annapolis. In: Environmental Research Foundation, 1996.
18. Montague P. Major causes of ill health. *Rachel's Environment & Health Weekly #584.* Annapolis. In: Environmental Research Foundation, 1998.
19. Rainwater L, Smeeding T. *Doing Poorly: the Real Income of American Children in a Comparative Perspective.* Working Paper 127, Luxembourg Income Study, 1995. On-line at http://lissy.ceps.lu/wpa-persentire.htm; then ftp://lissy.ceps.lu/127.pdf.
20. Townsend M. *Health and Wealth: How Social and Economic Factors Affect Our Well-being.* Toronto: Lorimer, 1999. Available through http://www.policyalternatives.ca.
21. Wolff EN. *Top Heavy: The Increasing Inequality of Wealth in America and What Can Be Done about It.* New York: The New Press, 1995.
22. Yalnizyan A. *The Growing Gap: A Report on Growing Inequality Between the Rich and Poor in Canada.* Toronto: Centre for Social Justice, 1998. Available through http://www.socialjustice.org.
23. Yalnizyan A. *Canada's Great Divide: The Politics of the Growing Gap Between Rich and Poor in the 1990s.* Toronto: Centre for Social Justice, 2000. Available through http://www.socialjustice.org.
24. Terris M. Determinants of Health: A Progressive Political Platform. *J Pub Health Policy.* 1994. 15: 5–17.
25. Wilkinson RG. *Unhealthy Societies: The Afflictions of Inequality.* New York: Routledge, 1996.
26. US Department of Health and Human Services. *Health, United States, 1998: Socioeconomic Status and Health Chartbook.* Washington DC, 1998. On-line at http://www.cdc.gov/nchs/products/pubs/pubd/hus/2010/ 98chtbk.htm.
27. Wilkins R, Adams OB. Health expectancy in Canada, late 1970's: demographic, regional and social dimensions. *Am J Pub Health.* 1983. 73: 1073–1080.

28. Marmot MG, Rose G, Shipley M, Hamilton, PJS. Employment Grade and Coronary Heart Disease in British Civil Servants. *J Epidemiol Com Health.* 1978. 32: 244–249.

29. Feldman JJ, Makuc DM, Kleinman JC, Cornoni-Huntley J. National trends in educational differentials in mortality. *Am J Epidemiol.* 1989. 129: 919–933.

30. Lantz PM, House JS, Lepkowski JM, Williams DR, Mero RP, Chen J. Socioeconomic Factors, Health Behaviors, and Mortality. *J Am Med Assoc.* 1998. 279: 1703–1708.

31. Health Canada. *Taking Action on Population Health: A Position Paper for Health Promotion and Programs Branch Staff.* Ottawa, 1998. On-line at http://www.hc-sc.gc.ca/main~hppb/phdd/resource.htm.

32. Evans RG, Barer M, Marmor TR. editors. *Why Are Some People Healthy and Others Not?: The Determinants of Health of Populations.* New York: Aldine De Gruyter, 1995.

33. Coburn D. Income inequality and health status: The role of neo-liberalism. *Soc Sci Med.* 2000. 51: 135–146.

34. International Health Program. Health and Income Equity Web Site. University of Washington and Health Alliance International, 2000. On-line at http://depts.washington.edu/eqhlth.

35. Raphael D. Health effects of inequality. *Can Rev Soc Pol.* 1999. 44: 25–40.

36. Lynch JW, Davey Smith G. Kaplan GA, House JS. Income inequality and mortality: importance to health of individual income, psychosocial environment, or material conditions. *BMJ.* 2000. 320: 1200–1204.

37. Sram I, Ashton J. Millennium report to Sir Edwin Chadwick. *BM J.* 1998. 317: 592–596. On-line at: http://www.bmj.com.

38. Townsend P, Davidson N, Whitehead M, editors. *Inequalities in Health: The Black Report and the Health Divide.* New York: Penguin, 1992.

39. Acheson D. *Independent inquiry into inequalities in health.* London: Stationary Office, 1998. On-line at http://www.official-documents.co.document/doh/ih/contents.htm.

40. Gordon D, Shaw M, Dorling D, Davey Smith G, editors. *Inequalities in Health: The Evidence Presented to the Independent Inquiry into Inequalities in Health.* Bristol, UK: The Policy Press, 1999. Available through http://amazon.co.uk.

41. Pantazis C., Gordon D, editors. *Tackling Inequalities: Where Are We Now and What Can Be Done?* Bristol, UK: The Policy Press, 2000.

42. Shaw M, Dorling D, Gordon D, Davey Smith G. *The Widening Gap: Health Inequalities and Policy in Britain.* Bristol, UK: The Policy Press, 1999.

43. Raphael D. Public health responses to health inequalities. *Can J Pub Health.* 1998. 89: 380–381.

44. Raphael D. Health inequalities in Canada: current discourses and implications for public health action. *Crit Pub Health.* 2000. 10: 193–216.

45. Raphael D. From increasing poverty to societal disintegration: Low economic inequality affects the health of individuals and communities. In: Armstrong H, Armstrong P, Coburn D, editors. *Unhealthy Times: The Political Economy of Health and Health Care in Canada*. Toronto: Oxford University Press, in press.

46. Kawachi I, Kennedy BP. The relationship of economic inequality to mortality. *Soc Sci Med*. 1997 45: 1121–1127.

47. Kawachi I, Levine S, Miller SM, Lasch K, Amick B. *Income Inequality and Life Expectancy Theory, Research, and Policy*. Boston: Health Institute, New England Medical Centre, 1994.

48. Bartley M, Blane D, Montgomery S. Health and the life course: Why safety nets matter. *BMJ*. 314 (1997): 1194–1196.

49. Montgomery S, Bartley M, Cook D, Wadsworth M. Health and social precursors of unemployment in young men in Great Britain. *J Epidemiol Com Health*. 1996. 50: 415–422.

50. Smeeding TM. US income inequality in a cross-national perspective: why are we so different? In Auerbach J, Belous R, editors. *The Inequality Paradox: Growth of Income Disparity*, pp. 194–217. Washington, DC: National Policy Association, 1998.

51. World Health Organization. *Twenty Steps for Developing A Healthy Cities Project*. Copenhagen, 1995. On-line at http://www.who.dk/ healthy-cities/.

52. Raphael D, Steinmetz B, Renwick R, Philips S, Sehdev H, Smith T. The community quality of life project: a health promotion approach to understanding communities. *Health Promot Inter*. 1999. 14: 197–207.

53. Raphael D, Phillips S, Renwick R, Sehdev H. Government policies as a threat to health: findings from two community quality of life studies in Toronto. *Can J Pub Health*. 2000. 91: 181–185.

54. Leon DA, Vagero D, Otterblad O. Social class differences in infant mortality in Sweden: A comparison with England and Wales. *BMJ*. 1992. 305: 687–691.

55. Vagero D, Lundberg O. Health inequalities in Britain and Sweden. *Lancet*. 1989. 2: 33–36.

56. Lynch JW, Kaplan GA, Pamuk ER, Cohen R, Heck C, Balfour J, Yen I. Income inequality and mortality in metropolitan areas of the United States. *Am J Pub Health*. 1998: 1074–1080

57. Department of Health and Human Services. Health, United States, 199. Washington DC, 2000.

58. Kaplan JR, Pamuk E, Lynch JW, Cohen JW, Balfour JL Income inequality and mortality in the United States. *BMJ*. 1996. 312: 999–1003.

59. Wolfson M, Kaplan G, Lynch J, Ross N, Backlund E. Relation between income inequality and mortality: Empirical demonstration. *BMJ*. 1999. 312: 953–958.

60. BMJ. Editorial: The big idea. *BMJ*. 1999. 312: 985.

61. Kawachi I, Kennedy BP. Socioeconomic determinants of health: Health and social cohesion, why care about income inequality? *BMJ*. 1997. 314: 1037–1045.
62. Putnam R. *Making Democracy Work: Civic Traditions in Modern Italy.* Princeton, NJ: Princeton University Press, 1993.
63. Putnam R. *Bowling Alone: The Collapse and Revival of American Community.* New York: Simon and Schuster, 2000.
64. Ross N, Wolfson MC, Dunn JR, Berthelot JM, Kaplan GA, Lynch JW. Income inequality and mortality in Canada and the United States. *BMJ*. 2000. 320: 898–902.
65. Muntaner C, Lynch J, Oates GL. The social class determinants of income inequality and social cohesion. *Intl J Health Serv*. 1999. 29: 699–732.
66. Lynch JW, Kaplan GA, Salonene JT. Why do poor people behave poorly? Variation in adult health behaviours psychosocial characteristics by stages of the socioeconomic life course. *Soc Sci Med*. 1997. 44: 809–819.
67. Labonte R. *Health Promotion and Empowerment: Practice Frameworks.* Toronto Centre for Health Promotion and Participatory Action, 1993. Available through http://www.utoronto.ca/chp.
68. Tesh S. *Hidden Arguments: Political Ideology and Disease Prevention Policy.* New Brunswick, NJ: Rutgers University Press, 1990.
69. Davies J, Macdonald G. *Quality, Evidence, and Effectiveness in Health Promotion: Striving for Certainties.* London: Routledge, 1998.
70. Hancock T, Minkler M. Community Health Assessment or Healthy Community Assessment: Whose Community? Whose Health? Whose Assessment? In Minkler M, editor. *Community Organizing and Community Building for Health*, pp. 139–156. New Brunswick, NJ: Rutgers University Press, 1997.
71. Donaldson L. *Ten Tips for Better Health.* 1999.
72. Gordon D. *An Alternative 10 Tips for Better Health.* University of Bristol: Personal Communication, October, 12, 1999.
73. Williams RB. Lower socioeconomic status and increased mortality: Early childhood roots and the potential for successful interventions. *JAMA*. 1998. 279: 1745–1746.
74. Levitin LC, Snell E, McGinnis M. Urban issues in health promotion strategies. *Am J Pub Health*. 2000. 90: 863–866.
75. Terris M. The development and prevention of cardiovascular disease risk factors: socioenvironmental influences. *J Pub Health Policy*. 1996. 17: 426–441.
76. Anderson GF, Poullier J. Health spending, access, and outcomes: Trends in industrialized nations. *Health Affairs*. 1999. May/June. On-line at http://www.projhope.org/HA/bonus/180321.htm.
77. OECD. *OECD Health Data 98: A Comparative Analysis of Twenty-nine Countries. Paris, 1998.* On-line at http://www.projhope.org/HAlbonus/180321.htm.

78. World Health Organization. *WHO Issues New Healthy Life Expectancy Rankings.* Press Release, June 4, 2000. On-line at http://www. who.int/ inf-pr-zooo/en/pr2000-life.htm1.
79. Miringoff M, Miringoff ML. *The Social Health of the Nation.* New York: Oxford University Press, 1999.
80. Freeman RB. The Facts about Rising Economic Inequality. In: Auerbach J. Belous R, editors. *The Inequality Paradox: Growth of Income Disparity,* pp. 19–33. Washington, DC: National Policy Association, 1998.
81. Yellen C. Trends in Income Inequality. In Auerbach J, Belous R, editors. *The Inequality Paradox: Growth of Income Disparity,* pp. 7–17. Washington, DC: National Policy Association, 1998.
82. Reich RB. The Inequality Paradox. In Auerbach J, Belous R, editors. *The Inequality Paradox: Growth of Income Disparity,* pp. 1–6. Washington, DC: National Policy Association, 1998.
83. Lardner R. The Rich Get Richer: Why Those at the Top Are Leaving the Rest of Us Behind. *US News and World Report,* February 21, 2000. On-line at http://www.usnews.com/usnews/issue/ooozz~/r~ch.htm.
84. Fallows J. The Invisible Poor: In the Shadow of Wealth. *New York Times Magazine,* March 19, 2000. On-line at www.igc.apc.orglglob-alpolic). /socecon/inequal/uspoor.htm.
85. Office of Minority Health, Minnesota. *Populations of Color in Minnesota: Health Status Report.* Minneapolis: Minnesota Department of Health, 1997.
86. Krieger N. Shades of difference: Theoretical underpinnings of the medical controversy on black/white differences in the United States, 1830–1870. *Intl J Health Services.* 1987. 17: 259–278.
87. Pappas G, Queen S, Hadden W, Fisher G. The increasing disparity in mortality between socioeconomic groups in the United States, 1960 and 1986. *N Eng J Med.* 1993. 329: 103–109.
88. Williams DR, Yu Y, Jackson J. Racial differences in physical and mental health. *J Health Psych.* 1997. 2: 335–351.
89. Clark R, Anderson NB, Clark VR, Williams DR. Racism as a stressor for African Americans: A biopsychosocial model. *Am Psychologist.* 1999. 54: 805–816.
90. Krieger N. Discrimination and Health. In Berkman L, Kawachi I, editors. *Social Epidemiology,* pp. 36–75. Oxford: Oxford University Press, 2000.
91. Williams DR. Race, socioeconomic status, and health: The added effects of racism and discrimination. *Ann NY Aca. Sci.* 1999. 896: 173–188.
92. Krieger N, Rowley DL, Herman AA, Avery B, Phillips MT. Racism, sexism, and social class: Implications for studies of health, disease, and well-being. *Am J Prev.Med.* 1993. 9(suppl): 82–122.
93. Glyn A, Millibrant D. *Paying for Inequality: The Economic Cost of Social Injustice.* London: IPPR/Rivers Press, 1994.

94. Orfield M. *Metropolitics: a Regional Agenda for Community and Stability.* Washington, DC: Brookings Institution Press, 1997.
95. Badcock B. *Unfairly Structured Cities.* Oxford: Basil Blackman, 1984.
96. Waitzman NJ, Smith KR. Separate but lethal: the effects of economic segregation on mortality in metropolitan America. *Milbank Q.* 1998. 76: 341–373.
97. Rosen, J. The lost promise of school integration. *New York Times Week in Review*, April 2, 2000. On-line at http://www.nytimes.com/learning/generaYfeatured~articles/ooo~o~monday.html.
98. Fannie Mae Foundation. *Interstate System and Dominance of the Automobile Influence in Past; Income Gap Disparities Is Main Influence in Future.* Press release, October 21, 1999. On-line at www.fanniemaefoundation.org/news/release/topten~o~~~~.html.
99. Jackson SA, Anderson RT, Johnson NJ, Sorlie D. The relation of residential segregation to all-cause mortality: A study in Black and White. *A J Pub Health.* 2000. 90: 615–617.
100. Raphael D. Letter from Canada: An end of the millennium update from the birthplace of the Healthy Cities Movement. *Health Prom Int.* 2001. 16: 99–101.
101. Raphael D. Paradigms, politics, and principles: A cautionary tale from Toronto, Canada, birthplace of the Healthy Cities Movement. In Issue #13 of *Research for Healthy Cities Newsletter* of the WHO Collaborating Centre for Research on Healthy Cities, Universiteit Maastricht, Netherlands, 1999.
102. Keating DP, Hertzman C. editors. *Developmental Health and the Wealth of Nations.* New York: Guilford Press, 1999.
103. Brooks-Gunn J, Duncan GJ, Britto PR. Are socioeconomic gradients for children similar to those for adults?: Achievement and health of children in the United States. In Keating DP, Hertzman C, editors. *Developmental Health and the Wealth of Nations*, pp. 94–124. New York: Guilford Press, 1999.
104. Association of Community Organizations for Reform. ACORN'S Living Wage Web Site, 2000. On-line at http://www.livingwagecampaign.org.
105. Epp J. *Achieving Health for All: A Framework for Health Promotion.* Ottawa: Health and Welfare Canada, 1986. On-line at http://www.hc-sc.gc.ca/hppb/hpo/ahfa.htm.
106. Lalonde M. *A New Perspective on the Health of Canadians: A Working Document.* Ottawa: Health and Welfare Canada, 1974. On-line at http://www.hc-sc.gc.ca/hppb/phdd/perintrod.htm.
107. Canadian Public Health Association. *Inequities in Health.* Ottawa, Canada, 1993.
108. Canadian Public Health Association. *Health Impacts of Social and Economic Conditions: Implications for Public Policy.* Ottawa, Canada, 1997.
109. Health Canada. *The Statistical Report on the Health of Canadians.* Ottawa, Canada, 1998. On-line at http://www.hc-sc.gc.ca/main/hppb/phdd/resource.htm.

110. Lessard, R. *Social Inequalities in Health: Annual Report of the Health of the Population.* Montreal: Direction De La Sante Publique, 1997. On-line at http://www.santepub-mtl.qc.ca/Communiques/Autres/rap-portan.html.
111. Federation of Canadian Municipalities. *Quality of Life Reporting System: Quality of Life in Canadian Communities.* Ottawa: Author, 1999. On-line at http://www.fcm.ca/pdfs/fcmeng.pdf.
112. Johnston D. Taxes Are Cut, and the Rich Get Richer. *New York Times*, Oct. 5, 1997.

To Mitigate, Resist, or Undo:
Addressing Structural Influences
on the Health of Urban Populations

Arline T. Geronimus, ScD

Young to middle-aged residents of impoverished urban areas suffer extraordinary rates of excess mortality, to which deaths from chronic disease contribute heavily. Understanding of urban health disadvantages and attempts to reverse them will be incomplete if the structural factors that produced modern minority ghettos in central cities are not taken into account.

Dynamic conceptions of the role of race/ethnicity in producing health inequalities must encompass (1) social relationships between majority and minority populations that privilege the majority population and (2) the autonomous institutions within minority populations that members develop and sustain to mitigate, resist, or undo the adverse effects of discrimination. Broad social and economic policies that intensify poverty or undermine autonomous protections can reap dire consequences for health.

Following from this structural analysis and previous research, guiding principles for action and suggestions for continued research are proposed. Without taking poverty and race/ethnicity into account, public health professionals who hope to redress the health problems of urban life risk exaggerating the returns that can be expected of public health campaigns or overlooking important approaches for mounting successful interventions.

A compounding series of changes in the urban socioeconomic and demographic landscape since World War II has resulted in staggering and increasing rates of excess mortality in urban areas of concentrated poverty.[1-3] By 1990, African American youths in some urban areas faced lower probabilities of surviving to 45 years of age than White youths nationwide faced of surviving to 65 years. Popularized images emphasize the role of homicide among urban youth, although chronic diseases in early and middle adulthood are key contributors to these health inequalities and to their growth. For example, among young and middle-aged men in Harlem, the number of excess deaths attributed to homicide per 100,000 persons remained stable between 1980 and 1990 and then began to decline. In contrast, throughout the 1980s, excess deaths attributed to circulatory disease or cancer each doubled among young and middle-aged Harlem men.[3]

Attempts to understand, and to reverse, these growing health inequalities will be partial without consideration of the socioeconomic factors and, even more critical, the historical and structural factors that have produced modern ghettos in central cities with predominantly minority populations. About 80% of the residents of high-poverty urban areas in the United States are minorities; the figure is over 90% in the largest metropolitan areas. African Americans alone account for 50% of residents of high-poverty urban areas nationally and between 80% and 90% of the population in some of the largest urban ghettos, such as in Detroit and Chicago.[4] A range of policies, some now old and all apparently disconnected from health considerations, have reaped dire consequences for the health of these urban residents. In the wake of these policies, unless public health professionals take poverty and race/ethnicity into account, they risk exaggerating the returns that can be expected of narrow or conventional public health campaigns or overlooking important targets, approaches, and resources for mounting successful interventions.

Poverty

Central city populations are characterized by extreme, persistent, and pervasive poverty that intensified in the late 20th century. There was a decline in the real value of working-class wages and government transfers and, by extension, of the material resources available through the pooling of income across kin networks; at the same time, the cost of living increased.

The association between health and poverty (or, more broadly defined, socioeconomic position) is among the most robust findings of social epidemiology.[5-9] Consider the list of social and psychosocial factors that have demonstrated associations with morbidity and mortality, and consider that those in poverty suffer from increased exposure to most of them. These factors include material hardships, psychosocial conditions of acute and chronic stress or of overburdened or disrupted social supports, and toxic environmental exposures.[10-14] Generally and persistently difficult psychosocial conditions contribute to the increased tendency of the poor to engage in some unhealthy behaviors, suffer depression, or engage in persistent high-effort coping, which in itself is a risk factor for stress-related diseases in low-income populations.[10-13,15-17] As Link et al.[18] have outlined, those of a lower socioeconomic position also have less ability than others to gain access to information, services, or technologies that could protect them from or ameliorate risks. Further, there appears to be a "dose-response" relationship: long-term poverty is more devastating to health than short poverty spells, both for children and for adults.[19,20] For impoverished African Americans, excess morbidity and mortality increase over the young and middle adult years, suggesting the cumulative health impact of persistent disadvantage.[13]

While poverty has intensified in central city areas, it has also come to interact with characteristics of the urban environment to produce a particularly lethal combination. Several social and environmental factors are likely contributors to this phenomenon. First, economic restructuring away from a manufacturing to a service economy resulted in extraordinarily high levels of urban unemployment and the loss of well-paying, unionized jobs. Those now employed in the service sector often face unreliable and shifting part-time hours and have little or no health or retirement benefits. Second, there is a lack of adequate housing in major urban areas: increased housing prices have been a formidable problem for those whose already low incomes have failed to keep pace. The scarcity of housing has been exacerbated by reductions in municipal services, including fire department closings, which, among other consequences, have resulted in large numbers of burned-out buildings and the deterioration of the remaining housing stock.[21]

Third, massive reductions in outlays to maintain and supervise public parks in urban areas have led to the dramatic deterioration of these facilities and their use for illicit purposes.[22] One can imagine the cascade of events, as suggested by Wallace and Wallace,[21] that has been triggered by reductions in city services in low-income minority neighborhoods in New York City: an upsurge in family homelessness; the profound disruption of social networks, as those network members who lose their homes and can avert homelessness do so by fleeing or doubling up with other families; and the movement of drug users and traffickers into burned-out buildings and dilapidated public play spaces. These service reductions allowed urban areas to become the staging ground for the violence we have come to associate with urban neighborhoods and for other severe public health problems, including the crack and HIV/AIDS epidemics and the reemergence of tuberculosis. That stress-related diseases are on the increase hardly seems surprising. Meanwhile, the urban poor have confronted new challenges in gaining access to medical care.[23-26]

This description suggests that poverty and urban decay are among the causes of early health deterioration and excess mortality among residents of distressed urban areas. It also suggests several program and policy levers for improving the health of urban populations, among them (1) implementing job programs and measures to raise family incomes, (2) improving the quality, quantity, and affordability of housing, (3) improving municipal services, (4) redressing environmental inequities, and (5) expanding health insurance coverage and increasing the number of physicians in depressed urban areas. Each of these measures deserves serious attention. However, without addressing the question of how urban decay, with its attendant health problems, was allowed to happen, and that of the role of race in this process, the promise of such policies may be limited. Socioeconomic characteristics of urban populations are unlikely to be transformed in isolation; they are not associated with an otherwise level playing field.

Race/Ethnicity

For this discussion of the role of race/ethnicity in understanding poverty and urban health, race will be conceptualized in two intertwined ways. One is as a set of social relationships between majority and minority populations that have been institutionalized over time,[27] that privilege the majority population, and that are prior to the poverty that is associated with race.[28,29] The other is as a set of autonomous institutions within the minority population that are developed and maintained—even in the face of burdensome obligations or costs to individuals—because, on balance, they mitigate, resist, or undo the adverse effects imposed by institutionalized discrimination.

In terms of the first conceptualization, the current urban environment developed under the influence of race-conscious policies. A large-scale migration of African Americans from the South to northern urban locations began in the 1940s, initially in response to increased demand for labor to sustain the war effort. In northern urban destinations, European immigrant neighborhood groups, government officials, and developers worked to avoid the integration of African Americans with established immigrant neighborhoods, producing the outlines of urban Black ghettoes.[30] Highway construction and public housing projects isolated Black neighborhoods from other areas, while other policies prevented Blacks from moving to emerging suburbs. Following World War II, African Americans were effectively frozen out of suburbs by racial covenants, discriminatory mortgage practices, and racial steering. In contrast, Whites were offered low-cost homes in suburbs and low interest rates on government-subsidized home mortgages, and they benefited from publicly funded transportation projects that linked their suburban homes to employment and cultural centers.[31,32]

Such housing and transportation policies promoted segregation and prevented many African Americans from escaping poverty, as urban centers lost jobs (first as industry moved to the suburbs and later because of macroeconomic restructuring away from industrialized jobs). They also precluded Blacks from enjoying the accumulation of wealth associated with the vast appreciation of suburban housing values.[33] Meanwhile, there has been little sustained investment—public or private—in central city areas. Race has been an explicit factor in this circumstance.[30]

In terms of the second conceptualization of race/ethnicity, African Americans have historically participated in community networks of exchange and support in order to mitigate social and economic adversity.[34,35] These networks are dynamic systems that help to shore up material resources among members and also serve to provide social support and identity-affirming cultural frameworks across generations. In 1919, Du Bois wrestled with the "curious paradox" that without the strength of conviction and cultural identity forged through vital separate ethnic organizations, the determination of African Americans to fight against being segregated into an "ill-lighted, unpaved, unsewered ghetto" might have been dilute rather than resolute.[36,p.268] More recently, James[37] has speculated that members of minority groups find health-preserving protection in cultural frameworks that are alternatives to the dominant cultural framework in which they are marginalized. James proposes a model that can be interpreted to resolve the paradox Du Bois observed: as a minority group's economic strength diminishes, its ability to supply the protection conferred by social support and identity-affirming symbols may be especially critical to preserving the health of its members.

In a vexing double whammy, policies and macroeconomic realities that gave rise to the ghettoization of poor African Americans in urban areas may have also dealt a series of hard blows to their critical social network systems, leaving such networks with fewer resources to meet the increasing needs of their members. Joblessness; homelessness; doubling up in overcrowded, substandard housing; ill health; and early death all undermine the efforts of kin to provide mutual aid or cultural affirmation. In addition, African Americans must vie with the dominant American culture to define urban Black identity. The dominant culture often defines urban minorities in disconfirming, negative stereotypes or ones that are affirming only in a narrow, perverse, and self-serving way—for example, in corporate images of urban athletes in high-priced athletic shoes. Kelley summarizes this restricted and confusing menu of images as "the circulation of the very representations of race that generate terror in all of us at the sight of young black men and yet compels most of America to want to wear their shoes."[22,p.224]

Apart from this materialistic fantasy, few sincerely attempt to walk in the shoes of the urban African American poor. Instead, pervasive negative images inform policies with flawed logic. For example, the growing inability of community networks in poor urban areas to avert material hardship, violence, or disease is interpreted through the prism of the dominant cultural occupation with a perceived decline in personal responsibility and family values. Rather than consider the historical or structural precursors of urban decay, citizens and policymakers—liberal and conservative—identify the behavior of urban residents (and the disturbing values their behavior is thought to represent) as an important source of urban poverty and distress.[38] One hard-hitting extension of this reasoning is the reduction of antipoverty policy into welfare policy institutionalized in the Personal Responsibility and Work Opportunity Reconciliation Act of 1996 (PRWORA; welfare reform),[39] a bill misguided and demeaning in many of its fundamental premises about the goals and motivations of the poor.[40]

Implications for Public Health

Healthy People 2010[41] calls attention to socioeconomic disparities in health and, for the first time, boldly calls for the elimination—not simply the reduction—of racial/ethnic and socioeconomic disparities in health. The unfortunate truth is that descriptive documentation of these disparities is matched neither by well-tested explanations for them nor by evaluation research on socioeconomic interventions. Without progress in research, specific socioeconomic interventions cannot be confidently proposed. Still, the preceding "structural" analysis suggests some activities and leads to guiding principles for action and continued research.

First Do No (More) Harm

In a structural framework, policies that affect the context of urban poverty—such as the distribution of wealth, the built environment, segregation, and access to technologies, information, or other resources—influence fundamental causes of health inequality. So, too, do policies that affect the integrity of the autonomous institutions—formal organizations, informal networks, ideologies, and cultural frameworks—that members of oppressed groups work to develop and maintain in order to mitigate, resist, or undo the structural constraints they face. Policies that are likely to erode income, housing, or neighborhood conditions; fragment or impose new obligations on already overburdened networks; or proliferate demeaning and demoralizing stereotypes affect the material and psychosocial conditions of life for the urban poor and thus their health. Public health professionals can describe the health impact of proposed policies by evaluating the likelihood that they will do any of the above and can bring these considerations to the table.

For example, if such an analysis had been part of the deliberations on PRWORA, those concerned with its probable health impact would have noted not only its implications for Medicaid eligibility (which were considered) but also its likelihood of intensifying the material hardship, stress, and uncertainty faced by poor residents of urban areas (through, for example, its time-limits provisions) and its potential to impose further perturbations on the protective systems worked out by kin networks (through, for example, requiring all adult family members to work, no matter whether they then compete with each other for the same scarce low-wage jobs or whether this requirement depletes the reserve of kin members available to offer child care to others). By intensifying their exposure to risks and undermining their autonomous protections, PRWORA could further erode the health of the urban poor.

Similarly, a press to revitalize urban areas now comes from environmentalists and upper-middle-class Americans who, ironically, now bemoan the sprawl wrought by increasing suburbanization and White flight. However, if plans to reverse sprawl and reclaim urban areas for the socioeconomically advantaged have no equity component, they risk leading to the dispersion and fragmentation of poor inner city neighborhood residents as real estate prices increase. Already, evidence of this possibility is available in urban "success" sites such as downtown Atlanta, the South End of Boston, and San Francisco. On a more positive note, broad interest in reversing sprawl may offer opportunities for urban community leaders to build coalitions with environmentalists to galvanize interest in the revitalization of American cities.

Work to Alter Public Perspectives on Race

Negative stereotypic judgments of African Americans led to, and continue to re-inforce, ghettoization; affect the treatment decisions of health providers[42,43]; in-fluence the hiring practices of potential employers[44]; fuel distrust of public health initiatives[45]; weaken public support for initiatives to improve the health of urban populations; and deny young, urban African Americans health-promoting, identity-affirming symbols. In a structural framework, understanding what shapes public sentiment on race and determining how it might be influenced become critical public health objectives. Incorporating the historical under-pinnings of ghettoization and the deterioration of urban areas into discussions of urban life and health may alter the ways people think about the minority poor and their health. To the extent that social epidemiologists elucidate the social conditions and contexts that trigger unhealthy behaviors among the urban poor, these should be described to broad audiences to alter public un-derstanding of these behaviors. For example, as King points out, high smoking rates in urban poor communities may be, in part, a response to pervasive psy-chosocial stress and to the targeting of these communities by tobacco compa-nies for advertising.[46]

When social epidemiologists find evidence that, in the face of formidable structural impediments to success, there is a physical price attached even to coping in socially approved ways, this information should also be disseminated. For example, James has suggested and found evidence of a culturally salient behavioral predisposition among African Americans to engage in persistent high-effort coping with social and economic adversity ("John Henryism"). In low-income African American populations, individuals who exhibit high levels of John Henryism are the ones most apt to be hypertensive.[15,16] This evidence contradicts demeaning stereotypic notions that fatalism and indolence precipi-tate cardiovascular disease among low-income African Americans. Put another way, the empirical evidence on John Henryism suggests that low-income African Americans who work hard to cope with or surmount structural barriers to their achievement also express values and take actions that are in sync with the greater American ideological emphasis on self-control and a strong work ethic. However, these actions can exact a physical price whether or not they are successful in producing social mobility.

Distinguish Between "Ameliorative" and "Fundamental" Approaches

Positing that many social conditions are "fundamental causes" of disease, Link, Phelan, and colleagues[18,47,48] describe the social patterning of health and disease as a potent force that may take new shape but persists undeterred by the identi-fication and amelioration of the risk factors that express that patterning in a given time period. In the realm of intervention, this conceptual model implies a distinc-tion between "ameliorative" and "fundamental" actions. Ameliorative approaches target the risk factors that link socioeconomic position to health in a particular context, but they do not fundamentally alter the context (or underlying inequalities). Public health practitioners are often engaged in what can be seen, by this rubric, as ameliorative actions. A substantial literature assesses ameliorative interventions, including ones specific to the urban context.[49]

Continued implementation of and refinements in ameliorative approaches are necessary to avoid health disparities from widening uncontrollably. Certainly, it is wise to build on the accumulated base of knowledge on how best to implement health promotion initiatives or expand access to medical services; it is also wise to target and tailor them appropriately for urban and minority populations. Still, such initiatives and services alone will not result in the elimination of health disparities. As Link, Phelan, and colleagues[18,47,48] outline, energy put forth to address a specific risk factor will achieve limited success in improving the health of a disadvantaged population. The risk factor may be virtually inevitable in a given social context, or it may be only one of the many risk factors that follow from a set of social conditions. Even the eradication of specific risk factors may be followed by the emergence of new risks that, similar to the old risks, are more likely to be averted by a population in more favorable social circumstances than by the population one is trying to help. From this perspective, the only way to eliminate differentials in health is to address the underlying "social inequalities that so reliably produce them."[48,p.472]

It is easiest to understand individual behavior change strategies or the expansion of access to medical services (especially tertiary services) as falling under the rubric of ameliorative interventions. It is also important to recognize that community-based public health initiatives can also be ameliorative rather than fundamental. The value of community partners in research, the importance of community members on boards of local health care facilities, and the necessity of the participation and leadership of community members in social or policy change efforts is clear and has been well described elsewhere.[26,29,45,50] In fact, aspects of the structural paradigm urge working in partnerships with communities, engaging in "bottom-up" approaches, and recognizing that historically important and effective social movements derive their moral, political, and practical force from the autonomous networks and institutions developed and kindled within minority communities.

However, the paradigm also suggests a caveat regarding overreliance on community-centered approaches. As Halpern notes, one possible pitfall of overreliance on such approaches is that "those who have the least role in making and the largest role in bearing the brunt of society's economic and social choices [are left] to deal with the effects of those choices."[30,p.5] If social, political, and economic exclusion are among the distal causes of the disproportionate health burden absorbed by the urban minority poor, and if, as a result, community members own and control little, the prospects for local community initiatives to alter fundamental causes of morbidity and mortality may be modest. The comments of a community legal aid activist of the 1960s are cautionary: "We undoubtedly brought some solace and relief to many individual tenants. . . . Nevertheless in those same three years the housing situation in San Francisco became a great deal worse. . . . [It] might appear [that we made] the process a little more humane without having any effect on the underlying machinery."[51,p.146]

In addition to cautioning against unrealistic expectations of what community-based public health approaches can be expected to achieve, this caveat also suggests broadening the set of community-based networks and organizations that can be enlisted to address structural barriers to include organizations with substantial economic leverage. For example, the largest and wealthiest minority organizations include labor unions. In some cities, minority-run public sector unions are a major force in city/state politics and policy. More generally, altering fundamental causes of health inequality requires working at multiple levels and making connections between levels. The scope and target of public health activity can move (as it has, to an extent) from the individual to the family to the community and also encompass large societal institutions, pervasive and influential ideologies, intergroup relations, and macroeconomic policy.

Increase Attention to the Needs of Adults

Many public health activities target or favor the health and well-being of youths over those of adults, because youths are viewed either as being more deserving of our efforts or as more at risk. However, adults are critical to the vitality of families and communities, and research findings suggest the merit of stimulating increased attention to the needs of young and middle-aged adults in impoverished urban areas. As noted previously, social differentials in morbidity and mortality are most pronounced among adults of reproductive and working-age.[13,52]

Adults of these ages play critical social roles as economic providers and caretakers. Improving adult health in impoverished urban areas would reap advantages for residents of all ages. Some examples are straightforward, such as the importance of maternal health to infant health. In addition, high levels of health-induced disability among working-age African American men and women contribute to their relatively low rates of participation in the labor force and thereby to their ability to support families economically.[53] Meanwhile, extensive and competing obligations to family and larger social networks as well as to paid jobs lead to stress-related disease, particularly among women.[13,54] More speculatively, pervasive uncertainty regarding health among young adult and middle-aged members of a community shapes the expectations of youths and may influence the timing of childbearing toward earlier ages[13,40] or the propensity of some youths to engage in risk-taking behaviors.[55]

Continued Research

To inform efforts to reduce or eliminate urban health disadvantages, continued research should evaluate the impact of social and economic policies on the health of urban residents. In addition, evidence of important interactions of race, poverty, and locality in influencing health is growing,[3,56] but social epidemiologists more often look at general patterns of the relationship between socioeconomic position and health (e.g., providing estimates based on national or statewide averages or averaging across all residents of major metropolitan areas). Stepping up research on variation among local poor populations may prove beneficial to those hoping to remedy the effects of urban life on health.

Indicators of personal experience with racism and racialized stress have been added to the set of studied influences on health,[57] but few investigators have systematically considered the health consequences of the manifestations of racism in the structures of society.[8,25] Conceptually, research in this area would benefit from the development of dynamic and contextualized understandings of the role of culture in health. This development would replace static constructions of culture as an imported set of behaviors, practices, or values that are subject to change only inasmuch as they are traded in for the dominant set.

As part of this activity, investigators should become more attuned to the functioning of autonomous social institutions within communities and less concerned with their form. For example, classifying mothers as married or unmarried provides more questionable information about children's well-being or local social organization than does understanding who, in a broader social network, is expected and available to participate in the care and support of children. Classifying mothers as married or unmarried also overlooks important questions such as why autonomous caretaking systems evolved and how they are maintained.[34,35,40, 58] To this end, development and empirical testing of theories that draw from African American (or other urban ethnic) culture, history, and life experience to hypothesize links between structural barriers, personal and social coping mechanisms, and their physiologic effects and health manifestations offer more promise than studies that draw from political theories abstracted from the lived experience of urban Americans.

A deeper understanding of how culture relates to inequalities in health will also require evaluation of the role the dominant cultural system plays in the maintenance of inequality. The history of race-based ghettoization suggests that there is a cultural component to the perpetuation of poverty and that it comes, in the main, from the dominant culture, not from the poor. One interpretation is that the health of the African American poor has been sacrificed to maintain the core American myth that some people are more equal than others. In this myth, the populace is divided into those who are responsible members of civil society, deserving of its full benefits, and those who are deemed a threat to civil society and are to be segregated, marginalized, or even policed.[59]

These comments have focused on African American residents of impoverished urban areas because both real and imagined threats to public health emanate from the long-term ghettoization of African Americans. Historical processes underpin this ghettoization, but there are also emerging racial/ethnic challenges and opportunities that affect the landscape and dynamics of urban centers. The 1990s witnessed the greatest influx of immigrants in 50 years, and many of these immigrants moved into high-poverty urban areas. Whether they become long-term residents of ghettos or barrios, or whether, like some immigrant populations before them, they are enabled to move through these areas and into higher-income areas, is an open question. Meanwhile, their needs and perspectives deserve articulation, and the influence of intergroup dynamics, coalitions, and tensions on health must also be examined and incorporated into programs and policies to improve the health of urban residents. In the spirit of this structural analysis, a key part of the process of examination is to discern the ways dominant American cultural ideologies and institutions shape, relieve, or reinforce the tensions between new immigrant groups and urban African Americans. Otherwise, a race-based culture of exclusivity will continue to draw its support by taxing the health of African Americans.

Acknowledgments

The author received financial support for this work from the William T. Grant Foundation and from a Robert Wood Johnson Foundation Investigator in Health Policy Research Award.

In developing these ideas, I benefited tremendously from exchanges with J. Philip Thompson. I am also grateful to Sherman James, Sylvia Tesh, and Adam Becker for commenting on earlier drafts. The views expressed are my own.

References

1. McCord C, Freeman HP. Excess mortality in Harlem. *N Engl J Med.* 1990; 322:173–177.
2. Geronimus AT, Bound J, Waidmann TA, et al. Excess mortality among Blacks and Whites in the United States. *N Engl J Med.* 1996;335:1552–1558.
3. Geronimus AT, Bound J, Waidmann TA. Poverty, time and place: variation in excess mortality across selected US populations, 1980–1990. *J Epidemiol Community Health.* 1999;53:325–334.
4. Jargowsky PA. *Poverty and Place: Ghettos, Barrios, and the American City.* New York, NY: Russell Sage Foundation; 1997.
5. Antonovsky A. Social class, life expectancy and overall mortality. *Milbank Q.* 1967;45:31–73.
6. Kitagawa EM, Hauser PM. *Differential Mortality in the United States: A Study in Socioeconomic Epidemiology.* Cambridge, Mass: Harvard University Press; 1973.
7. Adler NA, Boyce T, Chesney MA, et al. Socioeconomic status and health: the challenge of the gradient. *Am Psychol.* 1994;49:15–24.
8. Williams DR, Collins C. US socioeconomic and racial differences in health: patterns and explanations. *Annu Rev Sociol.* 1995;21:349–386.

9. Backlund E, Sorlie PD, Johnson NJ. The shape of the relationship between income and mortality in the United States: evidence from the National Longitudinal Mortality Study. *Ann Epidemiol.* 1996;6:12–20.
10. Lantz PM, House JS, Lepowski JM, Williams DR, Mero RP, Chen J. Socioeconomic factors, health behaviors, and mortality: results from a nationally representative prospective study of US adults. *JAMA.* 1998;279:1703–1708.
11. Marmot MG, Kogevinas M, Elston MA. Social/economic status and disease. *Annu Rev Public Health.* 1987;8:111–135.
12. Williams DR, House JS. Stress, social support, control and coping: a social epidemiological view. *WHO Reg Publ Eur Ser.* 1991;37:147–172.
13. Geronimus AT. The weathering hypothesis and the health of African-American women and infants: evidence and speculations. *Ethn Dis.* 1992;2: 207–221.
14. Mohai P, Bryant B. Environmental injustice: weighing race and class as factors in the distribution of environmental hazards. *Univ Colo Law Rev.* 1992; 63:921–932.
15. James SA. John Henryism and the health of African-Americans. *Cult Med Psychiatry.* 1994;18:163–182.
16. James SA, Strogatz SB, Browning SR, Garrett JM. Socioeconomic status, John Henryism, and hypertension in Blacks and Whites. *Am J Epidemiol.* 1987;126:664–673.
17. Northridge ME, Morabia A, Ganz ML, et al. Contribution of smoking to excess mortality in Harlem. *Am J Epidemiol.* 1998;147:250–258.
18. Link BG, Northridge M, Phelan JC, Ganz M. Social epidemiology and the fundamental cause concept: On the structuring of effective cancer screens by socioeconomic status. *Milbank Q.* 1998;76:304–305, 375–402.
19. Lynch JW, Kaplan GA, Shema SJ. Cumulative impact of sustained economic hardship on physical, cognitive, psychological, and social functioning. *N Engl J Med.* 1997;337:1889–1895.
20. Miller JE, Korenman S. Poverty and children's nutritional status in the United States. *Am J Epidemiol.* 1994;140:233–243.
21. Wallace R, Wallace D. Origins of public health collapse in New York City: The dynamics of planned shrinkage, contagious urban decay and social disintegration. *Bull NY Acad Med.* 1990;66:391–434.
22. Kelley RDG. Playing for keeps: pleasure and profit on the postindustrial playground. In: Lubiano W, ed. *The House That Race Built.* New York, NY: Pantheon Books; 1997:195–231.
23. Fossett JW, Perloff JD, Peterson JA, Kletke PR. Medicaid in the inner city: the case of maternity care in Chicago. *Milbank Q.* 1990;68:111–141.
24. Fossett JW, Perloff JD. *The "New" Health Reform and Access to Care: The Problem of the Inner City.* Washington, DC: Kaiser Commission on the Future of Medicaid; December 1995.
25. Polednak AP. Segregation, discrimination and mortality in US Blacks. *Ethn Dis.* 1996;6:99–108.

26. Schlesinger M. Paying the price: medical care, minorities and the newly competitive health care system. *Milbank Q.* 1987;65(suppl 2):270–296.
27. O'Connor A. Historical perspectives on race and community revitalization. Paper presented at: Meeting of the Race and Community Revitalization Project of the Aspen Institute Roundtable on Comprehensive Community Initiatives; November 13–15, 1998; Wye River Conference Center, Queenstown, Md.
28. Cooper R, David R. The biological concept of race and its application in public health and epidemiology. *J Health Polit Policy Law.* 1986;11:97–116.
29. Thompson JP. Universalism and deconcentration: Why race still matters in poverty and economic development. *Polit Soc.* 1998;26:181–219.
30. Halpern R. *Rebuilding the Inner City: A History of Neighborhood Initiatives to Address Poverty in the United States.* New York, NY: Columbia University Press; 1995.
31. Oliver ML, Shapiro TM. *Black Wealth/White Wealth: A New Perspective on Racial Inequality.* New York, NY: Routledge; 1995.
32. Massey D, Denton N. *American Apartheid: Segregation and the Making of the Underclass.* Cambridge, MA: Harvard University Press; 1993.
33. Conley D. *Being Black, Living in the Red: Race, Wealth, and Social Policy in America.* Berkeley: University of California Press; 1999.
34. Stack CB. *All Our Kin.* New York, NY: Harper & Row; 1974.
35. Stack C, Burton LM. Kinscripts. *J Comp Fam Stud.* 1993;24:157–170.
36. Du Bois WEB. "Jim Crowe." In: Weinberg M, ed. *W.E.B. Du Bois: A Reader.* New York, NY: Harper & Row; 1970:267–268.
37. James SA. Racial and ethnic differences in infant mortality and low birth weight: a psychosocial critique. *Ann Epidemiol.* 1993;3:130–136.
38. Gans HJ. *The War Against the Poor.* New York, NY: Basic Books; 1995.
39. Pub L No. 104-193, 110 Stat 2105-2355 (1996).
40. Geronimus AT. Teenage childbearing and personal responsibility: An alternative view. *Political Sci Q.* 1997;112:405–430.
41. Healthy People 2010: Understanding and Improving Health. Washington, DC: US Dept of Health and Human Services; January 2000. DHHS publication 017-001-00543-6.
42. Chasnoff IJ, Landress HJ, Barrett ME. The prevalence of illicit-drug or alcohol use during pregnancy and discrepancies in mandatory reporting in Pinellas County, Florida. *N Engl J Med.* 1990;322:1202–1206.
43. Schulman KA, Berlin JA, Harless W, et al. The effect of race and sex on physicians' recommendations for cardiac catheterization. *N Engl J Med.* 1999;340:618–626.
44. Wilson WJ. *When Work Disappears: The World of the New Urban Poor.* New York, NY: Alfred A. Knopf; 1996.
45. Dalton H. AIDS in blackface. *Daedalus.* 1989; Summer:205–227.
46. King G. The "race" concept in smoking: a review of research on African Americans. *Soc Sci Med.* 1997;45:1075–1087.

47. Link BG, Phelan JC. Social conditions as fundamental causes of disease. *J Health Soc Behav*. 1995;Spec no.:80–94.
48. Link BG, Phelan JC. Understanding sociodemographic differences in health: The role of fundamental social causes. *Am J Public Health*. 1996;86:471–473.
49. Freudenberg N. Community-based health education for urban populations: An overview. *Health Educ Behav*. 1998;25:11–23.
50. Israel BA, Schulz AJ, Parker EA, Becker AB. Review of community-based research: assessing partnership approaches to improve public health. *Annu Rev Public Health*. 1998;18:173–202.
51. Carlin J. Storefront lawyers in San Francisco. In: Pilisuk M, Pilisuk P, eds. *How We Lost the War on Poverty*. New Brunswick, NJ: Transaction Books; 1973:136–158.
52. House JS, Lepkowski JM, Kinney AM, Mero RP, Kessler RC, Herzog AR. The social stratification of aging and health. *J Health Soc Behav*. 1994;35:213–234.
53. Bound J, Schoenbaum M, Waidmann T. Race differences in labor force attachment and disability status. *Gerontologist*. 1996;36:311–321.
54. LeClere FB, Rogers RG, Peters K. Neighborhood social context and racial differences in women's heart disease mortality. *J Health Soc Behav*. 1998;39:91–107.
55. Wilson M, Daly M. Life expectancy, economic inequality, homicide, and reproductive timing in Chicago neighbourhoods. *BMJ*. 1997;314:1271–1274.
56. Davey Smith G, Hart C, Watt G, et al. Individual social class, area-based deprivation, cardiovascular disease risk factors, and mortality: The Renfrew and Paisley Study. *J Epidemiol Com Health*. 1998;52:399–405.
57. Williams DR, Yu Y, Jackson JS, Anderson NB. Racial differences in physical and mental health: socioeconomic status, stress and discrimination. *J Health Psychol*. 1997;2:335–351.
58. Sharff JW. *King Kong on 4th Street*. Boulder, CO: Westview Press; 1998.
59. Brodkin K. *How Jews Became White Folks and What That Says About Race in America*. New Brunswick, NJ: Rutgers University Press; 1998.

Neighborhoods and Violent Crime: A Multilevel Study of Collective Efficacy

Robert J. Sampson, Stephen W. Raudenbush, Felton Earls

For most of this century, social scientists have observed marked variations in rates of criminal violence across neighborhoods of U.S. cities. Violence has been associated with the low socioeconomic status (SES) and residential instability of neighborhoods. Although the geographical concentration of violence and its connection with neighborhood composition are well established, the question remains: why? What is it, for example, about the concentration of poverty that accounts for its association with rates of violence? What are the social processes that might explain or mediate this relation?[1-3] In this article, we report results from a study designed to address these questions about crime and communities.

Our basic premise is that social and organizational characteristics of neighborhoods explain variations in crime rates that are not solely attributable to the aggregated demographic characteristics of individuals. We propose that the differential ability of neighborhoods to realize the common values of residents and maintain effective social controls is a major source of neighborhood variation in violence.[4,5] Although social control is often a response to deviant behavior, it should not be equated with formal regulation or forced conformity by institutions such as the police and courts. Rather, social control refers generally to the capacity of a group to regulate its members according to desired principles—to realize collective, as opposed to forced, goals.[6] One central goal is the desire of community residents to live in safe and orderly environments that are free of predatory crime, especially interpersonal violence.

In contrast to formally or externally induced actions (for example, a police crackdown), we focus on the effectiveness of informal mechanisms by which residents themselves achieve public order. Examples of informal social control include the monitoring of spontaneous play groups among children, a willingness to intervene to prevent acts such as truancy and street-corner "hanging" by teenage peer groups, and the confrontation of persons who are exploiting or disturbing public space.[5,7] Even among adults, violence regularly arises in public disputes, in the context of illegal markets (for example, prostitution and drugs), and in the company of peers.[8] The capacity of residents to control group-level processes and visible signs of social disorder is thus a key mechanism influencing opportunities for interpersonal crime in a neighborhood.

Informal social control also generalizes to broader issues of import to the well-being of neighborhoods. In particular, the differential ability of communities to extract resources and respond to cuts in public services (such as police patrols, fire stations, garbage collection, and housing code enforcement) looms large when we consider the known link between public signs of disorder (such as vacant housing, burned-out buildings, vandalism, and litter) and more serious crime.[9]

Thus conceived, neighborhoods differentially activate informal social control. It is for this reason that we see an analogy between individual efficacy and neighborhood efficacy: both are activated processes that seek to achieve an intended effect. At the neighborhood level, however, the willingness of local residents to intervene for the common good depends in large part on conditions of mutual trust and solidarity among neighbors.[10] Indeed, one is unlikely to intervene in a neighborhood context in which the rules are unclear and people mistrust or fear one another. It follows that socially cohesive neighborhoods will prove the most fertile contexts for the realization of informal social control. In sum, it is the linkage of mutual trust and the willingness to intervene for the common good that defines the neighborhood context of collective efficacy. Just as individuals vary in their capacity for efficacious action, so too do neighborhoods vary in their capacity to achieve common goals. And just as individual self-efficacy is situated rather than global (one has self-efficacy relative to a particular task or type of task),[11] in this paper we view neighborhood efficacy as existing relative to the tasks of supervising children and maintaining public order. It follows that the collective efficacy of residents is a critical means by which urban neighborhoods inhibit the occurrence of personal violence, without regard to the demographic composition of the population.

What Influences Collective Efficacy?

As with individual efficacy, collective efficacy does not exist in a vacuum. It is embedded in structural contexts and a wider political economy that stratifies places of residence by key social characteristics.[12] Consider the destabilizing potential of rapid population change on neighborhood social organization. A high rate of residential mobility, especially in areas of decreasing population, fosters institutional disruption and weakened social controls over collective life. A major reason is that the formation of social ties takes time. Financial investment also provides homeowners with a vested interest in supporting the commonweal of neighborhood life. We thus hypothesize that residential tenure and home-ownership promote collective efforts to maintain social control.[13]

Consider next patterns of resource distribution and racial segregation in the United States. Recent decades have witnessed an increasing geographical concentration of lower income residents, especially minority groups and female-headed families. This neighborhood concentration stems in part from macro-economic changes related to the deindustrialization of central cities, along with the out-migration of middle-class residents.[14] In addition, the greater the race and class segregation in a metropolitan area, the smaller the number of neighborhoods absorbing economic shocks and the more severe the resulting concentration of poverty will be.[15] Economic stratification by race and place thus fuels the neighborhood concentration of cumulative forms of disadvantage, intensifying the social isolation of lower income, minority, and single-parent residents from key resources supporting collective social control.[1,16]

Perhaps more salient is the influence of racial and economic exclusion on perceived powerlessness. Social science research has demonstrated, at the individual level, the direct role of SES in promoting a sense of control, efficacy, and even biological health itself.[17] An analogous process may work at the community level. The alienation, exploitation, and dependency wrought by resource deprivation act as a centrifugal force that stymies collective efficacy. Even if personal ties are strong in areas of concentrated disadvantage, they may be weakly tethered to collective actions.

We therefore test the hypothesis that concentrated disadvantage decreases and residential stability increases collective efficacy. In turn, we assess whether collective efficacy explains the association of neighborhood disadvantage and residential instability with rates of interpersonal violence. It is our hypothesis that collective efficacy mediates a substantial portion of the effects of neighborhood stratification.

Research Design

This article examines data from the Project on Human Development in Chicago Neighborhoods (PHDCN). Applying a spatial definition of neighborhood—a collection of people and institutions occupying a subsection of a larger community—we combined 847 census tracts in the city of Chicago to create 343 "neighborhood clusters" (NCs). The overriding consideration in formation of NCs was that they should be as ecologically meaningful as possible, composed of geographically contiguous census tracts, and internally homogeneous on key census indicators. We settled on an ecological unit of about 8000 people, which is smaller than the 77 established community areas in Chicago (the average size is almost 40,000 people) but large enough to approximate local neighborhoods. Geographic boundaries (for example, railroad tracks, parks, and freeways) and knowledge of Chicago's neighborhoods guided this process.[18]

The extensive racial, ethnic, and social-class diversity of Chicago's population was a major criterion in its selection as a research site. At present, whites, blacks, and Latinos each represent about a third of the city's population. Table 4-1 classifies the 343 NCs according to race or ethnicity and a trichotomized measure of SES from the 1990 census.[19] Although there are no low-SES white

TABLE 4-1   Racial and Ethnic Composition by SES Strata: Distribution of 343
            Chicago NCs in the PHDCN Design

	SES		
Race or ethnicity	Low	Medium	High
≥ 75% black	77	37	11
≥ 75% white	0	5	69
≥ 75% Latino	12	9	0
≥ 20% Latino and ≥ 20% white	6	40	12
≥ 20% Latino and ≥ 20% black	9	4	0
≥ 20% black and ≥ 20% white	2	4	11
NCs not classified above	8	15	12
Total	114	114	115

neighborhoods and no high-SES Latino neighborhoods, there are black neighborhoods in all three cells of SES, and many heterogeneous neighborhoods vary in SES. Table 4-1 at once thus confirms the racial and ethnic segregation and yet rejects the common stereotype that minority neighborhoods in the United States are homogeneous.

To gain a complete picture of the city's neighborhoods, 8782 Chicago residents representing all 343 NCs were interviewed in their homes as part of the community survey (CS). The CS was designed to yield a representative sample of households within each NC, with sample sizes large enough to create reliable NC measures.[20] Henceforth, we refer to NCs as "neighborhoods," keeping in mind that other operational definitions might have been used.

Measures

"Informal social control" was represented by a five-item Likert-type scale. Residents were asked about the likelihood ("Would you say it is very likely, likely, neither likely nor unlikely, unlikely, or very unlikely?") that their neighbors could be counted on to intervene in various ways if (i) children were skipping school and hanging out on a street corner, (ii) children were spray-painting graffiti on a local building, (iii) children were showing disrespect to an adult, (iv) a fight broke out in front of their house, and (v) the fire station closest to their home was threatened with budget cuts. "Social cohesion and trust" were also represented by five conceptually related items. Respondents were asked how strongly they agreed (on a five-point scale) that "people around here are willing to help their neighbors," "this is a close-knit neighborhood," "people in this neighborhood can be trusted," "people in this neighborhood generally don't get along with each other," and "people in this neighborhood do not share the same values" (the last two statements were reverse coded).

Responses to the five-point Likert scales were aggregated to the neighborhood level as initial measures. Social cohesion and informal social control were closely associated across neighborhoods ($r = 0.80$, $P < 0.001$), which suggests that the two measures were tapping aspects of the same latent construct. Because we also expected that the willingness and intention to intervene on behalf of the neighborhood would be enhanced under conditions of mutual trust and cohesion, we combined the two scales into a summary measure labeled collective efficacy.[21]

The measurement of violence was achieved in three ways. First, respondents were asked how often each of the following had occurred in the neighborhood during the past 6 months: (i) a fight in which a weapon was used, (ii) a violent argument between neighbors, (iii) a gang fight, (iv) a sexual assault or rape, and (v) a robbery or mugging. The scale construction for perceived neighborhood violence mirrored that for social control and cohesion. Second, to assess personal victimization, each respondent was asked "While you have lived in this neighborhood, has anyone ever used violence, such as in a mugging, fight, or sexual assault, against you or any member of your household anywhere in your neighborhood?"[22] Third, we tested both survey measures against independently recorded incidents of homicide aggregated to the NC level.[23] Homicide is one of the most reliably measured crimes by the police and does not suffer the reporting limitations associated with other violent crimes, such as assault and rape.

Ten variables were constructed from the 1990 decennial census of the population to reflect neighborhood differences in poverty, race and ethnicity, immigration, the labor market, age composition, family structure, homeownership, and residential stability (see Table 4-2). The census was independent of the PHDCN CS; moreover, the census data were collected 5 years earlier, which permitted temporal sequencing. To assess whether a smaller number of linear combinations of census characteristics describe the structure of the 343 Chicago neighborhoods, we conducted a factor analysis.[24]

Consistent with theories and research on U.S. cities, the poverty-related variables given in Table 4-2 are highly associated and load on the same factor. With an eigenvalue greater than 5, the first factor is dominated by high loadings (> 0.85) for poverty, receipt of public assistance, unemployment, female headed-families, and density of children, followed by, to a lesser extent, percentage of black residents. Hence, the predominant interpretation revolves around concentrated disadvantage—African Americans, children, and single-parent families are differentially found in neighborhoods with high concentrations of poverty.[25] To represent this dimension parsimoniously, we calculated a factor regression score that weighted each variable by its factor loading.

The second dimension captures areas of the city undergoing immigration, especially from Mexico. The two variables that define this dimension are the percentage of Latinos (approximately 70% of Latinos in Chicago are of Mexican descent) and the percentage of foreign-born persons. Similar to the procedures

TABLE 4-2   Oblique Rotated Factor Pattern
(Loadings ≥ 0.60) in 343 Chicago
Neighborhoods (data are from the
1990 census)

Variable	Factor Loading
Concentrated disadvantage	
Below poverty line	0.93
On public assistance	0.94
Female-headed families	0.93
Unemployed	0.86
Less than age 18	0.94
Black	0.60
Immigrant concentration	
Latino	0.88
Foreign-born	0.70
Residential stability	
Same house as in 1985	0.77
Owner-occupied house	0.86

for concentrated disadvantage, a weighted factor score was created to reflect immigrant concentration. Because it describes neighborhoods of ethnic and linguistic heterogeneity, there is reason to believe that immigrant concentration may impede the capacity of residents to realize common values and to achieve informal social controls, which in turn explains an increased risk of violence.[1,5,7]

The third factor score is dominated by two variables with high (> 0.75) loadings: the percentage of persons living in the same house as 5 years earlier and the percentage of owner-occupied homes. The clear emergence of a residential stability factor is consistent with much past research.[13]

Analytic Models

The internal consistency of a person measure will depend on the intercorrelation among items and the number of items in a scale. The internal consistency of a neighborhood measure will depend in part on these factors, but it will hinge more on the degree of intersubjective agreement among informants in their ratings of the neighborhood in which they share membership and on the sample size of informants per neighborhood.[26] To study reliability, we therefore formulated a hierarchical statistical model representing item variation within persons, person variation within neighborhoods, and variation between neighborhoods. Complicating the analysis is the problem of missing data: inevitably, some persons will fail to respond to some questions in an interview. We present our hierarchical model as a series of nested models, one for each level in the hierarchy.[27]

Level 1 model. Within each person, Y_{ijk}, the ith response of person j in neighborhood k, depends on the person's latent perception of collective efficacy plus error:

$$Y_{ijk} = \pi_{jk} \sum_{p=1}^{9} \alpha_p D_{pijk} + e_{ijk} \qquad (1)$$

Here D_{pijk} is an indicator variable taking on a value of unity if response i is to item p in the 10-item scale intended to measure collective efficacy and zero if response i is to some other item. Thus, α_p represents the "difficulty" of item p, and π_{jk} is the "true score" for person jk and is adjusted for the difficulty level of the items to which that person responded.[28] The errors of measurement, e_{ijk}, are assumed to be independent and homoscedastic (that is, to have equal standard deviations).

Level 2 model. Across informants within neighborhoods, the latent true scores vary randomly around the neighborhood mean:

$$\pi_{jk} = \eta_k + r_{jk}, r_{jk} \sim N(0, \tau_\pi) \qquad (2)$$

Here η_k is the neighborhood mean collective efficacy, and random effects r_{jk} associated with each person are independently, normally distributed with variance τ_π, that is, the "within-neighborhood variance."

Level 3 model. Across neighborhoods, each neighborhood's mean collective efficacy η_k varies randomly about a grand mean:

$$\eta_k = \gamma + \mu_k, \mu_k \sim N(0, \tau_\eta) \qquad (3)$$

where γ is the grand mean collective efficacy, μ_k is a normally distributed random effect associated with neighborhood k, and τ_η is the between-neighborhood variance. According to this setup, the object of measurement is μ_k. The degree of intersubjective agreement among raters is the intraneighborhood correlation, $\rho = \tau_\eta/(\tau_\eta + \tau_\pi)$. The reliability of measurement of μ_k depends primarily on ρ and on the sample size per neighborhood. The entire three-level model is estimated simultaneously via maximum likelihood.[26]

The results showed that 21% of the variation in perceptions of collective efficacy lies between the 343 neighborhoods.[29] The reliability with which neighborhoods can be distinguished on collective efficacy ranges between 0.80 for neighborhoods with a sample size of 20 raters to 0.91 for neighborhoods with a sample size of 50 raters.

Controlling response biases. Suppose, however, that informant responses to the collective efficacy questions vary systematically within neighborhoods as a function of demographic background (such as age, gender, SES, and ethnicity), as well as homeownership, marital status, and so on. Then variation across neighborhoods in the composition of the sample of respondents along these lines could masquerade as variation in collective efficacy. To control for such possible biases, we expanded the level 2 model (Eq. 2) by incorporating 11 characteristics of respondents as covariates. Equation 2 becomes

$$\pi_{jk} = \eta_k + \sum_{q=1}^{11} \delta_q X_{qjk} + r_{jk}, \; r_{jk} \sim N(0, \tau_\pi) \qquad (4)$$

where X_{qjk} is the value of covariate q associated with respondent j in neighborhood k and δ_q is the partial effect of that covariate on the expected response of that informant on the collective efficacy items. Thus, η_k is now the level of efficacy for neighborhood k after adjustment for the composition of the informant sample with respect to 11 characteristics: gender (1 = female, 0 = male), marital status (composed of separate indicators for married, separated or divorced, and single), homeownership, ethnicity and race (composed of indicators for Latinos and blacks), mobility (number of moves in past 5 years), years in neighborhood, age, and a composite measure of SES (the first principal component of education, income, and occupational prestige).

Association Between Neighborhood Social Composition and Collective Efficacy

The theory described above led us to expect that neighborhood concentrated disadvantage (con. dis.) and immigrant concentration (imm. con.) would be negatively linked to neighborhood collective efficacy and residential stability would be positively related to collective efficacy, net of the contributions of the 11 covariates defined in the previous paragraph. To test this hypothesis, we expanded the level 3 model (Eq. 3) to

$$\eta_k = \gamma_0 + \gamma_1 \, (\text{con. dis.})_k + \gamma_2 \, (\text{stability})_k + \gamma_3 \, (\text{imm. con.})_k + u_k, \; u_k \sim N(0, \tau_\eta) \; (5)$$

where γ_0 is the model intercept and γ_1, γ_2, and γ_3 are partial regression coefficients.

We found some effects of personal background (Table 4-3): High SES, homeownership, and age were associated with elevated levels of collective efficacy, whereas high mobility was negatively associated with collective efficacy. Gender, ethnicity, and years in neighborhood were not associated with collective efficacy.

At the neighborhood level, when these personal background effects were controlled, concentrated disadvantage and immigrant concentration were significantly negatively associated with collective efficacy, whereas residential stability was significantly positively associated with collective efficacy (for metric coefficients and t ratios, see Table 4-3). The standardized regression coefficients were –0.58 for concentrated disadvantage, –0.13 for immigrant concentration, and 0.25 for residential stability, explaining over 70% of the variability across the 343 NCs.

Table 4-3 Correlates of Collective Efficacy

Variable	Coefficient	SE	*t* ratio
Intercept	3.523	0.013	263.20
Person-level predictors			
Female	−0.012	0.015	−0.76
Married	−0.005	0.021	−0.25
Separated or divorced	−0.045	0.026	−1.72
Single	−0.026	0.024	−1.05
Homeowner	0.122	0.020	6.04
Latino	0.042	0.028	1.52
Black	−0.029	0.030	−0.98
Mobility	−0.025	0.007	−3.71
Age	2.09×10^{-3}	0.60×10^{-3}	3.47
Years in neighborhood	0.64×10^{-3}	0.82×10^{-3}	0.78
SES	3.53×10^{-2}	0.76×10^{-2}	4.64
Neighborhood-level predictors			
Concentrated disadvantage	−0.172	0.016	−10.74
Immigrant concentration	−0.037	0.014	−2.66
Residential stability	0.074	0.130	5.61
Variance components			
Within neighborhoods	0.320		
Between neighborhoods	0.026		
Percent of variance explained			
Within neighborhoods	3.2		
Between neighborhoods	70.3		

Collective Efficacy as a Mediator of Social Composition

Past research has consistently reported links between neighborhood social composition and crime. We assessed the relation of social composition to neighborhood levels of violence, violent victimization, and homicide rates, and asked whether collective efficacy partially mediated these relations.

Perceived violence. Using a model that paralleled that for collective efficacy (Eqs. 1, 4, and 5), we found that reports of neighborhood violence depended to some degree on personal background. Higher levels of violence were reported by those who were separated or divorced (as compared with those who were single or married), by whites and blacks (as opposed to Latinos), by younger respondents, and by those with longer tenure in their current neighborhood. Gender, homeownership, mobility, and SES were not significantly associated with responses within neighborhoods. When these personal background characteristics were controlled, the concentrations of disadvantage (t = 13.30) and immigrants (t = 2.44) were positively associated with the level of violence (see Table 4-4, model 1). The corresponding standardized regression coefficients are 0.75 and 0.11. Also, as hypothesized, residential stability was negatively associated with the level of violence (t = –6.95), corresponding to a standardized regression coefficient of –0.28. The model accounted for 70.5% of the variation in violence between neighborhoods.

Next, collective efficacy was added as a predictor in the level 3 model (Table 4-4, model 2). The analysis built in a correction for errors of measurement in this predictor.[30] We found collective efficacy to be negatively related to violence (t = –5.95), net of all other effects, and to correspond to a standardized coefficient of –0.45. Hence, after social composition was controlled, collective efficacy was strongly negatively associated with violence. Moreover, the coefficients for social composition were substantially smaller than they had been without a control for collective efficacy. The coefficient for concentrated disadvantage, al-

TABLE 4-4   Neighborhood Correlates of Perceived Neighborhood Violence, Violent Victimization, and 1995 Homicide Events

Variable	Model 1: Social Composition			Model 2: Social Composition and Collective Efficacy		
	Coefficient	SE	t	Coefficient	SE	t
*Perceived neighborhood violence**						
Concentrated disadvantage	0.277	0.021	13.30	0.171	0.024	7.24
Immigrant concentration	0.041	0.017	2.44	0.018	0.016	1.12
Residential stability	0.102	0.015	–6.95	–0.056	0.016	–3.49
Collective efficacy				–0.618	0.104	–5.95
Violent victimization[†]						
Concentrated disadvantage	0.258	0.045	5.71	0.085	0.054	1.58
Immigrant concentration	0.141	0.046	3.06	0.098	0.044	2.20
Residential stability	–0.143	0.050	–2.84	–0.031	0.051	–0.60
Collective efficacy				–1.190	0.240	–4.96
1995 homicide events[‡]						
Concentrated disadvantage	0.727	0.049	14.91	0.491	0.064	7.65
Immigrant concentration	–0.022	0.051	–0.43	–0.073	0.050	–1.45
Residential stability	0.093	0.042	2.18	0.208	0.046	4.52
Collective efficacy				–1.471	0.261	–5.64

*Estimates of neighborhood-level coefficients control for gender, marital status, homeownership, ethnicity, mobility, age, years in neighborhood, and SES of those interviewed. Model 1 accounts for 70.5% of the variation between neighborhoods in perceived violence, whereas model 2 accounts for 77.8% of the variation.
[†]Neighborhood-level coefficients are adjusted for the same person-level covariates listed in the first footnote. Model 1 accounts for 12.3% of the variation between neighborhoods in violent victimization, whereas model 2 accounts for 44.4%.
[‡]Model 1 accounts for 56.1% of the variation between neighborhoods in homicide rates, whereas model 2 accounts for 61.7% of the variation.

though still statistically significant, was 0.171 (as compared with 0.277). The difference between these coefficients (0.277 − 0.171 = 0.106) was significant (t = 5.30). Similarly, the coefficients for immigrant concentration and for residential stability were also significantly reduced: The coefficient for immigrant concentration, originally 0.041, was now 0.018, a difference of 0.023 (t = 2.42); the coefficient for residential stability, which had been −0.102, was now −0.056, a difference of −0.046 (t = −4.18). The immigrant concentration coefficient was no longer statistically different from zero. As hypothesized, then, collective efficacy appeared to partially mediate widely cited relations between neighborhood social composition and violence. The model accounted for more than 75% of the variation between neighborhoods in levels of violence.

Violent victimization.   Violent victimization was assessed by a single binary item (Y_{jk} = 1 if victimized by violence in the neighborhood and Y_{jk} = 0 if not). The latent outcome was the logarithmic odds of victimization π_{jk}. The structural model for predicting π_{jk} had the same form as before (Eqs. 4 and 5).[31] Social composition, as hypothesized, predicted criminal victimization, with positive coefficients for concentrated disadvantage and immigrant concentration and a negative coefficient for residential stability (Table 4-4, model 1). The relative odds of victimization associated with a 2-SD elevation in the predictor were 1.67, 1.33, and 0.750, respectively. These estimates controlled for background characteristics associated with the risk of victimization. When added to the model, collective efficacy was negatively associated with victimization (Table 4-4, model 2). A 2-SD elevation in collective efficacy was associated with a relative odds ratio of about 0.70, which indicated a reduction of 30% in the odds of victimization. Moreover, after collective efficacy was controlled, the coefficients associated with concentrated disadvantage and residential stability diminished to nonsignificance, and the coefficient for immigrant concentration was also reduced.

Homicide.   To assess the sensitivity of the findings when the measure of crime was completely independent of the survey, we examined 1995 homicide counts (Y_k is the number of homicides in neighborhood k in 1995). A natural model for the expected number of homicides in neighborhood k is $E(Y_k) = N_k \lambda_k$, where λ_k is the homicide rate per 100,000 people in neighborhood k and N_k is the population size of neighborhood k as given by the 1990 census (in hundreds of thousands). Defining $\eta_k = \log(\lambda_k)$, we then formulated a regression model for η_k of the type in Eq. 5. This is effectively a Poisson regression model with a logarithmic link with extra-Poisson variation represented by between-neighborhood random effects.[32]

Although concentrated disadvantage was strongly positively related to homicide, immigrant concentration was unrelated to homicide, and residential stability was weakly positively related to homicide (Table 4-4, model 1). However, when social composition was controlled, collective efficacy was negatively

TABLE 4-5 Predictors of neighborhood level violence, victimization, and homicide in 1995, with prior homicide controlled. For violence and victimization as outcomes, the coefficients reported in this table were adjusted for 11 person-level covariates (see Table 4-3), but the latter coefficients are omitted for simplicity of presentation.

Variable	Violence as outcome			Victimization as outcome			Homicide in 1995 as outcome		
	Coefficient	SE	t	Coefficient	SE	t	Coefficient	SE	t
Intercept	3.772	0.379	9.95	−2.015	0.042	−49.24	3.071	0.050	62.01
Concentrated disadvantage	0.157	0.025	6.38	0.073	0.060	1.22	0.175	0.072	2.42
Immigrant concentration	0.020	0.016	1.25	0.098	0.045	2.20	−0.034	0.044	−0.77
Residential stability	−0.054	0.016	−3.39	−0.029	0.052	−0.56	0.229	0.043	5.38
Collective efficacy	−0.594	0.108	−5.53	−1.176	0.251	−4.69	−1.107	0.272	−4.07
Prior homicide	0.018	0.014	1.27	0.017	0.049	0.34	0.397	0.070	5.64
Variance									
Between-neighborhood variance	0.030			0.091			0.207		
Percent of variance explained between neighborhoods	78.0			43.8			73.0		

related to homicide (Table 4-4, model 2). A 2-SD elevation in collective efficacy was associated with a 39.7% reduction in the expected homicide rate. Moreover, when collective efficacy was controlled, the coefficient for concentrated disadvantage was substantially diminished, which indicates that collective efficacy can be viewed as partially mediating the association between concentrated disadvantage and homicide.[33]

Control for prior homicide. Results so far were mainly cross-sectional, which raised the question of the possible confounding effect of prior crime. For example, residents in neighborhoods with high levels of violence might be afraid to engage in acts of social control (9). We therefore reestimated all models controlling for prior homicide: the 3-year average homicide rate in 1988, 1989, and 1990. Prior homicide was negatively related (P < 0.01) to collective efficacy in 1995 ($r = -0.55$) and positively related (P < 0.01) to all three measures of violence in 1995, including a direct association ($t = 5.64$) with homicide (Table 4-5). However, even after prior homicide was controlled, the coefficient for collective efficacy remained statistically significant and substantially negative in all three models.

Further Tests

Although the results have been consistent, there are still potential threats to the validity of our analysis. One question pertains to discriminant validity: how do we know that it is collective efficacy at work rather than some other correlated social process?[34] To assess competing and analytically distinct factors suggested by prior theory,[4,5] we examined the measure of collective efficacy alongside three other scales derived from the CS of the PHDCN: neighborhood services, friendship and kinship ties, and organizational participation.[35] On the basis of the results in Tables 4-3 to 4-5 and also to achieve parsimony, we constructed a violent crime scale at the neighborhood level that summed standardized indicators of the three major outcomes: perceived violence, violent victimization, and homicide rate.

Consistent with expectations, collective efficacy was significantly ($p < 0.01$) and positively related to friendship and kinship ties ($r = 0.49$), organizational participation ($r = 0.45$), and neighborhood services ($r = 0.21$). Nonetheless, when we controlled for these correlated factors in a multivariate regression, along with prior homicide, concentrated disadvantage, immigrant concentration, and residential stability, by far the largest predictor of the violent crime rate was collective efficacy (standardized coefficient = -0.53, $t = -8.59$). Collective efficacy thus retained discriminant validity when compared with theoretically relevant, competing social processes. Moreover, these results suggested that dense personal ties, organizations, and local services by themselves are not sufficient; reductions in violence appear to be more directly attributable to informal social control and cohesion among residents.[36]

A second threat stems from the association of racial composition with concentrated disadvantage as shown in Table 4-2. Our interpretation was that African Americans, largely because of housing discrimination, are differentially exposed to neighborhood conditions of extreme poverty.[15] Nonetheless, a counterhypothesis is that the percentage of black residents and not disadvantage accounts for lower levels of collective efficacy and, consequently, higher violence. Our second set of tests therefore replicated the key models within the 125 NCs where the population was more than 75% black (see the first row of Table 4-1), effectively removing race as a potential confound. Concentrated poverty and residential stability each had significant associations with collective efficacy in these predominantly black areas ($t = -5.60$ and $t = 2.50$, respectively). Collective efficacy continued to explain variations in violence across black NCs, mediating the prior effect of concentrated disadvantage. Even when prior homicide, neighborhood services, friendship and kinship ties, and organizational participation were controlled, the only significant predictor of the violent crime scale in black NCs was collective efficacy ($t = -4.80$). These tests suggested that concentrated disadvantage more than race per se is the driving structural force at play.

Discussion and Implications

The results imply that collective efficacy is an important construct that can be measured reliably at the neighborhood level by means of survey research strategies. In the past, sample surveys have primarily considered individual-level relations. However, surveys that merge a cluster sample design with questions tapping collective properties lend themselves to the additional consideration of neighborhood phenomena.

Together, three dimensions of neighborhood stratification—concentrated disadvantage, immigration concentration, and residential stability—explained 70% of the neighborhood variation in collective efficacy. Collective efficacy in turn mediated a substantial portion of the association of residential stability and disadvantage with multiple measures of violence, which is consistent with a major theme in neighborhood theories of social organization.[1-5]

After adjustment for measurement error, individual differences in neighborhood composition, prior violence, and other potentially confounding social processes, the combined measure of informal social control and cohesion and trust remained a robust predictor of lower rates of violence.

There are, however, several limitations of the present study. Despite the use of decennial census data and prior crime as lagged predictors, the basic analysis was cross-sectional in design; causal effects were not proven. Indicators of informal control and social cohesion were not observed directly but rather inferred from informant reports. Beyond the scope of the present study, other dimensions of neighborhood efficacy (such as political ties) may be important, too. Our analysis was limited also to one city and did not go beyond its official boundaries into a wider region.

Finally, the image of local residents working collectively to solve their own problems is not the whole picture. As shown, what happens within neighborhoods is in part shaped by socioeconomic and housing factors linked to the wider political economy. In addition to encouraging communities to mobilize against violence through "self-help" strategies of informal social control, perhaps reinforced by partnerships with agencies of formal social control (community policing), strategies to address the social and ecological changes that beset many inner-city communities need to be considered. Recognizing that collective efficacy matters does not imply that inequalities at the neighborhood level can be neglected.

References and Notes

1. For a recent review of research on violence covering much of the 20th century, including a discussion of the many barriers to direct examination of the mechanisms explaining neighborhood-level variations, see R. J. Sampson and J. Lauritsen, in *Understanding and Preventing Violence: Social Influences*, vol. 3, A. J. Reiss Jr. and J. Roth, Eds. (National Academy Press, Washington, DC, 1994), pp. 1–114.

2. J. F. Short. *Poverty, Ethnicity, and Violent Crime*. (Westview, Boulder, CO, 1997).

3. For a general assessment of the difficulties facing neighborhood-level research on social outcomes, see S. E. Mayer and C. Jencks, *Science* **243**, 1441 (1989).

4. R. Kornhauser, *Social Sources of Delinquency* (Univ. of Chicago Press, Chicago, IL, 1978); R. J. Bursik Jr., *Criminology* **26**, 519 (1988); D. Elliott et al., *J. Res. Crime Delinquency* **33**, 389 (1996).

5. R. J. Sampson and W. B. Groves, *Am. J. Sociol.* **94**, 774 (1989).

6. M. Janowitz, *ibid.* **81**, 82 (1975).

7. E. Maccoby, J. Johnson, R. Church, *J. Social Issues* **14**, 38 (1958); R. Taylor, S. Gottfredson, S. Brower, *J. Res. Crime Delinquency* **21**, 303 (1983); J. Hacker, K. Ho, C. Ross, *Social Problems* **21**, 328 (1974). A key finding from past research is that many delinquent gangs emerge from unsupervised spontaneous peer groups [F. Thrasher, *The Gang: A Study of 1,313 Gangs in Chicago* (Univ. of Chicago Press, Chicago, IL, 1963); C. Shaw and H. McKay, *Juvenile Delinquency and Urban Areas* (Univ. of Chicago Press, Chicago, IL, 1969), pp. 176–185; J. F. Short Jr. and F. Strodtbeck, *Group Process and Gang Delinquency* (Univ. of Chicago Press, Chicago, IL, 1965)].

8. For example, about half of all homicides occur among nonfamily members with a preexisting relationship: friends, neighbors, casual acquaintances, associates in illegal activities, or members of a rival gang. Illegal markets are especially high-risk settings for robbery, assault, and homicide victimization, whether by an associate or a stranger [A. J. Reiss Jr. and J. Roth, Eds. *Understanding and Preventing Violence* (National Academy Press, Washington, DC,

1993), pp. 18, 79; A. J. Reiss Jr., in *Criminal Careers and "Career Criminals,"* A. Blumstein, J. Cohen, J. Roth, C. Visher, Eds. (National Academy Press, Washington, DC, 1986), pp. 121–160].

9. W. Skogan, *Disorder and Decline: Crime and the Spiral of Decay in American Neighborhoods* (Univ. of California Press, Berkeley, CA, 1990).

10. J. Coleman, *Foundations of Social Theory* (Harvard Univ. Press, Cambridge, MA, 1990); R. Putnam, *Making Democracy Work* (Princeton Univ. Press, Princeton, NJ, 1993).

11. A. Bandura, *Social Foundations of Thought and Action: A Social Cognitive Theory* (Prentice-Hall, Englewood Cliffs, NJ, 1986).

12. See, generally, J. Logan and H. Molotch, *Urban Fortunes: The Political Economy of Place* (Univ. of California Press, Berkeley, CA, 1987).

13. See also J. Kasarda and M. Janowitz, *Am. Sociol. Rev.* **39**, 328 (1974); R. Sampson, *ibid.* **53**, 766 (1988).

14. W. J. Wilson, *The Truly Disadvantaged* (Univ. of Chicago Press, Chicago, IL, 1987).

15. D. Massey and N. Denton, *American Apartheid: Segregation and the Making of the Underclass* (Harvard Univ. Press, Cambridge, MA, 1993); D. Massey, *Am. J. Sociol.* **96**, 329 (1990).

16. J. Brooks-Gunn, G. Duncan, P. Kato, N. Sealand, *Am. J. Sociol.* **99**, 353 (1993); F. F. Furstenberg Jr., T. D. Cook, J. Eccles, G. H. Elder, A. Sameroff, *Urban Families and Adolescent Success* (Univ. of Chicago Press, Chicago, IL, in press), chap. 7. Research has shown a strong link between the concentration of female-headed families and rates of violence [see (*1*)].

17. D. Williams and C. Collins, *Annu. Rev. Sociol.* **21**, 349 (1995).

18. Cluster analyses of census data also helped to guide the construction of internally homogeneous NCs with respect to racial and ethnic mix, SES, housing density, and family organization. Random-effect analyses of variance produced intracluster correlation coefficients to assess the degree to which this goal had been achieved; analyses (*37*) revealed that the clustering was successful in producing relative homogeneity within NCs.

19. For purposes of selecting a longitudinal cohort sample, SES was defined with the use of a scale from the 1990 census that included NC-level indicators of poverty, public assistance, income, and education (*37*). Race and ethnicity were also measured with the use of the 1990 census, which defined race in five broad categories: "white," "black," "American Indian, Eskimo, or Aleut," "Asian or Pacific Islander," and "other." We use the census labels of white and black to refer to persons of European American and African American background, respectively. We use the term "Latino" to denote anyone of Latin American descent as determined from the separate census category of "Hispanic origin." "Hispanic" is more properly used to describe persons of Spanish descent (i.e., from Spain), although the terms are commonly used interchangeably.

20. The sampling design of the CS was complex. For purposes of a longitudinal study (37), residents in 80 of the 343 NCs were oversampled. Within these 80 NCs, a simple random sample of census blocks was selected and a systematic random sample of dwelling units within those blocks was selected. Within each dwelling unit, all persons over 18 were listed, and a respondent was sampled at random with the aim of obtaining a sample of 50 households within each NC. In each of the remaining NCs (n = 263), nine census blocks were selected with probability proportional to population size, three dwelling units were selected at random within each block, and an adult respondent was randomly selected from a list of all adults in the dwelling unit. The aim was to obtain a sample of 20 in these 263 NCs. Despite these differences in sampling design, the selected dwelling units constituted a representative and approximately self-weighting sample of dwelling units within every NC (n = 343). ABT Associates (Cambridge, MA) carried out the data collection with the cooperation of research staff at PHDCN, achieving a final response rate of 75%.

21. "Don't know" responses were recoded to the middle category of "neither likely nor unlikely" (informal social control) or "neither agree nor disagree" (social cohesion). Most respondents answered all 10 items included in the combined measure; for those respondents, the scale score was the average of the responses. However, anyone responding to at least one item provided data for the analysis; a person-specific standard error of measurement was calculated on the basis of a simple linear item-response model that took into account the number and difficulty of the items to which each resident responded. The analyses reported here were based on the 7729 cases having sufficient data for all models estimated.

22. Respondents were also asked whether the incident occurred during the 6 months before the interview; about 40% replied affirmatively. Because violence is a rare outcome, we use the total violent victimization measure in the main analysis. However, in additional analyses, we examined a summary of the prevalence of personal and household victimizations (ranging from 0 to four) restricted to this 6-month window. This test yielded results very similar to those based on the binary measure of total violence.

23. The original data measured the address location of all homicide incidents known to the Chicago police (regardless of arrests) during the months of the community survey.

24. The alpha-scoring method was chosen because we are analyzing the universe of NCs in Chicago and are interested in maximizing the reliability of measures [H. F. Kaiser and J. Caffry, *Psychometrika* **30**, 1 (1965)]. We also estimated an oblique factor rotation, allowing the extracted dimensions to covary. A principal components analysis with varimax rotation nonetheless yielded substantively identical results.

25. For a methodological procedure and empirical result that are similar but that used all U.S. cities as units of analysis, see K. Land, P. McCall, L. Cohen, *Am. J. Sociol.* **95**, 922 (1990).

26. S. W. Raudenbush, B. Rowan, S. J. Kang, *J. Educ. Stat.* **16**, 295 (1991).

27. D. V. Lindley and A. F. M. Smith, *R. Stat. Soc. J. Ser. B Methodol.* **34**, 1 (1972).

28. Although the vast majority of respondents answered all items in the collective efficacy scale, the measurement model makes full use of the data provided by those whose responses were incomplete. There is one less indicator, D_{pijk}, than the number of items to identify the intercept πjk.

29. This degree of intersubjective agreement is similar to that found in a recent national survey of teachers that assessed organizational climate in U.S. high schools [B. Rowan, S. Raudenbush, S. Kang, *Am. J. Educ.* **99**, 238 (1991)].

30. The analysis of collective efficacy and violence as outcomes uses a three-level model in which the level 1 model describes the sources of measurement error for each of these outcomes. The level 2 and level 3 models together describe the joint distribution of the "true scores" within and between neighborhoods. Given the joint distribution of these outcomes, it is then possible to describe the conditional distribution of violence given "true" collective efficacy and all other predictors, thus automatically adjusting for any errors of measurement of collective efficacy. See S. Raudenbush and R. J. Sampson (paper presented at the conference "Alternative Models for Educational Data," National Institute of Statistical Sciences, Research Triangle Park, NC, 16 October 1996) for the necessary derivations. This work is an extension of that of C. Clogg, E. Petkova, and A. Haritou [*Am. J. Sociol.* **100**, 1261 (1995)] and P. Allison (*ibid.*, p. 1294). Note that census blocks were not included as a "level" in the analysis. Thus, person-level and block-level variance are confounded. However, this confounding has no effect on standard errors reported in this manuscript. If explanatory variables had been measured at the level of the census block, it would have been important to represent blocks as an additional level in the model.

31. The resulting model is a logistic regression model with random effects of neighborhoods. This model was estimated first with penalized quasi-likelihood as described by N. E. Breslow and D. G. Clayton [*J. Am. Stat. Assoc.* **88**, 9 (1993)]. The doubly iterative algorithm used is described by S. W. Raudenbush ["Posterior modal estimation for hierarchical generalized linear models with applications to dichotomous and count data" (Longitudinal and Multilevel Methods Project, Michigan State Univ., East Lansing, MI, 1993)]. Then, using those results to model the marginal covariation of the errors, we estimated a population-average model with robust standard errors [S. Zeger, K. Liang, P. Albert, *Biometrics* **44**, 1049 (1988)]. Results were similar. The results based on the population-average model with robust standard errors are reported here.

32. The analysis paralleled that of criminal victimization, except that a Poisson sampling model and logarithmic link were used in this case. Again, the reported results are based on a population-average model with robust standard errors.

33. Although the zero-order correlation of residential stability with homicide was insignificant, the partial coefficient in Table 4-4 is significantly positive. Recall from Table 4-3 that stability is positively linked to collective efficacy. But higher stability without the expected greater collective efficacy is not a positive neighborhood quality according to the homicide data. See (*14*).

34. T. Cook, S. Shagle, S. Degirmencioglu, in *Neighborhood Poverty: Context and Consequences for Children*, vol. 2, J. Brooks-Gunn, G. Duncan, J. L. Aber, Eds. (Russell Sage Foundation, New York, in press).

35. "Neighborhood services" is a nine-item scale of local activities and programs (for example, the presence of a block group, a tenant association, a crime prevention program, and a family health service) combined with a six-item inventory of services for youth (a neighborhood youth center, recreational programs, after-school programs, mentoring and counseling services, mental health services, and a crisis intervention program). "Friendship and kinship ties" is a scale that measures the number of friends and relatives that respondents report are living in the neighborhood. "Organizational participation" measures actual involvement by residents in (i) local religious organizations; (ii) neighborhood watch programs; (iii) block group, tenant association, or community council; (iv) business or civic groups; (v) ethnic or nationality clubs; and (vi) local political organizations.

36. Similar results were obtained when we controlled for a measure of social interaction (the extent to which neighbors had parties together, watched each other's homes, visited in each others' homes, exchanged favors, and asked advice about personal matters) that was positively associated with collective efficacy. Again the direct effect of collective efficacy remained, suggesting that social interaction, like friendship and kinship ties, is linked to reduced violence through its association with increased levels of collective efficacy.

37. R. J. Sampson, S. W. Raudenbush, F. Earls, data not shown.

38. Major funding for this project came from the John D. and Catherine T. MacArthur Foundation and the National Institute of Justice. We thank L. Eisenberg and anonymous reviewers for helpful comments; S. Buka and A. J. Reiss Jr. for important contributions to the research design; and R. Block, C. Coldren, and J. Morenoff for their assistance in obtaining, cleaning, geocoding, and aggregating homicide incident data to the NC level. M. Yosef and D. Jeglum-Bartusch assisted in the analysis.

SECTION II

Introduction to the Built Environment

The *built environment* is an embodied and embedded term. *Embodied* connotes the sense of the built environment as bricks and mortar, steel and concrete, heating and ventilation systems; that is, the construction materials and elements of housing and transportation systems and of civic and commercial buildings, such as schools, libraries, recreation spaces, stores, shops, and workplaces. It also includes the design and condition of the built environment, such as pedestrian-friendly, well-maintained, heavily trafficked, abandoned, poorly lit, near waste sites, and so on. *Embedded* suggests the sense of the built environment as situated within local and regional places, whether in compact, connected, or fragmented forms. For example, housing is nested in a neighborhood; neighborhoods are nested in a city or spread out in sprawling suburbs; shops and offices are linked in a contiguous city center or separated in distinct malls and office parks that are joined by roads and highways; and so on. This section offers a series of chapters by authors who are expert in aspects of the built environment and health that are a focal point of much contemporary research, intervention, public interest, and policy.

In the first chapter of this section, Krieger and Higgins chart the waxing and waning of public health interest in housing as a determinant of health beginning with the nineteenth and early twentieth century activism around housing quality and sanitation, in response to housing-related infectious disease. They trace the history of issues that have compelled the current healthy housing movement. These include lead poisoning and the recent asthma epidemic; the crisis in homelessness and unaffordable housing; the recent focus on suburban sprawl and overweight; and the new wave of studies linking health with poor housing conditions, poor neighborhood design, and poor neighborhood conditions. They argue for public health collaboration with building code departments, developers, housing advocacy groups, and local planning and zoning boards for the sake of improved housing code, code enforcement, and housing quality. Samet and Spengler, in their chapter on the indoor environment, contend that human exposure to pollutants in U.S. society is more intensive and accumulative indoors compared to the outdoor ambient environment, in many, if not most, cases. The percent of time people spend indoors (at least 80% on average), the variety and concentration of contaminants indoors, and the little-regulated indoor environment (in comparison to the ambient environment)—all conspire to increase human exposure to pollutants in homes, schools, and offices. This chapter, like that of Krieger and Higgins, provides a comprehensive overview of decades of research on housing and health, as well as recommendations for current interdisciplinary research needs and policy concerns.

Urban renewal in the mid-twentieth century involved the taking and demolishing of low-income and working class neighborhoods in order to extend the central business district and build middle-class housing. Urban renewal had a disproportionately negative impact on African American communities, resulting in great losses of income, social networks, upward mobility and political power.[1] In other words, the individual and communal *social efficacy* of urban Blacks was grievously undermined and, so also, the mental and physical health of many African Americans henceforth, through generations. Urban sprawl, a phenomenon linked to the exodus of Whites from cities to suburbs since the late nineteenth century, accelerated after World War II and during urban renewal of the 1950s and 1960s. It resulted in a built environment of low-density homogeneous housing, separation of work and commerce from housing, dependency on the automobile, and certain social isolation and segregation. Some have noted that the trends in: (1) growth in suburbs; (2) increased reliance on the automobile; (3) increased concentration of poor and minorities in cities; (4) increasing overweight and obesity; (5) lower rates of physical exercise; and (6) increased asthma prevalence have considerable overlap in time. In Chapter 7, Howard Frumkin offers a rich and dense overview of research and analysis to argue for a community health framework to study the health effects of sprawl. In so doing, he rejoins urban and land use planning with public health, an organic relationship that began in nineteenth century industrial cities and continued into the early twentieth century with housing, sanitation, drinking water, and occupational health reforms.

In the final chapter of the section, Lopez and Hynes explore the paradox that, although inner-city neighborhoods have the built environment features missing in suburban design—sidewalks, access to public transportation, shops in walking distance of housing, and so on—inner-city residents are more overweight and less active than suburban counterparts. Much of the recent, creative interdisciplinary research joining architecture, urban planning, environmental design, and health has centered on the design and form of suburbs. The authors argue for a comparable research and intervention focus on urban, especially inner-city neighborhoods, that integrates economic development, neighborhood development, and community health programs.

References

1. Fullilove MT. *Root Shock: How Tearing Up City Neighborhoods Hurts America, and What We Can Do About It.* New York: Ballantine Books, 2004.

Housing and Health:
Time Again for Public Health Action

James Krieger, MD, MPH, Donna L. Higgins, PhD

Housing is an important determinant of health, and substandard housing is a major public health issue.[1] Each year in the United States, 13.5 million nonfatal injuries occur in and around the home,[2] 2900 people die in house fires,[3] and 2 million people make emergency room visits for asthma.[4] One million young children in the United States have blood lead levels high enough to adversely affect their intelligence, behavior, and development.[5] Two million Americans occupy homes with severe physical problems, and an additional 4.8 million live in homes with moderate problems.[6]

The public health community has grown increasingly aware of the importance of social determinants of health (including housing) in recent years,[7] yet defining the role of public health practitioners in influencing housing conditions has been challenging. Responsibility for social determinants of health is seen as lying primarily outside the scope of public health.

The quality and accessibility of housing is, however, a particularly appropriate area for public health involvement. An evolving body of scientific evidence demonstrates solid relations between housing and health. The public health community is developing, testing, and implementing effective interventions that yield health benefits through improved housing quality. Public health agencies have valuable expertise and resources to contribute to a multisectoral approach to housing concerns. Public health has a long (albeit intermittent) history of involvement in the housing arena, and this involvement is generally accepted by other housing stakeholders (e.g., building departments, community housing advocates). Housing related health concerns such as lead exposure and asthma are highly visible.

The public is also concerned about the quality and accessibility of housing as affordable housing becomes scarcer.[8] Elected officials and communities alike recognize that substandard housing is an important social justice issue that adversely influences health.

In this article, we describe some of the evidence linking housing conditions to health, place public health's role in addressing housing issues in an historical context, provide examples of contemporary local public health activities in the housing arena, and conclude with suggestions for public health action in the next decade.

Housing as a Determinant of Health

An increasing body of evidence has associated housing quality with morbidity from infectious diseases, chronic illnesses, injuries, poor nutrition, and mental disorders. We present some of this evidence in the following section.

Infectious Diseases

Features of substandard housing, including lack of safe drinking water, absence of hot water for washing, ineffective waste disposal, intrusion by disease vectors (e.g., insects and rats) and inadequate food storage have long been identified as contributing to the spread of infectious diseases.[9-11] Crowding is associated with transmission of tuberculosis[12] and respiratory infections.[13-16] Lack of housing and the overcrowding found in temporary housing for the homeless also contribute to morbidity from respiratory infections and activation of tuberculosis.[17-20]

Chronic Diseases

In more recent years, epidemiological studies have linked substandard housing with an increased risk of chronic illness. Damp, cold, and moldy housing is associated with asthma and other chronic respiratory symptoms, even after potentially confounding factors such as income, social class, smoking, crowding, and unemployment are controlled for.[21-31] Water intrusion is a major contributor to problems with dampness. In 1999, eleven million occupied homes in America had interior leaks and 14 million had exterior leaks.[6] Overcrowding and inadequate ventilation also increase interior moisture.[32] Damp houses provide a nurturing environment for mites, roaches, respiratory viruses, and molds, all of which play a role in respiratory disease pathogenesis.[33-39] Cross-sectional epidemiological studies have also established associations between damp and moldy housing and recurrent headaches, fever, nausea and vomiting, and sore throats.[37,40]

Old, dirty carpeting, often found in substandard housing, is an important reservoir for dust, allergens, and toxic chemicals.[41,42] Exposure to these agents can result in allergic, respiratory, neurological, and hematologic illnesses.

Pest infestations, through their association with asthma, provide another linkage between substandard housing and chronic illness. Cockroaches can cause allergic sensitization and have emerged as an important asthma trigger in inner-city neighborhoods. Children with asthma who are sensitized and exposed to cockroaches are at elevated risk for hospitalization.[43] Mouse allergen also acts as a clinically important cause of allergy and asthma morbidity.[44] Structural defects permit entry of cockroaches and rodents; leaking pipes and other sources of water provide them with water to drink. Inadequate food storage and disposal facilities provide them with opportunities for obtaining food. Dead spaces in walls harbor pests and permit circulation among apartments in multi-unit dwellings.[11]

Deviation of indoor temperature beyond a relatively narrow range has been associated with increased risk of cardiovascular disease.[45] Living in cold housing has been associated with lower general health status and increased use of health services.[46] These health concerns have contributed to the development of standards for thermal comfort.[47]

Exposure to toxic substances found in homes can result in chronic health problems. The association of passive exposure to indoor tobacco smoke with respiratory disease is well documented.[48–50] Poor ventilation may increase exposure to smoke.[37] Indoor exposure to nitrogen dioxide (from inadequately vented or poorly functioning combustion appliances) has been associated with asthma symptoms.[37] Exposure to volatile organic compounds (emitted by particle board and floor coverings) may be associated with asthma and sick building syndrome.[37] Moderately elevated levels of carbon monoxide (from poorly functioning heating systems) cause headache, whereas higher levels result in acute intoxication.[51] The relation between lead exposure (from leaded paints) and neurodevelopmental abnormalities is clearly established,[52,53] and additional evidence suggests an association with hypertension.[54] Asbestos exposure (from deteriorating insulation) can cause mesothelioma and lung cancer.[55] Polyvinyl chloride flooring and textile wall materials have been associated with bronchial obstruction during the first 2 years of life.[56] Residential exposure to radon, which is increased by structural defects in basements, can cause lung cancer.[57] Old carpeting can contain pesticide residues and other compounds such as polycyclic aromatic hydrocarbons.[58,59]

Injuries

The importance of designing homes to prevent injuries has received long-standing attention,[60] especially with regard to reducing burns and falls.[61] Attributes of substandard housing that increase the risk of injury include exposed heating sources, unprotected upper-story windows and low sill heights,[62] slippery surfaces,[63] breakable window glass in sites with a high likelihood of contact, and poorly designed stairs with inadequate lighting.[64] Building design and materials influence the risk of injury from fires. These hazards are frequently present in temporary accommodations provided to homeless women and young children.[20]

Childhood Development and Nutrition

Recent analyses of longitudinal cohorts of children have examined the influence of childhood housing conditions on the subsequent development of chronic diseases. A study conducted in Britain demonstrated modest associations of inadequate ventilation with overall mortality (respiratory mortality was not specifically examined) and type of water supply with coronary heart disease mortality, independent of other measures of deprivation.[65] Another cohort study suggested that recurrent periods of housing deprivation during the participants' first 33 years of life were associated with disability or severe ill health.[27]

Lack of affordable housing has been linked to inadequate nutrition, especially among children. Relatively expensive housing may force low-income tenants to use more of their resources to obtain shelter, leaving less for other necessities such as food.[66] Children from low-income families receiving housing subsidies showed increased growth compared with children whose families were on a subsidy waiting list, an observation consistent with the idea that subsidies provide a protective effect against childhood undernutrition.[67] Temporary housing for homeless children often lacks cooking facilities, leading to poor nutrition.[20]

Mental Health

Substandard housing may also adversely affect mental health, although the evidence is more tentative. Excessive indoor temperature has been linked with irritability and social intolerance.[68,69] Damp, moldy, and cold indoor conditions may be associated with anxiety and depression.[70] A study in Glasgow demonstrated that dampness was significantly and independently associated with poorer mental health.[71] Crowding was associated with psychological distress among women aged 25 to 45 in London.[72] Homelessness and living in substandard, temporary housing has been related to behavioral problems among children.[73] Substandard housing conditions may lead to social isolation because occupants are reluctant to invite guests into their homes. High-rise buildings may inhibit social interaction because they lack common spaces.[74]

In summary, substandard housing affects multiple dimensions of health. There is evidence that, in part, poor housing conditions contribute to increasing exposure to biological (e.g., allergens), chemical (e.g., lead) and physical (e.g., thermal stress) hazards, which directly affect physiological and biochemical processes. In addition, concerns about substandard housing and fear of homelessness are psychosocial stressors that can lead to mental health problems. Preliminary research has suggested that residents' perceptions of their homes (e.g., pride in and satisfaction with their dwelling and concerns about indoor air quality) are associated with self-rated health status.[75] Stress induced by substandard housing may also play a pervasive role in undermining health by increasing the allostatic load[76] on the body; this hypothesis merits further investigation. For example, excessive noise (common in poorly insulated housing units) has been associated with sleep deprivation that leads to psychological stress and activation of the hypothalamic–pituitary–adrenal axis and sympathetic nervous system. These factors are major contributors to allostatic load (the wear and tear accumulated by an organism as a result of physiological responses to environmental stressors).[77,78]

Neighborhood Effects

Beyond the condition of the housing unit itself, the site of the home may be a determinant of health. Neighborhood-level effects on health have been documented; these include elevated rates of intentional injury,[79,80] poor birth outcomes,[81] cardiovascular disease,[82] HIV,[83] gonorrhea,[84] tuberculosis,[85] depression,[86] physical inactivity,[87,88] and all-cause mortality[89–91] in neighborhoods of low socioeconomic status, independent of individual-level risk factors. Several features of these neighborhoods may contribute to poor health. Air quality may be poor because of their proximity to sources of vehicle exhaust emissions such as major roads, bus depots, airports, and trucking routes.[92] These sources also create substantial noise exposure, which may be associated with a range of adverse health effects.[93] Sites of improper waste disposal can harbor pests, which can then infest homes. Yet it is possible to design neighborhoods to promote health by considering sidewalk and street design, the presence of green spaces and recreational sites, and the location of schools, work, and shopping within walking distance of homes.[94,95]

Social dimensions of neighborhoods also affect health. Sampson and colleagues examined the relation between collective efficacy (a combination of trust, social cohesion, and informal social control) and violence in Chicago neighborhoods and concluded that rates of neighborhood violence were lower in areas with high collective efficacy.[79] In addition, physical insecurity and violence can cause people to stay in their homes,[96] thus limiting physical activity.

Neighbor's Smoking Combines with a Structural Defect

When 5-year-old Jose and his 3-year-old sister Maria suddenly developed breathing problems, their doctor was puzzled. The usual medical treatments didn't work, and the symptoms persisted even after their mother followed instructions to rid the apartment of rugs, dust, and cockroaches. The pediatrician initially disregarded the mother's frustration with her neighbor's smoking—until she realized that the smoke flowed right into Jose and Maria's apartment through a large hole in the living room wall.[1,p.8]

Disparities in Housing, Disparities in Health

Exposure to substandard housing is not evenly distributed across populations. People of color and people with low income are disproportionately affected. For example, Blacks and low-income people are 1.7 times and 2.2 times more likely, respectively, to occupy homes with severe physical problems compared with the general population.[6] People with low income are more likely to live in over-crowded homes. Disparities in asthma morbidity may be attributable, in part, to disproportionate exposure to indoor environmental asthma triggers associated with living in substandard housing.[97,98] Injuries occur more commonly in low-income households because of substandard conditions and a lack of resources to repair them. Clutter stemming from lack of storage space and hazardous cooking facilities also contribute to increased risk of injury from fire.[99] Homes of people with low income are more likely to be too warm or too cool because they are less well insulated, often have relatively expensive forms of heating such as electric baseboards, and frequently lack air conditioning.[100,101] Additionally, occupants often cannot afford to pay for the energy needed to make their homes comfortable. As housing and energy prices continue to climb, low- and moderate-income households make tradeoffs between having enough food, staying warm, and living in adequate housing, with resultant adverse effects on health.

Public Health and Housing: A Long-Standing Relationship

The notion of housing as a public health issue is not new. In the middle of the 19th century, pathologist Rudolf Virchow advised city leaders that poorly maintained, crowded housing was associated with higher rates of infectious disease transmission.[102] Engels, in his study of the working class in England, noted that "There is ample proof that the dwellings of the workers who live in the slums, combined with other adverse factors, give rise to many illnesses."[103] "Slum clearance" and improving the quality of housing and sanitation were important components of 19th- and early-20th-century campaigns to control typhus, tuberculosis, and other infectious diseases.[104–106]

Interest in housing as a determinant of health has fluctuated in response to housing-related infectious disease outbreaks (e.g., cholera in New York City in the 1830s), social unrest and class conflict, industrialist interest in maintaining a healthier workforce, and economic downturns leading to crises in housing availability and quality.[107] Thus, interest in housing and health increased in the early 19th century because of concerns regarding infectious diseases. Later in the century, the sanitary reform movement was spurred by urban industrialization and growing class conflict. The depression and social unrest of the 1930s brought renewed public health attention to housing. During the post–World War II period, a lack of affordable housing, exacerbated by the return of veterans and migration from the rural South, increased the prominence of the housing issue. In the 1960s through the 1980s, activists addressed racial disparities in housing, the civil rights movement resulted in legislation prohibiting discrimination in housing, and indoor lead exposure became a major public health concern. Although a comprehensive history of public health involvement in housing is beyond the scope of this article, we next provide several illustrative examples.

In the early 1800s, the relation between housing conditions and health was recognized among public health practitioners in the United States[108–112] and Europe[113–115] and led to the rise of the sanitary reform movement. Industrialization caused a rapid growth in urban populations that was not matched by a sufficient increase in adequate housing. Builders, eager to capitalize on the need for housing, built inferior housing in congested areas of cities. In 1844, Engels observed, "in a word, we must confess that in the workingmen's dwelling of Manchester [England], no cleanliness, no convenience, and consequently no comfortable family life is possible; that in such dwellings only [beings] robbed of all humanity, degraded, reduced morally and physically to bestiality, could feel comfortable and at home."[103] Common characteristics of the housing of the working poor throughout the 19th century and into the early 20th century included insufficient light and air, few toilet and bathing facilities, and overcrowding. In New York City, windows in many tenement rooms opened into an air shaft instead of directly to fresh air and hallways were reported to be "pitch-black."[116] It was reported that entire families lived in single rooms and that as many as 30 people occupied single rooms in lodging houses.[117] These conditions were graphically documented by Edwin Chadwick[118] in England and by John Griscom[119] and Jacob Riis[120] in New York City.

The response to this situation established the basis of public health action at the local and national levels and clearly established the link between public health and housing. In the United States, the sanitary reform movement was carried out by boards of health and in some cases by voluntary health associations consisting of physicians, public officials, and other civic-minded citizens. They educated the public on hygiene, lobbied for policy reform, and sought to eliminate "crowded, poorly ventilated, and filthy [housing], impure water supplies, inadequate sewerage, and unwholesome food."[102] In New York City, the

---

Overcrowding, Leaks, and Mold Lead to Asthma

I have a 6-year-old patient who presented with severe asthma (no previous history; no previous symptoms recognized by mom) after moving into a large multifamily dwelling. Public Health nurse described mold on walls, dripping faucets, one small window in the whole place, roach infestation, mom and 3 kids slept in one room on a mattress on the floor.[1,p.4]

Council of Hygiene's report on the sanitary conditions of the city resulted in the first health and housing laws in the nation (the New York Metropolitan Health Act of 1866 and the New York Tenement House Law of 1867). Multiple reports followed, as did legislation requiring windows that opened to outside air in place of air shafts, separate "water closets" for each apartment, functional fire escapes, adequate lighting in hallways, proper sewage connections, and regular waste removal. These reforms succeeded in controlling the epidemics of infectious diseases.

The recognition of lead-based paint as a health hazard is another important chapter in the history of public health involvement in housing. As early as 1914, the health consequences of lead exposure were discussed in the medical literature. By the mid-1920s, there was strong evidence that lead poisoned those exposed to it and was especially harmful to children.[121,122] In the early 1930s, the Baltimore Health Department responded to this threat by educating its constituents. It continued an aggressive campaign throughout the 20th century, providing free diagnostic tests for lead poisoning, inspecting houses, requiring the removal of lead by landlords, and mandating the inclusion of warning labels for lead-based paint.[122] Unfortunately, it was not until the 1940s and early 1950s that other state and local health departments began warning their constituents about the dangers of lead paint; this delay was due in part to the obstructionist actions of the Lead Industries Association.[121] Gradually, local bans were implemented across the United States. Ultimately, the Consumer Product Safety Commission prohibited the use of all lead paint after 1978.

The American Public Health Association (APHA) began its involvement in housing issues in 1937 with the formation of its Committee on Hygiene of Housing. In 1941, C. E. A. Winslow (president of APHA, editor of the Journal, and chair of the Hygiene and Public Health Committee) invigorated APHA's commitment. He observed,

> Thirty years ago, our major emphasis was transferred from the physical environment to the individual. Today, we must shift our gaze from the individual back to the environment, but in a broader sense . . . to the whole social and economic environment in which the individual lives and moves and has his being.[123]

He therefore led the Hygiene and Public Health Committee in an examination of the components of healthy housing in terms of physical, physiological, and psychological needs. The committee prepared a report called the "Basic Principles of Healthful Housing" and developed an evaluation procedure to "appraise existing housing in objective quantitative terms."[124] This assessment tool was used in many American cities to examine housing stock and was incorporated into urban planning efforts at the urging of the US Public Health Service. APHA has periodically updated these guidelines on healthy housing.[125-127] The last version was published in 1986.[128] In 1999 and 2000, APHA released policy statements concerning public health's role in codes regulating the design, construction, and use of buildings.[129,130]

Putting Health into Housing—
What Is Public Health Doing About It Today?

Current public health efforts to improve housing conditions include a continuation of these historical activities as well as new strategies based on emerging issues such as indoor environmental quality. We now describe some of the activities of Public Health—Seattle & King County (PHSKC) and of sister agencies in larger American cities.

Guidelines, Codes, and Enforcement

The development and enforcement of most housing codes are the responsibility of housing and construction departments. Our health department, like most others, issues and enforces housing codes that address a limited set of concerns (e.g., plumbing, sanitation, occupancy). Local codes are based on national uniform codes that set minimal standards for new housing construction, fire safety, plumbing, and mechanical systems. However, these codes consider only a subset of the conditions that affect housing quality. For the most part, they do not address the maintenance or remediation of substandard conditions in existing buildings. Many jurisdictions have promulgated general health and nuisance codes that allow public health to intervene in situations in which an immediate threat to health exists, although such codes are applied infrequently to substandard housing conditions. A major limitation on the usefulness of codes is the difficulty in implementing them. Resources for inspection and enforcement are spread across multiple agencies that lack adequate staff and do not coordinate efforts. Another constraint is the current political climate,

---

Family in Shelter to Avoid Lead Exposure

I just witnessed the reunification of a young mother with her 3 children in a homeless shelter. The family had previously lived together in an overcrowded apartment with other extended family members. When the 3 children (ages 2, 5, and 6) all tested high for lead, the mother voluntarily signed the children over to custody of the Department of Social Services so they could be placed in a lead-free home. The mother then tried and failed to find a safe and affordable apartment for her family; moving to a shelter became her only chance to live with her children in safety. She is now homeless, searching for affordable housing, with little hope for securing a unit. At least her children have their mother back. (Boston Medical Center Web site. Available at http://www.bmc.org/program/doc4kids/append.htm. Accessed March 1, 2002.)

which favors market-based solutions and individual legal action rather than public sector regulation and enforcement.

In 2000, members of APHA's Joint Housing and Health Committee met with officials from the International Code Council and NFPA International (formerly the National Fire Protection Association) to emphasize the need for more involvement from public health professionals in the development of national building standards and codes. As a result, APHA is now represented on several key NFPA International committees.[131]

At the local level, recent guideline development has been directed at indoor mold contamination. The New York City Department of Health has issued Guidelines on Assessment and Remediation of Fungi in Indoor Environments.[132] The California legislature passed the Toxic Mold Protection Act of 2001, which calls for setting standards for permissible levels of mold exposure and requires disclosure of mold contamination in real estate transactions. Some jurisdictions are using the more general health codes to address substantial mold contamination.

Healthy Homes

The emergence of asthma as a major public health issue has led to renewed interest in improving indoor environmental quality and in integrating these newer efforts with ongoing work addressing other indoor health hazards such as lead and injury risk factors. Our department and many other local health jurisdictions (e.g., Boston, Cambridge, Cleveland, Detroit, New York, Philadelphia, San Diego, San Francisco) have developed "Healthy Homes" initiatives as a response. These projects provide education and resources to support household members in taking actions to improve the quality and safety of their home environments. The Seattle–King County Healthy Homes Project[133,134] employs community health workers who use a home environmental checklist to assess exposures, knowledge, and actions related to indoor asthma triggers and indoor chemical hazards. The checklist guides the development of a specific, computer-generated home environmental action plan for each household. The community health worker makes 5 visits over 1 year in which she works with clients to carry out the action plan by offering education and social support, encouraging changes in habits (e.g., household cleaning, tobacco use), providing materials to reduce exposures (e.g., bedding covers, vacuum cleaners, doormats, cleaning kits, integrated pest management supplies), helping repair minor deficiencies (e.g., small holes that allow pests to enter, minor leaks), assisting tenants in working with their landlords or relocating if needed, and providing counseling and referral for other household concerns. The project's scope is being expanded to include injury hazards, and Healthy Homes projects in jurisdictions with higher prevalences of lead exposure have also integrated lead assessment and abatement.

In addition to community health workers, other public health workers promote Healthy Homes principles. For example, the PHSKC Home Health Hazards Project trained public health nurses to conduct in-home environmental assessments and education to address fall hazards, infant and toddler safety issues, and indoor air quality.

Limited resources have restricted the scope of most Healthy Homes projects to educating household members, asking them to take individual actions, and assisting them with minor repairs. However, more substantial structural remediation is often necessary to reduce sources of exposure. For example, we found structural deficits permitting water intrusion in over 20% of the low-income homes included in our Healthy Homes project. Remediation is often not completed given the lack of landlord interest or of resources to make the improvements (e.g., installation of ventilation systems, removal of water-damaged carpet or wallboard, replacement of windows).

Several Healthy Homes projects, with support from the Department of Housing and Urban Development (HUD), federal home loan programs, energy assistance grants, and other sources, are assessing the benefits of more aggressive structural remediation interventions. For example, with HUD support, PHSKC is remediating 70 homes at an average cost of $8000 each over the next 3 years. Examples of remediation activities include removing and replacing extensive mold- or water-damaged material, installing continuously operating whole-house exhaust ventilation systems, repairing plumbing leaks, and removing carpeting. We have considered landlord–tenant issues in the development of this project. Owners agree that rent will not be increased as a result of remediation and that tenants will be guaranteed the right to remain for at least 24 months after remediation, unless they violate the terms of the initial rental agreement. Boston and Cleveland are completing similar projects.

Additional support for lead control has come from the federal government. Congress enacted the Residential Lead-Based Paint Hazard Reduction Act of 1992 with the goal of eliminating lead-based paint hazard in all housing as expeditiously as possible and preventing further childhood lead poisoning. Federal funds are now provided to state and local health departments to determine the extent of childhood lead poisoning, screen children for elevated blood lead levels, help ensure that lead-poisoned infants and children receive medical and environmental follow-up, develop neighborhood-based efforts to prevent childhood lead poisoning, and safely remove lead from houses.[135,136]

Exposure Assessment and Consultation for Individuals

Local health departments offer indoor environmental quality assessment of homes through visual inspection and, in some cases, through quantitative measurement of exposure to biological contaminants and toxic substances such as pesticides and heavy metals. They also provide education on reducing exposure.

Community Assessment

One barrier to developing effective housing policy is the lack of information on housing quality at the community level. Although the US Census Bureau's American Housing Survey collects housing quality data for larger metropolitan areas every 6 years, smaller-area data for most municipalities and neighborhoods are not available. A few municipal housing departments collect supplemental local data (e.g., the New York City Department of Housing Preservation and Development). We are unaware of any American local health jurisdictions that systematically collect and analyze local data related to housing and health, although some have in the past.[10] British local health districts are more involved in housing assessment. More than one-half of their annual health reports include a discussion of housing issues.[137] The City of Glasgow conducted a comprehensive survey of housing conditions in the mid-1980s.[100] It revealed substantial proportions of homes with dampness and mold, deteriorated external structural envelopes, and inadequate heating systems.

Services for Homeless People

Public health agencies frequently offer clinical assessment and management services to homeless shelter clients. Some of these agencies are responsible for operating shelters. Efforts to return the homeless to stable housing or to prevent eviction in the first place are less common. For example, the San Francisco Department of Public Health purchases buildings and renovates them for supportive housing for homeless or near-homeless people with substance abuse, mental health, or other chronic health conditions. This activity requires the patching together of multiple funding sources from the state and local levels. The program has decreased the use of hospital-based acute care health services.

Collaboration

Typically public health agencies do not build, maintain, or own housing stock; nor do they design housing developments or issue building permits. To promote healthy housing, they must collaborate with other entities who are more directly involved in the housing sector. Our Healthy Homes Project works with the local public housing authority to increase its awareness of the impact of housing conditions on asthma. The housing authority moved Healthy Homes clients to the top of its waiting list and offered housing that met Healthy Homes criteria. For clients already living in public housing units, the agency immediately repaired unhealthy conditions, gave priority to eradication of roaches, and moved the tenant to a more suitable unit (e.g., a second-floor unit with less dampness) if necessary. The project also refers clients to local weatherization programs that have resources to improve ventilation and energy efficiency. The

New York City Department of Health is partnering with the housing authority to implement a pilot integrated pest management project to reduce exposure to pesticides and cockroach antigens. The Boston Healthy Homes Project works with a community development corporation to arrange grants to low-income home owners for remediation of conditions with adverse health effects. It is developing a decision-making tool to assist housing rehabilitators in incorporating affordable modifications that improve respiratory health. The health authority in Cornwall, England used National Health Service funds to install central heating in homes that were damp and inhabited by children with asthma. An uncontrolled evaluation demonstrated significant reduction in dampness in children's bedrooms and in asthma morbidity.[138]

Advocacy

Public health workers support individuals and communities seeking better housing. For example, when public health staff assisted Healthy Homes participants in asking their landlords to make repairs, the tenants' requests were often more adequately addressed than when tenants tried on their own. Home visitors from the New York City Department of Health assist tenants by encouraging landlords to correct hazardous conditions before enforcement action is initiated. Some local health departments have successfully advocated with local elected officials and agencies on behalf of increasing the availability of affordable, healthy housing. Public health workers have supported the efforts of community organizations fighting for improved housing conditions.[139]

Public health advocates can point to evidence demonstrating that residents of substandard housing who move to improved living environments enjoy better health outcomes. Low-income seniors who moved from deteriorated, single-room, roach-infested apartments with inadequate kitchen and bath facilities into a new, well-designed senior apartment building with a senior center had lower mortality and improved self-reported health status after 8 years than a comparison group who were eligible to live in the new building but did not move.[140] Low-income families who moved from substandard housing to newly constructed public housing made fewer outpatient medical visits than did a similar group who did not move.[141] A small Danish study showed that lung function, symptoms, and medication use improved among asthmatic, dust-mite–allergic patients who moved to homes with effective ventilation systems compared with others who did not move.[142] However, a recent review of the health effects of housing interventions found that "because of the methodological limitations of the studies, it is impossible to specify the nature and size of the health gain," even though most studies did report benefits.[143] Preliminary findings from a study in Boston (not included in the aforementioned review) indicate that families that received a housing subsidy experienced increased safety, fewer behavioral problems among boys, and improved health among heads of households.[144]

Public Education and Awareness

Public health agencies provide information to the public regarding ways to make homes healthier and safer. They participate in distribution of smoke detectors,[145] offer educational resources in print and on Web sites regarding indoor environmental quality, and help with efforts to eliminate hazardous wastes and toxins from homes.

What Next?

Public health workers continue to build on a long tradition of engagement with housing and health issues. Many of the efforts we have described are yielding benefits, although most are small in scale relative to the need. Expansion of capacity is an important priority and is dependent on securing adequate resources. We conclude by suggesting what this expanded capacity might look like and what it might accomplish.

Making Housing Codes Healthier

Refinement of housing codes to reflect current knowledge of healthful housing is urgently needed.[146] Enhanced national uniform codes or guidelines that address factors affecting health such as ventilation,[147,148] moisture, carpeting, molds, injury hazards,[99] exposure to toxic substances, privacy, noise, lighting and other factors that are applicable to both new and existing housing stock would be a valuable asset for local public health agencies seeking to upgrade local housing codes.[9] As noted above, APHA's Joint Housing and Health Committee has established a public health "foothold" in national standards and code development. Continued and expanded efforts by the committee will help to include public health practitioners in such national endeavors. It may also be useful for national organizations, expert panels, and local health departments to develop guidelines (rather than codes).

Revised codes and enhanced guidelines can lay the groundwork for an expanded public health role in housing quality consultation, education, and enforcement. Local public health agencies need guidelines in order to respond to concerns about housing quality brought to them by the public, community organizations (e.g., tenant unions and housing advocacy groups), and other service providers. These agencies must have the capacity to assess whether units meet standards, to educate property owners and builders about how to implement guidelines, and to impose sanctions if standards are not met. Some owners of substandard property, especially landlords who own only a few units, lack the resources to improve their properties. Public health can take the lead in advocating for policies and resources to assist them.

Sustaining and Expanding Healthy Homes Programs

Evidence is accumulating that Healthy Homes programs yield measurable health benefits. These programs are popular with the public and current capacity cannot meet demand. Options for expansion include increasing program staffing and incorporating Healthy Homes activities into the regular duties of other home visitors (e.g., public health nurses, environmental health professionals, and community health workers). Advocating for payment by health insurers for some of these activities (in the context of health assessment and education for patients with asthma) may help fund this expansion.

Assessment

Many state and local health departments produce community health assessment reports, yet few include measures of housing quality and resident satisfaction with housing. Special reports that describe housing status in more detail, using qualitative as well as quantitative methods and incorporating visual documentation of housing conditions, could be powerful tools to focus attention on housing issues. Such assessment data could be invaluable for housing advocates attempting to improve housing in their communities. For example, the documentation in prose and photos by Jacob Riis of tenement conditions in New York City in the late 1800s helped intensify the tenement reform movement.[120]

Collaboration and Cross-Sectoral Planning

At the Milbank Memorial Fund meeting on housing and health in 1950, a participant noted that "the knitting together of various local [city] departments in an attempt to solve a problem of mutual concern [housing] is an important and long overdue step forward in public administration."[124] This still holds true in 2008. A single public health agency cannot achieve the goal of ensuring access to healthy housing and building healthy neighborhoods. For example, the revision of housing codes and development of guidelines discussed above will require collaboration with other government agencies that regulate housing construction, tenants, community housing advocacy groups, nonprofit housing organizations, community development corporations, builders, home owners, landlords, architects, and urban planners.

Public health representatives can participate in local planning processes and offer consultation to housing agencies and developers. They can encourage the use of Health Impact Assessment[149,150] methods to consider the health implications of new construction and zoning decisions. They can encourage development of policies and actions that incorporate the principles of healthy housing into housing construction and maintenance. They can advocate for the design of healthy communities that offer opportunities for physical activity, social interaction, and community building activities.

Public health workers can collaborate with community housing advocates by providing them with assessment data, offering technical assistance (e.g., with program planning, evaluation, and fundraising), and endorsing their efforts. Working closely with advocates and residents, public health workers can also develop culturally appropriate educational materials that explain healthy housing guidelines.

Closer collaboration with public housing agencies will protect the health of the most vulnerable populations. Partnering to make public housing units safe and healthy, supporting health promotion and community building activities, and developing mechanisms to identify children whose health is adversely affected by housing conditions and to rehouse them promptly are only some of the possibilities.

Advocacy

Public health workers should take the lead in advocating for housing policies that ensure access to affordable, healthy housing units and the elimination or remediation of unhealthy housing stock. Burridge and Ormandy note:

> The deficiencies in the housing stock will not be remedied by the waving of some legislative wand. At best, legal intervention can provide some normative standards for fiscal or coercive action, and a framework for intervention. Deeper solutions lie in the political arena. There is a pressing need for a public housing policy which embraces the perspectives of public health and the maintenance of a healthy national housing stock.[151]

Other arenas for advocacy include providing energy assistance for people with low income, expanding medical insurance coverage for items that make homes healthier (e.g., allergy-control bedding encasements, radiator covers, window guards, home assessments), and providing subsidies in the form of rental vouchers for use in the private housing market.

The extent to which these efforts will actually occur is dependent on the resources and organizational capacity of public health agencies. Staff already working on housing-related issues (e.g., in environmental health and health assessment units) can form a multidisciplinary team to initiate housing and health activities. This team can develop a strategic plan to address housing issues in collaboration with other public health staff and external partners. Resources to implement local public health housing activities will come from a combination of local sources, federal agencies, and national foundations. An important challenge is to develop sustainable and increased funding. Public health housing advocates may be able to interest the Centers for Disease Control and Prevention, other federal agencies, local housing developers, and health care payers in supporting their efforts.

Political factors also influence the ability of public health to respond to housing issues. Substandard housing is an environmental justice issue. The inequitable socioeconomic distribution of substandard housing reflects underlying disparities in income, assets, and power. Tenants are often powerless to improve their housing conditions in the context of the low vacancy rates, high rental costs, weak tenant protection laws, and politically influential landlord associations commonly found in American cities. Public health assets can help remedy this imbalance in power. Yet these circumstances also constrain public health practitioners, many of whom are reluctant to antagonize powerful local political interests and the elected officials who support them. The absence of organized community advocacy groups that can effectively balance landlords' influence further inhibits public health action. The current political climate is not supportive of a proactive, regulatory approach to addressing housing issues. Moving beyond an advisory, incentive-based approach will require courageous public health officials who can ally themselves with supportive community organizations and local elected officials.

Today, several issues drive the housing and health agenda: increased asthma morbidity,[152,153] unaffordable urban housing, urban sprawl, and a renewed interest in social determinants of health. This new era of unaffordable housing and the health and social disintegration that accompanies it will demand further public health attention. Sprawl that began almost 50 years ago with "White flight" from urban areas is also beginning to have deleterious effects on health[154] and will likely result in an increased public health interest in housing, housing environments, and health. These issues, along with the growing interest in the return of public health to its roots in addressing social factors affecting health, are converging to establish housing as a priority public health issue.

We have learned much in the past decade about how to make homes healthier places in which to live. Public health has a long history of promoting healthy housing. In recent years, we have been less engaged. It is time for us to build on this groundwork and do our share in ensuring that everyone has a safe and healthy home.

Acknowledgments

We thank the following colleagues for their thoughtful comments on drafts of this manuscript and for providing information about their valuable efforts in addressing housing and health issues in their communities: Daniel Moran and David Williams (Public Health—Seattle & King County), Rajiv Bhatia (San Francisco Department of Public Health), Andrew Goodman and Jennifer Leighton (New York City Department of Health), Margaret Reid (Boston Public Health Commission), Elizabeth Fee (National Library of Medicine), Theodore M. Brown (University of Rochester), and Carolyn Beeker (Centers for Disease Control and Prevention).

References

1. Sharfstein J, Sandel M, eds. *Not Safe at Home: How America's Housing Crisis Threatens the Health of Its Children.* Boston, Mass: Boston University Medical Center; 1998.
2. Warner M, Barnes PM, Fingerhut LA. Injury and poisoning episodes and conditions. National Health Interview Survey, 1997. *Vital Health Stat 10.* 2000;No. 202.
3. Karter MJ. *Fire Loss in the United States During 1999.* Quincy, Mass: National Fire Protection Association; 2000.
4. *National Hospital Ambulatory Medical Care Survey: 1998 Emergency Department Summary. Advance Data 313.* Hyattsville, Md: National Center for Health Statistics; 2000. Publication PHS 2000-1250.
5. National Center for Environmental Health, Centers for Disease Control and Prevention Web site. Available at: http://www.cdc.gov/nceh/lead/about/about.htm. Accessed December 6, 2001.
6. US Census Bureau. American Housing Survey 1999. Available at: http://www.census.gov/hhes/www/ahs.html. Accessed February 19, 2002.
7. Marmot M, Wilkinson R. *Social Determinants of Health.* New York, NY: Oxford University Press, 1999.
8. *Rental Housing Assistance—The Worsening Crisis: A Report to Congress on Worst Case Housing Needs.* Washington, DC: US Dept of Housing and Urban Development; 1997.
9. Mood EW. Fundamentals of healthful housing: their application in the 21st century. In: Burridge R, Ormandy D, eds. *Unhealthy Housing: Research, Remedies and Reform.* New York, NY: Spon Press; 1993:303–337.
10. Marsh BT. Housing and health: the role of the environmental health practitioner. *J Environ Health.* 1982;45:123–128.
11. Howard M. The effects on human health of pest infestations in houses. In: Burridge R, Ormandy D, eds. *Unhealthy Housing: Research, Remedies and Reform.* New York, NY: Spon Press; 1993:256–282.
12. Stein L. A study of respiratory tuberculosis in relation to housing conditions in Edinburgh; the pre-war period. *Br J Soc Med.* 1950;4:143–169.
13. Fonseca W, Kirkwood BR, Victora CG, Fuchs SR, Flores JA, Misago C. Risk factors for childhood pneumonia among the urban poor in Fortaleza, Brazil: a case–control study. *Bull World Health Organ.* 1996;74:199–208.
14. Denny FW Jr. The clinical impact of human respiratory virus infections. *Am J Respir Crit Care Med.* 1995;152(4 Pt 2):S4–S12.
15. Murtagh P, Cerqueiro C, Halac A, Avila M, Salomon H, Weissenbacher M. Acute lower respiratory infection in Argentinian children: a 40 month clinical and epidemiological study. *Pediatr Pulmonol.* 1993;16:1–8.
16. Graham NM. The epidemiology of acute respiratory infections in children and adults: a global perspective. *Epidemiol Rev.* 1990;12:149–178.

17. Wood DL, Valdez RB, Hayashi T, Shen A. Health of homeless children and housed, poor children. *Pediatrics.* 1990;86:858–866.
18. Zolopa AR, Hahn JA, Gorter R, et al. HIV and tuberculosis infection in San Francisco's homeless adults. Prevalence and risk factors in a representative sample. *JAMA.* 1994;272:455–461.
19. Kermode M, Crofts N, Speed B, Miller P, Streeton J. Tuberculosis infection and homelessness in Melbourne, Australia, 1995–1996. *Int J Tuberc Lung Dis.* 1999;3:901–907.
20. Conway J. Ill-health and homelessness: the effects of living in bed-and-breakfast accommodation. In: Burridge R, Ormandy D, eds. *Unhealthy Housing: Research, Remedies and Reform.* New York, NY: Spon Press; 1993: 283–300.
21. Bornehag CG, Blomquist G, Gyntelberg F, et al. Dampness in buildings and health. Nordic interdisciplinary review of the scientific evidence on associations between exposure to "dampness" in buildings and health effects (NORDDAMP). *Indoor Air.* 2001;11:72–86.
22. Peat JK, Dickerson J, Li J. Effects of damp and mould in the home on respiratory health: a review of the literature. *Allergy.* 1998;53:120–128.
23. Hyndman S. Making connections between housing and health. In: Kearns R, Gesler W, eds. *Putting Health Into Place: Making Connections in Geographical Research.* Syracuse, NY: Syracuse University Press; 1998:191–207.
24. Robinson T, Russell P. Healthy indoor environments for energy efficient housing. In: *Health and Ecological Effects: Proceedings of the 9th World Clean Air Congress, August 30–September 4, 1992, Montreal, Quebec, Canada.* Pittsburgh, Pa: Air & Waste Management Associates; 1992.
25. Hunt S. Damp and mouldy housing: a holistic approach. In: Burridge R, Ormandy D, eds. *Unhealthy Housing: Research, Remedies and Reform.* New York, NY: Spon Press; 1993:67–93.
26. Strachan DP. Dampness, mould growth and respiratory disease in children. In: Burridge R, Ormandy D, eds. *Unhealthy Housing: Research, Remedies and Reform.* New York, NY: Spon Press; 1993:94–116.
27. Marsh A, Gordon D, Pantazis C, Heslop P. *Home Sweet Home? The Impact of Poor Housing on Health.* Bristol, England: The Policy Press; 1999.
28. Platt SD, Martin CJ, Hunt SM, Lewis CW. Damp housing, mould growth, and symptomatic health state. *BMJ.* 1989;298:1673–1678.
29. Dales RE, Zwanenburg H, Burnett R, Franklin CA. Respiratory health effects of home dampness and molds among Canadian children. *Am J Epidemiol.* 1991;134:196–203.
30. Brunekreef B, Dockery DW, Speizer FE, Ware JH, Spengler JD, Ferris BG. Home dampness and respiratory morbidity in children. *Am Rev Respir Dis.* 1989;140:1363–1367.
31. Williamson IJ, Martin CJ, McGill G, Monie RD, Fennerty AG. Damp housing and asthma: a case–control study. *Thorax.* 1997;52:229–234.

32. Markus TA. Cold, condensation and housing poverty. In: Burridge R, Ormandy D, eds. *Unhealthy Housing: Research, Remedies and Reform.* New York, NY: Spon Press; 1993:141–167.
33. Bierman CW. Environmental control of asthma. *Immunol Allergy Clin North Am.* 1996;16:753–765.
34. Billings CG, Howard P. Damp housing and asthma. *Monaldi Arch Chest Dis.* 1998;53:43–49.
35. Verhoeff AP, van Strien RT, van Wijnen JH, Brunekreef B. Damp housing and childhood respiratory symptoms: the role of sensitization to dust mites and molds. *Am J Epidemiol.* 1995;141:103–110.
36. Karim YG, Ijaz MK, Sattar SA, JohnsonLussenburg CM. Effect of relative humidity on the airborne survival of rhinovirus-14. *Can J Microbiol.* 1985;31:1058–1061.
37. Institute of Medicine. *Clearing the Air: Asthma and Indoor Air Exposures.* Washington, DC: National Academy Press; 2000.
38. Oie L, Nafstad P, Botten G, Magnus P, Jaakkola JK. Ventilation in homes and bronchial obstruction in young children. *Epidemiology.* 1999;10:294–299.
39. Eggleston PA, Arruda LK. Ecology and elimination of cockroaches and allergens in the home. *J Allergy Clin Immunol.* 2001;107(suppl 3):S422–S429.
40. Platt SD, Martin CJ, Hunt SM, Lewis CW. Damp housing, mould growth, and symptomatic health state. *BMJ.* 1989;298:1673–1678.
41. Vaughan JW, Platts-Mills TA. New approaches to environmental control. *Clin Rev Allergy Immunol.* 2000;18:325–339.
42. Roberts JW, Dickey P. Exposure of children to pollutants in house dust and indoor air. *Rev Environ Contam Toxicol.* 1995;143:59–78.
43. Rosenstreich DL, Eggleston P, Kattan M, et al. The role of cockroach allergy and exposure to cockroach allergen in causing morbidity among inner-city children with asthma. *N Engl J Med.* 1997;336:1356–1363.
44. Phipatanakul W, Eggleston PA, Wright EC, Wood RA. Mouse allergen, II: the relationship of mouse allergen exposure to mouse sensitization and asthma morbidity in inner-city children with asthma. *J Allergy Clin Immunol.* 2000;106:1075–1080.
45. Collins KJ. Low indoor temperatures and morbidity in the elderly. *Age Ageing.* 1986;15:212–220.
46. Evans J, Hyndman S, Stewart-Brown S, Smith D, Petersen S. An epidemiological study of the relative importance of damp housing in relation to adult health. *J Epidemiol Community Health.* 2000;54:677–686.
47. *Thermal Environmental Conditions for Human Occupancy.* Atlanta, Ga: American Society of Heating, Refrigerating, and Air-Conditioning Engineers; 1981. ASHRAE Standard ANSI/ASHRAE 55-1981.
48. *Respiratory Health Effects of Passive Smoking.* Washington, DC: Environmental Protection Agency; 1992. Publication EPA/600/6-90/006F.

49. Weitzman M, Gortmaker S, Walker DK, Sobol A. Maternal smoking and childhood asthma. *Pediatrics.* 1990;85:505–511.
50. Cook DG, Strachan DP. Health effects of passive smoking, III: parental smoking and prevalence of respiratory symptoms and asthma in school age children. *Thorax.* 1997;52:1081–1094.
51. Walker E, Hay A. Carbon monoxide poisoning. *BMJ.* 1999;319:1082–1083.
52. Rosen JF. Adverse health effects of lead at low exposure levels: trends in the management of childhood lead poisoning. *Toxicology.* 1995;97:11–17.
53. Needleman HL, Schell A, Bellinger D, Leviton A, Allred EN. The long-term effects of exposure to low doses of lead in childhood: an 11-year follow-up report. *N Engl J Med.* 1990;322:83–88.
54. Schwartz J. The relationship between blood lead and blood pressure in the NHANES II survey. *Environ Health Perspect.* 1988;78:15–22.
55. Landrigan PJ. Asbestos—still a carcinogen. *N Engl J Med.* 1998;338:1618–1619.
56. Jaakkola JJ, Oie L, Nafstad P, Botten G, Samuelsen SO, Magnus P. Interior surface materials in the home and the development of bronchial obstruction in young children in Oslo, Norway. *Am J Public Health.* 1999;89:188–192.
57. Lubin JH, Boice JD Jr. Lung cancer risk from residential radon: meta-analysis of eight epidemiological studies. *J Natl Cancer Inst.* 1997;89:49–57.
58. Lewis RG, Fortmann RC, Camann DE. Evaluation of methods for monitoring the potential exposure of small children to pesticides in the residential environment. *Arch Environ Contam Toxicol.* 1994;26:37–46.
59. Lewis RG, Fortune CR, Willis RD, Camann DE, Antley JT. Distribution of pesticides and polycyclic aromatic hydrocarbons in house dust as a function of particle size. *Environ Health Perspect.* 1999;107:721–726.
60. Ranson R. *Healthy Housing: A Practical Guide.* London, England: Spon Press and the World Health Organization Regional Office for Europe; 1991.
61. Home radiator burns among inner-city children: Chicago. *MMWR Morb Mortal Wkly Rep.* 1996;45:814–815.
62. American Academy of Pediatrics. Falls from heights: windows, roofs, and balconies. *Pediatrics.* 2001;107:1188–1191.
63. Nuffield Institute for Health and NHS Centre for Reviews and Dissemination. Preventing falls and subsequent injury in older people. *Eff Health Care.* 1996;2:1–16.
64. Tinetti ME, Speechley M, Ginter SF. Risk factors for falls among elderly persons living in the community. *N Engl J Med.* 1988;319:1701–1707.
65. Dedman DJ, Gunnell D, Davey Smith G, Frankel S. Childhood housing conditions and later mortality in the Boyd Orr cohort. *J Epidemiol Community Health.* 2001;55:10–15.

66. Ellaway A, Macintyre S, Fairley A. Mums on Prozac, kids on inhalers: the need for research on the potential for improving health through housing interventions. *Health Bull.* 2000;54:336–339.
67. Meyers A, Frank DA, Roos N, et al. Housing subsidies and pediatric undernutrition. *Arch Pediatr Adolesc Med.* 1995;149:1079–1084.
68. Collins KJ. Cold and heat-related illnesses in the indoor environment. In: Burridge R, Ormandy D, eds. *Unhealthy Housing: Research, Remedies and Reform.* New York, NY: Spon Press; 1993:117–140.
69. Heat-related deaths—Los Angeles County, California, 1999–2000, and United States, 1979–1998. *MMWR Morb Mortal Wkly Rep.* 2001;50: 623–625.
70. Hyndman SJ. Housing dampness and health amongst British Bengalis in east London. *Soc Sci Med.* 1990;30:131–141.
71. Hopton JL, Hunt SM. Housing conditions and mental health in a disadvantaged area in Scotland. *J Epidemiol Community Health.* 1996;50:56–61.
72. Gabe J, Williams P. Women, crowding and mental health. In: Burridge R, Ormandy D, eds. *Unhealthy Housing: Research, Remedies and Reform.* New York, NY: Spon Press; 1993:191–208.
73. Zima BT, Wells KB, Freeman, HE. Emotional and behavioral problems and severe academic delays among sheltered homeless children in Los Angeles County. *Am J Public Health.* 1994;84:260–264.
74. Gilloran JL. Social problems associated with "high living." *Med Officer.* 1968;120:117–118.
75. Dunn JR, Hayes MV. Social inequality, population health, and housing: a study of two Vancouver neighborhoods. *Soc Sci Med.* 2000;51:563–587.
76. McEwen BS, Seeman T. Protective and damaging effects of mediators of stress: elaborating and testing the concepts of allostasis and allostatic load [review]. *Ann N Y Acad Sci.* 1999;896:30–47.
77. Henkin RI, Knigge KM. Effects of sound on hypothalamic-pituitary-adrenal axis. *Am J Physiol.* 1963;204:701–704.
78. Van Cauter E, Spiegel K. Sleep as a mediator of the relationship between socioeconomic status and health: a hypothesis. *Ann N Y Acad Sci.* 1999;896: 254–261.
79. Sampson RJ, Raudenbush SW, Earls F. Neighborhoods and violent crime: a multilevel study of collective efficacy. *Science.* 1997;277:918–924.
80. Cubbin C, LeClere FB, Smith GS. Socioeconomic status and injury mortality: individual and neighbourhood determinants. *J Epidemiol Community Health.* 2000;54:517–524.
81. Pearl M, Braveman P, Abrams B. The relationship of neighborhood socioeconomic characteristics to birthweight among 5 ethnic groups in California. *Am J Public Health.* 2001;91:1808–1814.
82. Diez Roux AV, Merkin SS, Arnett D, et al. Neighborhood of residence and incidence of coronary heart disease. *N Engl J Med.* 2001;345:99–106.

83. Wallace R. Synergism of plagues: "planned shrinkage," contagious housing destruction, and AIDS in the Bronx. *Environ Res.* 1988;47:1–33.
84. Cohen D, Spear S, Scribner R, Kissinger P, Mason K, Wildgen J. "Broken windows" and the risk of gonorrhea. *Am J Public Health.* 2000;90:230–236.
85. Barr RG, Riez-Roux AV, Knirsch CA, Pablos-Mendez A. Neighborhood poverty and the resurgence of tuberculosis in New York City, 1984–1992. *Am J Public Health.* 2001;91:1487–1493.
86. Schulz A, William D, Israel B, et al. Unfair treatment, neighborhood effects, and mental health in the Detroit metropolitan area. *J Health Soc Behav.* 2000;41:314–332.
87. Centers for Disease Control and Prevention. Neighborhood safety and the prevalence of physical inactivity—selected states, 1996. *MMWR Morb Mortal Wkly Rep.* 1999;48;143–146.
88. Brownson RC, Baker EA, Housemann RA, Brennan LK, Bacak SJ. Environmental and policy determinants of physical activity in the United States. *Am J Public Health.* 2001;91:1995–2003.
89. Yen IH, Kaplan GA. Neighborhood social environment and risk of death: multilevel evidence from the Alameda County Study. *Am J Epidemiol.* 1999; 149:898–907.
90. Bosma H, van de Mheen D, Borsboom GJJM, Mackenbach JP. Neighborhood socioeconomic status and all-cause mortality. *Am J Epidemiol.* 2001;153: 363–371.
91. Haan M, Kaplan GA, Camacho T. Poverty and health: prospective evidence from the Alameda County Study. *Am J Epidemiol.* 1987;125: 989–998.
92. Perlin SA, Wong D, Sexton K. Residential proximity to industrial sources of air pollution: interrelationships among race, poverty, and age. *J Air Waste Manage Assoc.* 2001;51:406–421.
93. Stansfeld S, Haines M, Brown B. Noise and health in the urban environment. *Rev Environ Health.* 2000;15:43–82.
94. Jackson RJ, Kochtitsky C. *Creating a Healthy Environment: The Impact of the Built Environment on Public Health.* Washington, DC: Sprawl Watch Clearinghouse Mongraph Series; 2001.
95. Frumkin H. Beyond toxicity, I: human health and the natural environment. *Am J Prev Med.* 2001;20:234–240.
96. Fullilove MT, Heon V, Jimenez W, Parsons C, Green LL, Fullilove RE. Injury and anomie: effects of violence on an inner-city community. *Am J Public Health.* 1998;88:924–927.
97. Huss K, Rand CS, Butz AM, et al. Home environmental risk factors in urban minority asthmatic children. *Ann Allergy.* 1994;72:173–177.
98. Kane MP, Jaen CR, Tumiel LM, Bearman GM, O'Shea RM. Unlimited opportunities for environmental interventions with inner-city asthmatics. *J Asthma.* 1999;36:371–379.

99. Ranson R. Accidents at home: the modern epidemic. In: Burridge R, Ormandy D, eds. *Unhealthy Housing: Research, Remedies and Reform.* New York, NY: Spon Press; 1993:223–255.

100. *The Glasgow House Condition Survey.* Glasgow, Scotland: City of Glasgow; 1985.

101. Boardman B. Prospects for affordable warmth. In: Burridge R, Ormandy D, eds. *Unhealthy Housing: Research, Remedies and Reform.* New York, NY: Spon Press; 1993:282–400.

102. Rosen G. *A History of Public Health.* New York, NY: MD Publications; 1958.

103. Engels F. *The Condition of the Working Class in England.* New York, NY: Panther Books; 1969.

104. Byrne D, Keithley J. Housing and the health of the community. In: Burridge R, Ormandy D, eds. *Unhealthy Housing: Research, Remedies and Reform.* New York, NY: Spon Press; 1993:41–66.

105. Walker WF. Some relation between our health and our environment. *Am J Public Health.* 1923;13:897–914.

106. McKeown T. *The Role Of Medicine—Dream, Mirage or Nemesis.* London, England: Nuffield Provincial Hospitals Trust; 1976.

107. Jacobs M, Stevenson G. Health and housing: a historical examination of alternative perspectives. *Int J Health Serv.* 1981;1:105–122.

108. Rosner D, ed. *Hives of Sickness: Public Health and Epidemics in New York City.* New Brunswick, NJ: Rutgers University Press; 1995.

109. Veiller L. Housing as a factor in health progress in the past fifty years. In: Ravenel MP, ed. *A Half Century of Public Health.* New York, NY: American Public Health Association; 1921:323–334.

110. Duffy J. *A History of Public Health in New York City 1866–1966.* New York, NY: Russell Sage Foundation; 1974.

111. Galishoff S. *Newark: The Nation's Unhealthiest City 1832–1895.* New Brunswick, NJ: Rutgers University Press; 1988.

112. Melosi MV. *The Sanitary City: Urban Infrastructure in America From Colonial Times to the Present.* Baltimore, Md: Johns Hopkins University Press; 2000.

113. Wohl AS. *Endangered Lives: Public Health in Victorian Britain.* Cambridge, Mass: Harvard University Press; 1983.

114. Coleman W. *Death Is a Social Disease: Public Health and Political Economy in Early Industrial France.* Madison: University of Wisconsin Press; 1982.

115. Evans RJ. *Death in Hamburg: Society and Politics in the Cholera Years 1830–1910.* Oxford, England: Clarendon Press; 1987.

116. DeForest RW, Veiller L. The tenement house problem. In: DeForest RW, Veiller L. *The Tenement House Problem.* Vol 1. New York, NY: MacMillan Co; 1903:18.

117. *Sanitary Conditions of the City, Report of the Council of Hygiene and Public Health of the Citizens' Association of New York.* New York, NY: Council of Hygiene and Public Health of the Citizens' Association of New York; 1865.

118. Chadwick E. *Report on the Sanitary Condition of the Labouring Population of Gt. Britain, by Edwin Chadwick. 1842.* Flinn MW, ed. Edinburgh, Scotland: University Press. 1965.
119. Griscom JC. *The Sanitary Condition of the Laboring Population of New York With Suggestions for Its Improvement.* New York, NY: Harper and Bros; 1845.
120. Riis JA. *How the Other Half Lives: Studies Among the Tenements of New York.* New York, NY: Charles Schribner's Sons; 1890.
121. Markowitz G, Rosner D. "Cater to the children": the role of the lead industry in a public health tragedy, 1900–1955. *Am J Public Health.* 2000;90:36–46.
122. Fee E. Public health in practice: an early confrontation with the "silent epidemic" of childhood lead paint poisoning. *J Hist Med Allied Sci.* 1990;45:570–606.
123. Winslow CEA. *Health and housing.* In: *Housing for Health.* Lancaster, Pa: Science Press Printing Company; 1941.
124. *Housing and Health: The Proceedings of a Round Table* at the 27th Annual Conference of the Milbank Memorial Fund. New York, NY: Milbank Memorial Fund; 1951:5.
125. *Basic Principles of Healthful Housing.* New York, NY: American Public Health Association; 1938.
126. *Basic Health Principles of Housing and Its Environment; APHA-PHS Recommended Housing Maintenance and Occupancy Ordinance.* Washington, DC: American Public Health Association; 1971.
127. APHA Program Area Committee on Housing and Health, 1968. Basic health principles of housing and its environment. *Am J Public Health.* 1969;59:841–851.
128. Mood EW. *APHA-CDC Recommended Minimum Housing Standards.* Washington, DC: American Public Health Association; 1986.
129. APHA policy statements. 9916: public health role of codes regulating design, construction and use of buildings.
130. APHA policy statements. 200019: public health role of the National Fire Protection Association on setting codes and standards for the built environment. *Am J Public Health.* 2001;91:503–504.
131. Pauls J. APHA's growing involvement with international standards and codes development activity affecting the built environment. Injury Control and Emergency Health Services Section Newsletter, Fall 2000.
132. Guidelines on assessment and remediation of fungi in indoor environments.
133. Krieger JW, Song L, Takaro TK, Stout J. Asthma and the home environment of low-income urban children: preliminary findings from the Seattle-King County healthy homes project. *J Urban Health.* 2000;77:50–67.
134. Krieger J, Takaro T, Allen C, et al. The Seattle–King County Healthy Homes Project: implementation of a comprehensive approach to improving indoor environmental quality for low-income children with asthma. *Environ Health Perspect.* 2002;110(suppl 2):311–322.

135. Centers for Disease Control and Prevention. About lead. Available at: http://www.cdc.gov/nceh/lead/about/about.htm. Accessed February 19, 2002.

136. Dept of Housing and Urban Development. HUD awards over $67 million to protect children from dangerous lead and other environmental hazards. Available at: http://www.hud.gov/news/release.cfm?content=pr01-108.cfm. Accessed February 19, 2002.

137. Roderick P, Victor C, Connelly J. Is housing a public health issue? A survey of directors of public health. BMJ. 1991;302:157–160.

138. Somerville M, Mackenzie I, Owen P, Miles D. Housing and health: does installing heating in their homes improve the health of children with asthma? *Public Health.* 2000;114:434–439.

139. Freudenberg N. Community organization, housing, and health: a perspective for public health workers. *Bull N Y Acad Med.* 1990;66:451–462.

140. Carp FM. Impact of improved living environment on health and life expectancy. *Gerontologist.* 1977;17:242–249.

141. Wambem DB, Piland NF. Effects of improved housing on health in South Dos Palos, Calif. *Health Serv Rep.* 1973;88:47–58.

142. Harving H, Korsgaard J, Dahl R. Clinical efficacy of reduction in house-dust mite exposure in specially designed, mechanically ventilated "healthy" homes. *Allergy.* 1994;49:866–870.

143. Thomson H, Petticrew M, Morrison D. Health effects of housing improvement: systematic review of intervention studies. *BMJ.* 2001;323:187–190.

144. Katz LF, King JR, Liebman JB. The early impact of moving to opportunity in Boston. October 2000. Available at: http://www.wws.princeton.edu/~kling/mto/mto_boston_hudreport.pdf. Accessed November 10, 2001.

145. Douglas MR, Mallonee S, Istre GR. Comparison of community based smoke detector distribution methods in an urban community. *Inj Prev.* 1998;4:28–32.

146. Raw GJ, Prior J. The environmental assessment of new houses. In: Burridge R, Ormandy D, eds. *Unhealthy Housing: Research, Remedies and Reform.* New York, NY: Spon Press; 1993:361–381.

147. Wargocki P, Sundell J, Bischoff W, et al. Ventilation and health in nonindustrial environments. Report from a European Multidisciplinary Scientific Consensus Meeting. Clima 2000/Napoli 2001 World Congress, Napoli (I), 15–18 September 2001. *Indoor Air.* 2002. In press.

148. *Standards for Ventilation Required for Minimum Acceptable Indoor Air Quality.* Atlanta, Ga: American Society of Heating, Refrigerating, and Air-Conditioning Engineers; 1981. ASHRAE Standard ANSI/ASHRAE 62-1981.

149. Douglas MJ, Conway L, Gorman D, Gavin S, Hanlon P. Developing principles for health impact assessment. *J Public Health Med.* 2001;23:148–154.

150. Lock K. Health impact assessment. *BMJ.* 2000;320:1395–1398.

151. Burridge R, Ormandy D. The legal environment of housing conditions. In: Burridge R, Ormandy D, eds. *Unhealthy Housing: Research, Remedies and Reform.* New York, NY: Spon Press; 1993:420–423.

152. Mannino DM, Homa DM, Pertowski CA, et al. Surveillance for asthma—United States, 1960–1995. *Mor Mortal Wkly Rep CDC Surveill Summ.* 1998;47:1–27.
153. Gergen PJ. The increasing problem of asthma in the United States. *Am Rev Respir Dis.* 1992;146:823–824.
154. Pierce J, Orlando D, Hortman P, Risco, Powell KE, Division of Environmental Hazards and Health Effects, CDC. Corporate action to reduce air pollution—Atlanta, Georgia, 1998–1999. *MMWR Morb Mortal Wkly Rep.* 2000;49:153–156.

Indoor Environments and Health: Moving into the 21st Century

Jonathan M. Samet, MD, MS, John D. Spengler, PhD

Introduction

The publication of an issue of the *American Journal of Public Health* on "the built environment" signals a timely recognition of the relevance to health and well-being of the indoor environments where people spend most of their time. Even in temperate climates, including the United States, people spend most of their time indoors—at home, at work, in transportation, and in many other public and private places. The quality of these environments affects well being and productivity, and risks for diverse diseases are increased by indoor air pollutants, surface contamination with toxins and microbes, and contact among people in these places. These are not new problems; they have been the focus of research and of control efforts for decades. The emphasis on the built environment indicates a shift towards a more holistic approach to indoor environments and the public's health, a shift consistent with the broadening recognition of the multiple levels of environmental factors, from the personal to the global, that determine an individual's health.

In this commentary, we offer a perspective on this shifting emphasis that has led to a move from consideration of specific problems within indoor environments, such as radon and lung cancer, to a broader view that places greater emphasis on prevention. We recognize that some of the specific problems of indoor environments remain quite relevant and are a current focus for research, public concern, policy development, and even litigation. The health consequences of dampness and mold are a current example, and there are always emerging issues such as phthalates, organophosphates and pyrethroid pesticides. Our intent is not to cover these individual topics, which have been reviewed in depth elsewhere.[1] Rather, we offer an overview of nearly a century of research directed at understanding indoor environments and health; consider current research needs; and set out policy matters that need to be addressed, if we are to have the healthiest possible built environments. We note that the policy context for built environments extends beyond health considerations to include energy use for air conditioning, selection of materials for sustainability, and design for safety, security and productivity.

Historical Perspective: Problems Recognized

Theories have long been advanced with regard to building ventilation and health. At the start of the last century, ventilation was viewed as healthy and as decreasing risk for infection.[2] The important early work of Constantin Yaglou, reported in the 1930s, established a paradigm for using ventilation as the way to achieve thermal and odor comfort in the built environment.[3,4] For the next 50 years, dilution of human odors motivated mechanical design of buildings and guided the use of often large heating, ventilating and air conditioning (HVAC) systems. In the latter part of the 20th century as health and comfort problems associated with buildings became apparent, Ole Fanger and others pointed out that office equipment, materials and even the HVAC system itself add to the odor and contaminant load of buildings and cause discomfort to occupants.[5] In the 21st century, we have returned to concern for airborne spread of infection. With new analytical tools that can isolate specific strains of viruses from a room air sample or a specimen of nasal mucus, we can further advance our understanding of the role of ventilation and health and the potential for interrupting disease transmission in indoor environments. Perhaps the most dramatic demonstration of the need for new information on this issue was the dissemination of anthrax spores in postal facilities during the 2001 bioterrorism episode.

The more contemporary recognition of the relevance of the built environment to health came when measurements of levels of specific pollutants were first made in indoor air and the major contributions of indoor exposures to total personal exposures to air pollution were recognized. This recognition was broadened by such dramatic problems as mobile homes that could not be occupied because of extremely high levels of formaldehyde from building materials, the finding of homes with radon levels as high as those in underground uranium mines, and the appearance of a new clinical syndrome, often referred to as "sick-building syndrome," that was linked to the building environment.

Some of the first measurements of indoor air pollutants were made in the 1960s.[6] In 1965, for example, Biersteker and colleagues[7] made measurements of nitrogen dioxide in Dutch homes, finding that this outdoor air pollutant was also present at high levels in homes with gas-fired combustion devices. Some of the initial measurements of tobacco smoke components were made in the 1970s[8,9] and asbestos fibers were found in indoor air in public buildings and schools in the late 1970s and early 1980s.[10] Radon had been measured in indoor air as early as the 1950s, but gained prominence as large numbers of measurements were taken in the 1970s and 1980s and homes were found with dramatically high concentrations. The problem of lead paint and lead-contaminated surface dust in inner-city homes was recognized in the 1950s and 1960s.[11]

The health- and risk-relevant concept of total personal exposure to pollutants was introduced in the 1970s and provided a framework for integrating and interpreting pollutant measurements taken indoors and outdoors.[12] In the microenvironmental model, total personal exposure to a contaminant is the time-weighted average of pollutant concentrations in the various "microenvironments" where time is spent. In the 1980s, the US Environmental Protection Agency's Total Exposure Assessment Methodology (TEAM) Study used this model for comprehensive assessment of the contributions of indoor and outdoor exposures to total personal exposure for selected volatile organic chemicals, such as benzene.[13] This study yielded the then startling conclusion that indoor pollution sources are generally a far more significant contributor to total personal exposure for toxic volatile organic compounds than are releases by some industrial sources into outdoor air. The Harvard Six-Cities Study, known as a landmark investigation of outdoor air pollution, also proved to be an invaluable research platform for understanding residential indoor air pollution and its strong contributions to total personal exposures for a number of pollutants, including particles, sulfates, and nitrogen oxides.[14–16]

Some Problems Solved

The measurement of these and other indoor air pollutants was quickly followed by research directed at their health effects. Epidemiological studies of cross-sectional and cohort design focused on the risks of exposures at home and a more limited number considered workplace exposures, particularly to tobacco smoke. Case-control studies, and a few cohort studies, of secondhand smoke exposure and lung cancer risk in never smokers were carried out. The risks of cancer associated with asbestos and radon were estimated by extrapolating risks from studies of workers,[10,17] but ecological and case-control studies of indoor radon and lung cancer in the general population were also initiated as early as the late 1970s.[18] Studies of infants and children addressed adverse respiratory effects of nitrogen dioxide, secondhand tobacco smoke exposure, and biological agents, particularly indoor allergens. The earliest of these studies date to the late 1960s and research over the ensuing decades has provided convincing evidence for adverse effects of secondhand smoke, radon, and some biological agents. The evidence remains mixed for some other indoor pollutants: volatile organic compounds and nitrogen dioxide, for example.

For involuntary smoking, research on adverse effects on respiratory health of children began in the late 1960s; the first studies on involuntary smoking and lung cancer were published in 1981.[19,20] The possibility of preventing exposure through elimination of smoking indoors was always clear and as the epidemiologic evidence mounted, increasing numbers of municipalities and states implemented policies to reduce or ban smoking in public places and workplaces. By 1986, the U.S. Surgeon General and the National Research Council had concluded that involuntary smoking causes lung cancer and adverse effects on the respiratory health of children;[21,22] the list continues to expand, now including coronary heart disease as well. With these causal conclusions, the debate over tobacco use shifted from the rights of an individual to use a product to the right of the public to breathe clean indoor air. Increasingly stringent control measures have resulted with broad impact; the majority of workplaces are now smokefree in the United States, as are almost all commercial air flights, and levels of cotinine, the tobacco smoke biomarker, have declined sharply in the United States in recent years.[23] Reducing involuntary smoking in the home is a remaining challenge, one that can be addressed primarily through education. Unfortunately, passive smoking remains a worldwide problem, particularly for women and children.[24]

Indoor radon, labeled as "the colorless, odorless killer," gained notoriety in the United States in the early 1980s, after media reports of a Pennsylvania home with such high levels that the nuclear power plant worker who lived there triggered the radiation monitoring system at the plant as he arrived at work. In the subsequent 20 years, we have gained an increasingly complete picture of the risks posed by indoor radon.[25] A pooled analysis of data from 11 cohort studies of underground miners was carried out to estimate the risks of indoor radon, with complementary evidence gained from case-control studies of lung cancer in the general population.[18,26] Elegant experimental models, involving irradiation of single cells with single alpha particles, provide results consistent with a linear non-threshold relationship between typical concentrations of indoor radon and lung cancer risk.[27,28] The source of most indoor radon, soil gas, is well characterized and radon concentrations can be measured cheaply and with reasonable accuracy. In spite of the abundant scientific evidence supporting strategies for radon control, including measuring and mitigating homes with high levels and building radon-resistant homes, the voluntary initiatives of the Environmental Protection Agency have had limited acceptance by the public.[29–31] Since the mid-1980s, the Agency reports that 18 million U.S. homes have been tested and 50,000 homes mitigated.[32] The voluntary approach is strengthened where radon testing is a standard requirement in purchase and sales agreements for homes.

Asbestos, another inhaled carcinogen, was widely used in the United States through the 1970s as an insulating material in public and commercial buildings; it has also been used to insulate piping in residences and there is a potential for exposures in homes if the asbestos-containing material is friable. Concern about asbestos indoors first followed the recognition that insulating materials in many schools contained asbestos and some of the first measurements in schools indicated the possibility of unsafe levels in air. Under the Asbestos Hazard Emergency Response Act (AHERA),[33] school systems had the option of either removing the asbestos or of maintaining it in place. Initially, asbestos-containing material was removed from many schools at substantial expense but this approach was re-evaluated as further measurements were obtained and options for managing asbestos-containing materials in commercial buildings were considered. A risk assessment carried out by the Health Effects Institute proved pivotal in pushing control towards in-place management.[10] Concerns about asbestos indoors may arise again after it becomes widely known that tremolite asbestos fibers, from the Libby Montana mine, are in Zonolite insulation used in millions of homes, businesses and schools.[34]

Nitrogen dioxide, one of the first pollutants measured indoors, can adversely affect the lungs at high concentrations and consequently when it was found to be emitted by such ubiquitous appliances as gas stoves, epidemiological studies were initiated on its effects on the respiratory health of children and adults.[35,36] The findings of these studies have not provided consistent evidence for adverse effects of nitrogen dioxide and levels in homes have declined as stoves with electronic ignition have replaced older stoves with gas pilot lights and cooking patterns in the United States have moved towards increasing use of microwaves and less cooking generally. Some higher level exposures persist, however. Gas stoves are still used for supplemental heating, particularly by those in public housing who are often not sub-metered for gas use. Also, quite high levels of nitrogen dioxide have been measured in poorly ventilated indoor ice rinks that are resurfaced with machines powered by gasoline or diesel engines.[37]

Biological agents have proved challenging; they are myriad and cause disease through infectious and non-infectious mechanisms. Nonetheless, we have sufficient evidence to prevent the disease caused by some specific agents. The transmission of *Legionella* species through inadequately maintained cooling equipment for HVAC systems and building water systems is well recognized and building-related[38] (as well as cruise ship) epidemics of *Legionella* infection can be avoided through proper cleaning and maintenance. Numerous indoor allergens have been measured and some linked to exacerbation and possibly causation of allergic diseases, including asthma. Control measures can reduce exposures to some of the agents, e.g., cockroach and mite antigens, but substantial benefits to health have not been readily shown, in part because of the difficulties of maintaining reduced levels.[39]

Approaching the Problems Remaining to be Solved

The single most pervasive and harmful indoor air problem worldwide is the oldest—smoke from fires. Domestic cooking and heating with biomass fuels of wood, crop residues, dried animal dung or with charcoal and coal can produce substantial concentrations of particles, carbon monoxide and polycyclic aromatic hydrocarbon indoors. The World Health Organization's 2002 report[40] on global burden of disease considered the almost daily exposures of billions of people, primarily women and young children, as the eighth leading cause of disability adjusted life years (DALYs) lost, accounting for nearly 3% of the world's total burden of disease. For over two decades we have known that improving stove efficiency, providing working flue vents, or improving fuel quality, e.g., switching to propane or liquefied petroleum gas (LPG), could dramatically reduce acute respiratory infections, chronic lung and heart disease, and blindness. Stove improvement programs on a massive scale in China have been successful. Land reclamation programs in India have demonstrated that investments in bio-gas digesters and liquefied natural gas cook stoves will be made as economic prosperity increases. But the prospects for improvements for those trapped in third world poverty are dim as the costs of less polluting cooking and heating fuels or stoves are prohibitive.

Many of the recognized indoor air quality problems facing developed countries are avoidable. If achieving a healthy indoor environment were a specific design criterion for buildings, many of the recurring problems of mold, pest allergens, radon, organic compounds, nitrogen dioxide and carbon monoxide could be controlled. Tobacco smoking indoors has been reduced but achieving effective control in the home remains a challenge; educational strategies are needed, particularly for protecting those at greatest risk, such as infants and children with asthma. Attention should be focused on particularly critical building environments; schools are one obvious example as children spend substantial time in them but ventilation and maintenance may be inadequate.

One lesson that has been learned repeatedly is the need to approach the built environment with multidisciplinary teams, whether for research, design and problem-solving, or for planning for the future. There is far too much isolation of the involved professions, which include public health and medical scientists and researchers, architects, engineers, city planners, building managers, and others, and there is insufficient engagement with the needs of the population itself. We have convened interdisciplinary meetings to address indoor air quality issues and have been impressed with the immediate recognition among the participants of the necessity for interdisciplinary interactions on such issues as sick-building syndrome, air cleaning, and the level of optimal humidity.[41,42] Over the last several decades, the profession of indoor air quality specialist has developed and there are private firms providing indoor air quality services that include problem-solving and management. Since 1978, the *Indoor Air* conferences have offered an international venue for scientific exchange among the many disciplinary experts concerned with the built environment. Some of the critical topics have been addressed by committees of the National Research Council, the Institute of Medicine, and other organizations.[18,43,44]

With an ever growing research base available, the scientific evidence on indoor air should inform the process of designing and maintaining buildings. All too often, well-intended inclusion of indoor air quality as a consideration is reduced to a simple checklist of general items to be avoided and to compliance with ventilation codes. This approach reflects a "dumbing down" of the complex ways in which humans interact with the environment. A more comprehensive rethinking is needed on the physiological, sociological, ergonomic, and psychological characteristics of the built environment that affect health and well-being. Many building codes and design criteria are not soundly based in their consequences for human performance (e.g., lighting requirements). Ventilation requirements for buildings have been assessed, along with those for temperature and humidity more on the basis of meeting comfort criteria than with an orientation towards health or even productivity. Remarkably, there has never been a comprehensive study on the role of ventilation and health and comfort in homes. The current guidelines of the American Society of Heating, Refrigerating, and Air Conditioning Engineers (ASHRAE)[45] recommend a minimum air exchange rate of 35% per hour for homes. However, associations of homebuilders have resisted attempts to specify mechanical means to achieve this recommended exchange rate or to have higher exchange rates for homes, even though the majority of time is spent in homes.

New issues related to the built environment will inevitably emerge. On the current short-list of chemicals likely to be of concern are several synthetic organic compounds: polychlorinated biphenyls in building materials; phthalates in polyvinyl chloride materials used in flooring, wall coverings, cables, foam and other products involving plastic; polybrominated diphenyl esters, which are fire retardants used in many products including computers; pesticide residues including the recently introduced family of pyrethroids; and cleaning agents such as those with phenol among other potentially sensitizing compounds.

The current concern about intentionally introduced viruses and other infectious organisms as acts of bioterrorism will advance research on the role of building ventilation and air cleaning in the transmission of pathogenic organisms. As more multi-disciplinary research on health and buildings is carried out, the effects of space characteristics, materials, lighting and air quality on stress and performance should become better understood. Studies of workforce health complaints related to the building environments have been methodologically complicated by the nonspecificity of most complaints and separating causal effects of engineering and design factors from job stress, personal stress, and perception of unsatisfactory indoor environmental conditions is often impossible. A recently published research agenda for indoor environments and worker health emphasized building-related asthma and allergic diseases in addition to communicable respiratory infections and nonspecific building-related symptoms.[46]

While research continues, for some problems the public, the Congress, and the lawyers will not await more certainty from scientific investigations. For example, state and federal legislation on toxic mold has been proposed. Many individuals, building owners, and insurance companies have been affected by the consequences of water damage and molds and there is uncertainty as to health risks and control approaches. Effective policy approaches are urgently needed for the problem of indoor molds and moisture. The current situation is reminiscent of the past tumultuous debates and litigation around asbestos in buildings. In the 1980s and early 1990s expensive removal of asbestos-containing material was the first course of action regardless of whether the presence of that material actually exposed occupants to asbestos fibers. Currently insurance companies are attempting to write policies excluding mold liability or simply refusing to insure in states where mold claims are widespread. This situation needs resolution through science-based policies and perhaps legislation, but the needed research has yet to be carried out.

We are hopeful that the new focus on built environment and health will contribute to developing the research and policy agenda for improving the built environment. Unfortunately, this topic has received inadequate emphasis, particularly when comparison is made to the substantial resources directed at outdoor air pollution.

References

1. Spengler JD, Samet JM, McCarthy JF, editors. *Indoor Air Quality Handbook.* New York: McGraw-Hill, 2000.
2. Addington DM. The history and future of ventilation. In: Spengler JD, Samet JM, McCarthy JF, editors. *Indoor Air Quality Handbook.* New York: McGraw-Hill, 2000: 2.1–2.16.
3. Yaglou CP, Riley EC, Coggins DI. Ventilation requirements. Heating, Piping and Air Conditioning. *ASHRAE J* 1936; 65–76.
4. Yaglou CP, Witheridge WN. Ventilation requirements, Part 2. Heating, Piping and Air Conditioning. *ASHRAE J* 1937; 1–4.
5. Fanger PO, Valbjorn O. Indoor climate: effects on human comfort, performance, and health in residential, commercial, and light-industry buildings. Copenhagen: Danish Building Research Institute, 1979.
6. National Research Council (NRC), Committee on Indoor Pollutants. Indoor pollutants. 1981. Washington, D.C., National Academy Press.
7. Biersteker K, de Graaf H, Nass CAG. Indoor air pollution in Rotterdam homes. *International Journal of Air, Water, and Pollution* 1965; 9:343–350.
8. Hinds WC, First MW. Concentrations of nicotine and tobacco smoke in public places. *N Engl J Med* 1975; 75(16):844–845.
9. Repace JL, Lowrey AH. Indoor air pollution, tobacco smoke, and public health. *Science* 1980; 80(4443):464–472.
10. Health Effects Institute, Asbestos Research Committee, Literature Review Panel. Asbestos in public and commercial buildings: A literature review and a synthesis of current knowledge. 1991. Cambridge, Massachusetts, Health Effects Institute.
11. Markowitz G, Rosner D. *Denial and Deceit. The Deadly Politics of Industrial Pollution.* Berkeley, CA: University of California Press, 2002.
12. National Research Council (NRC), Committee on Advances in Assessing Human Exposure to Airborne Pollutants. *Human Exposure Assessment for Airborne Pollutants: Advances and Opportunities.* 1991. Washington, D.C., National Academy Press.
13. Wallace LR. The total exposure assessment methodology (TEAM) study: Summary and analysis. Washington, D.C.: Office of Research and Development. U.S. Environmental Protection Agency, 1987.

14. Speizer FE, Ferris BG, Jr., Bishop YM, Spengler JD. Respiratory disease rates and pulmonary function in children associated with NO2 exposure. *Am Rev Respir Dis* 1980; 121:3–10.
15. Dockery DW, Pope CA, III, Xu X, Spengler JD, Ware JH, Fay ME et al. An association between air pollution and mortality in six U.S. cities. *N Engl J Med* 1993; 329:1753–1759.
16. Ware JH, Dockery DW, Spiro A, III. Passive smoking, gas cooking, and respiratory health of children living in six cities. *Am Rev Respir Dis* 1984; 129:366–374.
17. National Research Council (NRC), Committee on the Biological Effects of Ionizing Radiation. *Health Risks of Radon and Other Internally Deposited Alpha-Emitters: BEIR IV.* 1988. Washington, D.C., National Academy Press.
18. National Research Council (NRC), Committee on Health Risks of Exposure to Radon, Board on Radiation Effects Research, Commission on Life Sciences. *Health Effects of Exposure to Radon (BEIR VI).* 1998. Washington, D.C., National Academy Press.
19. Hirayama T. Non-smoking wives of heavy smokers have a higher risk of lung cancer: A study from Japan. *Br Med J* 1981; 282:183–185.
20. Trichopoulos D, Kalandidi A, Sparros L, MacMahon B. Lung cancer and passive smoking. *Int J Cancer* 1981; 27(1):1–4.
21. US Department of Health and Human Services (USDHHS). The health consequences of involuntary smoking: A report of the Surgeon General. DHHS Publication No. (CDC) 87-8398. 1986. Washington, D.C., U.S. Government Printing Office.
22. National Research Council (NRC), Committee on Passive Smoking. Environmental tobacco smoke: Measuring exposures and assessing health effects. 1986. Washington, D.C., National Academy Press.
23. Centers for Disease Control and Prevention (CDC). *Second National Report on Human Exposure to Environmental Chemicals. Results.* NECH Publication No. 02–0716. Atlanta, GA, 2003.
24. Samet JM, Yang G. Passive smoking, women and children. In: Samet JM, Yoon S-Y, editors. *Women and the Tobacco Epidemic. Challenges for the 21st Century.* Geneva: World Health Organization, 2001: 17–45.
25. Samet JM, Eradze GR. Radon and lung cancer risk: taking stock at the millenium. *Environ Health Perspect* 2000; 108 Suppl 4:635–641.
26. Lubin JH, Boice JD, Jr., Edling C, Hornung RW, Howe G, Kunz E et al. *Radon and Lung Cancer Risk: A Joint Analysis of 11 Underground Miners Studies.* Bethesda, MD: U.S. Department of Health and Human Services, Public Health Service, National Institutes of Health, 1994.
27. Zhou H, Randers-Pehrson G, Waldren CA, Vannais D, Hall EJ, Hei TK. Induction of a bystander mutagenic effect of alpha particles in mammalian cells. *Proc Natl Acad Sci U S A* 2000; 97(5):2099–2104.

28. Zhou H, Suzuki M, Randers-Pehrson G, Vannais D, Chen G, Trosko JE et al. Radiation risk to low fluences of alpha particles may be greater than we thought. *Proc Natl Acad Sci U S A* 2001; 98:14410–14415.

29. US Environmental Protection Agency (EPA). *A Citizen's Guide to Radon. The Guide to Protecting Yourself and Your Family from Radon.* 2nd ed. Washington, D.C.: U.S. Government Printing Office, 1992.

30. US Environmental Protection Agency (EPA). *A Citizen's Guide to Radon. What It Is and What to Do About It.* 2nd ed. Washington D.C.: U.S. Government Printing Office, 1992.

31. Cole LA. *Elements of Risk: the Politics of Radon.* Washington, D.C.: AAAS Press, 1993.

32. Gregory B, Jalbert PP. National radon results: 1985 to 1999. Washington, D.C., U.S. Environmental Protection Agency, 2001.

33. Asbestos Hazard Emergency Response Act (AHERA). H.R. 5073, 1986.

34. Bowker M. *Fatal Deception. The untold story of asbestos. Why it is still legal and still killing us.* Emmaus, PA: Rodale, 2003.

35. Samet JM, Basu R. A review of the epidemiological evidence on health effects of nitrogen dioxide exposure from gas stoves. *J Environ Med* 1999; 1:173–187.

36. Samet JM, Utell MJ. The risk of nitrogen dioxide: What have we learned from epidemiological and clinical studies? *Toxicol Ind Health* 1990; 6(2): 247–262.

37. Brauer M, Spengler JD. Nitrogen dioxide exposures inside ice skating rinks. *Am J Public Health* 1994; 84:429–433.

38. Barry BE. Legionella. In: Spengler JD, Samet JM, McCarthy JF, editors. *Indoor Air Quality Handbook.* New York: McGraw-Hill, 2000: 48.1–48.15.

39. Burge HA. An update on pollen and fungal spore aerobiology. *J Allergy Clin Immunol* 2002; 110(4):544–552.

40. *Global estimates of burden of disease caused by the environment.* World Health Organization, 2002.

41. American Thoracic Society. Environmental controls and lung disease. Report of the ATS workshop on environmental controls and lung disease, Santa Fe, New Mexico, March 24–26. *Am Rev Respir Dis* 1988; 142:915–939.

42. American Lung Association, American Thoracic Society. Achieving Healthy Indoor Air. Report of the American Thoracic Society Workshop. Sante Fe, New Mexico, November 16–18, 1995. *Am J Resp Crit Care Med* 1997.

43. Institute of Medicine, Committee on the Health Effects of Indoor Allergens, Division of Health Promotion and Disease Prevention. *Indoor Allergens: Assessing and Controlling Adverse Health Effects.* Washington, D.C.: National Academy Press, 1993.

44. Institute of Medicine, Committee on the Assessment of Asthma and Indoor Air. *Clearing the Air: Asthma and Indoor Air Exposures.* Washington, D.C.: National Academy Press, 2000.

45. *The Human Equation: Health and Comfort.* Atlanta, Georgia: American Society of Heating, Refrigerating and Air Conditioning Engineers (ASHRAE), 1989.
46. Mendell MJ, Fisk WJ, Kreiss K, Levin H, Alexander D, Cain WS et al. Improving the health of workers in indoor environments: priority research needs for a national occupational research agenda. *Am J Public Health* 2002; 92(9):1430–1440.

Urban Sprawl and Public Health

Howard Frumkin

W hen regular steam ferry service between Brooklyn and Manhattan began in 1814, the first commuter suburb became possible.[1] Suburbs continued to develop slowly but steadily during the 19th and early 20th centuries, thanks to transportation advances such as commuter trains and streetcars, the innovations of early real estate developers, and the urge to live in pastoral tranquility rather than in urban squalor. As automobile ownership became widespread starting in the 1920s, suburban growth continued, a trend that accelerated greatly during the second half of the 20th century. One in two Americans now lives in the suburbs.[2]

In recent years, the rapid expansion of metropolitan areas has been termed "urban sprawl"—referring to a complex pattern of land use, transportation, and social and economic development. As cities extend into rural areas, large tracts of land are developed in a "leapfrog," low-density pattern. Different land uses—housing, retail stores, offices, industry, recreational facilities, and public spaces such as parks—are kept separate from each other, with the separation enforced by both custom and zoning laws. Extensive roads need to be constructed; for suburban dwellers, most trips, even to buy a newspaper or a quart of milk, require driving a car. Newly built suburbs are relatively homogeneous in both human and architectural terms, compared with the diversity found in traditional urban or small town settings. With the expansion of suburbs, capital investment and economic opportunity shift from the center to the periphery. Regional planning and coordination are relatively weak.[1,3-7]

Clearly, the move to the suburbs reflects a lifestyle preference shared by many Americans. Such a major shift in the nation's demographics and in the form of our environment might also be expected to have health implications, both positive and negative. Some of these effects relate directly to heavy reliance on automobiles: air pollution, automobile crashes, and pedestrian injuries and fatalities. Other effects relate to land use patterns that typify sprawl: sedentary lifestyles, threats to water quantity and quality, and an expansion of the urban heat island effect. Finally, some mental health and social capital effects are mediated by the social dimensions of sprawl. Many of these health effects are individually recognized as environmental health issues, and certain aspects of sprawl, such as reliance on automobiles, have been analyzed as public health issues.[8,9] Yet the broad phenomenon of sprawl, a complex of issues related to land use, transportation, urban and regional design, and planning, has been the intellectual "property" of engineers and planners. Public health professionals have provided neither an intellectual framework nor policy guidance. This is a striking departure from the legacy of the 19th and early 20th centuries, when public health and urban design were overlapping and largely indistinguishable concerns.[10–12]

This article offers a public health framework for understanding the consequences of urban sprawl. For each of the health outcomes noted earlier, available evidence about the health effect and its connection with sprawl is presented, and issues that require further research are identified. Because the adverse impacts of sprawl do not fall equally across the population, the distribution of health impacts across the population and resulting equity concerns are addressed. Finally, some solutions are discussed.

Direct Effects of Reliance on Automobiles

One of the cardinal features of sprawl is driving, reflecting a well-established, close relationship between lower density development and more automobile travel.[4,13–16] For example, in the Atlanta metropolitan area, one of the nation's leading examples of urban sprawl, the average person travels 34.1 miles in a car each day—an average that includes the entire population, both drivers and non-drivers.[17] More densely populated metropolitan areas have far lower per capita daily driving figures than Atlanta, e.g., 16.9 miles for Philadelphia, 19.9 for Chicago, and 21.2 for San Francisco.[17] On a neighborhood scale, the same pattern is observed. In the Los Angeles, San Francisco, and Chicago metropolitan areas, vehicle miles traveled increase as neighborhood density decreases.[18]

Automobile use offers extraordinary personal mobility and independence. However, it is also associated with health hazards, including air pollution, motor vehicle crashes, and pedestrian injuries and fatalities.

Air Pollution

Motor vehicles are a leading source of air pollution.[19,20] Even though automobile and truck engines have become far cleaner in recent decades, the sheer quantity of vehicle miles driven results in large releases of carbon monoxide, carbon dioxide, particulate matter, nitrogen oxides, and hydrocarbons into the air.[21] Nitrogen oxides and hydrocarbons, in the presence of sunlight, form ozone.

Nationwide, "mobile sources" (mostly cars and trucks) account for approximately 30% of emissions of oxides of nitrogen and 30% of hydrocarbon emissions.[22] However, in automobile-dependent metropolitan areas, the proportion may be substantially higher. In the 10-county metropolitan Atlanta area, for example, on-road cars and trucks account for 58% of emissions of nitrogen oxides and 47% of hydrocarbon emissions, figures that underestimate the full impact of vehicle traffic because they exclude emissions from related sources, such as fuel storage facilities and filling stations.[23]

In various combinations, the pollutants that originate from cars and trucks, especially nitrogen oxides, hydrocarbons, ozone, and particulate matter, account for a substantial part of the air pollution burden of American cities. Of note, the highest air pollution levels in a metropolitan area may occur not at the point of formation but downwind, due to regional transport. Thus, air pollution is a problem not only alongside roadways (or in close proximity to other sources) but also on the scale of entire regions.

The health hazards of air pollution are well known.[24] Ozone is an airways irritant. Higher ozone levels are associated with higher incidence and severity of respiratory symptoms, worse lung function, more emergency room visits and hospitalizations, more medication use, and more absenteeism from school and work.[24] Although healthy people may demonstrate these effects, people with asthma and other respiratory diseases are especially susceptible. Particulate matter is associated with many of the same respiratory effects and, in addition, with elevated mortality.[25-27] People who are especially susceptible to the effects of air pollution include the elderly, the very young, and those with underlying cardiopulmonary disease.

An additional driving-related emission is carbon dioxide, the end product of burning fossil fuels such as gasoline. Carbon dioxide is the major greenhouse gas, accounting for approximately 80% of emissions with global warming potential.[28] Motor vehicles are also a major source of other greenhouse gases, including methane, nitrogen oxides, and volatile organic compounds. As a result, automobile traffic is a major contributor to global climate change, accounting for approximately 26% of U.S. greenhouse gas emissions.[28] During the decade of the 1990s, greenhouse gases from mobile sources increased 18%, primarily a reflection of more vehicle miles traveled.[28] In turn, global climate change threatens human health in a number of ways, including the direct effects of heat, enhanced formation of some air pollutants, and increased prevalence of some infectious diseases.[29-32]

Thus, the link between sprawl and respiratory health is as follows: Sprawl is associated with high levels of driving, driving contributes to air pollution, and air pollution causes morbidity and mortality. In heavily automobile-dependent cities, air pollution can rise to hazardous levels, and driving can account for a majority of the emissions. Although ongoing research is exploring the pathophysiology of air pollution exposure and related issues, there are also important research questions that revolve around prevention. Technical issues include such challenges as the development of low-emission vehicles and other clean technologies. Policy research needs to identify approaches to land use and transportation that would reduce the need for motor vehicle travel. Behavioral research needs to identify factors that motivate people to choose less-polluting travel behaviors, such as walking, carpooling, or use of more efficient vehicles.

Motor Vehicle Crashes

Automobiles now claim more than 40,000 lives each year in the United States, a number that has slowly declined from about 50,000 per year in the 1960s.[33] Rates of automobile fatalities and injuries per driver and per mile driven have fallen thanks to safer cars and roads, seat belt use, laws that discourage drunk driving, and other measures, but the absolute toll of automobile crashes remains high. Automobile crashes are the leading cause of death among people 1–24 years old, account for 3.4 million nonfatal injuries annually, and cost an estimated $200 billion annually.[34]

The relationship between sprawl and motor vehicle crashes is complex. At the simplest level, more driving means greater exposure to the dangers of the road, translating to a higher probability of a motor vehicle crash.[35] Suburban roads may be a particular hazard, especially major commercial thoroughfares and "feeder" roads that combine high speed, high traffic volume, and frequent "curb cuts" for drivers to use in entering and exiting stores and other destinations.[36] However, available data from the National Highway Traffic Safety Administration (NHTSA) show fatal crashes aggregated into only two categories of roads: urban (accounting for approximately 60% of fatalities) and rural (approximately 40%).[33]

The NHTSA data do permit comparison of automobile fatality rates by city.[33] In general, denser cities with more extensive public transportation systems have lower automobile fatality rates (including drivers and passengers, but excluding pedestrians) than more sprawling cities: 2.45 per 100,000 population in San Francisco, 2.30 in New York, 3.21 in Portland, 6.67 in Chicago, and 5.26 in Philadelphia, compared with 10.08 in Houston, 16.15 in Tampa, 12.72 in Atlanta, 11.35 in Dallas, and 9.85 in Phoenix.[33] (There are notable exceptions to this pattern, such as 5.79 per 100,000 population in Los Angeles and 10.93 per 100,000 in Detroit.[33])

According to the American College of Emergency Physicians, "Traffic crashes are predictable and preventable, and therefore are not 'accidents.'"[37] In fact, the determinants of motor vehicle injuries and fatalities are well recognized. For some of these, public health interventions, from seat belts to traffic signals, have achieved dramatic reductions in injury and fatality rates in the three-quarters of a century since automobile use became widespread. A relatively overlooked risk factor, however, is the simple fact of driving and the number of miles driven. Primary prevention would consist of decreasing exposure, an approach that is currently impractical in many metropolitan areas.

Pedestrian Injuries and Fatalities

On December 14, 1995, 17-year-old Cynthia Wiggins rode the public bus to her job at the Walden Galleria in suburban Cheektowaga, New York, outside of Buffalo. The bus did not stop at the mall itself, so Cynthia had to cross a seven-lane highway on foot to complete her trip to work. On that day, she had made it across six lanes when a dump truck crushed her.[38] Her death received national media attention; it was seen as exemplifying inadequate mass transportation links, pedestrian-hostile roadways, and the disproportionate impact of these factors on members of minority groups.

Each year, automobiles cause about 6,000 fatalities and 110,000 injuries among pedestrians nationwide. Pedestrians account for about one in eight automobile-related fatalities.[39,40] Data from Atlanta show that as the city sprawled in recent years, the pedestrian fatality rate increased even as the national rate declined slightly.[41] The most dangerous stretches of road were those built in the style that typifies sprawl: multiple lanes, high speeds, no sidewalks, long distances between intersections or crosswalks, and roadways lined with large commercial establishments and apartments blocks.[41] Across the country, the pattern seen for driver and passenger fatalities is repeated for pedestrian fatalities, with lower annual rates in denser cities: 1.89 per 100,000 population in Portland, 2.22 in New York, 2.52 in Chicago, and 2.57 in Philadelphia, compared with 3.03 in Dallas, 3.61 in Atlanta, 4.08 in Phoenix, and 6.60 in Tampa. However, this pattern is not as consistent as for driver and passenger fatalities, and there are exceptions, e.g., 2.60 per 100,000 population in Los Angeles, 2.61 in Houston, 3.86 in San Francisco, and 4.73 per 100,000 in Detroit.[33]

While many factors contribute to the high toll of pedestrian fatalities, including alcohol abuse, inadequate lighting, and pedestrian behavior, the proliferation of high-speed, pedestrian-hostile roads in expanding metropolitan areas likely plays an important part. Walking offers important public health benefits, but safe and attractive sidewalks and footpaths are needed to attract walkers and assure their safety. Much of the knowledge needed to make progress is available, but further research might help clarify the best and most cost-efficient ways to build walkways and the most successful approaches to zoning, financing, and other incentives.

Effects of Land Use Decisions

Land use and travel patterns are closely linked. If distinct land uses are separated, if the distances between them are great, and if roads are more available than sidewalks and paths, then people shift from walking and bicycling to driving. Accordingly, the U.S. is a nation of drivers, in which only 1% of trips are on bicycles and 9% are on foot.[42] For comparison, in the Netherlands 30% of all trips are on bicycles and 18% are on foot, and in England the corresponding figures are 8% and 12%.[42] Approximately 25% of all trips in the U.S. are shorter than one mile; of these, 75% are by car.[43]

Physical Activity

A considerable body of research establishes that sprawl—as measured by low residential density, low employment density, low "connectivity," and other indicators—is associated with less walking and bicycling and with more automobile travel than denser communities.[13,44–48]

Low levels of physical activity threaten health both directly and indirectly. A sedentary lifestyle is a well-established risk factor for cardiovascular disease, stroke, and all-cause mortality,[49–53] whereas physical activity prolongs life.[54,55] Men in the lowest quintile of physical fitness have two to three times the risk of dying overall, and three to five times the risk of dying of cardiovascular disease, compared with men who are more fit.[56] Among women, walking 10 blocks per day or more is associated with a 33% lower risk of cardiovascular disease.[57] The risk associated with poor physical fitness is comparable to, and in some studies greater than, the risk associated with hypertension, high cholesterol, diabetes, and even smoking.[56,58] Among diabetic patients, the higher the blood sugar, the more protective is physical fitness.[59] Physical activity also appears to be protective against cancer.[60–63]

In addition to its direct effects on health, lack of physical activity is also a risk factor for being overweight. Sedentary lifestyles may help explain the rapid increase in the prevalence of overweight in recent years. In 1960, 24% of Americans were overweight (defined as a Body Mass Index ≥ 25 kg/m^2), and by 1990 that proportion had increased to 33%.[64] During the same interval, the prevalence of obesity (defined as a Body Mass Index ≥ 30 kg/m^2) nearly doubled.[65] According to data from the Behavioral Risk Factor Surveillance System, this trend continued during the 1990s, with the prevalence of obesity rising from 12.0% in 1991 to 17.9% in 1998.[66,67]

Being overweight is itself a well-established risk factor for a number of diseases: ischemic heart disease (overweight increases the risk up to fourfold in the 30–44 age group, less at older ages[68]), hypertension, stroke, dyslipidemia, osteoarthritis, gall bladder disease, and some cancers. Overweight people die at as much as 2.5 times the rate of non-obese people.[51,68–71] Being overweight increases the risk of Type 2 diabetes up to fivefold, and the current epidemic of Type 2 diabetes tracks closely with the increase in being overweight.[72]

Sprawl does not fully account for Americans' increasingly sedentary lives, and physical inactivity does not tell the entire story of the national epidemic of being overweight. However, by contributing to physical inactivity and therefore to overweight and associated health problems, sprawl has negative health consequences. Further research will help provide a more complete understanding of the association between sprawl and physical inactivity.[73] In theory, a randomized trial might assign some people to live in walkable neighborhoods and others to live in subdivisions without sidewalks or nearby schools, stores, or workplaces. Then, the two groups might be followed for physical activity patterns and related health outcomes. Such residential randomization is, of course, impossible. Observational studies are underway to characterize the relationships among land use, travel patterns, and physical activity.[74] However, such research is challenging. People living in walkable neighborhoods may have chosen to live there because of better health and a greater inclination to walk. Because children do not choose their neighborhoods, an alternative might be to study adult physical activity and travel patterns according to the type of neighborhood of origin to test the hypothesis that childhood access to walkable neighborhoods predicts lifelong travel preferences and activity patterns. Research is also needed on design issues (how to build more walkable communities), policy issues (how to put incentives in place to encourage needed environmental and behavioral changes), and behavior issues (how to motivate more physical activity, including walking).

Water Quantity and Quality

Americans take for granted the availability of clean, plentiful, and cheap water. Indeed, the development of an excellent water supply—the result of social policy, civil engineering, and health advocacy over more than a century—is credited with a central role in improving public health during the first half of the 20th century.[12,75]

Sprawl may threaten both the quantity and quality of the water supply. As forest cover is cleared and impervious surfaces built over large areas, rainfall is less effectively absorbed and returned to groundwater aquifers.[76] Instead, relatively more stormwater flows to streams and rivers and is carried downstream. One study found that about 4% of rainfall on undeveloped grassland, compared with 15% of rainfall on suburban land, was lost as runoff.[77] The same is true for snowmelt, especially early in the melting process.[78] Modeling shows that higher density development patterns can reduce peak flows and total runoff volumes.[79] With less groundwater recharge, communities that depend on groundwater for their drinking water—about one-third of U.S. communities[80]— may face shortages.

Water quality may be affected in several ways. With better control of "point sources" of water pollution—factories, sewage treatment plants, and similar facilities—"non-point source" water pollution has emerged as the major threat to water supplies. Non-point source water pollution occurs when rainfall or snowmelt moves over and through the ground, picking up contaminants and depositing them into surface water (lakes, rivers, wetlands, and coastal waters) and groundwater. Much of this problem is specific to agricultural land, the primary source of contamination by fertilizers, herbicides, and insecticides. However, growing forms of non-point source pollution include oil, grease, and toxic chemicals from roadways, parking lots, and other surfaces, and sediment from improperly managed construction sites, other areas from which foliage has been cleared, or eroding stream banks. Studies of the movement of polycyclic aromatic hydrocarbons,[81] zinc,[82] and organic waste[83] suggest that suburban development is associated with high loading of these contaminants in nearby surface water.

Both water quantity and water quality are directly affected by land use and development patterns, and evidence suggests that sprawl contributes to these problems in specific ways. Further evidence is needed to identify the precise features of land use that best predict non-point source pollution, the impact of this pollution on drinking water quality, and the optimal control methods.

The Heat Island Effect

On warm days, urban areas can be 6°–8° F warmer than surrounding areas, an effect known as an urban heat island. The heat island effect is caused by two factors. First, dark surfaces such as roadways and rooftops efficiently absorb heat from sunlight and reradiate it as thermal infrared radiation; these surfaces can reach temperatures of 50°–70° F higher than surrounding air. Second, urban areas are relatively devoid of vegetation, especially trees, that would provide shade and cool the air through "evapotranspiration." As cities sprawl outward, the heat island effect expands, both in geographic extent and in intensity. This is especially true if the pattern of development features extensive tree cutting and road construction.[84,85] NASA satellite imagery, available for public viewing on the Web, documents the heat island effect for several cities.[86]

Metropolitan expansion involves a positive feedback loop that may aggravate the heat island effect. Sprawling metropolitan areas, with greater travel distances, generate a large amount of automobile travel. This, in turn, results in more fuel combustion, with more production of carbon dioxide, and consequent contributions to global climate change.[87] Global climate change, in turn, may intensify the heat island effect in metropolitan areas. Thus, not only does the morphology of metropolitan areas contribute to warming, but so may the greenhouse gas production that results from increased driving.

The magnitude of the contribution of sprawl to urban heat episodes is unclear. Data from the last half century show a clear increasing trend in extreme heat events in U.S. cities.[88] While global warming may contribute to this trend, the rate of the increase far exceeds the rate of global warming, suggesting that urban growth patterns may be a primary determinant.[89] Further research on this phenomenon is required.

Heat is of concern because it is a health hazard.[90] Relatively benign disorders include heat syncope, or fainting; heat edema, or swelling, usually of dependent parts such as the legs; and heat tetany, a result of heat-induced hyperventilation. Heat cramps are painful muscle spasms that occur after strenuous exertion in a hot environment. Heat exhaustion is a more severe acute illness that may feature nausea, vomiting, weakness, and mental status changes. The most serious of the acute heat-related conditions is heat stroke, which represents the body's failure to dissipate heat. The core body temperature may exceed 104°F, muscle breakdown occurs, and renal failure and other profound physiologic derangements may follow. The fatality rate is high.

There are several well-known risk factors for developing heat stroke or dying during a heat wave, including being elderly, bedridden, homebound, or socially isolated, having certain diseases or using certain medications, and living on an upper floor.[91,92] Poverty and minority race or ethnicity are also risk markers.[93]

Heat also has indirect effects on health, mediated through air pollution. As the temperature rises, so does the demand for energy to power air conditioners, requiring power plants to increase their output. The majority of U.S. power plants burn fossil fuels, so increased summer demand results in higher emissions of the pollutants they generate, including carbon dioxide, particulate matter, sulfur oxides, nitrogen oxides, and air toxics. Ozone formation from its precursors, nitrogen oxides and hydrocarbons, is enhanced by heat. In summary, through both the direct and indirect effects of heat, sprawl has potential adverse health consequences.

Social Aspects of Sprawl

Mental Health

One of the original motivations for migration to the suburbs was access to nature.[1] People like trees, birds, and flowers, and these are more accessible in the suburbs than in denser urban areas. Moreover, contact with nature may offer benefits beyond the purely aesthetic; it may benefit both mental health and physical health.[94] In addition, the sense of escaping from the turmoil of urban life to the suburbs, the feeling of peaceful refuge, may be soothing and restorative to some people. In these respects, there may be health benefits to suburban lifestyles.

On the other hand, certain aspects of sprawl, such as commuting, may exact a mental health toll. For some time, automobile commuting has been of interest to psychologists as a source of stress, stress-related health problems, and even physical ailments. Evidence links commuting to back pain, cardiovascular disease, and self-reported stress.[95] As people spend more time on more crowded roads, an increase in these health outcomes might be expected.

One possible indicator of such problems is road rage, defined as "events in which an angry or impatient driver tries to kill or injure another driver after a traffic dispute."[96] Even lawmakers may be involved; one press account described a prominent attorney and former Maryland state legislator who knocked the glasses off a pregnant woman after she had the temerity to ask him why he had bumped her Jeep with his.[97]

Available data do not make clear whether road rage is on the rise. The only longitudinal study available in the U.S., published by the AAA Foundation for

Traffic Safety in 1997, reported a 51% increase in reported annual incidents of road rage during the interval from 1990 to 1996.[98] The Foundation documented 10,000 reports of such incidents, resulting in 12,610 injuries and 218 deaths. A variety of weapons was used, including guns, knives, clubs, fists, or feet, and in many cases the vehicle itself. However, since the data sources included police reports and newspaper accounts, it is possible that the apparent increase reflected growing public awareness and media attention rather than a true increase in the number or rate of road rage incidents.

Road rage is not well understood, and there is a multiplicity of reasons for its occurrence. Stress at home or work may combine with stress while driving to elicit anger.[99,100] Data from Australia[101] and Europe[102] suggest that both traffic volume and travel distance are risk factors. Long delays on crowded roads are likely to be a contributing factor.

Episodes of road rage may reflect a reservoir of frustration and anger on the roads. In national telephone surveys conducted by Mississippi State University in 1999 and 2001,[103,104] large numbers of respondents reported both engaging in aggressive behaviors while driving and being the objects of such behavior (see Table 7-1). The surveys did not identify respondents who lived in suburban locations, although the responses differed in several respects across the geographic categories used (rural, small town, small city, and large city), suggesting an influence of density and other "built environment" factors on aggressive driving behavior. A similar survey, conducted for NHTSA in 1998, found somewhat lower but comparable numbers.[105] In the NHTSA survey, the two leading reasons cited for aggressive driving were (a) being rushed or being behind schedule (23% of respondents), and (b) increased traffic or congestion (22%)—common experiences on the crowded roadways of sprawling cities. Moreover, 30% of the NHTSA respondents perceived that aggressive driving—their own and others'—was increasing over time, and only 4% thought it was decreasing. More recently, Curbow and Griffin[106] surveyed 218 women employed by a telecommunications company. This was a stable, professional population; 67% of the respondents had more than a high school education, 76% were parents, and the average job seniority was 18 years. Among these women, 56% reported driving aggressively, 41% reported yelling or gesturing at other drivers while commuting, and 25% reported taking out their frustrations from behind the wheel of their cars. Aggressive driving behavior appears to be a widespread problem.

It seems reasonable to hypothesize that anger and frustration among drivers are not restricted to their cars. When angry people arrive at work or at home, what are the implications for work and family relations? If the phenomenon known as commuting stress affects well-being and social relationships both on the roads and off, and if this set of problems is aggravated by increasingly long and difficult commutes on crowded roads, then sprawl may in this manner threaten mental health.

TABLE 7-1   Prevalence of Self-Reported Driving Behaviors, 1999 and 2001 National Highway Safety Surveys

Percent of respondents by response choice

How often do you . . . (1999)	Never	Rarely	Sometimes	Often
Say bad things to yourself about other drivers	15.3	22.9	39.5	22.1
Complain or yell about other drivers to a passenger in your vehicle	25.5	22.2	39.0	13.1
Give another driver a dirty look	41.8	17.6	32.7	7.7
Honk or yell at someone through the window to express displeasure	61.1	17.9	17.9	2.9
Keep someone from entering your lane because you are angry	80.2	12.9	5.9	0.8
Make obscene gestures to another driver	83.7	9.2	6.1	0.8
Think about physically hurting another driver	89.0	5.4	4.4	1.1
Make sudden or threatening moves to intimidate another driver	94.6	4.0	1.1	0.1
Follow or chase another driver in anger	96.5	3.2	0.3	0.0

Percent of respondents by place of residence

Within the last year, another driver . . . (2001)	Rural	Small town	Small city	Large city	Total
Made an obscene gesture at you	39.7	37.1	44.9	44.3	41.8
Made a threatening move with car	25.4	23.5	30.0	25.9	26.4
Tailgated you	69.1	61.3	70.3	69.8	66.8
Followed or chased you in anger	9.9	6.4	9.9	11.5	9.4
Got out of car to argue with you	5.8	5.8	4.2	8.3	5.9
Cut you off	32.0	33.7	38.6	48.0	38.1

Source: Adapted from references 103 and 104.

Social Capital

Since World War II, social commentators have ascribed to suburban living a sense of social isolation and loneliness,[107–114] although some of these claims have recently been challenged.[115] "It is no coincidence," observes Yale architecture professor Philip Langdon, "that at the moment when the United States has become a predominantly suburban nation, the country has suffered a bitter harvest of individual trauma, family distress, and civic decay."[116] Indeed, a perceived erosion of civic engagement and mutual trust—a loss of what is called "social capital"—has been widely noted and discussed in recent years.[117,118] Some authors have attributed this decline, in part, to suburbanization and sprawl.[119,120]

A full discussion of the complex sociology of suburban life is beyond the scope of this article. Several facts bear mention, however. First, as Robert Putnam argues in Bowling Alone, the simple fact of more driving time means less time with family or friends, and less time to devote to community activities, from neighborhood barbecues to PTA meetings.[118] Putnam estimates that each additional 10 minutes of driving time predicts a 10% decline in civic involvement.[118] Second, suburban development patterns often feature considerable economic stratification. Many housing developments are built to specific price ranges, so that buyers of $250,000 homes are effectively segregated from buyers of $500,000 homes (and those at the bottom of the economic ladders are excluded altogether).[121] This pattern creates income homogeneity within neighborhoods but may intensify income inequality across metropolitan areas. Third, both polling data and voting records have demonstrated that suburban residents prefer more individualized, less collective solutions to social problems relative to rural, small town, and urban voters, with the possible exception of schools.[122–125] Finally, suburban neighborhoods with capacious houses and lawns offer few options for older adults once their children have grown up and moved from the home. These "empty nesters" typically have to change neighborhoods if they wish to find smaller, lower maintenance homes. The inability to remain in a single neighborhood through the life cycle may also undermine community cohesiveness. Collectively, these trends suggest that certain features of sprawl tend toward greater social stratification and less social capital.

A large literature has explored the relationship between social relationships and health, focusing both on the individual level (one's own relationships) and on the societal level (social capital).[126] In general, a higher quantity and quality of social relationships is associated with health benefits. Conversely, social stratification, in particular income inequality, is associated with higher all-cause mortality, higher infant mortality, and higher mortality from a variety of specific causes, independent of income and poverty, according to data from the United States[127–130] and Great Britain.[131,132] There is evidence that this effect is mediated, at least in part, through effects on social capital.[133,134] Therefore, to the extent that sprawl is associated with social stratification and loss of social capital and these phenomena are in turn associated with increased morbidity and mortality, sprawl may have a negative health impact on this broad scale.

Environmental Justice Considerations

Research over the last 15 years has suggested that poor people and members of minority groups are disproportionately exposed to environmental hazards.[135–137] Could any adverse health consequences of sprawl disproportionately affect these same populations?

In general, the pattern of urban development of which sprawl is a part may deprive the poor of economic opportunity. When jobs, stores, good schools, and other resources migrate outward from the core city, poverty is concentrated in the neighborhoods that are left behind.[138–142] A full discussion of the impact of urban poverty on health is beyond the scope of this article, but a large literature explores this relationship.[143–147] To the extent that sprawl aggravates poverty, at least for selected groups of people, it may contribute to the burden of disease and mortality.

More specifically, there is evidence that several of the specific health threats related to sprawl affect minority populations disproportionately. Air pollution is one example. Poor people and people of color are disproportionately impacted by air pollution for at least two reasons: disproportionate exposure, and higher prevalence of underlying diseases that increase susceptibility. Members of minority groups are relatively more exposed to air pollutants than whites, independent of income and urbanization.[148,149] Environmental Protection Agency data show that black people and Hispanics are more likely than white people to live in areas that violate air quality standards.[150] As asthma continues to increase, asthma prevalence and mortality remain higher in minority group members than in white people.[151] The cumulative prevalence of asthma is 122 per 1,000 in black people and 104 per 1,000 in white people, and asthma mortality is approximately three times as high in black people as in white people.[152] Similarly, asthma prevalence is more than three times as high among Puerto Rican children as among non-Hispanic children.[153] Among Medicaid patients, black children are 93% more likely, and Latino children 34% more likely, than white children to have multiple hospitalizations for asthma.[154] Although some of this excess is related to poverty, the excess persists in analyses controlled for income.[155] Asthma prevalence and mortality are especially high, and rising, in inner cities, where minority populations are concentrated.[156,157] Both exposure to air pollution and susceptibility to its effects appear to be concentrated disproportionately among the poor and people of color. As sprawl contributes to air pollution in metropolitan areas, these populations may be disproportionately affected.

Heat-related morbidity and mortality also disproportionately affect poor people and members of minority groups. In the 1995 Chicago heat wave, black residents had a 50% higher heat-related mortality rate than white residents.[158] Similar findings have emerged following heat waves in Texas,[159] Memphis,[160] St. Louis,[161] and Kansas City[161] and are reflected in nationwide statistics.[162] Of special interest in the context of urban sprawl, one heat wave study considered transportation as a risk factor and found that poor access to transportation—a correlate of poverty and non-white race[163]—was associated with a 70% higher rate of heat-related death.[92]

There are significant racial/ethnic differences in motor vehicle fatality rates. Results from the National Health Interview Survey revealed motor vehicle fatality rates of 32.5 per 100,000 person-years among black men, 10.2 among Hispanic men, 19.5 among white men, 11.6 among black women, 9.1 among Hispanic women, and 8.5 among white women.[164] Much of the disparity was associated with social class.[164] However, differences in neighborhood design, road quality, automobile quality, and behavioral factors may be important, and need to be better understood.

Pedestrian fatalities disproportionately affect members of minority groups and those at the bottom of the economic ladder.[164] In Atlanta, for instance, pedestrian fatality rates during 1994–1998 were 9.74 per 100,000 for Hispanics, 3.85 for black people, and 1.64 for white people.[41] In suburban Orange County, California, Latinos represent 28% of the population but account for 43% of pedestrian fatalities.[165] In the Virginia suburbs of Washington, Hispanics represent 8% of the population but account for 21% of pedestrian fatalities.[166] The reasons for this disproportionate impact are complex and may involve the probability of being a pedestrian (perhaps related to low access to automobiles and public transportation), road design in areas where members of minority groups walk, and behavioral and cultural factors (such as being unaccustomed to high speed traffic).

These examples illustrate that the health effects of sprawl may have disparate impacts on different sub-populations. In other cases, there is less evidence of disparities in the health outcomes associated with sprawl, or when such disparities exist, they are likely to relate to factors other than land use and transportation. Examples include physical activity, water-related health outcomes, and mental health outcomes.

Physical activity and overweight vary by ethnic and racial group. People of color are more likely to be overweight[164,167] and more likely to lead sedentary lifestyles[168,169] than white people.[170–173] In the Third National Health and Nutrition Examination Survey (NHANES-III), for example, 40% of Mexican Americans and 35% of blacks reported no leisure time physical activity, compared with 18% of white people.[174] In this same survey, the mean Body Mass Index was 29.2 among black people, 28.6 among Mexican Americans, and 26.3 among white people.[170] The relationships among race/ethnicity, genetic factors, social class, the environment, diet, physical activity, and body weight are complex. There is no evidence that sprawl disproportionately affects people of color with regard to physical activity. In fact, poorer people may be less likely to own cars and therefore more likely to walk than wealthier people. Given the public health importance of overweight, obesity, and related health conditions, and the fact that relatively little research has addressed disparities in environmental contributors such as sprawl, further data on these relationships are needed.

In contrast, there is no evidence that sprawl-related threats to the water supply disproportionately affect poor people or members of minority groups. Similarly, there is no evidence that the mental health consequences of sprawl, such as road rage, affect various racial/ ethnic groups differently. In the driving behavior survey data cited previously, no racial/ethnic differences were found in self-reported aggressive behavior. Although black people were slightly less likely to be the victims of aggression than white people or members of other racial/ethnic groups, this difference was not statistically significant.[103,104]

In summary, some of the health consequences of sprawl appear disproportionately to affect vulnerable subpopulations, while others do not demonstrate this pattern. In many cases we do not have sufficient data to reach firm conclusions. Given the significance of the health outcomes involved, the moral imperative of eliminating racial and ethnic health disparities, and the steady increase in sprawl, these associations deserve continued public health attention.

Solutions

As discussed above, further research is needed to clarify the complex relationships among land use, transportation, and health. What approaches to urban planning, design, and construction are most likely to reduce air pollution, reduce urban heat, encourage physical activity, reduce automobile-related morbidity and mortality, and promote mental health and a sense of community? Although this article has focused on the health consequences of sprawl, other forms of built environment—dense cities, remote rural areas, and small towns— all have advantages and disadvantages that need to be assessed. It is likely that many different kinds of built environments can promote health, and that optimal approaches will borrow elements of cities, suburbs, and small towns.

Some interventions may be relatively simple, such as planting more trees or providing more sidewalks. Others are more complex and expensive to implement, such as mass transit and mixed-use zoning. For each of these, standard health research methods—ranging from clinical trials to observational epidemiology—may offer insights. This research will require innovative partnerships with other professionals, such as urban planners, architects, and real estate developers.

It is especially important for health researchers to recognize and study "natural experiments." Patterns of urban land use are changing, with migration back into inner cities, urban growth boundaries that restrict development to certain areas, development of mixed-use projects, innovations in mass transportation, green space programs, and related initiatives. Such efforts offer opportunities for health researchers who can examine their effects on relevant health endpoints.

As we recognize and understand the health costs of urban sprawl, we can begin to design solutions. Many potential solutions are found in an urban planning approach that has come to be known as "smart growth," characterized by higher density; more contiguous development; preserved green spaces; mixed land uses with walkable neighborhoods; limited road construction balanced by transportation alternatives; architectural heterogeneity; economic and racial/ ethnic heterogeneity; a balance of development and capital investment between central city and periphery; and effective, coordinated regional planning.[116,175–178] Importantly, many of the health-related benefits that could flow from this approach—less air pollution, more physical activity, lower temperatures, fewer motor vehicle crashes—would also yield collateral benefits, such as a cleaner environment and more livable neighborhoods. If the health consequences of sprawl represent a "syndemic"[179]—a combination of synergistic epidemics that contributes to the population burden of disease—then solutions may also operate synergistically, ameliorating several health problems.

Health professionals can play an important role in designing and implementing transportation and land use decisions. Similarly, those who have traditionally managed these issues—urban planners, architects, engineers, developers, and others—should recognize the important health implications of their decisions and seek collaboration with health professionals.

Conclusions

Urban sprawl is a longstanding phenomenon. It began with the expansion of cities into rural areas and accelerated greatly during the last half of the 20th century. As the 21st century begins, approximately half of Americans live in suburbs,[2] and the features of sprawl—low-density land use, heavy reliance on automobiles for transportation, segregation of land uses, and loss of opportunity for some groups, especially those in inner cities—are widespread and familiar.

This article has discussed the relationship between sprawl and health based on eight considerations: air pollution, heat, physical activity patterns, motor vehicle crashes, pedestrian injuries and fatalities, water quality and quantity, mental health, and social capital. The data show both health benefits and health costs. As is true for most public health hazards, the adverse impacts of sprawl do not fall equally across the population, and those who are most affected deserve special attention.

As we address sprawl on a variety of levels, from personal transportation decisions to local zoning ordinances, from regional mass transit and land use decisions to federal regulations, it is essential to incorporate health considerations into policy making. Because the health effects of sprawl are unevenly distributed across the population, it is equally essential to incorporate considerations of social justice and equity.

Preparation of an earlier version of this paper was partially supported by the Atlanta Transportation Equity Project (ATEP) at Clark Atlanta University, under a grant from the Turner Foundation. The author thanks Robert Bullard, PhD, Richard Jackson, MD, MPH, and Larry Frank, PhD, for invaluable comments.

References

1. Jackson KT. *Crabgrass frontier: the suburbanization of the United States.* New York: Oxford University Press; 1985.
2. Census Bureau (US), Population Division, Population Estimates Program. *Population estimates of metropolitan areas, metropolitan areas inside central cities, metropolitan areas outside central cities, and nonmetropolitan areas by state for July 1, 1999 and April 1, 1990 population estimates base* [cited 2002 Jul 30]. Available from: URL: http://www.census.gov/population/estimates/metro-city/ma99-06.txt

3. Garreau J. *Edge city: life on the new frontier.* New York: Doubleday; 1991.
4. Cervero R. *America's suburban centers: the land use-transportation link.* Boston: Unwin Hyman; 1989.
5. Fishman R. *Bourgeois utopias: the rise and fall of suburbia.* New York: Basic Books; 1987.
6. Bullard RD, Johnson GS, Torres AO. *Sprawl city: race, politics and planning in Atlanta.* Washington (DC): Island Press; 2000.
7. Gillham O. *The limitless city: a primer on the urban sprawl debate.* Washington (DC): Island Press; 2002.
8. British Medical Association. *Road transport and health.* London: BMA; 1997.
9. Dora C, Phillips M. *Transport, environment and health.* WHO Regional Publications, European Series, No. 89. Copenhagen: World Health Organization, Regional Office for Europe; 2000.
10. Rosen G. *A history of public health.* Expanded ed. Baltimore: Johns Hopkins University Press; 1993.
11. Duffy J. *The sanitarians: a history of American public health.* Urbana: University of Illinois Press; 1990.
12. Melosi MV. *Sanitary city: urban infrastructure in America from colonial times to the present.* Baltimore: Johns Hopkins University Press; 2000.
13. Frank LD, Pivo G. Impacts of mixed use and density on utilization of three modes of travel: single-occupant vehicle, transit, and walking. *Transportation Res Rec* 1995; 1466:44–52.
14. Kenworthy JR, Laube FB. *An international sourcebook of automobile dependence in cities, 1960–1990.* Boulder: University Press of Colorado; 1999.
15. Benfield FK, Raimi MD, Chen DDT. *Once there were greenfields: how urban sprawl is undermining America's environment, economy and social fabric.* Washington (DC): Natural Resources Defense Council and Surface Transportation Policy Project; 1999.
16. Environmental Protection Agency (US). *Our built and natural environments: a technical review of the interactions between land use, transportation, and environmental quality.* Washington (DC): EPA; 2001. Pub. No.: EPA 231-R-01-002.
17. Texas Transportation Institute. *2002 annual urban mobility study.* Urban mobility data [cited 2002 Aug 11]. Available from: URL: http://mobility.tamu.edu/ums/study/mobility_data/
18. Holtzclaw J, Clear R, Dittmar H, Goldstein D, Haas P. Location efficiency: neighborhood and socio-economic characteristics determine auto ownership and use-studies in Chicago, Los Angeles and San Francisco. *Transportation Plan Technol* 2002; 25(1):1–27.
19. Environmental Protection Agency (US). *Air quality criteria for O^3 and other photochemical oxidants*: EPA/600/P-93-004aF through EPA/600/P-93-004cF. Washington (DC): EPA; 1996 Jul.
20. Kennedy D, Bates RR, editors. *Air pollution, the automobile, and public health.* Washington (DC): National Academy Press; 1989.

21. Easas S, Samdahl D, editors. *Transportation, land use, and air quality: making the connection.* Reston (VA): American Society of Civil Engineers; 1998.
22. Environmental Protection Agency (US). *National Emission Inventory. Air pollutant emission trends.* Current emissions trend summaries [cited 2002 Jul 30]. Available from: URL: http://www.epa.gov/ttn/chief/trends/index.html
23. Environmental Protection Agency (US), Office of Air Quality Planning and Standards. *AIRData: access to air pollution data.* NET tier report, 1999 [cited 2002 Aug 11]. Available from: URL: http://www.epa.gov/air/data/index.html
24. Committee of the Environmental and Occupational Health Assembly, American Thoracic Society. Health effects of outdoor air pollution. *Am J Respir Crit Care Med* 1996; 153:3–50,477–98.
25. Goldsmith CA, Kobzik L. Particulate air pollution and asthma: a review of epidemiological and biological studies. *Rev Environ Health* 1999; 14:121–34.
26. Dockery DW, Pope CA III, Xu X, Spengler JD, Ware JH, Fay ME, et al. An association between air pollution and mortality in six U.S. cities. *N Engl J Med* 1993; 329:1753–9.
27. Pope CA III, Thun MJ, Namboodiri MM, Dockery DW, Evans JS, Speizer FE, Heath CW Jr. Particulate air pollution as a predictor of mortality in a prospective study of U.S. adults. *Am J Respir Crit Care Med* 1995; 151:669–74.
28. Environmental Protection Agency (US). *Inventory of U.S. greenhouse gas emissions and sinks: 1990-1999.* Washington (DC): EPA; 2001 Apr. Pub. No.: USEPA 236-R-01-001.
29. National Assessment Synthesis Team. *Climate change impacts on the United States: the potential consequences of climate variability and change.* New York: Cambridge University Press; 2000.
30. Patz JA, Engelberg D, Last J. The effects of changing weather on public health. *Annu Rev Public Health* 2000; 21:271–307.
31. Epstein PR. Is global warming harmful to health? *Sci Am* 2000; 283:50–7.
32. Patz JA, McGeehin MA, Bernard SM, Ebi KL, Epstein PR, Grambsch A, et al. The potential health impacts of climate variability and change for the United States: executive summary of the report of the health sector of the U.S. National Assessment. *Environ Health Perspect* 2000; 108:367–76.
33. National Highway Traffic Safety Administration (US), National Center for Statistics and Analysis. *Traffic safety facts 2000: a compilation of motor vehicle crash data from the Fatality Analysis Reporting System and the General Estimates System.* Washington (DC): NHTSA; 2001 Dec. Pub. No.: DOT HS 809 337.
34. Motor-vehicle safety: a 20th century public health achievement. *MMWR Morb Mortal Wkly Rep* 1999; 48:369–74.
35. Lourens PF, Vissers JA, Jessurum M. Annual mileage, driving violations, and accident involvement in relation to drivers' sex, age, and level of education. *Accid Anal Prev* 1999; 31:593–7.

36. Ossenbruggen PJ, Pendharkar J, Ivan J. Roadway safety in rural and small urbanized areas. *Accid Anal Prev* 2001; 33:485–98.
37. Peterson TD, Jolly BT, Runge JW, Hunt RC. Motor vehicle safety: current concepts and challenges for emergency physicians. *Ann Emerg Med* 1999; 34:384–93.
38. Mall accused of racism in a wrongful death trial in Buffalo. *New York Times* 1999 Nov 15; Sect. B:4.
39. Cohen BA, Wiles R, Campbell C, Chen D, Kruse J, Corless J. *Mean streets: pedestrian safety and reform of the nation's transportation law.* Washington: Surface Transportation Policy Project and Environmental Working Group; 1997. Also available from: URL: http://www.ewg.org/pub/home/reports/meanstreets/mean.html [cited 2002 Jul 30].
40. McCann B, DeLille B. *Mean streets 2000: pedestrian safety, health and federal transportation spending.* Washington: Surface Transportation Policy Project; 2000.
41. Hanzlick R, McGowan D, Havlak J, Bishop M, Bennett H, Rawlins R, et al. Pedestrian fatalities—Cobb, DeKalb, Fulton, and Gwinnett Counties, Georgia, 1994–98. *MMWR Morb Mortal Wkly Rep* 1999; 8:601–5.
42. Pucher J. Bicycling boom in Germany: a revival engineered by public policy. *Transportation Q* 1997; 1:31–46.
43. Koplan JP, Dietz WH. Caloric imbalance and public health policy. *JAMA* 1999; 82:1579–81.
44. Newman PWG, Kenworthy J. Transport and urban form in thirty-two of the world's principal cities. *Transport Rev* 1991; 1:249–72.
45. Cervero R, Gorham R. Commuting in transit versus automobile neighborhoods. *J Am Planning Assoc* 1995; 1:210–25.
46. Cervero R, Kockelman K. Travel demand and the three Ds: density, diversity, and design. *Transportation Res Part D* 1997; 2:199–219.
47. Frank LD. Land use and transportation interactions: implications on public health and quality of life. *J Planning Educ Res* 2000; 0:6–22.
48. Berrigan D, Troiano RP. The association between urban form and physical activity in U.S. adults. *Am J Prev Med* 2002; 23(2 Suppl 1):74–9.
49. Department of Health and Human Services (US). *Physical activity and health: a report of the Surgeon General.* Atlanta: Centers for Disease Control and Prevention; 1996.
50. National Institutes of Health Consensus Development Panel on Physical Activity and Cardiovascular Health. NIH Consensus Conference: physical activity and cardiovascular health. *JAMA* 1996; 276:241–6.
51. Wannamethee SG, Shaper AG, Walker M, Ebrahim S. Lifestyle and 15-year survival free of heart attack, stroke, and diabetes in middle-aged British men. *Arch Intern Med* 1998; 158:2433–40.
52. Wannamethee SG, Shaper AG. Physical activity and the prevention of stroke. *J Cardiovasc Risk* 1999; 6:213–16.

53. Pate RR, Pratt M, Blair SN, Haskell WL, Macera CA, Bouchard C, et al. Physical activity and public health: a recommendation from the Centers for Disease Control and Prevention and the American College of Sports Medicine. *JAMA* 1995; 273:402–7.

54. Lee IM, Paffenbarger RS Jr. Associations of light, moderate, and vigorous intensity physical activity with longevity: the Harvard Alumni Health Study. *Am J Epidemiol* 2000; 151:293–9.

55. Wannamethee SG, Shaper AG, Walker M. Changes in physical activity, mortality and incidence of coronary heart disease in older men. *Lancet* 1998; 351:1603–8.

56. Wei M, Kampert JB, Barlow CE, Nichaman MZ, Gibbons LW, Paffenbarger RS, et al. Relationship between low cardiorespiratory fitness and mortality in normal-weight, overweight, and obese men. *JAMA* 1999; 282:1547–53.

57. Sesso HD, Paffenbarger RS, Ha T, Lee IM. Physical activity and cardiovascular disease risk in middle-aged and older women. *Am J Epidemiol* 1999; 150:408–16.

58. Blair SN, Kampert JB, Kohl HW III, Barlow CE, Macera CA, Paffenbarger RS Jr, Gibbons LW. Influences of cardiorespiratory fitness and other precursors on cardiovascular disease and all-cause mortality in men and women. *JAMA* 1996; 276:205–10.

59. Kohl HW III, Gordon NF, Villegas JA, Blair SN. Cardiorespiratory fitness, glycemic status, and mortality risk in men. *Diabetes Care* 1992; 15: 184–92.

60. Kampert JB, Blair SN, Barlow CE, Kohl HW III. Physical activity, physical fitness, and all-cause and cancer mortality: a prospective study of men and women. *Ann Epidemiol* 1996; 6:452–7.

61. Lee IM, Sesso HD, Paffenbarger RS Jr. Physical activity and risk of lung cancer. *Int J Epidemiol* 1999; 28:620–5.

62. Slattery ML, Edwards SL, Boucher KM, Anderson K, Caan BJ. Lifestyle and colon cancer: an assessment of factors associated with risk. *Am J Epidemiol* 1999; 150:869–77.

63. Oliveria SA, Christos PJ. The epidemiology of physical activity and cancer. *Ann N Y Acad Sci* 1997; 833:79–90.

64. Kuczmarski RJ, Flegal KM, Campbell SM, Johnson CL. Increasing prevalence of overweight among US adults: the National Health and Nutrition Examination Surveys, 1960 to 1991. *JAMA* 1994; 272:205–11.

65. Flegal KM, Carroll MD, Kuczmarksi RJ, Johnson CL. Overweight and obesity in the United States: prevalence and trends, 1960-1994. *Int J Obes Related Metab Disord* 1998; 22:39–47.

66. Mokdad AH, Serdula MK, Dietz WH, Bowman BA, Marks JM, Koplan JP. The spread of the obesity epidemic in the United States, 1991–1998. *JAMA* 1999; 282:1519–22.

67. Mokdad AH, Bowman BA, Ford ES, Vinicor F, Marks JS, Koplan JP. The continuing epidemics of obesity and diabetes in the United States. *JAMA* 2001; 286:1195–1200.
68. Must A, Spadano J, Coakley EH, Field AE, Colditz G, Dietz WH. The disease burden associated with overweight and obesity. *JAMA* 1999; 282:1523–9.
69. Willett WC, Dietz WH, Colditz GA. Guidelines for healthy weight. *N Engl J Med* 1999; 341:427–34.
70. Sesso HD, Paffenbarger RS Jr, Lee IM. Physical activity and breast cancer risk in the College Alumni Health Study (United States). *Cancer Causes Control* 1998; 9:433–9.
71. Shaper AG, Wannamethee SG. Walker M. Body weight: implications for the prevention of coronary heart disease, stroke, and diabetes mellitus in a cohort study of middle aged men. *BMJ* 1997; 314:1311–17.
72. Mokdad AH, Ford ES, Bowman BA, Nelson DE, Engelgau MM, Vinicor F, et al. Diabetes trends in the U.S.: 1990–1998. *Diabetes Care* 2000; 23:1278–83.
73. Sallis JF, Bauman A, Pratt M. Physical activity interventions: environmental and policy interventions to promote physical activity. *Am J Prev Med* 1998; 15:379–97.
74. SMARTRAQ [cited 2002 Jul 30]. Available from: URL: http://www.smartraq .net/
75. McKeown T. *The role of medicine: dream, mirage, or nemesis?* Princeton: Princeton University Press; 1979.
76. Noble C. Lifeline for a landscape: Baltimore–Washington area. *Am Forests* 1999; 105:37–9.
77. Stephenson D. Comparison of the water balance for an undeveloped and a suburban catchment. *Hydrol Sci J* 1994; 39:295–307.
78. Buttle JM, Xu F. Snowmelt runoff in suburban environments (Ontario, Canada). *Nordic Hydrol* 1988; 19:19–40.
79. Zheng PQ, Baetz BW. GIS-based analysis of development options from a hydrology perspective. *J Urban Plann Dev* 1999; 25:164–80.
80. Environmental Protection Agency (US). Public drinking water systems programs. Public drinking water system: facts and figures [cited 2002 Aug 12]. Available from: URL: http://www.epa.gov/safewater/pws/factoids.html
81. Van Metre PC, Mahler BJ, Furlong ET. Urban sprawl leaves its PAH signature. *Environ Sci Technol* 2000; 34;4064–70.
82. Callender E, Rice KC. The urban environmental gradient: anthropogenic influences on the spatial and temporal distributions of lead and zinc in sediments. *Environ Sci Technol* 2000; 34:232–8.
83. Dierberg FE. Non-point source loadings of nutrients and dissolved organic carbon from an agricultural-suburban watershed in east central Florida. *Water Res* 1991; 25:363–74.

84. Oke TR. City size and the urban heat island. *Atmospheric Environ* 1973; 7:769–79.
85. Ackerman B. Temporal march of the Chicago heat island. *J Climatol Appl Meteorol* 1987; 26:427–30.
86. EPA-NASA Urban Heat Island Pilot Project. Heat island [cited 2002 Jul 30]. Available from: URL: http://wwwghcc.msfc.nasa.gov/urban/urban_heat_island.html
87. McGeehin MA, Mirabelli M. The potential impacts of climate variability and change on temperature-related morbidity and mortality in the United States. *Environ Health Perspect* 2001; 109(Suppl 2):185–9.
88. Gaffen DJ, Ross RJ. Increased summertime heat stress in the U.S. *Nature* 1998; 396:529–30.
89. Gallo KP, Owen TW, Easterling DR, Jamason PF. Temperature trends of the U.S. historical climatology network based on satellite-designated land use/ land cover. *J Climate* 1999; 12:1344–8.
90. Nadel E, Cullen MR. Thermal stressors. In: Rosenstock L, Cullen MR, editors. *Textbook of clinical occupational and environmental medicine.* Philadelphia: Saunders; 1994. p. 658–66.
91. Kilbourne EM, Choi K, Jones TS, Thacker SB. Risk factors for heatstroke: a case-control study. *JAMA* 1982; 247:3332–6.
92. Semenza JC, Rubin CH, Falter KH, Selanikio JD, Flanders WD, Howe HL, et al. Heat-related deaths during the July 1995 heat wave in Chicago. *N Engl J Med* 1996; 335:84–90.
93. Klinenberg E. *Heat wave: a social autopsy of disaster in Chicago.* Chicago: University of Chicago Press; 2002.
94. Frumkin H. Beyond toxicity: the greening of environmental health. *Am J Prev Med* 2001; 20:47–53.
95. Koslowsky M, Kluger AN, Reich M. *Commuting stress: causes, effects, and methods of coping.* New York: Plenum Press; 1995.
96. Rathbone DB, Huckabee JC. *Controlling road rage: a literature review and pilot study.* Washington (DC): AAA Foundation for Traffic Safety; 1999 Jun.
97. Vest J, Cohen W, Tharp M, Mulrine A, Lord M, Koerner BI, Murray B, Kaye SD. Road rage. Tailgating, giving the finger, outright violence— Americans grow more likely to take out their frustrations on other drivers. *U.S. News & World Rep* 1997 Jun 2.
98. Mizell L. Aggressive driving. In: *Aggressive driving: three studies.* Washington (DC): AAA Foundation for Traffic Safety; 1997 Mar.
99. Hartley L, el Hassani J. Stress, violations and accidents. *Appl Ergon* 1994;25: 221–30.
100. Novaco R. Aggression on roadways. In: Baenninger R, editor. *Targets of violence and aggression.* Amsterdam: Elsevier; 1991.
101. Harding RW, Morgan FH, Indermaur D, Ferrante AM, Blagg H. Road rage and the epidemiology of violence: something old, something new. *Stud Crime Crime Prev* 1998; 7:221–8.

102. Parker D, Lajunen T, Summala H. Anger and aggression among drivers in three European countries. *Accid Anal Prev* 2002; 34:229–35.
103. Snow RW. *1999 National Highway Safety Survey: monitoring Americans' attitudes, opinions, and behaviors.* January 2000. Mississippi State University, Social Science Research Center [cited 2002 Aug 11]. Available from: URL: http://www.ssrc.msstate.edu/publications/srrs2000-1.pdf
104. Snow RW. *2001 National Highway Safety Survey: monitoring Americans' attitudes, opinions, and behaviors.* January 2002. Mississippi State University, Social Science Research Center [cited 2002 Aug 11]. Available from: URL: http://www.ssrc.msstate.edu/publications/2001nationalhighwaysafety survey.pdf
105. National Highway Traffic Safety Administration (US). Volume II: Driver attitudes and behavior. In: *National survey of speeding and other unsafe driving actions.* Washington (DC): NHTSA; 1998. Pub. No.: DOT HS 808 749. Also available from: URL: http://www.nhtsa.dot.gov/people/injury/aggressive/unsafe/att-beh/cov-toc.html [cited 2002 Aug 11].
106. Curbow B, Griffin J. *Road rage or road benefit? Relationships with demographic, home and work variables.* Presented at the 1999 American Psychological Association/ National Institute of Occupational Safety and Health Conference; 1999 March 11–13; Baltimore.
107. Riesman D. *The lonely crowd: a study of the changing American character.* New Haven: Yale University Press; 1950.
108. Mills CW. *White collar: the American middle classes.* New York: Oxford University Press; 1951.
109. Keats J. *The crack in the picture window.* Boston: Houghton Mifflin; 1956.
110. Friedan B. *The feminine mystique.* New York: Norton; 1963.
111. Baumgartner MP. *The moral order of a suburb.* New York: Oxford University Press; 1989.
112. Baldassare M. *Trouble in paradise: the suburban transformation in America.* New York: Columbia University Press; 1986.
113. Gaines D. *Teenage wasteland: suburbia's dead-end kids.* Chicago: University of Chicago Press; 1998.
114. Suarez R. *The old neighborhood: what we lost in the great suburban migration, 1966–1999.* New York: Free Press; 1999.
115. Baxandall R, Ewen E. *Picture windows: how the suburbs happened.* New York: Basic Books; 2000.
116. Langdon P. *A better place to live: reshaping the American suburb.* Amherst: University of Massachusetts Press; 1994.
117. Etzioni A. *The spirit of community: the reinvention of American society.* New York: Crown Publishers; 1993.
118. Putnam R. *Bowling alone: the collapse and revival of American community.* New York: Simon & Schuster; 2000.
119. Mo R, Wilkie C. *Changing places: rebuilding community in the age of sprawl.* New York: Henry Holt and Co.; 1997.

120. Calthorpe P. *The next American metropolis: ecology, community, and the American dream.* Princeton: Princeton Architectural Press; 1993.

121. Haar CM. *Suburbs under siege: race, space, and audacious judges.* Princeton: Princeton University Press; 1998.

122. Greenberg D. *The politics of privilege: governing the affluent suburb.* Lanham (MD): University Press of America; 1993.

123. Thomas GS. *The United States of Suburbia: how the suburbs took control of America and what they plan to do with it.* Amherst (NY): Prometheus Books; 1998.

124. Teaford JC, Kilpinen JT. *Post-suburbia: government and politics in the edge cities.* Baltimore: Johns Hopkins University Press; 1997.

125. Oliver JE. *Democracy in suburbia.* Princeton: Princeton University Press; 2001.

126. House JS, Landis KR, Umberson D. Social relationships and health. *Science* 1988; 241:540–5.

127. Kennedy BP, Kawachi I, Prothrow-Stith D. Income distribution and mortality: cross sectional ecological study of the Robin Hood Index in the United States. *BMJ* 1996; 312:1004–7.

128. Lynch JW, Kaplan GA, Pamuk ER, Cohen RD, Heck KE, Balfour JL, et al. Income inequality and mortality in metropolitan areas of the United States. *Am J Public Health* 1998; 88:1074–80.

129. Kaplan GA, Pamuk E, Lynch JW, Cohen RD, Balfour JL. Income inequality and mortality in the United States. *BMJ* 1996; 312:999–1003.

130. Lynch JW, Smith GD, Kaplan GA, House JS. Income inequality and mortality: importance to health of individual income, psychosocial environment, or material conditions. *BMJ* 2000; 320;1200–4.

131. Stanistreet D, Scott-Samuel A, Bellis MA. Income inequality and mortality in England. *J Public Health Med* 1999; 21:205–7.

132. Wilkinson RG. *Unhealthy societies: the afflictions of inequality.* London: Routledge; 1996.

133. Kawachi I, Kennedy BP, Lochner K, Prothrow-Stith D. Social capital, income inequality, and mortality. *Am J Public Health* 1997; 87:1491–8.

134. Kawachi I, Kennedy BP. Income inequality and health: pathways and mechanisms. *Health Serv Res* 1999; 34(1 Pt 2):215–27.

135. United Church of Christ, Commission for Racial Justice. *Toxic wastes and race in the United States: a national report on the racial and socioeconomic characteristics of communities with hazardous waste sites.* New York: Public Data Access; 1987.

136. Bryant B, Mohai P, editors. *Race and the incidence of environmental hazards.* Boulder (CO): Westview Press; 1992.

137. Bullard R. *Dumping in Dixie: race, class, and environmental quality.* 3rd ed. Boulder (CO): Westview Press; 2000.

138. Wilson WJ. *The truly disadvantaged: the inner city, the underclass and public policy.* Chicago: Review Press; 1987.

139. Frey WH, Fielding EL. Changing urban populations: regional restructuring, racial polarization and poverty concentration. *Cityscape* 1995; 1(2): 1–66.

140. Wilson WJ. *When work disappears: the world of the new urban poor.* New York: Knopf; 1996.

141. Squires GD. *Capital and communities in black and white: the intersections of race, class, and uneven development.* Albany (NY): SUNY Press; 1994.

142. Jargowsky PA. *Poverty and place: ghettos, barrios, and the American city.* New York: Russell Sage Foundation; 1998.

143. Wilkinson RG, editor. *Class and health: research and longitudinal data.* London: Tavistock; 1986.

144. Adler NE, Marmot M, McEwen BS, Stewart J, editors. Socioeconomic status and health in industrial nations: social, psychological and biological pathways. *Ann N Y Acad Sci* 1999; 896:1–503.

145. Kaplan G, Haan M, Syme LH, Miszcynski M. Socioeconomic status and health. *Am J Prev Med* 1987; 3(Suppl):125–31.

146. Feinstein JS. The relationship between socioeconomic status and health: a review of the literature. *Milbank Q* 1993; 71:279–321.

147. Adler NE, Ostrove JM. Socioeconomic status and health: what we know and what we don't. *Ann N Y Acad Sci* 1999; 896:3–15.

148. Mohai P, Bryant B. Environmental racism: reviewing the evidence. In: Bryant B, Mohai P, editors. *Race and the incidence of environmental hazards.* Boulder (CO): Westview Press; 1992. p. 163–76.

149. Perlin SA, Sexton K, Wong DW. An examination of race and poverty for populations living near industrial sources of air pollution. *J Exposure Analysis Environ Epidemiol* 1999; 9:29–48.

150. Wernette DR, Nieves LA. Breathing polluted air: minorities are disproportionately exposed. *EPA Journal* 1992; 18:16–17.

151. Persky VW, Slezak J, Contreras A, Becker L, Hernandez E, Ramakrishnan V, et al. Relationships of race and socioeconomic status with prevalence, severity, and symptoms of asthma in Chicago school children. *Ann Allergy Asthma Immunol* 1998; 81:266–71.

152. National Heart, Lung, and Blood Institute Working Group. Respiratory diseases disproportionately affect minorities. *Chest* 1995; 108:1380–92.

153. Metzger R, Delgado JL, Herrell R. Environmental health and Hispanic children. *Environ Health Perspect* 1995; 103(Suppl 6):539–50.

154. Chabra A, Chavez GF, Adams EJ, Taylor D. Characteristics of children having multiple Medicaid-paid asthma hospitalizations. *Matern Child Health J* 1998; 2:223–9.

155. Litonjua AA, Carey VJ, Weiss ST, Gold DR. Race, socioeconomic factors, and area of residence are associated with asthma prevalence. *Pediatr Pulmonol* 1999; 28:394–401.

156. Carr W, Zeitel L, Weiss S. Variations in asthma hospitalizations and deaths in New York City. *Am J Public Health* 1992; 82:59–65.

157. Wing JS. Asthma in the inner city: a growing health concern in the United States. *J Asthma* 1993; 30:427–30.
158. Whitman S, Good G, Donoghue ER, Benbow N, Shou W, Mou S. Mortality in Chicago attributed to the July 1995 heat wave. *Am J Public Health* 1997; 87:1515–18.
159. Greenberg JH, Bromberg J, Reed CM, Gustafson TL, Beauchamp RA. The epidemiology of heat-related deaths, Texas—1950, 1970–79, and 1980. *Am J Public Health* 1983;73:805–7.
160. Applegate WB, Runyan JW Jr, Brasfield L, Williams ML, Konigsberg C, Fouche C. Analysis of the 1980 heat wave in Memphis. *J Am Geriatr Soc* 1981; 29:337–42.
161. Jones TS, Liang AP, Kilbourne EM, Griffin MR, Patriarca PA, Wassilak SG, et al. Morbidity and mortality associated with the July 1980 heat wave in St. Louis and Kansas City, Mo. *JAMA* 1982; 247:3327–31.
162. Martinez BF, Annest JL, Kilbourne EM, Kirk ML, Lui KJ, Smith SM. Geographic distribution of heat-related deaths among elderly persons: use of county-level dot maps for injury surveillance and epidemiologic research. *JAMA* 1989; 262:2246–50.
163. Bullard RD, Johnson GS, editors. *Just transportation: dismantling race and class barriers to mobility*. Gabriola Island (BC): New Society Publishers; 1997.
164. Cubbin C, LeClere F, Smith GS. Socioeconomic status and the occurrence of fatal and nonfatal injury in the United States. *Am J Public Health* 2000; 90:70–7.
165. Marosi R. Pedestrian deaths reveal O.C.'s car culture clash; safety: Latinos, 28% of Orange County's population, are victims in 40% of walking injuries, 43% of deaths. *Los Angeles Times* 1999 Nov 28:1.
166. Moreno S, Sipress A. Fatalities higher for Latino pedestrians; area's Hispanic immigrants apt to walk but unaccustomed to urban traffic. *Washington Post* 1999 Aug 27;Sect. P:A01.
167. Kumanyika S. Special issues regarding obesity in minority populations. *Ann Intern Med* 1993; 119:650–4.
168. Adams-Campbell LL, Rosenberg L, Washburn RA, Rao RS, Kim KS, Palmer J. Descriptive epidemiology of physical activity in African-American women. *Prev Med* 2000; 30:43–50.
169. Brownson RC, Eyler AA, King AC, Brown DR, Shyu YL, Sallis JF. Patterns and correlates of physical activity among US women 40 years and older. *Am J Public Health* 2000; 90:264–70.
170. Winkleby MA, Kraemer HC, Ahn DK, Varady AN. Ethnic and socioeconomic differences in cardiovascular disease risk factors. *JAMA* 1998; 280:356–62.
171. Johnson JL, Heineman EF, Heiss G, Hames CG, Tyroler HA. Cardiovascular disease risk factors and mortality among black women and white women aged 40–64 years in Evans County, Georgia. *Am J Epidemiol* 1986; 123:209–19.

172. Sprafka JM, Folsom AR, Burke GL, Edlavitch SA. Prevalence of cardio-vascular disease risk factors in blacks and whites: the Minnesota Heart Study. *Am J Public Health* 1988; 78:1546–9.

173. Shea S, Stein AD, Basch CE, Lantigua R, Maylahn C, Strogatz DS, Novick L. Independent associations of educational attainment and ethnicity with behavioral risk factors for cardiovascular disease. *Am J Epidemiol* 1991; 134:567–82.

174. Crespo CJ, Smit E, Andersen RE, Carter-Pokras O, Ainsworth BE. Race/ethnicity, social class and their relation to physical inactivity during leisure time: results from the Third National Health and Nutrition Examination Survey, 1988–1994. *Am J Prev Med* 2000; 18:46–53.

175. Calthorpe P, Fulton W. *The regional city: planning for the end of sprawl.* Washington (DC): Island Press; 2001.

176. Bollier D. *How smart growth can stop sprawl.* Washington (DC): Essential Books; 1998.

177. Newman P, Kenworthy J. *Sustainability and cities: overcoming automobile dependence.* Washington (DC): Island Press; 1999.

178. Congress for the New Urbanism. *Charter for the new urbanism.* New York: McGraw-Hill; 2000.

179. CDC Syndemics Prevention Network. *Spotlight on syndemics* [cited 2002 Jul 30]. Available from: URL: http://www.cdc.gov.ezproxy.bu.edu/syndemics/

Obesity, Physical Activity, and the Urban Environment: Public Health Research Needs

Russell P. Lopez and H. Patricia Hynes

Introduction

Persistent trends in overweight and obesity among adults and children in the United States have alarmed health care clinicians and public health practitioners. This heightened concern has yielded a rapid research effort focused strongly on the built environment, physical activity, and overweight. While much of this research is still in its infancy, certain disparities in obesity and overweight, physical activity, and research focus have emerged that are important to address.

This paper examines racial/ethnic disparities in obesity and physical activity. It then summarizes the current state of research on the built environment and health, which has been predominately suburban in focus. Next it explores the urban form—health relationship in the context of inner city environments. The paper then presents a paradox: research would predict that people of color and low income individuals would have lower obesity rates and higher physical activity rates because they live in neighborhoods that promote healthier life styles. But contrary to what theory would predict, these populations are less likely to be physically active and more likely to be obese. The paper explores the reasons for this paradox. It draws from and augments the framework of factors identified in studies of primarily suburban residential neighborhoods in order to pose a set of research questions concerning the nexus of built environment and public health in inner-city communities. We link conditions of the urban built environment to co-related social factors, including poverty, income inequality, racial segregation and economic isolation. These interlinked factors may necessitate research on more holistic and multi-sector public health policy responses and interventions in order to improve minority health impacted by the built environment of the inner city.

Disparities in Obesity and Overweight and Physical Activity

US surveys including the Behavioral Risk Factor Surveillance System (BRFSS) and the National Health and Nutrition Examination Survey (NHANES) reveal that inner-city residents are more overweight, less physically active, and less healthy overall than the general population. Moreover, they suffer higher rates of diseases associated with obesity, namely diabetes and cardiovascular disease.[1] Data from the National Health Interview Survey (1997–1998) found that men living in center cities were more likely to be obese (39.4%) than suburban men (35.5%). Similarly, 20.6% of center city dwelling women were obese vs. 19.1% of suburban dwelling women.[2] Urban–suburban differences in physical activity were found among all adults with the urban propensity for inactivity greatest among low income people.[3]

The initial flux of built environment and health research culminated in a series of articles in joint editions of the *American Journal of Public Health* and the *American Journal of Health Promotion* in 2003.[4] The research hypotheses examined the role of sprawl, dependence on the car, and the design and form of suburbs on physical activity and overweight. The resultant findings were largely suburban in focus. The role of urban environment factors in overweight, physical inactivity and poor health of urban and minority residents has been less studied.[6] Contextualizing research on overweight, physical activity and the urban built environment within the reality of political, social and demographic inequality of inner cities has yet to be done.

Built Environment and Health: What Have We Learned?

Studies on sprawl and public health have found that increased levels of sprawl are associated with increased obesity, decreased physical activity[7,8] and poorer health[9,10] including the risk of motor vehicle and pedestrian fatalities.[11] While studies on sprawl and obesity have tended to control for race, ethnicity and other individual factors, none has distinguished between effects of sprawl on inner city and suburban populations.

Evidence is mounting that the design and form of many, if not most, U.S. suburbs contribute to the growing prevalence of obesity and overweight among children and adults. Certain features of the built environment—such as the presence of sidewalks, streetlights, interconnectivity of streets, population density and use mix—appear to encourage physical activity and thus reduce the risk of obesity and related health problems. Other factors—such as cul de sacs, lack of parks, high speed traffic and automobile focused transport—may function to discourage activity and ultimately increase obesity risk.[12] Studies find that people who live close to parks are more likely to use them and to be physically active than those who live farther from them.[13] Neighborhoods with a mixture of land use types including commercial, industrial, residential and office, also appear to promote physical activity,[14] while neighborhoods consisting exclusively of housing seem to dampen physical activity.[15]

The built environment can affect social connectivity, motivating and stimulating interaction with others, and increasing people's trust in society and government. Alternatively, it can discourage connections with neighbors, reduce social capital, and foster a distrust of neighbors and government.[16]

An Urban–Suburban Paradox

Given a built environment in many US inner cities and urban neighborhoods that includes sidewalks and mixed land uses; that offers parks, playgrounds and public transportation; and that has a traditional gridded street pattern (small blocks with streets at right angles to each other) which fosters connectivity, we might expect that rates of physical activity and trends in obesity would be more favorable in inner city neighborhoods. But there appears instead a paradox whereby obesity, physical inactivity and associated diseases of diabetes and cardiovascular disease, are more prevalent among inner-city residents than among suburbanites. Some, if not much, of this discrepancy may be explained by other documented health risks such as the stress of poverty, racism, and violence; discrimination in health services; food insecurity; and so on. We propose that other factors of the urban built and physical environment may undermine the positive potential for being physically active in inner cities, even though urban form may, in principle, facilitate being active. We hypothesize that many factors of the environment in inner cities—including built, physical and social factors—may exert a net negative influence on the health of inner city residents and that it may be mediated in ways that are different or function differently from those in suburban neighborhoods. These factors and conditions include problem land use issues, such as waste sites; infrastructure maintenance and investment issues; and social realities, such as neighborhood crime, that can result in a neighborhood environment where outdoor exercise and recreation are risky or unappealing and are, thus, avoided (Table 8-1).

Research on the impediments to physical activity in inner cities is needed to determine what barriers urban neighborhoods share with suburban neighborhoods and what barriers are unique to inner cities. Better understanding of the potential interaction between social and built environment factors would allow for a more fine-grained examination of the role of the built environment on the health of inner city residents. Further, research is needed to determine if a different set of design and policy responses are called for in inner cities than those aimed at reducing the obstacles to physical activity in the suburban built environment.

The issues raised in this paper are not all inclusive; nor are they always exclusive to the inner-city. They are discussed here in order to stimulate increased debate and more targeted research that may ultimately assist inner-city populations.

Land Use Issues

The loss of commercial and industrial employers in cities has increased the physical distance between inner city residents and available jobs.[17] At one time, US metropolitan areas had strong downtown commercial districts surrounded by dense residential areas with industrial areas also close to worker housing. But

TABLE 8-1   A Taxonomy of Urban Environmental Issues

Type of Issues	Representative Risk Factors	Potential Pathways of Effect
Land use issues	Business and job loss	Lengthens commutes, reduces walking
	Proximity of toxic facilities	Pollution may discourage outdoor activities
	Lack of supermarkets	May be more difficult to access healthy diets
	Abandoned buildings	Reduces density, increases crime
Infrastructure, maintenance and service issues	Sidewalks and street trees	Lack of pedestrian amenities
	Lighting	Fear of crime keeps people indoors
	Transit projects	Lack of transit makes people more dependent on driving
Social environment issues	Poverty and income	Poor areas suffer from disinvestments
	Racial segregation	May promote "redlining," the denial of loans to certain communities
	Crime	Unsafe areas may result in less physical activity, lower overall health status

decades of de-industrialization and suburbanization have resulted in a large transfer of jobs away from inner city neighborhoods towards suburban employment centers.[18,19] The result is that inner city communities are no longer close to employment opportunities, a phenomenon that economists characterize as "spatial mismatch."[20] One consequence of this mismatch is that fewer inner city residents can walk or take local public transportation to work. They have long commutes, particularly the significant numbers that do not own cars, which ultimately could leave them little free time to be physically active or to socialize with their neighbors. To a great extent, this mismatch is not the result of zoning or government land use decisions that separate land uses in suburban areas. Rather it is the result of disinvestment and job loss in inner cities that has also contributed to the impoverishment of inner city governments and residents. Many of these economic changes have also resulted in a "loss of place" in that neighborhoods take on a tooth-gapped appearance with empty storefronts, abandoned buildings and vacant lots,[21] likely making them less attractive for walking or for children playing outside.

In suburbs, solutions to the problem of special mismatch might include zoning reform and design guideline changes to allow mixed use development and encourage the development of office and commercial properties close to residential areas.[22] Inner city remedies, on the other hand, may require a different set of policy solutions, such as renewed investment in inner city neighborhoods, greater training and educational opportunities to increase skill match with existing jobs, and aggressive redevelopment of brownfields (contaminated urban parcels) for commercial/industrial development. Case studies and evaluation research of inner city neighborhood and brownfield redevelopment would help answer the question of whether and how resident physical activity is impacted by economic and neighborhood revitalization, and would garner lessons from neighborhood development models that are conducive to walking and other forms of physical exercise.

Of the non-residential land uses remaining in inner cities, many may well discourage walking and physical activity. Numerous studies have documented that hazardous waste facilities and factories that are required to report their toxic releases to the federal government (i.e., larger facilities) are disproportionately located in poor neighborhoods and communities of color.[23] An early study in Houston showed that solid waste dumps were more likely to be found in Black neighborhoods.[24] Toxic facilities in Los Angeles are more likely to be sited in minority and working class communities than in more affluent, White neighborhoods of the city.[25] A recent study of hazardous and solid waste sites, power plants, and polluting industrial facilities in Massachusetts cities and towns, found that low income communities were cumulatively exposed to environmentally hazardous facilities and sites at four times the rate of high income communities. For high minority communities, the rate was twenty times that of low minority communities.[26] Comparative studies of inner-city neighborhoods by health factors, such as exercise and prevalence of overweight, and by environmental factors, such as density and type, size, and proximity of polluting facility, would help identify the impact of local polluting facilities on residents' physical activity and overweight.

Coinciding with the health risk of physical inactivity in inner cities is the reality of food insecurity. Many older inner-city neighborhoods no longer have a local supply of fresh, healthful food and they often lack transportation access to more remote supermarkets.[27] Supermarkets are less likely to locate in inner cities and small stores are more likely to sell low quality, non-fresh food and have higher prices, a situation that would contribute to poorer nutrition and lower health status.[28] The separation of residential areas from commercial services and goods, such as large supermarkets in inner cities, is not the result of intentional zoning policy as in suburbs; rather it is a consequence of social and economic trends, including business flight, that have impoverished older urban neighborhoods. Studies of diet and nutrition among inner city residents need to include research on the prevalence of, proximity to, and transportation access to large supermarkets, as well as comparisons of price and food quality between urban and suburban food markets.

Decades of racial change, segregation, economic disinvestment and discriminatory lending and insurance practices have resulted in a severe reduction of the housing stock in many urban communities, often accompanied by new construction in distant areas.[29] The social effect of abandonment has been termed "the broken window syndrome": Neighborhoods with broken windows and dilapidated housing encourage crime, pose safety hazards, isolate residents and reduce trust in the ability of the neighborhood to meet its challenges.[30] One study has linked these factors of neighborhood quality to the risk of acquiring sexually transmitted diseases.[31] Another consequence of this constellation of risks from a moldering environment would likely be reduced walking, physical activity and recreation in public.

Comparative studies of building conditions, rates of children's play out-of-doors and resident walking could reveal a relationship between residential conditions and physical activity. Poor built environment conditions beg the research question: What is the relationship between building condition, building tenancy, building abandonment and rates of physical activity and obesity?

Even when abandoned buildings are demolished, the resulting vacant land poses problems to the environment.[32] If untended, these lots usually become overgrown with weeds and covered with litter, an invitation for illegal dumping (including demolition and construction debris, hazardous chemicals and medical wastes), and foster criminal activity. Does vacancy contribute to less walking, playing, and other physical activity in the affected neighborhood? This question, like its companion regarding abandoned housing, has yet to be examined.

If low density is a factor implicated in physical inactivity as some have posited it is important for policy implications to distinguish between lower density neighborhoods caused by abandonment and those resulting from zoning and land use decisions. While the latter is the intentional result of government decision-making, the former is a consequence of a more complex mixture of forces that include public and private sector lending and insurance practices as well as social relations among races in the United States. Solutions, which have centered around increased investment, elimination of discriminatory lending practices and the creation of new, beneficial land uses in inner city communities, such as side lot disposition programs, community gardens, and housing rehabilitation,[33] ought to be evaluated for their potential impact on multiple forms of physical activity, such as more time spent outdoors in walking, gardening, biking, and so on.

Infrastructure, Maintenance, and Service Issues

The social context of the inner city environment, specifically inequity, can affect the quality of infrastructure and how new improvements are planned and implemented[34]. Standardized tests over time for recreation, is resulting in less gym and recess in the school day. Cyclic decay in urban parks and playgrounds has rendered some of them unuseable and dangerous havens for criminal activity. The net effect is to reduce the utility of local recreational facilities for many inner city residents and reduce opportunities for social interaction. These factors will only be addressed by a change in government priority and investment and by social mobilizing to preserve, maintain and enhance physical activity opportunities. Evaluation research is needed on the community health benefits of restoring degraded parks and playgrounds with regular recreational opportunities for children and adults in order to support the lobby for more public investment in parks and playgrounds.

The authors are familiar with programs that have restored inner city schoolyard environments. The Boston Schoolyard Initiative (BSI) is a creative example of private–public partnership that has restored 60 Boston public school playgrounds for recreation and play using community collaborative design.[35] While none of the renovated schoolyards has been evaluated for change in physical activity by amount or kind, the BSI does intend to measure activity change in students using a set of validated questionnaires and observational tools.

A Harlem Hospital physician who documented the increase in child injury on debilitated school and parks department playgrounds and a gardener for the New York City Department of Parks and Recreation developed a collaborative venture called The Greening of Harlem. They renovated numerous school playgrounds, turning them from cracked and jagged concrete and blacktop surfaces with broken metal play equipment into safe and creative performance and play spaces with vegetable and flower gardens.[36] Evaluation of inner-city interventions is often sacrificed because scarce resources are spent on projects and programs that are desperately needed and inherently challenging to accomplish.

A related series of observational studies of the built and natural environment in Chicago public housing, one of the starkest of urban built environments, found that greater numbers of people gathered in outdoor spaces with trees than in those without trees,[37] the distance to each being equal. A companion study of Chicago public housing play space found that children in highly vegetated spaces played more (by a factor of two) than children in non-vegetated areas, and that they played more creatively and interacted more with adults.[38] These studies raise the question of the role and value of trees, vegetation and nearby nature in inner cities in promoting physical activity and play. Is their presence sufficient? Are factors such as their condition and maintenance and their proportion to the recreational space important in their effect of promoting play and activity?

Over decades, unimproved sidewalks decay as utility crews dig up concrete, tree roots push up paved areas, and weather erodes surfaces. Many cities lack the resources to repave or replace sidewalks as frequently as needed; and many urban neighborhoods lack the political clout to have their sidewalks prioritized for repair or reconstruction. As a result, urban neighborhoods frequently have broken or impassable pedestrian sidewalks. While sharply contrasting with the problem of no sidewalks in many suburban communities, broken sidewalks in inner cities likely have a similar outcome, less leisure walking.[39] Sidewalk replacement and repair in city neighborhoods provides an opportunity to study the question of whether passable sidewalks result in more local walking.

Street trees, along with other pedestrian amenities, have been found to be a promoting factor in physical activity.[40] In many urban areas, street canopies are disappearing as disease, age, and lack of maintenance of new trees, slowly reduce the number of trees. When cities suffer fiscal constraints, the budgets of parks and recreation departments are generally the first to be cut; and replacement of urban street becomes a low priority. Further, evidence suggests that trees are more likely to be replaced in higher income communities than in neighborhoods with more poor households and people of color.[41]

Solutions to the decay of street and sidewalk infrastructure depend on improving the fiscal environment of inner cities.[42] Unless center cities have access to adequate capital and operating funds, the physical environment will continue to decay. This decline in infrastructure is more likely to be concentrated in poor and minority neighborhoods and has been documented for a wide range of services including fire stations and hospitals.[43,44]

Traffic lights can both improve and inhibit pedestrian activity. When they are well timed and placed to reduce traffic flows and improve pedestrian safety, they may encourage physical activity and social interaction. But when they are timed to improve traffic speeds or are missing, they can discourage pedestrian activity.[45] Bus shelters, public transportation and "traffic calming" can be a net boon to pedestrian activity. Conversely, intersections engineered for cars, increased speeds in residential and commercial areas, and even large parking lots can result in local people spending less time outdoors and doing less physical activity.[46] Older cities are increasingly being redeveloped with the same engineering standards of newer, automobile-focused suburbs rather than in keeping with older, pedestrian-oriented communities. The new roads and parking facilities do not promote physical activity in the way older streets once did.[47] Policy research on redevelopment in inner cities could examine and reconcile the transportation design in inner city redevelopment with emerging pedestrian-friendly design guidelines for suburban development.

Transportation improvements, like other types of infrastructure investments, take place in the context of political and social decision making. To the extent that poor inner city neighborhoods lack the ability to make their transportation needs a political priority, they can suffer from a decline in services or a lack of access to new or existing improvements. In Los Angeles, the Metropolitan Transit Authority shifted investments to commuter rail and large subway lines that served more affluent communities to the detriment of the buses that had traditionally provided services to lower income neighborhoods.[48] In Boston, new suburban rail lines that will serve up to 5000 passengers per day have received more funding than new public transport for inner city communities designed to serve 50,000, even when investments were promised and owed to inner city residents as replacement for the 20 year loss of a preexisting subway.[49] Increasing transportation options for inner city residents, who are often the most transit dependent population and less likely than suburbanites to own cars, needs to be made at least as high a priority as suburban transportation investment. Research on the impacts of local and regional transportation investments on physical activity and health will add evidence to support more equitable transportation policy.

Federal highway construction that mushroomed together with the suburban housing boom after World War II bifurcated many older communities and devastated others. In numerous metropolitan areas, neighborhoods with large numbers of minorities, poor and working class were specifically targeted for new highways that connected expanding suburbs with existing downtowns. Neighborhood businesses and affordable housing were razed by state land taking under the power of eminent domain; and the new highways functioned as physical barriers within neighborhoods for those without a car. Miami's Overtown neighborhood was devastated—churches demolished, commercial districts destroyed and residential areas literally severed from each other—by the construction of Interstate 95.[50] Similarly, New Orleans's Black community suffered from highway construction with neighborhood institutions destroyed, affordable housing lost and residents displaced.[51] Wherever cities make major transportation infrastructure changes, studies of local populations are vital to document the impact on their physical mobility and activity, their stress level and quality of life.

Social Environment Issues

Both low income and increased income inequality have been found to be associated with a decrease in physical activity and an increased likelihood of poor health.[52,53] Living in economic isolation, that is a neighborhood with a high percentage of low income people, has also been found to be a risk factor for poor health.[54] People with low incomes likely have less time to be physically active because they are working multiple jobs, and because they are more likely to be concentrated in neighborhoods without the amenities (or with deteriorated amenities) found in more affluent communities.[55] Likewise, income inequality, which has been increasing since the early 1970s,[56] may result in poor communities having fewer recreational resources and ones of lower quality than would be the case where income inequality is less extreme. Assessing and addressing the burdens of inequality, which fall most heavily on the poor and near poor, can only help to improve the health of inner city residents. Results can help identify underserved neighborhoods and prioritizing them for physical activity intervention programs.

Residential racial segregation, the physical separation of people based on skin color or ethnic origin, has declined slightly from its peak in the 1950s but continues to be a substantial problem in many metropolitan areas.[57] Interestingly, the greater the Black–White segregation, the more likely all residents, both Black and White, are to be physically inactive or otherwise unhealthy.[58] Segregation has also been found to influence the impact of infectious diseases, reducing overall health status and further decreasing physical activity levels.[59] Segregation has also been linked to increased air pollution, potentially increasing risk to cardiovascular and respiratory health.[60] Higher levels of segregation are linked with increased exposure to violence, less time outdoors and an overall increase in the allostatic load, that is the sum of ill health, as a result of increased stress.[61] Increased stress, when sustained over time, is known to have immune related consequences and to increase the risk of cardiovascular disease and other health problems.[62] Additional research is needed regarding the impact of segregation on rates of physical activity, obesity and access to recreational resources and nutritious food.

Crime and the fear of crime are a reality in many inner city communities. Crime erodes community trust, marginalizes residents, and further stresses people and the environment.[63] Fear of crime is likely to keep people indoors, particularly the old and the young, and discourage physical activity. Results from a recent asthma research project in one of Boston's most distressed public housing developments, which had also experienced a series of murders in or near the development, revealed that 63% of those interviewed were afraid of violence in the neighborhood and 60% did not allow their children to play outside because of neighborhood violence. This was a significantly higher response when compared with residents of housing developments in other neighborhoods, which had not experienced the wave of violent crime.[64]

Increasing physical activity among inner city people may hinge significantly on increasing people's sense of neighborhood security. Many research questions arise here: Does change in local crime rates affect change in rates of local physical activity? Do positive neighborhood activities, such as community gardens, park cleaning, and crime watch, result in changed rates of crime, leisure walking, socializing, playing outdoors, and more walking trips to local destination points such as library, stores, and so on?

Discussion

Given the overall burden of poverty, discrimination, and prevalence of crime in many older inner-city neighborhoods, it is no surprise that health status is lower in these communities. Built environment also may play a role in poor health, by discouraging physical activity, recreation, and social interaction and by limiting access to nutritious food. Problems in the built environment may interact with and compound other social and health issues and thus magnify the community health effects.[65] The challenge is to identify the nature and extent of the activity-

and health-related built environment factors in inner-city neighborhoods—
many of which have been studied in suburbs—and also to create new measures
of the built environment that incorporate the unique social and physical characteristics of urban inner city environments.[66]

Improving the built environment in inner cities was crucial before the recent public health awareness of the correlation between built environment and
obesity with its health-related diseases. However, policy initiatives that reduce
barriers to physical activity in middle class and affluent suburbs do not assuredly
translate to improvements in inner city health.[67] Some policies, such as better
designs that encourage mixed use development and traffic calming,[68] may be applicable in both suburb and city, especially in the context of urban redevelopment. In fact, these design policies prevailed in original inner city master plans.
However, other needed interventions are unique to urban cores. These include:
investment in inner city development that also builds social capital, prioritizing
brownfield redevelopment, renewing efforts to reduce racial segregation and
economic isolation, and addressing the trend in income inequality in cities.[69]
Government policies on urban renewal and redevelopment have had the historical effect of displacing and isolating people of color and reducing their ability
to move to healthier communities, a consequence of which is severe health disparities between people of color and others.[70,71]

Studies of the impact of sprawl on inner cities need to be designed to identify specific effects on urban form and resident physical activity, as has been
done for metropolitan areas and suburbs.[72,73] In addition, community-based initiatives that can incorporate the energy and experience of inner city residents,
and the special knowledge of community-based institutions are needed to assure
that interventions and policy initiatives are effective in identifying solutions to
the epidemic of obesity and related chronic disease in inner cities.[74,75]

Effective research on urban areas must involve the people and communities
being studied. Community-based Participatory Research (CBPR) provides a
framework for researchers interested in the urban built environment. Briefly,
the CBPR principles that should guide research include: neighborhoods should
have input into the types of issues being studied as well as study design; researchers should take care to communicate the results of these studies back to
the neighborhoods where the research took place; and studied communities
should benefit from research.[76] Using the expertise of residents can energize research and neighborhood change. Research on inner city communities has
sometimes been seen as problematic in these neighborhoods with problems
ranging from inappropriate burdens on time placed on already overburdened
individuals and institutions to research that bypasses local residents all together.
Consultation with local residents can help researchers better target their research and help find the right balance between involvement and resource use.

Issues of scale and neighborhood definition complicate efforts to research
and intervene on the urban environment. Neighborhood definitions can be
fluid, and even a given individual's concept of neighborhood can vary over time,

place, or issue. Furthermore, neighborhoods do not exist in isolation but are subunits of larger city, county, metropolitan, state, national, or even transnational entities. Given the enormous potential impact of these other scales, it is important to study the effects of neighborhood in context. In practice, this may necessitate using multilevel modeling or other techniques to fully capture local and regional effects. In any case, researchers should be explicit in their definitions of neighborhood and clearly state the type of urban/suburban environment that is being studied.

It is also important to remember that the current conditions in a neighborhood reflect past policies, conditions, and events. Individuals and institutions sometimes carry a memory of the past and sometimes neighborhoods undergoing demographic change may no longer carry an understanding of history. As part of the process of studying or improving communities, researchers can help neighborhoods learn the historical precedents of contemporary environments as well as utilize the knowledge of current residents, particularly elders, to develop a more thorough understanding of a neighborhood's history. Gathering oral histories, searches of archival databases (including public records), focus groups, or detailed questionnaires targeting key individuals can assist in these efforts.

Studies of built environment—health interactions represent a reconnection of the intersection of public health and urban planning. But these are not the only disciplines that should be included in this line of research. To fully utilize the potential of the built environment to better the health of urban communities, it will be necessary to consult economists, sociologists, anthropologists, education specialists, among others. Landscape architects, urban historians, traffic engineers, and botanists all should be involved in the effort to study and improve urban environments. Multidisciplinary teams and transdisciplinary research are best for addressing the multi-dimensional issues confronting our urban areas.

Conclusion

Recent research on the health impacts of the built environment has led to a better understanding of how contemporary land use planning may influence physical activity, obesity and related chronic diseases. Much of the focus of this research has been on suburban development design and form. Comparable research on the relationship of the built environment and health is needed for urban, especially inner city, neighborhoods. The research should be designed to include the web of social and political factors that contribute to the conditions of the built environment of inner cities, if the consequent solutions and policy initiatives to increase physical activity and promote health are to succeed.

Acknowledgments

This publication was made possible in part by grant number 3 R25 ES012084-03S1 from the National Institute of Environmental Health Sciences (NIEHS),

NIH. Its contents are solely the responsibility of the authors and do not necessarily represent the official views of the NIEHS, NIH.

References

1. Keberhadt M, Pamuk E. The importance of place of residence: Examining health in rural and nonrural areas. *Am J Public Health.* 2004; 94(10): 1682–1686.
2. Schoenborn C, Adams P, Barnes P. *Body weight status of adults: United States, 1997–98.* Hyattsville MD: National Center for Health Statistics; 2002.
3. Parks S, Housemann R, Brownson R. Differential correlates of physical activity in urban and rural adults of various socioeconomic backgrounds in the United States. *J Epidemiol Com Health* 2003; 57(1):29–35.
4. Jackson R. The impact of the built environment on health: an emerging field. *Am J Public Health* 2003; 93(9):1382–1384.
5. O'Donnell M. Health promoting community design. *Am J Health Promot* 2003; 18(1):iv–v.
6. Diez-Roux A, Merikin S, Arnett D, et al. Neighborhood of residence and incidence of coronary heart disease. *NEJM* 2001; 345(2):99–106.
7. Ewing R, Schmid T, Killingsworth R, Zlot A, Raudenbush S. Relationship between urban sprawl and physical activity, obesity, and morbidity. *Am J Health Promo* 2003; 18(1):47–57.
8. Lopez R. Urban sprawl and risk for being overweight or obese. *Am J Public Health* 2004; 94(9):1574–1579.
9. Cohen D, Sturm R. Urban Sprawl and Chronic Medical Problems. *Public Health* 2004, 118(7):488–496.
10. Kelly-Schwartz A, Stockard J, Doyle S, Schlossberg M. Is sprawl unhealthy? A multi-level analysis of the relationship of metropolitan sprawl to the health of individuals. *J Plann Ed Res* 2004.
11. Ewing R, Schieber R, Zegeer C. Urban sprawl as risk factor in motor vehicle occupant and pedestrian fatalities. *Am J Public Health* 2003; 93(9):1541–1545.
12. Berrigan D, Troiano R. The association between urban form and physical activity in U.S. adults. *Am J Prev Med* 2002; 23(2S):74–79.
13. Giles-Corti B, Giles-Corti R. The relative influence of individual, social and physical environment determinants of physical activity. *Soc Sci Med* 2002; 54:1793–1812.
14. Frank L, Schmid T, Sallis J, Chapman J, Saelens B. Linking objectively measured physical activity with objectively measured urban form: findings from SMARTRAQ. *Am J Prev Med* 2005; 28(Supplement 2):117–125.
15. Cervero R, Duncan M. Walking, bicycling, and urban landscapes: evidence from the San Francisco Bay Area. *Am J Public Health* 2003; 93(9): 1478–1483.
16. Freeman L. The effects of sprawl on neighborhood social ties. An explanatory analysis. *J Am Plann Assoc* 2001; 67(1):69–77.

17. Collins W, Margo R. Residential segregation and socioeconomic outcomes: when did ghettos go bad? *EconLett* 2000; 69:239–243.
18. Jargowsky P. Take the money and run: economic segregation in U.S. metropolitan areas. *Am Soc Rev* 1996; 61:984–998.
19. Kasarda J. Industrial restructuring and the changing location of jobs. *State of the union: America in the 1990s. Volume 1. Economics trends.* Vol 1. New York: Russell Sage Foundation; 1995:215–267.
20. Kain J. The spatial mismatch hypothesis: Three decades later. *Housing Policy Debate.* 1992; 3(2):371–460.
21. Fullilove M, Fullilove R. Place matters. In: Hofrichter R, ed. *Reclaiming the environmental debate: The politics of health in a toxic culture.* Cambridge MA: MIT Press; 2000.
22. King W, Brach J, Belle S, Killingsworth R, Fenton M, Kriska A. The relationship between convenience of destinations and walking levels in older women. *Am J Health Promot* 2003; 18(1):74–82.
23. UCC. *Toxic waste and race in the United States: A national report on the racial and socioeconomic characteristics of communities with hazardous waste sites.* New York: United Church of Christ; 1987.
24. Bullard R. Solid waste sites and the Black Houston community. *Soc Inq* 1983; 53:273–288.
25. Morello-Frosch R, Pastor M, Sadd J. Environmental justice and Southern California's 'riskscape': the distribution of Air Toxics exposures and health risks among diverse communities. *Urb Aff Rev* 2001; 36(4):551–578.
26. Faber D, Krieg E. *Unequal exposure to ecological hazards 2005: Environmental injustices in the Commonwealth of Massachusetts.* Boston: Philanthropy and Environmental Justice Research Project, Northeastern University; October 12, 2005.
27. Committee NAUA. *Urban agriculture and community food security in the United States: farming from the city center to the urban fringe.* Venice CA: Community Food Security Coalition; 2003.
28. Morland K, Wing S, Diez-Roux A, Poole C. Neighborhood characteristics associated with the location of food stores and food service places. *Am J Pre Med* 2001; 22(1):23–29.
29. Bullard R, Johnson G, Torres A. *Sprawl city. Race, politics and planning in Atlanta.* Washington DC: Island Press; 2000.
30. Wilson J, Kelling G. Broken windows. *Atlantic* 1982; 249(3):29–38.
31. Cohen D, Spear S, Scribner R, Kissinger P, Mason K, Wildgen J. "Broken windows" and the risk of gonorrhea. *Am J Public Health* 2000; 90(2): 230–236.
32. Cohen D, Farley T, Mason K. Why is poverty unhealthy? Social and physical mediators. *Soc Sci Med.* 2003; 57(9):1631–1641.
33. Bullard R. Environmental justice: it's more than waste facility siting. *Soc Sci Q* 1996; 77(3):493–499.

34. Smith N, Caris P, Wyly E. The "Camden syndrome" and the menace of suburban decline. Residential disinvestment and its discontents in Camden County, New Jersey. *Urb Aff Rev* 2001; 36(4):497–531.

35. Howard J. Extreme makeover: sixty-one Beantown school playgrounds get new lives. *Landscape Architecture Magazine* 2004(July):118–127.

36. Hynes HP. *A patch of Eden: America's inner-city gardeners.* White River Junction VT: Chelsea Green Publishing Company; 1996.

37. Levine-Coley R, Kuo F, Sullivan W. Where does the community grow? The social context created by nature in urban public housing. *Environ Beh* 1997; 29(4):468–494.

38. Taylor AF, Wiley A, Kuo FE, Sullivan SC. Growing up in the inner city: green spaces as places to grow. *Environ Beh* 1998; 30(1):3–27.

39. Owen N, Humpel N, Leslie E, Bauman A, Sallis J. Understanding environmental influences on walking: review and research agenda. *Am J Prev Med* 2004; 27(1):67–76.

40. Wetter A, Goldberg J, King A, et al. How and why do individuals make food and physical activity choices? *Nutr Rev* 2001; 59(3):S11–S20.

41. Perkins H, Heynen N. Inequitable access to urban reforestation: the impact of urban political economy on housing tenure and urban forests. *Cities* 2004; 21(4):291–299.

42. Harwood S. Environmental justice on the streets: Advocacy planning as a tool to contest environmental racism. *J Plann Ed Res* 2003; 23(1):24–38.

43. Sager A. Why urban voluntary hospitals close. *Health Serv Res.* 1983; 18(3): 451–481.

44. Wallace R. A synergism of plagues: Planned shrinkage, contagious housing destruction and AIDS in the Bronx. *Environ Res* 1988; 47(1):1–33.

45. Frank L, Engelke P, Schmid T. *Health and community design: the impact of the built environment on physical activity.* Washington DC: Island Press; 2003.

46. Sallis J, Rochaska J, Taylor W. A review of correlates of physical activity of children and adolescents. *Medi Sc Sports Exer* 2000; 32(5):963–975.

47. Duany A, Plater-Zyberk E, Speck J. *Suburban nation.* New York: North Point Press; 2000.

48. Mann E. Los Angeles bus riders derail the MTA. In: Bullard R, Johnson G, Torres A, eds. *Highway robbery: Transportation racism and new routes to equity.* Cambridge MA: South End Press; 2004.

49. Horst N, Moscufo N, Pierotti D, Valentine A. *Investment decisions of the MBTA: The Silver Line and the Greenbush project.* Boston: Boston University; 2003.

50. Mohl R. The second ghetto: Thesis and the power of history. *J Urb Hist* 2003; 29(3):243–256.

51. Wright B. New Orleans neighborhoods under siege. In: Bullard R, Johnson G, eds. *Just Transportation: Dismantling race and class barriers to mobility.* Stony Creek CT: New Society Publishers; 1997.

52. Diez-Roux A. Residential environments and cardiovascular risk. *J Urb Health* 2003; 80(4):569–589.
53. Kawachi I, Kennedy B, Lochner K, Prothow-Stith D. Social capital, income inequality, and mortality. *Am J Public Health* 1997; 87(9):1491–1498.
54. Gold R, Kennedy B, Connell F, Kawachi I. Teen births, income inequality, and social capital: developing an understanding of the causal pathway. *Health Place* 2002; 8:77–83.
55. Kahn H, Tatham L, Pamuk E, Heath C. Are geographic regions with high income inequality associated with risk of abdominal weight gain? *Soc Sci Med* 1998; 47(1):1–6.
56. Jones A, Weinberg D. *The changing shape of the nation's income distribution 1947–1998*. Washington DC: U.S. Department of Commerce Economics and Statistics Administration U.S. Bureau of the Census; June 2000.
57. Denton N. Half empty or half full: segregation and segregated neighborhoods 30 years after the Fair Housing Act. *Cityscape* 1999; 4(3):107–122.
58. Litake DG, Sudano J, Colabianchi N. Understanding the effects of racial residential segregation on health status. *J Gen Int Med* 2004; 18(Supplement 1):180.
59. Acevedo-Garcia D. Residential segregation and the epidemiology of infectious diseases. *Soc Sci Med* 2000; 51(8):1143–1161.
60. Lopez R. Segregation and Black/White differences in exposure to air toxics in 1990. *Environl Health Perspect* 2002; 110(Supplement 2):289–295.
61. Massey D. Segregation and stratification: a biosocial perspective. *Du Bois Rev* 2004; 1(1):1–19.
62. Collins C, Williams D. Segregation and mortality: the deadly effects of racism. *Soc Forum* 1999; 14(3):495–523.
63. CDC. Neighborhood safety and the prevalence of physical inactivity—selected states 1996. *JAMA* 1999; 281(15):1373.
64. Levy J, Welker-Hood L, Cougherty J, Dodson R, Steinbach S, Hynes HP. Lung function, asthma symptoms, and quality of life for children in public housing in Boston: a case-series analysis. *Environ Health*; Forthcoming.
65. Northridge M, Sclar E, Biswas P. Sorting out the connections between the built environment and health: a conceptual framework for navigating pathways and planning healthy cities. *J Urb Health* 2003; 80(4):556–568.
66. Dannenberg A, Jackson R, Frumkin H, et al. The impact of community design and land-use choices on public health: a scientific research agenda. *Am J Public Health* 2003; 93(9):1500–1508.
67. Perdue W, Gostin L, Stone L. Public health and the built environment: historical, empirical, and theoretical foundations for an expanded role. *J Law Med Ethics* 2003; 31(4):557–566.
68. Jackson R, Kochtitzky C. *Creating a healthy environment: the impact of the built environment on public health*. Washington DC: Sprawl Watch Clearinghouse; 2002.

69. Swanstrom T, Casey C, Flack R, Dreier P. *Pulling apart: Economic segregation among suburbs and central cities in major metropolitan areas.* Washington DC: The Brookings Institution; 2004.
70. Jones-Correa M. The origins and diffusion of racial restrictive covenants. *Pol Sci Q* 2000/2001; 115(4):541–568.
71. Silver C. The racial origins of zoning in American cities. In: Manning-Thomas J, Ritzdorf M, eds. *Urban Planning and the African American community. In the shadows.* Thousand Oaks CA: Sage; 1997.
72. Saelens B, Sallis J, Black J, Chen D. Neighborhood-based differences in physical activity: an environmental scale evaluation. *Am J Public Health* 2003; 93(9):1552–1558.
73. Srinivasan S, O'Fallon L, Dearry A. Creating healthy communities, healthy homes, healthy people: initiating a research agenda on the built environment and public health. *American Journal of Public Health* 2003; 93(9): 1446–1450.
74. Voorhees C, Young D. Personal, social, and physical environmental correlates of physical activity levels in urban Latinas. *Am J Prev Med* 2003; 25(3Si):61–68.
75. Corburn J. Confronting the challenges in reconnecting urban planning and public health. *Am J Public Health* 2004; 94(4):541–546.
76. Brugge D, Hynes H. *Community Research in Environmental Health: Studies in Science, Advocacy and Ethics.* Burlington VT: Ashgate; 2005.

SECTION III

Introduction to the Physical Environment

Nature in cities has had a deeply embattled history, with severe consequences for the urban poor and working class. Rivers and their flood-
plains were the sustenance of indigenous peoples and early settlers. Like
interstate highways and flyways today, waterways carried people, raw materials,
and finished goods to and from distant markets. Virtually every city of renown is
built along the water, and gained character, identity, and wealth from its river.
Yet by the early twentieth century, cities had severely polluted their rivers and
by mid-century segregated them from nearby neighborhoods by constructing
commercial port facilities, wastewater treatment plants, railroads, highways,
warehouses, and factories along riverfronts. In some cases, urban rivers were
rerouted or buried.[1] In what was a precursor to the market trade in pollution,
philanthropists who built their industrial wealth on the banks of city rivers
chose to preserve rivers elsewhere—wild and scenic rivers, and upstream rural
stretches of city rivers—for elite recreation, sports fishing, and tourism.

Horticulture has always been practiced in cities: In our ancestors' transition
from nomadic to settled existence, gardens eventually gave birth to cities. The
earliest market gardens were sited on riverine plains and deltas that were renewed by the annual silt-bearing floods of the Nile, the Tigris and Euphrates,
the Indus, and the Yangtze; and from their largesse, farmers built the first cities.
For thousands of years, built and cultivated environments coexisted: Homes,
markets, public buildings, and sacred spaces were interspersed with kitchen gardens, farms, and common grazing lands for animals. Not until the Industrial
Revolution were dooryard and market gardens, orchards and town commons
usurped by brick, mortar, and asphalt.[2] Horticulture, after being virtually eliminated from nineteenth-century factory neighborhoods, was then restored in select urban open spaces as an antidote to the monotony, noise, congestion and
poor ventilation of industrial factories and tenements. In the mid nineteenth
century, large "natural" landscaped parks on whose perimeter the wealthy built
residences, such as New York City's Central Park, became the American city's
counterpoint to the gritty, hardscape factory neighborhoods that had replaced
local market gardens and green spaces.

Environmental geography in metropolitan areas inevitably reflects social inequality. New Orleans, under the siege of a hurricane of extreme intensity, uniquely mirrored these patterns: 84 percent of the nearly 30 percent of the city's poor were Black; and the White and well off of the flood-prone city lived on high ground while the poor lived in the bottom land. "Hydrology joined sociology," one journalist wrote of the disastrous flooding and the plight of the car-less and money-less poor. Contrasting "broken levees" and "unbroken social barriers," he ruminated: Levees will be rebuilt; what will become of segregationist barriers?[3]

In this section on the physical environment of cities we include studies of air pollution, vacant and underused industrial sites (brownfields), and commercial hazardous waste facilities, all of which employ conceptual approaches and novel methods to document the disproportionate and unjust burden of pollution on people of lower income and people of color. In Chapter 9, authors O'Neill et al. aim to introduce readers to promising research approaches that connect the fields of air pollution and social epidemiology. They propose theories and hypotheses about how air pollution and socioeconomic factors may interact to influence health. Drawing on studies conducted worldwide, they discuss issues in the design and analysis of studies to determine whether and how the health effects of exposure to ambient air pollution are worsened for poorer people. The authors propose specific steps that will advance knowledge in this field, fill information gaps, and apply research results to improve the collaboration between public health and affected communities.

In Chapter 10, authors Litt et al. describe an approach to characterize both vacant and underutilized industrial and commercial properties in Southeast Baltimore and also the health and well being of communities living near these properties. We have included this chapter because brownfield redevelopment can be a key component of our national efforts to address environmental justice and health disparities within urban communities. Brownfield redevelopment is critical to urban revitalization and can help with the curbing of urban sprawl. The authors argue that incorporating public health into brownfields-related cleanup and land-use decisions will increase the likelihood of success of urban neighborhood redevelopment with long-term public health benefits.

An update of the landmark environmental justice study, *Toxic Wastes and Race*, was recently published by the United Church of Christ. Chapter 11 is taken from the 2007 update, which uses new spatial methods to determine the proximity of hazardous waste facilities to U.S. metropolitan neighborhoods by socioeconomic status, race, and ethnicity. According to *Toxic Wastes and Race at Twenty: 1987–2007*, commercial hazardous waste facilities licensed by the U.S. EPA to store, treat, and dispose of hazardous waste are located in greater proportion in neighborhoods of color. This environmental injustice is magnified in neighborhoods with clusters of facilities, where two-thirds of the residents are people of color. Race, the author Robin Saha finds, "continues to be a stronger predictor of [hazardous waste] facility locations than other factors often considered to be associated with race," such as income and education.

In the final chapter of this section, authors Hynes and Howe describe a broad-based community gardening and greening movement which has spawned a rich variety of social, economic, health, and educational benefits in hundreds of cities and towns across the United States. A companion food security movement has promoted urban–rural linkages, urban agriculture, and farmers' markets. The authors provide an overview of studies which have shown that community gardens and farms and nearby green space in cities are an important response to needs for nutritious and affordable food, psychological and physiological health, social cohesion, crime prevention, recreation, and life satisfaction, particularly for low-income communities.

References

1. MacBroom, JG. *The River Book.* Hartford, CT: Department of Environmental Protection; 1999.
2. Warner SB. *To Dwell Is to Garden: A History of Boston's Community Gardens.* Boston: Northeastern University Press; 1987.
3. DeParle, J. What happens to a race deferred? *The New York Times.* September 4, 2005. Section 4:1,4.

Health, Wealth, and Air Pollution: Advancing Theory and Methods

*Marie S. O'Neill, Michael Jerrett, Ichiro Kawachi,
Jonathan I. Levy, Aaron J. Cohen, Nelson Gouveia,
Paul Wilkinson, Tony Fletcher, Luis Cifuentes,
and Joel Schwartz, with input from participants of the
Workshop on Air Pollution and Socioeconomic Conditions*

Introduction

Numerous epidemiologic studies have found associations between socioeconomic position (SEP) and health, with gradients observed for outcomes including mortality, infectious and chronic diseases, and psychiatric disorders.[1–3] Ambient air pollution has also been linked with a broad range of health effects, including mortality and morbidity from heart and lung disease, impaired lung function, and lung cancer.[4] Because of the importance of SEP as a determinant of health, and because air pollution exposure can vary according to socioeconomic circumstances, SEP has been included as a potential confounder[5,6] and an effect modifier[7–9] in epidemiologic studies. In this article, we describe current knowledge, hypotheses and theories, methodologic approaches, and research needs related to the effects and interactions of air pollution and socioeconomic conditions on human health and well-being. We structure the discussion with an interpretative framework based on three related propositions. First, groups with lower SEP may receive higher exposure to air pollution. Second, because lower-SEP groups already experience compromised health status due to material deprivation and psychosocial stress, they may be more susceptible to the health effects of air pollution. Third, because of the combination of greater exposure and susceptibility, these groups are likely to suffer greater health effects from air pollution exposure.

International organizations have identified both air pollution and poverty as priority areas for public health intervention,[10] and the intersection of these pressing problems requires strategic attention from researchers and policy makers.

These concerns affect the lives of many people—approximately 1 billion people live in poverty.[11] An estimated 1.5 billion people currently live in polluted urban areas, and 65% of the world's population is projected to live in cities by 2025.[12] More than 40% of the world's children are estimated to live in polluted cities of the developing world.[13] At the same time, evidence indicates that air pollution is an even more serious health concern than previously thought, with associations seen with reduced life expectancy, increased daily mortality and hospital admissions, birth outcomes, and asthma.[4,14–16] These effects appear to be without thresholds,[17] suggesting large attributable risks in both the developing and developed world.[18]

Experts attending a recent international workshop recommended further research and collaboration on issues including vulnerability to air pollution exposure.[19] The U.S. National Research Council has called the identification of subpopulations at elevated risk a priority research concern,[20] and persons with low SEP are one potential subpopulation. To support and better focus public health action in alleviating economic disparities and reducing air pollution, reliable estimates of the health effects of both, as well as potential confounding or effect modification one may exert on the other, are required.

Several steps to improving understanding of the interaction between socioeconomic disparities and air pollution exposures have already been taken. Research and initiatives to reduce inequities in pollution exposure and consequent health effects have increased in the United States since the early 1990s, partly as a result of the environmental justice movement.[21] Community partnerships in research and decision making have been recommended to improve the relevance of scientific results and enhance understanding of the varied concerns of those affected.[22] Accumulated environmental exposure from multiple sources (noise, water quality, crowding, housing quality, and neighborhood conditions) has been offered as one potential explanation for observed health gradients by SEP.[23] Although we focus on ambient air pollution, we believe that a thorough examination of one class of pollution may illuminate the studies of how other contaminants may affect and be affected by SEP.

Despite international interest in the effects of socioeconomic disparities and ambient air pollution on health, and growing awareness of the importance of considering both in epidemiologic research, few studies have looked carefully at how these factors interact with one another. In this review, we introduce readers to underlying approaches in both fields, articulate hypotheses of how air pollution and socioeconomic factors could interact to influence health, and recommend research methods for investigating these hypotheses.

A Primer on the Health Effects of SEP and Air Pollution

An analysis of the health effects of SEP and air pollution can and should consider all levels of the potential causal chain, from molecular mechanisms, to individual risk factors (including personal behaviors), to contextual factors (including economic and social policy). This holistic view has been articulated in recent publications.[24–26] We will familiarize researchers with either social determinants of health or air pollution health effects, review available evidence on effect modification of air pollution health effects by SEP, and draw the literatures together under the hypotheses that explain why SEP may modify the health effects of air pollution.

SEP and Health

There are four widely agreed upon facts and principles about the relationship between SEP and health. First, the relationship between SEP and poor health is not confined to poor people alone. Although it is clear that the highest risks of premature mortality and morbidity are concentrated among the poor, studies have also repeatedly demonstrated the existence of a graded relationship between low SEP (whether measured by income or educational attainment) and worse health outcomes. At each step of the socioeconomic hierarchy, individuals tend to have better health compared with those immediately below them. This gradient extends well into the range of incomes that can be termed "middle class."

Second, SEP can be conceptualized and measured at both the individual level and the area level (e.g., neighborhoods). Evidence suggests that each level exerts an independent influence on an individual's chances of health. In other words, an individual with the same level of income or educational attainment could experience different chances of health depending upon the SEP of his or her neighbors. Area-level SEP may pattern an individual's access to opportunities for good health. Examples of such patterning include differential access to the service environment (e.g., health clinics, supermarkets, sanitation or waste disposal), the physical environment (e.g., traffic burden, crowding, clean water for drinking or bathing), and the social environment (crime rate, social cohesion, and vandalized public areas).[27]

Third, in addition to the dimension of context or place, the dimension of time is important for conceptualizing and measuring SEP effects on health. SEP rarely remains static across the life course, and the measurement of income, for example, at a single point in time is unlikely to capture the dynamic as well as the cumulative effects of SEP on health. Childhood socioeconomic circumstances are now believed to exert an effect on adult health, independently of SEP attained in adulthood.[28] Income dynamics (e.g., downward social mobility, or accumulated spells of poverty) have been shown to predict mortality and other health outcomes.[29] We now understand that wealth (or some other measure of permanent income) is much more strongly related to health than is a single measure of income.[30] A further important aspect of time relates to the history of a geographical location; migration in and out of areas will affect the health status profiles, behaviors, and possibly accumulated exposures of local population groups and should be accounted for in associative analyses.

Finally, social epidemiologists now stress the importance of distinguishing the concept of SEP from race. This point is particularly pertinent to the United States, where official statistics often conflate racial disparities in health with socioeconomic disparities. The two are not the same, despite the fact that racial minorities in the United States are overrepresented among lower-SEP groups. Race and SEP have been shown to have independent effects on health, and interpretation of studies using these variables should acknowledge that one variable may be a poor proxy of the other.

Air Pollution and Health

This section covers salient aspects of the associations between air pollution and health, focusing on three central topics: sources and emissions, concentrations and exposures, and health effects assessment.

Commonly studied pollutants include primary and secondary airborne particles and gases, including ozone, carbon monoxide, sulfur dioxide, and nitrogen oxides. The term "secondary" here refers to compounds (gases or particles) that are not directly emitted into the atmosphere but rather form because of reactions in the atmosphere, often driven by ultraviolet light. These pollutants frequently form at some distance from the site of emission of their precursor compounds. Because lead has been the subject of a number of reviews and is no longer added to the gasoline in many countries, we do not consider it here, but it remains an important air pollutant in countries where leaded gasoline is still used.

Air pollution health studies assign exposure based on measurements at or near the individual's breathing zone or at ambient monitors intended to represent community exposure. The validity of ambient monitors as a reflection of actual personal exposure for epidemiologic studies varies by the nature of the air pollutant of interest, the epidemiologic study design, and the measurement technology.[31,32] In general, ambient monitoring data are fairly good surrogates for daily fine particle personal exposures but less so for gases such as nitrogen dioxide that display small-area spatial variation. For long-term exposure, it is unknown how well ambient monitors predict personal exposure, but available evidence suggests a potential for exposure measurement error.[33]

Air pollution epidemiology has addressed several health outcomes, including mortality and morbidity, acute infections, lung cancer, impairments of lung function, hospitalization, chronic respiratory diseases, and reproductive anomalies.[4] Study designs include time-series analyses, in which daily measures of pollution are evaluated with respect to daily counts of morbidity and mortality outcomes; panel studies, wherein a defined group of subjects is followed longitudinally to assess responses to pollution exposure; ecologic studies using group contrasts in mortality and exposure (but no information on individual risk factors); and cohort studies in which associations between long-term exposure to pollution and health outcomes are evaluated within cities or across geographic regions with differing pollutant profiles. Although some contradictory results have emerged, overall significant positive associations between air pollution and various health outcomes have been established.[4] Because some laws—for example, the U.S. Clean Air Act—require that air quality standards protect "sensitive" populations, special attention has been paid to studying susceptibility related to age, disease status, and factors such as smoking status.

Evidence on SEP Modification of Air Pollution Health Effects

Several recent studies have addressed whether SEP modifies the health effects of particulate air pollution. These studies were chosen to illustrate recent research, not comprehensively review it. Several factors evaluated are not direct measures of SEP but rather medical conditions that are differentially distributed by SEP, or race, which can have independent effects on health outcomes. The majority of studies evaluating individual-level characteristics did show effect modification with higher effects (in general) among those of lower SEP, by race, or in those having medical characteristics associated with lower SEP. Low educational attainment seems to be a particularly consistent indicator of vulnerability in these studies. Those studies using group/county level indicators did not show important effect modification, as a whole; these results may relate to the relatively coarse resolution of these variables.

Although many of the studies reported effect modification via SEP variables, few have explicitly examined why SEP may modify this environmental health effect. In the next section we propose three possible explanations for potential effect modification.

Hypotheses and Theories

We hypothesize that the effects of air pollution exposure on health are differentially distributed by SEP and that, under most conditions, people in lower SEPs are at greater risk. Additionally, some of the observed disparities in health outcomes by SEP may be explained by air pollution exposure. We base this general hypothesis on three possible routes through which air pollution exposure may result in greater health effects among those in disadvantaged circumstances. These routes are as follows: a) air pollution exposure is differentially distributed by SEP; b) low SEP may directly increase susceptibility to air pollution-related health consequences; and c) some health conditions and traits that cause vulnerability to air pollution are linked to SEP. We recognize that there can be some blurring between categories b and c, but we feel these warrant separate consideration to underscore different aspects of the pathway from air pollution exposure to health effects.

Exposure Differentials Related to Socioeconomic Conditions

The intersection of late-twentieth-century social movements against racism and the degradation of the environment focused attention on issues of environmental justice and environmental equity. Researchers have investigated processes (e.g., land use; political, cultural, and economic structures) leading to unequal exposures.[34] Outcome-focused research evaluates whether unequal exposure exists, without considering the processes that might have led to disparities. The scientific community, often working directly with disadvantaged communities, has documented disproportionate exposures to some pollutants in communities characterized by low SEP and/or "minority" racial composition. Explanations range from housing market dynamics[35] to systemic racism and class bias in land use decisions that push noxious facilities away from wealthy neighborhoods toward poor ones with more racial minorities.[36] Regardless of racial or social composition, high land costs that discourage purchase for industrial uses in more affluent areas are likely to affect distribution of pollutant sources, over and above the effects of political and social influence and discrimination. Internationally, politically weaker and usually poorer nations may become repositories for pollution or waste generated in wealthier countries, or polluting facilities may be sited there because of lower labor costs or less stringent environmental regulations. In keeping with the health effects focus of this article, we emphasize studies that evaluate outcomes of unequal pollution exposure distribution, not necessarily those that seek to describe the processes leading to those results. A common hypothesis of such studies is that socially disadvantaged groups suffer greater exposures that explain, in part, persistent inequalities in health observed along social and racial gradients.[23,37]

Heterogeneity of exposure over space and thus the potential for inequity in exposure varies markedly by pollutant type. Fine particles are distributed fairly homogeneously over large urban areas),[38,39] due mostly to the contribution of small, long-range transport particles. Thus, central air pollution monitors can be good surrogates for personal exposure, despite some variation in people's activities. Ultrafine particles can, however, have elevated concentrations (from traffic sources) adjacent to roadways.[40,41] Significant spatial variation has also been seen for diesel-related pollutants, as indicated by elemental carbon and polycyclic aromatic hydrocarbon levels.[42–44] Gaseous traffic-related pollutants such as NO_2 and CO display variations in concentration across small areas[45,16] and probably cluster close to emission sources on roadways.[46–48] O_3 can be lower closer to areas with dense traffic because of scavenging by NO_2[49] but generally has fairly homogeneous distributions over large areas.

Reviews of the empirical findings on ambient air pollution exposure and socioeconomic level support the idea that disadvantaged groups are more highly exposed to some pollutants).[50,51] In some cases, the evidence is indirect. A number of studies have not been pollutant specific but have shown differences in health impacts as a function of proximity to a roadway.[52–54] If proximity to traffic depresses property values, as suggested by the hedonic pricing literature,[55] then it is likely that the lower dwelling values will attract residents of lower SEP.[35] Thus, higher ambient exposure is experienced by relatively disadvantaged groups living near roadways. Over larger areas, major roadways may also be routed through lower-income areas because of reduced political and economic power of these residents to oppose such siting. Indeed, lower values of dwellings were strongly associated with higher particle levels in one Canadian study.[56] However, urban development may cause secondary roads to become busier, putting relatively expensive housing stock in the midst of high traffic volume.

European and Scandinavian studies show differential personal exposures to particles and traffic pollutants by occupation and education.[57,58] Studies in Helsinki, Finland; Mexico City, Mexico; Los Angeles, California; and the U.S. Great Lakes region have shown differences in exposure to gaseous pollutants by occupation, education, minority status, and income.[59-62] Although these studies suggested that people of lower SEP have higher exposure, O_3 exposure can be substantially higher among wealthier people who live farther from traffic sources. For example, in southern Mexico City, where more wealthy people reside, O_3 levels are substantially higher than in the poorer northern part of the city.[63] Interpretation of studies that use personal exposure measures should take into account possible selection bias for participants. In Basel, Switzerland, and Helsinki, participants were more likely to be female, older, and better educated and to live in areas with lower traffic volume.[64]

Many studies on exposure differentials rely on proximity to sources or ambient monitoring networks that are limited in number and location. Other studies have collected specific monitoring at additional locations, particularly for NO_2, and modeled exposure over finer geographic levels using data on population density, traffic density, location of residence, and so forth.[47,65,66] One effort in Stockholm, Sweden, used 11,000 residential addresses to estimate individual cumulative exposure to air pollutants from traffic and home heating over several decades, using reconstructed emissions data and dispersion modeling.[67] This process yielded wide ranges of exposure for the 11,000 individuals. Although few of these studies have focused on differential exposure by SEP, methods for deriving individual-specific exposure data could provide a useful basis for examining modification of chronic pollution exposure effects by socioeconomic factors, both individual and contextual.

The exposure assessment literature describes several techniques, from more advanced exposure modeling to use of geographic information systems (GIS) and residential addresses, that improve our ability to evaluate whether gradients in exposure exist and are associated with socioeconomic gradients. Studies that involve more complex exposure modeling should consider type of pollutant and the pollutants' physicochemical behavior in the environment, in addition to residential settlement patterns, time–activity patterns, and the behavior of the subjects whose exposure is being estimated. Because human settlement patterns and behaviors as well as pollutant sources and composition differ across local, national, and international scales, studies examining exposure in a variety of geographic regions are desirable. Many other methodologic issues can influence the assessment of inequity in exposure, but these have been the subject of recent reviews[68,69] and therefore are not included here.

Susceptibility Directly Related to Social Position

Susceptibility has been classified as encompassing "intrinsic" factors that include age, sex, genetics, and ethnicity or race, and "acquired," which include factors such as chronic medical conditions, health care access, nutrition, fitness, other pollutant exposures, and drug and alcohol use.[70] The boundaries between susceptibility acquired because of some aspect of social position and intrinsic susceptibility coincident with it are not clearly defined, and timing of a person's socioeconomic experience can play an important role. Susceptibility may result from a whole cascade of events. For example, diagnosis with a chronic lung or heart condition could result in reduced income due to job change or loss, which in turn could initiate a cascade of damaging coping behaviors (increased smoking, drinking) that might lead to further deterioration of health.

People in lower socioeconomic circumstances may be more susceptible to air pollution for reasons directly related to their relative disadvantage and psychosocial stress. For example, they may lack access to grocery stores that sell fresh fruits and vegetables[71] or the income to buy them, resulting in reduced intake of antioxidant vitamins that can protect against adverse consequences of air pollution exposure.[72] Another possibility is reduced access to medical care, so poor people may not have the appropriate prescription for a respiratory condition such as asthma. Medication can alleviate symptoms aggravated by pollution exposure, and more consistent use of corticosteroids lowers baseline inflammation, potentially lowering responsiveness to proinflammatory pollutants. An additional hypothesis is that psychosocial stress and violence, which can be higher among those of lower SEP, can increase susceptibility.[73,74]

Characteristics of neighborhoods can affect susceptibility. In four U.S. communities, residence in a disadvantaged neighborhood was associated with coronary heart disease (CHD) incidence, even after controlling for established CHD risk factors and personal income, education, and occupation.[75] With current emphasis on cardiac effects of air pollution exposure, this finding is particularly relevant to the study of the air pollution and socioeconomic interaction. Because lower-income people are more likely to live closer to roadways, there is also evidence that increased traffic density has been associated with lack of neighborhood communication and collaboration (thereby reducing available social networks).[76]

Another potential mechanism of susceptibility directly related to social position is coexposure to other pollutants, including indoor pollutants. A person with a relatively high dose of other pollutants may be "weakened" and less able to withstand the additional insult of ambient air pollution. People with less wealth are more likely to be employed in dirtier occupations[51] and in developing countries, they may also be more likely to be exposed to pollutants indoors from heating and cooking.[77] Workers in the coke oven and farm industries and children who are in the workforce may suffer increased susceptibility due to cumulative lifetime dose.[78] Workers in blue-collar occupations may also be more exposed to environmental tobacco smoke than are white-collar workers in cases where regulations limiting indoor smoking in the workplace are not applied consistently. Housing stock in poorer communities with high rates of crowding can have higher levels of certain allergens as well as other risk factors for asthma sensitization and exacerbation.[79,80] These differing allergen profiles may affect whether individuals sensitized to certain allergen burdens will be more responsive to air pollution exposure, and lower-income households may have difficulty obtaining follow-up asthma care that could reduce the severity of responses to air pollution.[81]

Although much research on susceptible subpopulations in air pollution epidemiology focuses on traits such as preexisting disease, age, and sex, evidence is growing that exposure to particular socioeconomic conditions can affect susceptibility through mechanisms (psychological, nutritional, etc.) that have not been widely studied in air pollution epidemiology.

Susceptibility from Predisposing Health Conditions, Behaviors, or Traits

Several studies have shown that people with diabetes are more sensitive to the health effects of air pollution than is the general population.[82-84] In the United States, diabetes is more common among the elderly, non-Hispanic blacks, and Mexican Americans and among people living in or near a central city. U.S. residents with non-insulin-dependent diabetes mellitus, or type 2 diabetes, usually have less education, lower income, and higher unemployment rates, adjusting for age, than do nondiabetics.[85] In Mexico, type 2 diabetes was more prevalent among low-income individuals, and in the United Kingdom, early childhood deprivation is a risk factor.[86] Thus, diabetes can be associated with several of the indicators of lower SEP, as well as with more advanced age, which also contributes to vulnerability. Even precursors to diabetes are differentially distributed by social level. Among civil service workers in the United Kingdom, risk factors for diabetes and coronary disease were higher among those employed in lower-paid occupations, independent of health-related behaviors.[87]

Mechanisms hypothesized to contribute to the extra sensitivity of diabetics to air pollution include their lower heart rate variability and higher levels of inflammatory markers in their blood; these factors have also been linked to vulnerability to air pollution in other studies.[88,89] More prevalent among diabetics, obesity is a condition that increases with age and is associated with increased systemic inflammation, including markers of cardiovascular risk.[90,91]

Both diabetes and asthma are differentially distributed by socioeconomic level in international comparative studies. In 12 European countries, the prevalence of asthma and diabetes was higher in countries with lower gross national product.[92] Other international studies show, in general, much higher asthma prevalence in more industrialized countries, although prevalence is increasing overall.[93] Lower asthma prevalence has been seen in countries closer to the equator, compared with higher-latitude countries.[92,94]

However, factors determining patterns of prevalence require additional investigation. One recent analysis found a gradient of increasing prevalence of coexistent asthma and hay fever among people with increasing levels of education, but decreasing prevalence of asthma without hay fever as educational level increased.[95] In some areas, asthma prevalence is higher in inner-city areas more likely to have large indoor and outdoor pollution burdens.[96] Asthma is widely accepted to be aggravated by air pollution exposure,[97] although new evidence suggests that O_3 may also contribute to asthma onset in children.[15]

In addition to diabetes and asthma, some genetic traits that may affect response to air pollution exposure are differentially distributed by race and/or ethnicity.[78] These traits include fast versus slow acetylation, which affects the ability of the body to remove toxins; deficiency in glucose-6-phosphate dehydrogenase, an enzyme that affects the red blood cell membrane; and sickle cell trait (more common in those of West African descent), which can cause health problems even in heterozygous individuals when exposure to pollutants such as CO occurs.[78]

Smoking behavior is unequally distributed across socioeconomic levels. In the United States, smoking has become concentrated among individuals in lower socioeconomic strata, as measured by income and educational attainment.[98] This contrasts with Mexico, where a national survey showed that higher income households consumed more tobacco in the form of cigarettes.[99]

Smoking-related lung conditions can affect uptake and response to exposure. Deposition of particles is relatively higher among persons who have chronic obstructive pulmonary disease, especially in the part of the lung that is functional.[100] Lung function can decrease among smokers, resulting in increased ventilation-perfusion inhomogeneity, which can in turn affect delivered dose of particles. Smoking behavior may not necessarily result in heightened sensitivity; several studies have observed that smokers may experience less of an impact from air pollution because of a "healthy smoker" effect,[131] wherein individuals who might be sensitive to air pollution effects will choose not to begin smoking because the inhaled smoke causes discomfort or irritation, or smokers experience physiologic changes such as thickening of bronchial mucosa, which make them less responsive to additional pollutant exposure.

The examples of diabetes, asthma, genetic characteristics, and smoking demonstrate that certain traits, health conditions, and behaviors that affect susceptibility to air pollution distribute differentially by SEP. Evaluation of whether air pollution causes adverse health effects to a greater extent among those of relative disadvantage can benefit from insights into biomedical and behavioral characteristics of those in different socioeconomic strata.

Conceptual Model

If both exposures and susceptibilities vary across socioeconomic gradients, these factors are likely to act together to influence the health response of groups classified by socioeconomic level. An air pollution epidemiology study that considers air pollution exposure, SEP measures, and potentially other factors related to SEP (disease status, sex, behaviors) must be based, implicitly or explicitly, on a conceptual model that accounts for complex relationships among these factors. Such a model can guide hypothesis development as well as choice of statistical methods. These models show that race, ethnicity, and sex may be associated with SEP and are therefore useful to consider. In turn, both differences in vulnerability and exposure may influence or be influenced by SEP and each other. Both exposure and vulnerabilities may lead to disparate health outcomes, which then can cycle back to affect SEP, as in the example cited above where a disabling illness affects one's ability to work.

The conceptual model developed for a given study will depend on the pollutant being considered and the health outcome. For example, plausible mechanisms for asthma exacerbation may differ from mechanisms for cardiac arrest, and will also depend on what pollutant or combination of pollutants are under consideration. Availability of data and indicators will also affect the pathways that can be explored for a research study.

Methodologic Issues in Research Design and Analysis

Data Sources

Current Approaches and Challenges.   An important step in research design is choosing variables that capture characteristics fundamental to the hypothesis being addressed. Published research on SEP and air pollution interactions has employed common individual-level indicators of SEP, including occupational status, income, educational attainment, and wealth; or area-level variables, including neighborhood compositional measures (e.g., percentage of households below the poverty threshold) as well as indices of deprivation (e.g., presence of overcrowding).[2,103,104] Many of these commonly used variables are measured cross-sectionally, but using socioeconomic measures that incorporate the time dimension (e.g., childhood socioeconomic circumstances, migration history, income dynamics, and/or accumulated monetary resources over time, i.e., wealth) provides a more complete picture of the patterning of health by SEP. In addition to the temporal dimension, space is a critical component of many SEP variables. Recent articles examined which individual- and group-level variables provide the most robust indicators of an association with mortality, a defined and well-measured health outcome. Using longitudinal data from the U.S. Panel Study of Income Dynamics, Daly et al.[30] examined education, occupation, income, and wealth as predictors of mortality. Wealth and recent family income were the most strongly associated with mortality.[30]

In an examination of U.S. area-based SEP measurements with respect to cancer incidence and mortality detected socioeconomic gradients by block group and census tract, but using zip codes, Krieger et al.[105] detected either no gradients or they were in the opposite direction. Economic poverty measures were more robust and sensitive indicators than were education and indices of deprivation.[105]

A novel measure of SEP attempts to determine people's subjective perceptions of their socioeconomic standing. The question asks people to place themselves on an imaginary "ladder" with 10 rungs.[106] Respondents are told that this ladder is a visual representation of people's "standing" within their community to society (based on prestige, wealth, education, etc.), after which they are asked to put themselves on one of the rungs. First developed by the MacArthur Network on Socioeconomic Status and Health, this measure of subjective SEP has now been asked on several cross-sectional and cohort studies. This subjective placement appears to predict health status independently of income, education, and occupational status. Interestingly, people's position on the ladder correlates only moderately (about 0.3–0.4) with objective indicators of SEP, such as income and education. However, further work is required to understand the exact meaning of responses to this question, as well as mechanisms underlying its empirical association with health outcomes.[107] Other important aspects of perception relate to the physical and service environment. For example, perceived excessive noise, heavy traffic, inadequate lighting, and limited access to public transportation were associated with increased risk of physical impairment among older adults.[108]

As mentioned above, many epidemiology studies use air pollution data obtained from outdoor monitors that typically measure a few key pollutants, such as particles, O_3, and SO_2. Personal exposure is measured using portable samplers,[109] although this kind of study is much more expensive than using routinely collected community-level data. Many of the limitations and advances in air pollution exposure estimation have been discussed in the preceding section on exposure differentials. Health outcome data can be taken from administrative records of vital statistics (births, deaths, hospital admissions)[110–112] or measured directly using methods including spirometry (for lung function),[72] electrocardiograms (for heart function),[88] symptom diaries,[114] and clinical assays of biologic samples such as blood.[17]

Recommendations.   Choice of data sources and specific variables should be guided by development of hypotheses for the potential joint effects of individual and neighborhood effects, specifying the relevant geographic areas and their characteristics, and considering longitudinal/life-course features of socioeconomic exposures.[115] For administrative reasons, data are often collected at the resolution of counties or postal codes. Researchers should evaluate whether these divisions encompass community units or neighborhoods that are of interest or relevance for health outcome studies.[105] Although research using census data or commonly measured individual SEP indicators aid comparisons and generalizability across study settings, air pollution researchers should also consider using some of the more innovative SEP indicators described previously and tap existing databases with advanced or high-resolution SEP indicators, such as those that allow linkage of detailed survey data on social cohesion and other contextual exposures, for example.[116] Linking health outcome data from various sources, such as surveys and vital statistics records, can also enable more complete control of such characteristics as medical history in studies of SEP/air pollution interactions.[117]

Another approach is to use innovative metrics for evaluating both socioeconomic and environmental inequalities. The Gini coefficient is a commonly used measure of inequality, taking on a value of zero for perfect equality and one for total inequality. Several researchers have proposed the application of Gini coefficients to measure environmental inequality, and some suggest that environmental inequalities be measured within groups of comparable income, under the assumption that people should be compensated as a way of "making up" for increased environmental exposure.[118] This approach could be applied to air pollution exposure in cases where the pollutants of interest vary enough within or between communities to give an indication of how uneven the distribution of pollution is among different social groups.

Although we have identified and discussed a number of articles, still little is known about differences in personal exposure patterns across socioeconomic groups. Further exposure assessment work that explicitly includes SEP as a selection criterion for participation would be useful. Other factors to consider include diurnal patterns in exposure, traffic density, and proximity to schools.

Statistical Analyses

Current Approaches and Challenges. A number of challenges exist relating to the conduct and interpretation of health inequities studies using area-based socioeconomic variables. Greenland[119] reviewed some of the potential sources of bias and problems in interpretation in studying contextual exposures and suggested multilevel study design as an appropriate method to address some of the identified concerns. Multilevel analysis evaluates the effects of individual-level and group-level exposure variables on individual-level outcomes at the same time.[120] Researchers have applied such models to assess whether the effects of income inequality in a society are associated with poor health outcomes beyond what individual income attainment does, and whether this contextual effect is independent of a given individual's income.[121] The approach has also been described for air pollution studies.[122] Diez Roux[120] provided a comprehensive introduction to these models and various hypotheses they can address.

Contextual SEP indicators may be affected by a common concern pertinent to area-based statistics: the "modifiable areal unit problem."[123] Modifying the scale of aggregation zones (e.g., postal codes, counties, grids) and which geographic units are aggregated together can change study results by masking heterogeneity within them, among other problems.[124]

Air pollution exposure also has a strong spatial component. Most studies of air pollution and health outcomes have neither analyzed nor reported whether the residuals from regression models had spatial autocorrelation).[68] In one study that has applied spatial regression techniques,[56] control for autocorrelation through the application of simultaneous autoregression models affected not only which variables were significant but also the overall prediction accuracy of the model.

Examining geographic patterns of inequity using GIS systems can be informative and visually illustrate the problem. In southeast England, for example, traffic density and most air pollutants are highest in east London, where many poorer population groups live, often with substantial ethnic minority communities and higher prevalences of cardiorespiratory illness; wealthier populations, with lower underlying disease prevalence but greater car ownership, tend to reside in the lower-pollution areas of the suburbs and surrounding areas.[102]

Innovative study designs such as "case crossover"[125] have recently been applied to air pollution epidemiology. The case-crossover design allows assessment of the effect of transient exposures on the risk of an acute event. Using a bidirectional approach where control data are obtained both before and after the health event of interest, factors such as temporal trends, season, day of week, and changes in population size and composition are controlled by design. But its greatest advantage is that individual-level characteristics such as SEP are controlled by design but can be analyzed as effect modifiers.[126]

A final statistical challenge relates to the study of effect modification. In the air pollution literature, multiplicative scale interactions (i.e., difference in relative risks across population subgroups) have been commonly evaluated. These are conceptually justified because, for example, a doubling of the population would be expected to result in a doubling of the incremental number of cases. However, additive scale effect modification may be useful for risk assessment. This is because results can be expressed in terms of numbers of deaths or hospitalizations attributable to air pollution exposure, compared with the percentage of changes that may be the same in two different population groups who have different baseline rates of the health event. For example, blacks in some areas have higher rates of asthma hospital admissions than do whites, so for the same percentage of excess admissions associated with pollution, more blacks than whites are actually affected, despite no evidence of differential susceptibility.[8,127] Indeed, two studies that evaluated multiplicative-scale interaction offered the baseline differences as one possible explanation for why little difference was seen.[128,9]

Recommendations.   In light of the additive versus multiplicative effect modification issues, studies should account for baseline differences in health response across socioeconomic strata and consider reporting risk/rate differences in addition to ratios. In addition, statistical methods should account for spatial correlation in both pollution and SEP variables. Characterizing spatial relationships more systematically would also be useful, ideally using methods of exposure estimation that take account of the movement of individuals through the urban environment rather than relying on static geography alone. And, innovative statistical approaches including case crossover should be employed for studying air pollution and SEP interaction. Our final suggestion is that multilevel modeling be more widely applied to studies of this nature. Below we provide a theoretical example of a multilevel model approach applied to a study of O_3 and daily mortality.

Consider a cohort study of n subjects with information about individual-level measures of SEP and medical history (including smoking) as well as contextual (e.g., density of liquor stores, parks, fast food) and compositional (e.g., literacy rates) variables pertaining to the neighborhood where they live. Air quality data can be modeled using regression or dispersion modeling to the level of individual address, including workplace exposures and indoor exposures based on questionnaires. Because people move around but spend more time out of their houses in their community than in distant communities, a contextual air pollution variable can then also be constructed. In such a scenario, consider a survival model where the risk ratio for mortality is modeled as

$$
\begin{aligned}
\log RR_{ij} = \beta_0 + \beta_1 \\
\times \text{personal risk factors}_i + \beta_2 \\
\times O_{3j} + \beta_3 \times (O_{3i} - O_{3j}) + \beta_4 \\
\times O_{3i} \times SEP_i + V_j + U_j \times O_{3j},
\end{aligned}
\tag{1}
$$

where i represents an individual in the jth area; V_j represents a random area effect capturing variations in risk, not explained by personal risk factors, that cluster within geographic areas; and U_j represents variation in the slope of O_3, not explained by the individual level interaction terms, which cluster geographically by areas. β_2 measures the effect of areawide O_3 exposure and β_3 the effect of the difference from that areawide exposure for the ith individual. β_4 represents the effect modification of individual SEP on the response to O_3. Because of the large number of groups, it is customary to treat the U_j and V_j as random. The second level of the multilevel model assumes that

$$
\begin{aligned}
U_j = \alpha_j + \gamma_1 \\
\times \text{contextual/compositional variable } 1 \\
+ \dots \gamma_p \\
\times \text{contextual/compositional variable } p
\end{aligned}
\tag{2}
$$

$$
\begin{aligned}
V_j = \sigma_j + \eta_1 \\
\times \text{contextual/compositional variable } 1 \\
+ \dots \eta_p \\
\times \text{contextual/compositional variable } p.
\end{aligned}
\tag{3}
$$

Here α_j and σ_j represent the remaining heterogeneity in baseline risk or pollution slope unexplained by the contextual/compositional variables. Fitting such models requires extensions to standard Cox regression packages [some of which do incorporate U_j (frailty models) but not V_j]. However, a proportional hazard model can be fit as a two-stage generalized linear model, allowing the use of generalized linear mixed model procedures. This approach has the additional advantage of allowing the use of flexible functions to examine the potential for nonlinear dependence of risk on some of the covariates. Of course, in reality, not all of the above data may be available or affordable, and in any case, power considerations will certainly limit the number of interactions than can be considered. For continuous, binomial, or count outcomes these models can be fit using generalized linear mixed models.

Conclusions

Research may show that groups most likely to be made ill from air pollution also receive the highest exposure, and this exposure then exerts larger effects on their health than it does on the average or reference population. The public health and regulatory implications of such a finding could be significant because most air pollution standards aim to reduce average exposure over large regions, rather than targeting exposure reduction and mitigation programs to those areas receiving the highest exposure.[56,129] Thus, targeting exposure reduction would be justified on the grounds of maximizing public health benefits. Differential distribution of adverse health effects (as addressed in this article) also need to be considered alongside differential distribution of the benefits (e.g., employment or car ownership) related to the emission sources. In one of the few studies that has assessed the impact of air quality regulations, the overall conclusion was that poor people and communities tend to benefit most from air quality improvements.[130]

Including both air pollution and socioeconomic variables in epidemiologic studies can help inform public policy that aims to protect those most vulnerable to air pollution exposure; identify cost-effective, targeted mitigation efforts; ensure equitable protection from health risks; and develop physiologic explanations for the observed associations with SEP. As researchers evaluate how socioeconomic disparities and pollution exposure can affect health and quality of life, their work can benefit through careful consideration of the themes addressed in this article. First, researchers can clearly define their working hypotheses, considering exposures and susceptibilities and both temporal and spatial dimensions. Second, new collaborations can be formed among environmental and social epidemiologists, exposure assessment experts, and other researchers to aid selection of appropriate tools and data sets. Third, research ideas can be developed in collaboration with affected communities and policy makers tasked with environmental and health protection, as well as social and economic policies. Finally, international perspectives and collaborative studies can enhance understanding and improve public health action by showing how the complex relationships among SEP, pollution, and health vary across communities and nations.

Acknowledgments

Funding was provided by the Health Effects Institute, a training grant from the National Institute for Environmental Health Sciences, 5 T32 ES07069-22, NIEHS ES00002, and EPAR827353.

The views expressed in this article are those of the authors and do not necessarily reflect those of the Health Effects Institute or its sponsors.

References

1. Haan M, Kaplan GA, Camacho T. Poverty and health. Prospective evidence from the Alameda County Study. *Am J Epidemiol* 1987; 125:989–998.
2. Krieger N, Williams DR, Moss NE. Measuring social class in U.S. public health research: concepts, methodologies, and guidelines. *Annu Rev Public Health* 1997; 18:341–378.
3. Marmot M. Inequalities in health. *N Engl J Med* 2001; 345:134–136.
4. Brunekreef B, Holgate ST. Air pollution and health. *Lancet* 2002; 360: 1233–1242.
5. Bobak M, Leon DA. The effect of air pollution on infant mortality appears specific for respiratory causes in the postneonatal period. *Epidemiology* 1999; 10:666–670.
6. Dockery DW, Pope CA III, Xu X, Spengler JD, Ware JH, Fay ME, et al. An association between air pollution and mortality in six U.S. Cities. *N Engl J Med* 1993; 329:1753–1759.
7. Gouveia N, Fletcher T. Time series analysis of air pollution and mortality: effects by cause, age and socio-economic status. *J Epidemiol Community Health* 2000; 54:750–755.
8. Gwynn RC, Thurston GD. The burden of air pollution: impacts among racial minorities. *Environ Health Perspect* 2001; 109(suppl 4):501–506.
9. Zanobetti A, Schwartz J, Gold D. Are there sensitive subgroups for the effects of airborne particles? *Environ Health Perspect* 1000; 108:841–845.
10. Ezzati M, Lopez AD, Rodgers A, Vander Hoorn S, Murray CJ, Comparative Risk Assessment Collaborating Group. Selected major risk factors and global and regional burden of disease. *Lancet* 2002; 360:1347–1360.
11. World Bank. Millennium Development Goals: Eradicate Extreme Poverty and Hunger. 2002. Available: http://www.developmentgoals.org/Poverty .htm [accessed 13 August 2003].
12. WHO. *Air Quality Guidelines for Europe*. Copenhagen: World Health Organization, Regional Office for Europe; 2000.
13. Davis DL, Saldiva PHN. *Urban Air Pollution Risks to Children: A Global Environmental Health Indicator.* Internal Report. Washington, DC: World Resources Institute; 1999. Available: http://pdf.wri.org/urbanair_health.pdf [accessed 7 October 2003].
14. Clancy L, Goodman P, Sinclair H, Dockery DW. Effect of air-pollution control on death rates in Dublin, Ireland: an intervention study. *Lancet* 2002; 360:1210–1214.
15. McConnell R, Berhane K, Gilliland F, London SJ, Islam T, Gauderman WJ, et al. Asthma in exercising children exposed to ozone: a cohort study. *Lancet* 2002; 359:386–391.

16. Ritz B, Yu F, Fruin S, Chapa G, Shaw GM, Harris JA. Ambient air pollution and risk of birth defects in Southern California. *Am J Epidemiol* 2002; 155:17–25.
17. Schwartz J. Air pollution and blood markers of cardiovascular risk. *Environ Health Perspect* 2001; 109:405–409.
18. Working Group on Public Health and Fossil-Fuel Combustion. Short-term improvements in public health from global-climate policies on fossil-fuel combustion: an interim report. *Lancet* 1997; 350:1341–1349.
19. Bell ML, Davis D, Cifuentes L, Cohen A, Gouveia N, Grant L, et al. International Expert Workshop on the Analysis of the Economic and Public Health Impacts of Air Pollution: workshop summary. *Environ Health Perspect* 2002; 110:1163–1168.
20. National Research Council. *Research Priorities for Airborne Particulate Matter I. Immediate Priorities and a Long-range Research Portfolio.* Washington, DC: National Academy Press; 1998.
21. Bullard RD, Wright BH. Environmental justice for all: community perspectives on health and research needs. *Toxicol Ind Health* 1993; 9:821–841.
22. Israel BA, Schulz AJ, Parker EA, Becker AB. Review of community-based research: assessing partnership approaches to improve public health. *Annu Rev Public Health* 1998; 19:173–202.
23. Evans GW, Kantrowitz E. Socioeconomic status and health: the potential role of environmental risk exposure. *Annu Rev Public Health* 2002; 23: 303–331.
24. Kaplan GA. The role of epidemiologists in eradicability of poverty. *Lancet* 1998; 352:1627–1628.
25. McMichael AJ. The role of epidemiologists in eradicability of poverty [Letter]. *Lancet* 1998; 352:1627.
26. Susser M. Does risk factor epidemiology put epidemiology at risk—peering into the future. *J Epidemiol Community Health* 1998; 52:608–611.
27. Kawachi I, Berkman L. *Neighborhoods and Health.* New York: Oxford University Press; 2003.
28. Davey Smith G, Gunnell D, Ben-Shlomo Y. Life-course approaches to socio-economic differentials in cause-specific adult mortality. In: *Poverty, Inequality and Health: An International Perspective* (Leon D, Walt G, eds). Oxford, UK: Oxford University Press; 2001, 88–124.
29. McDonough P, Duncan GJ, Williams D, House J. Income dynamics and adult mortality in the United States, 1972 through 1989. *Am J Public Health* 1997; 87:1476–1483.
30. Daly MC, Duncan GJ, McDonough P, Williams DR. Optimal indicators of socioeconomic status for health research. *Am J Public Health* 2002; 92:1151–1157.
31. Janssen NA, Hoek G, Brunekreef B, Harssema H, Mensink I, Zuidhof A. Personal sampling of particles in adults: relation among personal, indoor, and outdoor air concentrations. *Am J Epidemiol* 1998; 147:537–547.

32. Samet JM, Dominici F, Curriero FC, Coursac I, Zeger SL. Fine particulate air pollution and mortality in 20 U.S. cities, 1987-1994. *N Engl J Med* 2000; 343:1742–1749.
33. Liu LJ, Delfino R, Koutrakis P. Ozone exposure assessment in a Southern California community. *Environ Health Perspect* 1997; 105:58–65.
34. Pijawka DJ, Blair J, Guhathakurta SLS, Ashur S. Environmental equity in central cities: socioeconomic dimensions and planning strategies. *J Plan Educ Res* 1998; 18:113–123.
35. Been V. What's fairness got to do with it? Environmental justice and the siting of locally undesirable land uses. *Cornell Law Rev* 1993; 78: 1001–1036.
36. Pulido L. Rethinking environmental racism: white privilege and urban development in Southern California. *Ann Assoc Am Geogr* 2000; 90:12–40.
37. Sexton K, Adgate JL. Looking at environmental justice from an environmental health perspective. *J Expo Anal Environ Epidemiol* 1999; 9:3–8.
38. Burton RM, Suh HH, Koutrakis P. Spatial variation in particulate concentrations within metropolitan Philadelphia. *Environ Sci Technol* 1996; 30: 400–407.
39. Suh HH, Allen GA, Koutrakis P, Burton RM. Spatial variation in acidic sulfate and ammonia concentrations within metropolitan Philadelphia. *J Air Waste Manage* 1995; 45:442–451.
40. Buckeridge D, Glazier R, Harvey B, Escobar M, Amrhein C, Frank J. Effect of motor vehicle emissions on respiratory health in an urban area. *Environ Health Perspect* 2002; 110:293–300.
41. Zhu YF, Hinds WC, Kim S, Shen S, Sioutas C. Study of ultrafine particles near a major highway with heavy-duty diesel traffic. *Atmos Environ* 2002; 36:4323–4335.
42. Hitchins J, Morawska L, Wolff R, Gilbert D. Concentrations of submicrometre particles from vehicle emissions near a major road. *Atmos Environ* 2000; 34:51–59.
43. Kinney PL, Aggarwal M, Northridge ME, Janssen NA, Shepard P. Airborne concentrations of PM2.5 and diesel exhaust particles on Harlem sidewalks: a community-based pilot study. *Environ Health Perspect* 2000; 108:213–218.
44. Nielsen T. Traffic contribution of polycyclic aromatic hydrocarbons in the center of a large city. *Atmos Environ* 1996; 30:3481–3490.
45. Hewitt CN. Spatial variations in nitrogen dioxide concentrations in an urban area. *Atmos Environ* 1991; 25B:429–434.
46. Briggs D, Collins S, Elliott P, Fischer P, Kingham S, Lebert E, et al. Mapping urban air pollution using GIS: a regression-based approach. *Int J Geogr Inf Sci* 1997; 11:699–718.
47. Hoek G, Fischer P, VanDenBrandt P, Goldbohm S, Brunekreef B. Estimation of long-term average exposure to outdoor air pollution for a cohort study on mortality. *J Expo Anal Environ Epidemiol* 2001; 11:459–469.

48. Rijnders E, Janssen NA, van Vliet PH, Brunekreef B. Personal and outdoor nitrogen dioxide concentrations in relation to degree of urbanization and traffic density. *Environ Health Perspect* 2001; 109(suppl 3):411–417.
49. Godish T. *Air Quality*, 2nd ed. Chelsea, MI: Lewis Publishers; 1991.
50. Institute of Medicine. *Toward Environmental Justice: Research, Education, and Health Policy Needs.* Washington, DC: National Academy Press; 1999.
51. Sexton K, Gong H Jr, Bailar JC, Ford JG, Gold DR, Lambert WE, et al. Air pollution health risks: do class and race matter? *Toxicol Ind Health* 1993; 9:843–878.
52. Brunekreef B, Janssen NA, de Hartog J, Harssema H, Knape M, van Vliet P. Air pollution from truck traffic and lung function in children living near motorways. *Epidemiology* 1997; 8:298–303.
53. English P, Neutra R, Scalf R, Sullivan M, Waller L, Zhu L. Examining associations between childhood asthma and traffic flow using a geographic information system. *Environ Health Perspect* 1999; 107:761–767.
54. Weiland SK, Mundt KA, Ruckmann A, Keil U. Self-reported wheezing and allergic rhinitis in children and traffic density on street of residence. *Ann Epidemiol* 1994; 4:243–247.
55. Graves P, Murdock JC, Thayer MA, Waldman D. The robustness of hedonic price estimation: urban air quality. *Land Econ* 1988; 64:220–233.
56. Jerrett M, Burnett RT, Kanaroglou P, Eyles J, Finkelstein N, Giovis C, et al. 2001. A GIS-environmental justice analysis of particulate air pollution in Hamilton, Canada. Environ Plan A 33:955–973.
57. Rotko T, Koistinen K, Hanninen O, Jantunen M. Sociodemographic descriptors of personal exposure to fine particles (PM2.5) in Expolis Helsinki. *J Expo Anal Environ Epidemiol* 2000; 10:385–393.
58. Rotko T, Hanninen O, Jantunen MJ. Time used in traffic by sociodemographic groups in Expolis-Helsinki. *Epidemiology* 2002; 13:S256–257.
59. Korc ME. A socioeconomic assessment of human exposure to ozone in the south coast air basin of California. *J Air Waste Manage* 1996; 46:547–557.
60. Pellizzari E, Perritt R, Clayton C. National human exposure assessment survey (NHEXAS): exploratory survey of exposure among population subgroups in EPA Region V. *J Expo Anal Environ Epidemiol* 1999; 9:49–55.
61. Romieu I, Ramirez M, Meneses F, Ashley D, Lemire S, Colome S, et al. Environmental exposure to volatile organic compounds among workers in Mexico City as assessed by personal monitors and blood concentrations. *Environ Health Perspect* 1999; 107:511–515.
62. Rotko T, Kousa A, Alm S, Jantunen M. Exposures to nitrogen dioxide in Expolis-Helsinki: microenvironment, behavioral and sociodemographic factors. *J Expo Anal Environ Epidemiol* 2001; 11:216–223.
63. Castillejos M, Gold DR, Damokosh AI, Serrano P, Allen G, McDonnell WF, et al. Acute effects of ozone on the pulmonary function of exercising schoolchildren in Mexico City. *Am J Respir Crit Care Med* 1995; 152: 1501–1507.

64. Oglesby L, Rotko T, Krutli P, Boudet C, Kruize H, Nen MJ, et al. Personal exposure assessment studies may suffer from exposure-relevant selection bias. *J Expo Anal Environ Epidemiol* 2000; 10:251–266.
65. Gehring U, Cyrys J, Sedlmeir G, Brunekreef B, Bellander T, Fischer P, et al. Traffic-related air pollution and respiratory health during the first 2 years of life. *Eur Respir J* 2002; 19:690–698.
66. Pikhart H, Bobak M, Gorynski P, Wojtyniak B, Danova J, Celko MA, et al. Outdoor sulphur dioxide and respiratory symptoms in Czech and Polish school children: a small-area study (SAVIAH). Small-area variation in air pollution and health. *Int Arch Occup Environ Health* 2001; 74:574–578.
67. Bellander T, Berglind N, Gustavsson P, Jonson T, Nyberg F, Pershagen G, et al. Using geographic information systems to assess individual historical exposure to air pollution from traffic and house heating in Stockholm. *Environ Health Perspect* 2001; 109:633–639.
68. Bowen W. An analytical review of environmental justice research: what do we really know? *Environ Manage* 2002; 29:3–15.
69. Maantay J. Zoning, equity, and public health. *Am J Public Health* 2001; 91:1033–1041.
70. Sexton K. Sociodemographic aspects of human susceptibility to toxic chemicals: do class and race matter for realistic risk assessment? *Environ Toxicol Pharmacol* 1997; 4:261–269.
71. Morland K, Wing S, Diez Roux A, Poole C. Neighborhood characteristics associated with the location of food stores and food service places. *Am J Prev Med* 2002; 22:23–29.
72. Romieu I, Meneses F, Ramirez M, Ruiz S, Perez Padilla R, Sienra JJ, et al. Antioxidant supplementation and respiratory functions among workers exposed to high levels of ozone. *Am J Respir Crit Care* 1998; 158: 226–232.
73. Wright RJ, Rodriguez M, Cohen S. Review of psychosocial stress and asthma: an integrated biopsychosocial approach. *Thorax* 1998; 53:1066–1074.
74. Wright RJ, Steinbach SF. Violence: an unrecognized environmental exposure that may contribute to greater asthma morbidity in high risk inner-city populations. *Environ Health Perspect* 2001; 109:1085–1089.
75. Diez Roux AV. Investigating neighborhood and area effects on health. *Am J Public Health* 2001; 91:1783–1789.
76. Appleyard D. *Livable Streets.* Berkeley: University of California Press; 1981.
77. Smith KR, Samet JM, Romieu I, Bruce N. Indoor air pollution in developing countries and acute lower respiratory infections in children. *Thorax* 2000; 55:518–532.
78. Rios R, Poje GV, Detels R. Susceptibility to environmental pollutants among minorities. *Toxicol Ind Health* 1993; 9:797–820.
79. Krieger JW, Song L, Takaro TK, Stout J. Asthma and the home environment of low-income urban children: preliminary findings from the Seattle-King County healthy homes project. *J Urban Health* 2000; 77:50–67.

80. Leaderer BP, Belanger K, Triche E, Holford T, Gold DR, Kim Y, et al. Dust mite, cockroach, cat, and dog allergen concentrations in homes of asthmatic children in the northeastern United States: impact of socioeconomic factors and population density. *Environ Health Perspect* 2002; 110: 419–425.

81. Kattan M, Mitchell H, Eggleston P, Gergen P, Crain E, Redline S, et al. Characteristics of inner-city children with asthma: the national cooperative inner-city asthma study. *Pediatr Pulm* 1997; 24:253–262.

82. Bateson TF, Schwartz J. Who is sensitive to the effects of particles on mortality? A case-crossover analysis. *Epidemiology*. In press.

83. Goldberg MS, Burnett RT, Brook J, Bailar JC III, Valois MF, Vincent R. Associations between daily cause-specific mortality and concentrations of ground-level ozone in Montreal, Quebec. *Am J Epidemiol* 2001; 154: 817–826.

84. Zanobetti A. Cardiovascular damage by airborne particles: are diabetics more susceptible? *Epidemiology* 2002; 13:588–592.

85. Cowie CC, Eberhardt MS. *Sociodemographic characteristics of persons with diabetes. In: Diabetes in America*, 2nd ed. NIH Publication No. 95-1468. Bethesda, MD: National Diabetes Data Group, National Institute of Diabetes and Digestive and Kidney Diseases; 1995.

86. Ekoe JM, Zimmet P, Williams R, eds. *The Epidemiology of Diabetes Mellitus: An International Perspective*. Chichester, UK: John Wiley & Sons, Ltd.; 2001.

87. Brunner EJ, Marmot MG, Nanchahal K, Shipley MJ, Stansfeld SA, Juneja M, et al. Social inequality in coronary risk: central obesity and the metabolic syndrome. Evidence from the Whitehall II study. *Diabetologia* 1997; 40:1341–1349.

88. Gold DR, Litonjua A, Schwartz J, Lovett E, Larson A, Nearing B, et al. Ambient pollution and heart rate variability. *Circulation* 2000; 101: 1267–1273.

89. Peters A, Frohlich M, Doring A, Immervoll T, Wichmann HE, Hutchinson WL, et al. Particulate air pollution is associated with an acute phase response in men; results from the Monica-Augsburg study. *Eur Heart J* 2001; 22:1198–1204.

90. Visscher TL, Seidell JC. The public health impact of obesity. *Annu Rev Public Health* 2001; 22:355–375.

91. Visser M, Bouter LM, McQuillan GM, Wener MH, Harris TB. Elevated C-reactive protein levels in overweight and obese adults. *JAMA* 1999; 282:2131–2135.

92. Bach JF. Mechanisms of disease: the effect of infections on susceptibility to autoimmune and allergic diseases. *N Engl J Med* 2002; 347:911–920.

93. Pearce N, Beasley R, Burgess C, Crane J, eds. *Asthma Epidemiology: Principles and Methods*. New York: Oxford University Press; 1998.

94. Hassan MR, Kabir AR, Mahmud AM, Rahman F, Hossain MA, Bennoor KS, et al. Self-reported asthma symptoms in children and adults of Bangladesh: findings of the national asthma prevalence study. *Int J Epidemiol* 2002; 31:483–488.
95. Chen JT, Krieger N, Van Den Eeden SK, Quesenberry CP. Different slopes for different folks: socioeconomic and racial/ethnic disparities in asthma and hay fever among 173,859 U.S. men and women. *Environ Health Perspect* 2002; 110(suppl 2):211–216.
96. Lin RS, Sung FC, Huang SL, Gou YL, Ko YC, Gou HW, et al. Role of urbanization and air pollution in adolescent asthma: a mass screening in Taiwan. *J Formos Med Assoc* 2001; 100:649–655.
97. Norris G, Larson T, Koenig J, Claiborn C, Sheppard L, Finn D. Asthma aggravation, combustion, and stagnant air. *Thorax* 2000; 55:466–470.
98. Centers for Disease Control and Prevention. Cigarette smoking among adults—United States, 1999. *Morb Mortal Wkly Rep* 2001; 50:869–873.
99. Vazquez-Segovia LA, Sesma-Vazquez S, Hernandez-Avila M. Tobacco consumption in Mexican households: results from the national household income and expenditure survey, 1984–2000. *Salud Publica Mex* 2002; 44:S76–S81.
100. MacNee W, Donaldson K. Exacerbations of COPD: environmental mechanisms. *Chest* 2000; 117:390S–397S.
101. Census Dissemination Unit. 1991 *Area Statistics*. 1999. Available: http://census.ac.uk/cdu/Datasets/1991_Census_datasets/Area_Stats/ [accessed 30 October 2003].
102. ESRC. Environmental Justice: Rights and Means to a Healthy Environment for All. Special Briefing No. 7. Swindon, UK:Economic and Social Research Council, Global Environmental Change Programme; 2001. Available: http://www.foe.co.uk/resource/reports/environmental_justice.pdf [accessed 7 October 2003].
103. Liberatos P, Link BG, Kelsey JL. The measurement of social class in epidemiology. *Epidemiol Rev* 1988; 10:87–121.
104. Lynch J, Kaplan J. Socioeconomic position. In: *Social Epidemiology* (Berkman L, Kawachi I, eds). New York: Oxford University Press; 2000, 13–35.
105. Krieger N, Waterman P, Chen JT, Soobader MJ, Subramanian SV, Carson R. ZIP code caveat: bias due to spatiotemporal mismatches between zip codes and US census-defined geographic areas—the Public Health Disparities Geocoding Project. *Am J Public Health* 2002; 92:1100–1102.
106. John D. and Catherine T. MacArthur Research Network on Socioeconomic Status and Health. *Network Research*. 2003. Available: http://www.macses.ucsf.edu/Research/overview.htm [accessed 13 August 2003].
107. Goodman E, Adler NE, Kawachi I, Frazier AL, Huang B, Colditz GA. Adolescents' perceptions of social status: development and evaluation of a

new indicator. *Pediatrics* 2001; 108:E31. Available: http://pediatrics.aap publications.org/cgi/content/full/108/2/e31 [accessed 7 October 2003].

108. Balfour JL, Kaplan GA. Neighborhood environment and loss of physical function in older adults: evidence from the Alameda County study. *Am J Epidemiol* 2002; 155:507–515.

109. Chang LT, Koutrakis P, Catalano PJ, Suh HH. Hourly personal exposures to fine particles and gaseous pollutants—results from Baltimore, Maryland. *J Air Waste Manage* 2000; 50:1223–1235.

110. Borja-Aburto VH, Loomis DP, Bangdiwala SI, Shy CM, Rascon-Pacheco RA. Ozone, suspended particulates, and daily mortality in Mexico City. *Am J Epidemiol* 1997; 145:258–268.

111. Ritz B, Yu F, Chapa G, Fruin S. Effect of air pollution on preterm birth among children born in Southern California between 1989 and 1993. *Epidemiology* 2000; 11:502–511.

112. Zanobetti A, Schwartz J, Dockery DW. Airborne particles are a risk factor for hospital admissions for heart and lung disease. *Environ Health Perspect* 2000. 108:1071–1077.

113. Tolbert PE, Mulholland JA, MacIntosh DL, Xu F, Daniels D, Devine OJ, et al. Air quality and pediatric emergency room visits for asthma in Atlanta, Georgia, USA. *Am J Epidemiol* 2000; 151:798–810.

114. Castillejos M, Gold DR, Dockery D, Tosteson T, Baum T, Speizer FE. Effects of ambient ozone on respiratory function and symptoms in Mexico City schoolchildren. *Am Rev Respir Dis* 1992; 145:276–282.

115. Diez Roux AV, Merkin SS, Arnett D, Chambless L, Massing M, Nieto FJ, et al. Neighborhood of residence and incidence of coronary heart disease. *N Engl J Med* 2001; 345:99–106.

116. Sampson RJ, Raudenbush SW, Earls F. Neighborhoods and violent crime: a multilevel study of collective efficacy. *Science* 1997; 277:918–924.

117. Finkelstein M, Jerrett M, De Luca P, Finkelstein N, Verma DK, Chapman K, et al. Environmental justice: a cohort study of income, air pollution and mortality. *Can Med Assoc J* 2003; 169:397–402.

118. Millimet DL, Slottje D. An environmental Paglin-Gini. *Appl Econ Lett* 2002; 9:271–274.

119. Greenland S. Ecologic versus individual-level sources of bias in ecologic estimates of contextual health effects. *Int J Epidemiol* 2001; 30:1343–1350.

120. Diez Roux AV. Multilevel analysis in public health research. *Annu Rev Public Health* 2000; 21:171–192.

121. Kawachi I. Income inequality and health. In: *Social Epidemiology* (Berkman LF, Kawachi I, eds). New York: Oxford University Press; 2000, 76–94.

122. Navidi W, Thomas D, Stram D, Peters J. Design and analysis of multilevel analytic studies with applications to a study of air pollution. *Environ Health Perspect* 1994; 102(suppl 8):25–32.

123. Ratcliffe JH, McCullagh MJ. Hotbeds of crime and the search for spatial accuracy. *Geogr Syst* 1999; 1:385–398.

124. Anderton D, Anderson J, Oakes J, Fraser M. Environmental equity: the demographics of dumping. *Demography* 1994; 31:229–248.

125. Maclure M. The case-crossover design: a method for studying transient effects on the risk of acute events. *Am J Epidemiol* 1991; 133:144–153.

126. Pope CA III. Mortality and air pollution: associations persist with continued advances in research methodology. *Environ Health Perspect* 1999; 107: 613–614.

127. Rothman KJ, Greenland S, eds. *Modern Epidemiology*, 2nd ed. Philadelphia: Lippincott-Raven; 1998.

128. HEI. *Reanalysis of the Harvard Six Cities Study and the American Cancer Society Study of Particulate Air Pollution and Mortality.* Cambridge, MA: Health Effects Institute; 2000. Available: http://www.healtheffects.org/Pubs/ReanExecSumm.pdf [accessed 7 October 2003].

129. Levy JI, Greco SL, Spengler JD. The importance of population susceptibility for air pollution risk assessment: a case study of power plants near Washington, DC. *Environ Health Perspect* 2002; 110:1253–1260.

130. Bae CHC. The equity impacts of Los Angeles' air quality policies. *Environ Plan A* 1997; 29:1563–1584.

131. Nyberg F, Gustavsson P, Jarup L, Bellander T, Berglind N, Jakobsson R, et al. Urban air pollution and lung cancer in Stockholm. *Epidemiology* 2000; 11:487–495.

Examining Urban Brownfields
Through the Public Health "Macroscope"

Jill S. Litt, Nga L. Tran, and Thomas A. Burke

Introduction

Since the mid-1970s, legislative and policy boundaries have been drawn around the management of hazardous waste and the protection of the public health and the environment from the adverse effects of hazardous waste contamination. While myriad sites have been enrolled in federal and state hazardous waste management programs and subsequently tracked, evaluated, and, in many instances, remediated, hundreds of thousands of waste sites remain that are outside the reach of existing programs yet may pose significant public health and environmental risks.

Over the past decade, interest has been renewed in putting to use vacant industrial land, also referred to as brownfields, which the U.S. Environmental Protection Agency (U.S. EPA) defines as "abandoned, idled, or under-used industrial and commercial facilities where expansion or redevelopment is complicated by real or perceived environmental contamination."[1] Through new and amended environmental legislation and policies, government agencies are developing long-term strategies to link the cleanup of vacant land to redevelopment. These efforts aim to reduce liability for potential purchasers and lending institutions and to increase flexibility in the cleanup and reuse of vacant or underused properties. The U.S. Department of Housing and Urban Development estimated that over 90% of states have established some aspect of a voluntary cleanup program to ease the redevelopment of brownfields sites.[2] The new administration also has singled out brownfields cleanup and redevelopment as a top environmental priority.[3] Finally, on 11 January 2002, President Bush signed the Small Business Liability Relief and Brownfields Revitalization Act into law that aims to facilitate cleanup activities and redevelopment.[4]

The potential benefits of reusing urban land, redirecting development away from pristine areas and increasing opportunities for neighborhood revitalization and economic expansion in distressed neighborhoods, are widely recognized. However, questions and concerns remain about whether new policies will protect the communities most affected by such measures and whether local health officials, regulators, and communities are prepared for the potential short- and long-term hazards of brownfields given the paucity of environmental data on these properties and the exposure risks that may ensue if we do not implement adequate technology-based and institutional controls and sustain them over time. Technology-based controls are pollution control requirements for point sources (municipal wastewater treatment plants and industrial discharges) and nonpoint sources of pollution that are required by federal, state, or local environmental laws. The U.S. EPA defines "institutional controls" as they relate to hazardous waste sites as "legal mechanisms designed to control exposures to chemicals in environmental media, including soil and groundwater."[5]

The cleanup and redevelopment of vacant industrial land are issues that will affect poor, working-class, and minority communities, for better or worse.[6,7] At first glance, the prospects of cleanup and concomitant redevelopment may be tantalizing given the promised economic benefits. At second glance, however, expedited cleanup and redevelopment may come at the community's expense—environmental, social, economic, and public health harm—given the environmental unknowns of brownfields and the sensitive populations living in affected areas.[7]

This study provides a starting point for investigators to examine brownfields through a public health lens—that is, to examine the potential hazards of brownfields both at a site-specific and at neighborhood levels and to identify opportunities for prevention and short- and long-term public health planning. Specifically, in this article we evaluate brownfields in Southeast Baltimore by tracing the historic operations of 182 vacant industrial sites. We screened sites for their hazard potential, drawing on hazard identification information, chemical persistence data, and physical characteristics of sites. Statistical models characterize the health of communities living near hazardous brownfields areas.

Methods

Study Area Profile

Census Data.   We used data at the census-tract level for this research project. Census-tract boundaries, as defined by the U.S. Census Bureau, represent approximately 4,000 persons. Baltimore has 203 census tracts, 28 of which define the Southeast Baltimore study area. In terms of equity analyses, researchers have shown that the geographic extent of a study area (e.g., county, ZIP code, census tract, census block group, census block) may influence findings about the communities of concern, particularly as it relates to the location of the impact area that may be the basis for an inequitable situation.[8,9] For this project, we chose the census tract as a starting point for characterizing brownfields communities. While these lines are political in nature, they provide basic information about the social and economic characteristics of Southeast Baltimore and were consistent with the impact area of interest—industrial brownfields properties and the geographic scale necessary to protect confidentiality of individual health information and preempt problems introduced by small numbers of cases and consequently unstable death rates.

For this research, we created and evaluated indicators using the 1990 census data to provide this broader context from which the "brownfields" issue can be considered and evaluated. These indicators included age, poverty status, population density, percent minority, percent working class, percentage of adults with less than a high school degree, percent vacant homes, percentage of families with income greater than $50,000, and percent owner-occupied homes. The indicators aimed to capture community assets and economic strengths. For example, evaluating income levels at the neighborhood level may miss important insights about "family assets" that influence residential mobility and consequently neighborhood stability. In this instance, we considered home ownership a reasonable proxy for wealth and included it in this analysis.[10-14]

Health Data. We obtained data on the leading causes of mortality for the population 45 years of age and older in Baltimore City for 1990–1996. These end points included heart disease, cancer, stroke, chronic obstructive pulmonary disease (COPD), diabetes, influenza and pneumonia, and liver disease. We selected these end points to capture the diseases that bear the greatest public health impact on Baltimore's communities for populations 45 years of age and older and that have been identified in the literature as being plausibly determined or influenced by environmental exposures.[15-18] We developed age-adjusted mortality rates and mapped them at the U.S. census tract scale using ArcView, a geographic information system.[19] We used the 1940 standard population for direct adjustment to facilitate comparisons with state and national data. Because the denominator consists of population 45 years of age and older, we readjusted the 1940 population standard weights accordingly. We calculated population estimates for intercensal years 1991 through 1996 by linear interpolation between the 1990 and 1997 U.S. census figures.[20]

Building the Brownfields Scoring Algorithm

The methodology to rank brownfields involved a stepwise approach. It encompassed the development of scores specific to substance, site, and census tract, which the following four subsections discuss.

Step 1: Site Inventory. The Baltimore City Planning Department's inventory of vacant and underused parcels was the starting point for developing a brownfields-scoring algorithm. Site-specific address information, parcel size, current occupancy, land value, and several other parameters were available for each site. To trace past uses of these sites and construct a comprehensive profile of the study properties, we consulted the following resources: Baltimore City

Real Estate Tax Assessments (1935–1997); the Baltimore City Health Department archives; the Maryland Department of Environment Divisions of Waste Management, Air and Radiation, Water Management, and Technical and Regulatory Services, and Baltimore Manufacturing Directories, among other resources. Details about these data sources and the data collected are described elsewhere.[21]

Step 2: Substance Score.   From the review of facility files and other reference materials, we developed a chemical substance database. This database included chemicals used in past processes or released on site, as recorded in facility files or other industrial records. We then populated the database with information on the hazard potential and chemical persistence. This screening algorithm is limited by available testing data and thus provides a first step in understanding the range of hazards associated with urban brownfields.

For each chemical, we assigned hazard scores and chemical persistence weights and combined them to derive scores for each substance:

$$\text{Substance score}_n = \text{hazard score}_n \times \text{chemical persistence weight}_n \qquad [1]$$

We derived this type of weighting algorithm, in part, from the U.S. EPA Hazard Ranking System,[22] which the Superfund program uses to characterize hazards at hazardous waste sites, and the U.S. EPA Toxics Release Inventory Relative Risk-Based Environmental Indicator Initiative.[22,23] It also draws on Tran et al.'s[24] application of a proportional weighting scheme to evaluate the acute and chronic health risks for military personnel deployed overseas.

The following subsections discuss the individual components of Equation 1. Table 10-1 summarizes these components, their chemical characteristics, the assigned weights, and the data sources.

Hazard score.   Hazard scoring methods using quantitative metrics such as the LC_{50}, LD_{50}, reference dose, or cancer slope factor have been used for risk ranking and screening purposes.[22,23] We considered these approaches, but LC_{50} and LD_{50} were not applicable for chronic effects, and reference dose and cancer slope factor were not available for a majority of chemicals present at the brownfields sites included in the study. To capture the full range of substances of concern in the study, we developed a semiquantitative approach using the qualitative "weight of evidence" information on thousands of chemicals included in the Environmental Defense's Scorecard Initiative[25] and the quantitative weighting schemes.

For each substance in the scorecard database, the "weight of evidence" for 12 broad categories of health is captured as a "recognized" and/or "suspected" toxicant. A recognized toxicant refers to agents that have been studied by national or international authoritative and scientific regulatory hazard identification efforts.[26] Suspected toxicants are agents that have been shown to have target organ toxicity in either humans or two mammalian species by a relevant

Table 10-1 Description of Hazard Potential-Persistence Algorithm Components

Parameter	Description	Weight Assignments	Source
Chemical persistence	K_{oc}: The measure of a chemical's tendency "to absorb to soil or sediment organic matter"[30]	$K_{oc} > 10{,}000 = 1{,}000$ $1{,}000 < K_{oc} < 10{,}000 = 100$ $100 < K_{oc} = 10$	(44) (45)
Hazard potential	Recognized toxicant. An agent that has been studied by national or international authoritative and scientific regulatory hazard identification efforts. Information on recognized toxicants was available for three broad categories of health effects: cancer, reproductive, and developmental	Recognized toxicant = 10	(25–27)
	Suspected toxicant. Agents that have been shown to have target organ toxicity in either humans or two mammalian species by a relevant route of exposure. Information on suspected toxicants related to the following broad categories of health effects: cardiovascular/blood, developmental, endocrine, gastrointestinal/liver, immunologic, kidney, musculoskeletal, neurological, reproductive, respiratory, skin/sense organs, and cancer.	Suspected toxicant = 5	

route of exposure.[27] Together, these data provided a means to use toxicologic information for screening purposes and maximize information on a wide range of chemical substances.

To quantify the scorecard's weight of evidence, we assigned a "suspected" effect a weight of 5 and a "recognized" health effect a weight of 10. The aim of this weighting system was to emphasize the proportional differences between recognized and suspected toxicants. We considered ordinal ranking schemes for this analysis, but they were limited in illustrating the relative differences in hazard potential between substances. Table 10-1 defines recognized and suspected toxicants and describes the weights assigned to these substances.

Multiple recognized or suspected health effects are associated with each substance in the brownfields chemical database. Thus, by summing the weights associated with the effects, a hazard score for each substance can be derived. These scores will be limited by the availability and extent of toxicity data. Lead provides an example of a substance that is associated with more than one health effect and is classified as both a recognized and a suspected toxicant. Based on the scientific literature, it is recognized as a carcinogen as well as a reproductive and developmental toxicant and is suspected to be toxic to the respiratory, neurologic, gastrointestinal/liver, skin and sense organ, cardiovascular and blood organ, kidney, immunologic, and endocrine systems. Based on the weight of evidence, we derived the following hazard score for lead as follows:

$$\text{Hazard score for lead} = (3 \text{ recognized effects} \times 10) \\ + (8 \text{ suspected effects} \times 5) = 70 \quad [1a]$$

Chemical persistence. Soil contamination from past industrial uses is one of the major exposure pathways for local residents, remediation crews, construction workers, and current occupants of brownfields properties. Therefore, we selected a metric of chemical persistence (K_{oc}) as a proxy for substance's fate in the environment. A chemical with high adsorptive capacity is less likely to volatilize into the air. The K_{oc} has been adopted by the U.S. EPA in its soil screening guidance[28] and applied to the Superfund chemical data matrix.[29]

We assigned proportional weights to the K_{oc} value associated with each substance,[30] which are described in Table 10-1. Substances with a K_{oc} greater than 10,000 are recognized to adsorb to soil organic carbon. Substances within the middle range may or may not adsorb, depending on other physical–chemical characteristics associated with the substance and the soil. Finally, substances with a low K_{oc} will not adsorb to organic carbon.[30,31]

Metals such as chromium, lead, nickel, iron compounds, copper compounds, and aluminum are recognized to be highly persistent compounds that do not degrade in the environment.[32] Therefore, we applied a weight of 1,000 to each of these compounds to capture their persistence in the environment.

Step 3: Site-Specific Score. For each brownfields site, we calculated a total score representing all substances (n) found at each site (Equation 2a). Once we developed a site score, we weighted it by other site-specific information such as duration of operation for each property by use and parcel size (Equation 2b). Where this information was missing, we assigned the average duration of operation (i.e., 46 years). We applied the weight as a multiplier to each site score.

$$\text{Site score A} = ..._n(\text{substance score})_n \quad [2a]$$
$$\text{Site score B} = \text{site score A} \times \text{years of operation} \times \text{acreage} \quad [2b]$$

Step 4: Tract-Specific Score and Rank. We calculated a score for each tract by aggregating the site-specific scores (j) in each census tract (Equation 3a). At the tract level, we applied a weight for adjusted density of sites (total sites per square mile minus acreage of parkland and waterways) as a multiplier to derive tract-specific scores (Equation 3b).

$$\text{Tract score A} = \ldots \text{A}_j(\text{site score B})_j \qquad [3a]$$
$$\text{Tract score B} = \text{tract score A} \times \text{site density} \qquad [3b]$$

We ranked the tract-specific scores and grouped them into ranges using the SAS RANK procedure.[33] The three groups or "zones" represented 16 tracts with a low hazard potential (zone 1), five tracts with a medium hazard potential (zone 2), and seven tracts with a high hazard potential (zone 3). These three zones formed the basis for a newly created categorical variable, referred to as a brownfields indicator, to be used in the statistical analysis as described in the following section.

Multivariate Statistical Modeling

We used log-linear models to evaluate health status across brownfields zones. The following sections describe the independent and dependent variables and the statistical models.

Independent Variables

Brownfields indicator.   The brownfields indicator was the independent variable of interest, which we created from the tract-specific score as discussed in the previous section. We classified the census tracts into zones 1–3 as described above.

Social class and demographic indicators.   We evaluated the socioeconomic variables for correlation and narrowed to two principal components to simplify the regression model.[34] The first two principal components accounted for 75% of the variance of the five variables. Upon examining the loadings, the first principal component (PC1) represented percent owner-occupied homes, poverty status, and minority populations and the second principal component (PC2) represented percent working class and educational attainment. We then included these factors in the log-linear regression model as the socioeconomic covariates.

Dependent Variables.   The leading causes of mortality were the dependent variables. We obtained these data from the Baltimore City Health Department for years 1990 through 1996. We also restricted the data to deaths for the population 45 years of age and older. The end points included leading cause of death index, cancer (all-cause, lung, colon, bladder, stomach, oral, head and neck, skin), heart disease, COPD, diabetes, cerebrovascular disease, influenza and pneumonia, and liver disease.

Log-Linear Model.   The base statistical model included the brownfields indicator (categorical) and population age (categorical). An extended model considered the contributions of population age, socioeconomic factors (PC1 and PC2), and area of census tracts:

$$
\begin{aligned}
\text{Log(expected deaths)} = \beta_0 &+ \beta_1 \text{ (brownfields indicator)} \\
&+ \beta_2 \text{(population age)} \\
&+ \beta_3 \text{ (area of census tract)} \qquad [4]\\
&+ \beta_4 \text{ (PC1)} + \beta_5 \text{ (PC2)}
\end{aligned}
$$

We used SAS GENMOD to estimate regression coefficients, with age-specific population estimates as the offset term. The model assumed a log link and a Poisson distribution. We used chi-square tests and residual plots to evaluate the fit of the models and calculated the odds ratios as measures of association by exponentiating the ß coefficient. We present the results of each model as odds ratios with 95% confidence intervals.[35]

Results

Study Area Profile

Figure 10-1 displays the brownfields inventory for Baltimore City and provides a delineation of the study area and the spatial extent of the three brownfields zones within the study area based on the results of the brownfields algorithm. Table 10-2 provides average percentages for each socioeconomic indicator for Baltimore City (excluding Southeast Baltimore) and Southeast Baltimore, averages by brownfields zones in Southeast Baltimore, and the spatial display of these indicators are in Figure 10-2 and 10-3. Figure 10-3A and B compares age-adjusted mortality rates in Southeast Baltimore with rates for the rest of the city, for Maryland, and for the United States. The data illustrate that, for key causes of death, Baltimore (both Southeast Baltimore and the rest of the city) suffers from excess mortality for heart disease, total cancers (specifically cancers of the lung, colon, stomach, and bladder), COPD, diabetes, influenza and pneumonia, and liver disease. Figure 10-3C–H presents the spatial distribution of the age-adjusted rates by census tract across Baltimore City using a geographic information system.[19] These data together paint a picture of baseline health status in Baltimore and provide a context from which to consider these trends by comparing them with those for Maryland and the United States.

Brownfields Ranking Results

Substance-Specific Score.   For this analysis, we identified persistence data for 90 of the 122 substances (74%). "Weight-of-evidence" hazard information from the scorecard database was available for 105 substances included in the brownfields chemical inventory (85%). For example, of the 105 substances, 71

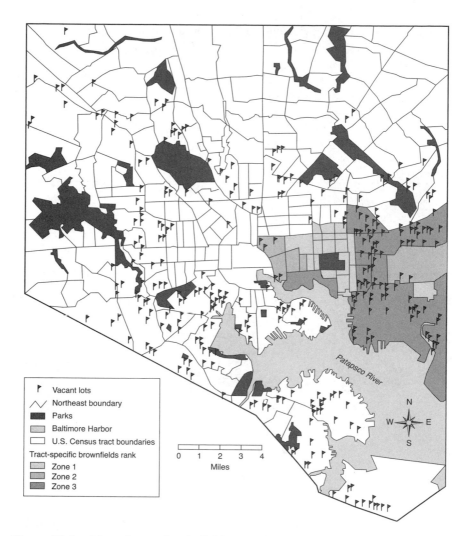

Figure 10-1. Map of vacant lots in Baltimore City

TABLE 10-2   Summary of Socioeconomic Indicators in Baltimore (percent)

Variable	Rest of City	Southeast	Southeast (brownfields zone)		
			Zone 1	Zone 2	Zone 3
Minority population	62	32	37	62	5
Poverty status	22	26	27	50	15
Less than high school degree	28	45	44	38	63
Owner-occupied homes	48	51	62	25	59
Family income $50K or higher	21	16	16	14	20
Working class	70	73	75	71	69

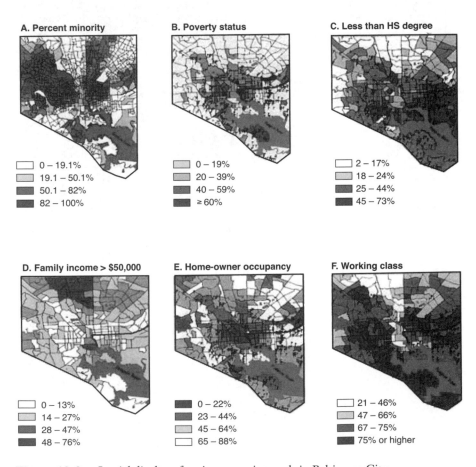

Figure 10-2.   Spatial display of socioeconomic trends in Baltimore City

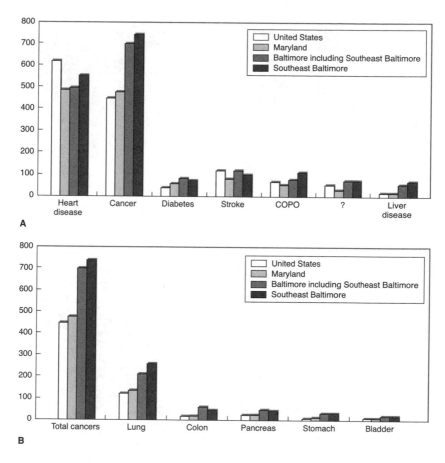

Figure 10-3. Age-adjusted mortality rates (per 100,000) for leading causes of death in Baltimore City's population 45 years of age and older

(68%) have indications of respiratory effects, and 69 substances (66%) have indications of neurologic effects. Table 10-3 lists the complete number of chemicals in this study's database and the associated health categories.

On the basis of the hazard identification-chemical persistence score, lead, polychlorinated biphenyls (PCBs), nickel, chromium, copper compounds, iron compounds, phthalates, toluene diisocyanate (TDI), and naphthalene comprised the top 10 substances associated with brownfields sites. When ranking the substances on hazard information, the leading substances were lead, benzene, cadmium, PCBs, ethylene oxide, TDI, pentachlorophenol, toluene, acrylonitrile, and beryllium. When ranking the substances on chemical persistence information, the top 10 substances were lead, PCBs, nickel, chromium, iron compounds, copper compounds, butyl benzyl phthalate, dioctyl phthalate, TDI,

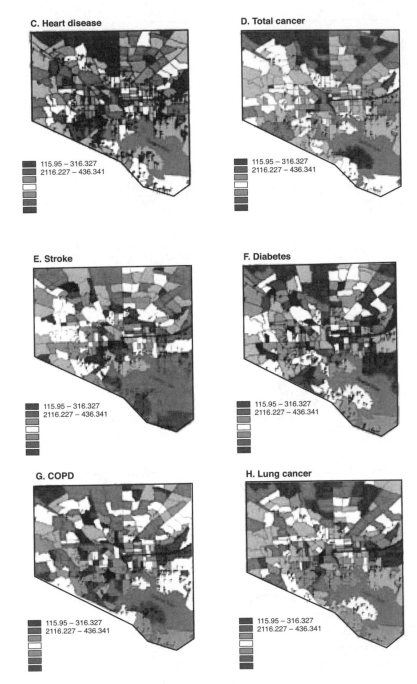

Figure 10-3. Map of Age-Adjusted Mortality Rates *(Continued)*

TABLE 10-3   Number of Chemicals in Study Database and Associated Toxicologic
End Points

Toxicologic End Point	Number of Chemicals in Study Database
Respiratory toxicity	71
Neurologic toxicity	69
Gastrointestinal and liver toxicity	58
Skin or sense organ toxicity	58
Cardiovascular and blood toxicity	49
Renal toxicity	35
Cancer	25
Immunologic toxicity	19
Endocrine toxicity	14
Developmental toxicity	10
Reproductive toxicity	4
Musculoskeletal toxicity	3

naphthalene, and creosote. These lists constitute the same actors, with a higher ranking of heavy metals when ranking on chemical persistence alone.

Site-Specific Score.   For the study area analysis, we evaluated 173 of the 182 sites (95%) identified by the ranking methodology. Information on site acreage was available for all 182 sites. We determined duration of operation for 66% of the sites. The top 10 past uses included scrap metal recycling, bottle cap manufacturing, chemical manufacturing (e.g., inorganic pigments, plastics, synthetic rubber, industrial organics, fertilizers, and pesticides), steel manufacturing, and warehousing. Figure 10-4 provides a spatial display of these properties relative to the other properties in the site inventory. Of the facilities examined in the study, over 20% were once regulated or are currently regulated under state or federal environmental regulatory programs, including hazardous and solid waste programs, air management, and clean water programs. We conducted sensitivity analyses to understand the contributions of each variable to the overall site-specific score. We provide a summary of such findings below and discuss the results from our final score.

The primary chemical substances driving the high-ranking properties included heavy metals (lead, nickel, copper iron, and chromium), plasticizers (PCBs) used for metal castings, aromatic hydrocarbons (benzene, toluene, ethylbenzene, and naphthalene), iron compounds, and solvents (tetrachloroethylene). When ranking properties on their hazard potential, the list of top 10 facilities captured the city's paint and chemical manufacturers, which concentrated in Southeast Baltimore. When ranking the properties on chemical persistence alone, the top 10 facilities included a larger percentage of primary and secondary metals operations and waste disposal sites. When including other

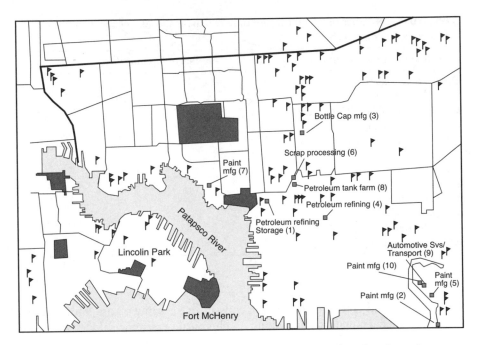

Figure 10-4. Spatial display of top 10 sites (numbered 1–10) based on hazard-persistence score

characteristics of the sites, such as duration of operation and parcel size, the list broadened in its coverage to include the petroleum refining industries and past railroad operations. These establishments occupy larger tracts of land and represent over 100 years of operations.

Tract-Specific Score.   The tract scores reflected information on site-specific hazard potential and chemical persistence, total site acreage per tract, and total number of sites per tract. Figure 10-5 displays the tracts, based on the hazard-persistence scores. The two highest-ranking tracts contain approximately 66% of all the brownfields sites considered in the analysis. The past uses of these sites include petroleum refining, primary and secondary metals industries, paint manufacturing, and service industries such as dry cleaning establishments, gasoline service stations, and auto repair shops. The highest ranking tracts are located in the most industrial areas of Southeast Baltimore and are surrounded by Baltimore's active and currently regulated industrial operations.

Brownfields and Community Health

We developed four statistical models to examine the relationship between key variables and mortality in Southeast Baltimore. The base model included the

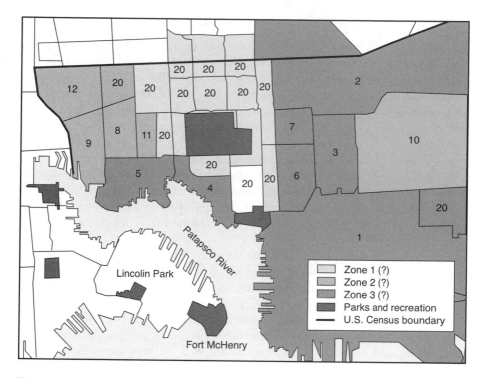

Figure 10-5. Spatial display of tract-specific brownfields rankings for southeast Baltimore

brownfields indicator, population age, and area of census tract (after adjusting for parkland and water). We then expanded these models to adjust for socioeconomic factors that may be strong determinants of community health.

In Southeast Baltimore, communities living in the highest brownfields zone (zone 3), when compared with communities living in low brownfields zones (zone 1), experienced statistically higher mortality rates due to cancer (27% excess), lung cancer (33% excess), respiratory diseases (39% excess), and the major causes of death (index of liver, diabetes, stroke, COPD, heart disease, cancer, injury, and influenza and pneumonia; 20% excess). We observed these differences after adjusting for well-known risk factors such as population age and socioeconomic status. For end points such as diabetes, heart disease, and stroke, we observed no statistically significant differences across the brownfields zones. Additionally, although we observed declines in health between zone 3 and zone 2 and between zone 2 and zone 1, we observed no significant differences within these comparisons. The model used for this analysis was useful in capturing extreme differences between neighborhoods. However, further enhancements to the model and refined classification of sites may improve our understanding of more subtle differences among zones that were not detectable by the existing statistical model.

Discussion

Historical records, toxicologic information, and environmental fate data, in general, illustrated that brownfields properties are not benign. Despite their dormant status, brownfields properties may pose potential chemical and physical risks to Baltimore's communities. Given the absence of population exposure data and site monitoring data, the methods developed for this analysis demonstrate that it is possible to screen and rank brownfields properties based on their hazard potential and consider brownfields at both a site-specific and neighborhood-specific level. The socioeconomic indicators evaluated for this analysis highlighted the constellation of economic and class issues that define communities living in close proximity to historic brownfields hazards. The health information provided important insights about the vitality of and cumulative environmental risks facing affected communities and revealed disparities in health across brownfields zones.

Importantly, these data underscore the need for a coordinated public health and community-based planning approach to brownfields redevelopment. Opportunities for prevention and public health planning must begin with improved environmental health surveillance to track historic hazards in the environment, population exposures to chemical and physical hazards, and priority health conditions in the population. From an emergency response perspective, such tracking information will help uncover past industrial and commercial practices at hundreds of sites and thus aid frontline responders to prepare for events including fire, injury, or unintended population exposures that may occur at these sites. Furthermore, by identifying priority substances of concern, public health officials and environmental regulators, together with affected communities, can develop strategies for biomonitoring or area monitoring if they deem it necessary to better understand population exposures.

Finally, better environmental health tracking information can facilitate plans for future land use and the appropriateness of institutional controls to protect communities over the long term. Public health screening data, for example, can be used to set site cleanup standards and inform local environmental policies, particularly where cause-and-effect relationships between environmental exposures and health effects are difficult to establish yet where public health concerns are real and environmental pollution and degradation persist. Below we describe other examples that illustrate the utility of environmental health information.

In 1998, the Public Interest Law Center of Philadelphia developed an Environmental Justice Protocol to protect communities with substandard health from local sources of pollution, regardless of the cause of the substandard health, and to assure that permit reviews, future land use decision making, and community development are transparent and reflect the needs of affected communities. The center, in its proposed protocol, calls for the establishment of public health standards to guide permit reviews and other local environmental decision making based on an assessment of age-adjusted all-cause mortality rates, age-adjusted cancer mortality rates, infant mortality rates, and low-birth-weight rates.[36]

In Massachusetts, the legislature is currently considering language to establish an Environmental Justice Designation program. Similar to 1975 Massachusetts legislation that designates "areas of critical environmental concern," this legislative act would enable the Massachusetts Executive Office of Environmental Affairs to designate areas of environmental justice concern based partly on community health information.[37] Finally, the Boston Public Health Commission has included language in its regulations on waste container lots to consider the cumulative impacts of environmental pollution on public health and safety when reviewing industrial and commercial permits.[38] In Baltimore, such approaches would allow for the inclusion of community health concerns such as excess deaths from respiratory-related illness in the design and implementation of redevelopment strategies for aging industrial areas, thus reorienting environmental policies to be responsive to local issues and affected communities.

More broadly, the creation and persistence of brownfields in Baltimore underscore the need for a balanced policy approach that includes both people and place strategies—one that focuses on the rebuilding of social capital (e.g., neighborhood cohesion), human capital (e.g., professional skills), physical capital (e.g., infrastructure), and natural capital (e.g., natural resources and living systems) to improve community health and restore neighborhood vitality.[39–41] Sviridoff[42] once noted, "[E]conomic incentives alone are unlikely to transform workers with few skills into productive assets, nor chaotic environments into profitable commercial or industrial sites." Fullilove and Fullilove[43] have opined that "the decline in [community] health is the inevitable outcome of the collapse of place." Rebuilding brownfields neighborhoods through an integrative public health and planning approach will be essential for improving the odds for sustainable redevelopment and securing long-term gains in public health.

References and Notes

1. U.S. Environmental Protection Agency. *Brownfields Glossary of Terms.* 1997. Available: http://www.epa.gov/swerosps/bf/glossary.htm [accessed 15 September 1997].
2. ICF Consulting, The E.P. Systems Group I. *Assessment of State Initiatives to Promote Redevelopment of Brownfields.* HC 5966, Task Order 13. Washington, DC: U.S. Department of Housing and Urban Development, 1999.
3. Bush GW. *Address of the President to the Joint Session of Congress.* Washington, DC: White House Office of the Press Secretary, 27 February 2001.
4. U.S. Congress. *Small Business Liability Relief and Brownfields Revitalization Act of 2002.* Public Law 107-118.
5. U.S. EPA. *Guidance for Institutional Controls at Hazardous Waste Cleanups.* Washington, DC: U.S. Environmental Protection Agency, 2000.

6. Greenberg MR, Lee C, Powers C. Public health and brownfields: reviving the past to protect the future. *Am J Public Health* 1998; 88:1759–1760.
7. Arnold CA. Planning milagros: environmental justice and land use regulation. *Denver Univ Law Rev* 1998; 76:1–153.
8. Zimmerman R. Issues of classification in environmental equity: how we manage is how we measure. *Fordham Urban Law J* 1994; 21:633–669.
9. Anderton DL, Anderson AB, Rossi PH, Oakes M, Fraser MR. Hazardous waste facilities: environmental equity issues in metropolitan areas. *Eval Rev* 1994; 18:123.
10. Krieger N, Williams DR, Moss NE. Measuring social class in US public health research: concepts, methodologies, and guidelines. *Annu Rev Public Health* 1997; 18:341–378.
11. Kitagawa E, Hauser PM. *Differential Mortality in the United States. A Study in Socioeconomic Epidemiology.* Cambridge, MA: Harvard University Press, 1973.
12. Marmot MG, Bobak M, Smith GD. *Explanations for social inequalities in health.* In: *Society and Health* (Amick BC, Levine S, Tarlov AR, Walsh DC, eds). New York: Oxford University Press, 1995; 172–210.
13. Syme SL. Social determinants of disease. *Ann Clin Res* 19(2):44–52.
14. Jerrett M, Eyles J, Cole D. Socioeconomic and environmental covariates of premature mortality in Ontario. *Soc Sci Med* 1998; 47:33–49.
15. Hardy RJ, Schroder GD, Cooper SP, Buffler PA, Prichard HM, Crane M. A surveillance system for assessing health effects from hazardous exposures. *Am J Epidemiol* 1990; 132:S32–S42.
16. Lybarger JA, Spengler RF. *Introduction.* In: *Priority Health Conditions* (Lybarger JA, Spengler RF, DeRosa CT, eds). Atlanta: U.S. Department of Health and Human Services, 1993; 1–11.
17. Rios R, Poje G, Detels R. Susceptibility to environmental pollutants among minorities. *Toxicol Ind Health* 1993; 9:797–820.
18. Rothwell CJ, Hamilton CB, Leaverton PE. Identification of sentinel health events as indicators of environmental contamination. *Environ Health Perspect* 1991; 94:261–263.
19. Environmental Systems Research Institute, Inc. ArcView 3.2. Redlands, CA: Environmental Systems Research Institute, Inc., 2001.
20. Shryock HS, Siegel JS, Stockwell EG. *The Methods and Materials of Demography.* New York: Academic Press, 1976.
21. Litt JS. *An Evaluation of the Public Health and Environmental Aspects of Urban Brownfields.* Baltimore: Johns Hopkins School of Public Health and Hygiene, 2000.
22. U.S. EPA, Office of Emergency and Remedial Response. *The Hazard Ranking System Guidance Manual; Interim Final.* EPA/540/R-92/026. Washington, DC: U.S, Environmental Protection Agency, 1992.
23. Bouwes NW, Hassur SM. *Toxics Release Inventory Relative Risk-Based Environmental Indicators Methodology.* Washington, DC: U.S. Environmental Protection Agency, 1997.

24. Tran N, Burke TA, Fox MA, Litt JS, Shalauta N, Ruscio B. Environmental health risk assessment methodology for overseas military deployment. *Johns Hopkins APL Tech Dig* 1999; 20:405–414.
25. Environmental Defense. *Scorecard.* New York: Environmental Defense, 2000.
26. Environmental Defense. *How the Scorecard Identifies Health Hazards of Toxic Chemicals.* New York: Environmental Defense, 28 June 2001.
27. Environmental Defense. *EDF's Project to Identify Suspected Health Hazards.* New York: Environmental Defense, 28 June 2001.
28. U.S. EPA. Soil Screening Guidance: Technical Background Document. EPA/540/R95/128. Washington, DC: U.S. Environmental Protection Agency, 1996.
29. U.S. Environmental Protection Agency. *Superfund Chemical Data Matrix.* EPA/540/R-96/028. Washington, DC: U.S. Environmental Protection Agency, 1996.
30. Ney RE. *Where Did That Chemical Go?* New York: Van Nostrand Reinhold, 1990.
31. Asante-Duah DK. Contaminant fate and transport in the environment. In: *Managing Contaminated Sites: Problem Diagnosis and Development of Site Restoration.* Chichester, UK: John Wiley & Sons, 1996; 36–49.
32. Salvato J. *Environmental Engineering and Sanitation.* New York: John Wiley & Sons, 1992.
33. SAS Institute Inc. *SAS Version 8.0.* Cary, NC: SAS Institute, 2001.
34. Hatcher L, Stepanski EJ. Principal component analysis. In: *A Step-by-Step Approach to Using the SAS System for Univariate and Multivariate Statistics.* Cary, NC: SAS Institute Inc., 1994; 449–504.
35. McCullagh P, Nelder JA. *Generalized Linear Models.* New York: Chapman and Hall, 1989.
36. Balter J. The EPA needs a workable environmental justice protocol. *Tulane Environ Law J* 1999; 12:357–371.
37. Wilkerson D. *An Act to Establish an Environmental Justice Designation Program.* Sec 1145, 2001. Available: http://www.environmentalleague.org/issues/environmental-justice/EJFACT.htm [accessed 14 May 2001].
38. Boston Public Health Commission. *Waste Container Lot, Junk Yard and Recycling Facilities.* Sec 2, subsecs 2.01–2.19, 1998.
39. Furstenberg FF, Hughes ME. The influence of neighborhoods on children's development. In: *Neighborhood Poverty: Policy Implications in Studying Neighborhoods*, Vol 2 (Brooks-Gunn J, Duncan GJ, Aber L, eds). New York: Russell Sage Foundation, 1997; 23–47.
40. Brenner MH. Political economy and health. In: *Society and Health* (Amick BC, Levine S, Tarlov AR, Walsh DC, eds). New York: Oxford University Press, 1995; 211–246.
41. Hawken P, Lovins A, Lovins LH. *Natural Capitalism: Creating the Next Industrial Revolution.* Boston: Little, Brown and Company, 1999.

42. Sviridoff, M. The seeds of urban revival. *Public Interest* 1994; (Winter):82–103.
43. Fullilove MT, Fullilove RM III. Place matters. In: *Reclaiming the Environmental Debate: The Politics of Health in a Toxic Culture* (Hofrichter R, ed). Cambridge: Massachusetts Institute of Technology, 2000; 77–91.
44. U.S. Department of Energy. *Risk Assessment Information System.* Oak Ridge, TN: Department of Energy, 1999.
45. Syracuse Research Corporation. *LogKow Program.* Syracuse, NY: Syracuse Research Corp., 2000.

A Current Appraisal of Toxic Wastes and Race in the United States—2007

Robin Saha

Note: This research was supported by a grant from the Sociology and Geography Program and Regional Science Program of the National Science Foundation (#0099123). The author extends thanks to Dr. Paul Mohai of the University of Michigan School of Natural Resources and Environment (SNRE) for his helpful comments on drafts of this manuscript, and to Dr. Robert Bullard of Clark Atlanta University's Environmental Justice Resource Center, who along with the United Church of Christ's Justice and Witness Ministries initiated *Toxic Wastes and Race at Twenty*, the 20-year commemoration and update of the 1987 landmark report *Toxic Wastes and Race in the United States*.

Distance-based methods reveal racial and socioeconomic disparities in the location of the nation's commercial hazardous waste facilities that are much greater than previously reported. Compared to approaches used in prior research, these new methods are more reliable and accurate because they count persons living within the same proximity to each hazardous waste facility as part of the impacted population.[1,2]*

This article utilizes distance-based methods and 2000 census data to assess the current extent of racial and socioeconomic disparities for the nation as a whole. Disparities also are examined by region and state, and separate analyses are conducted for metropolitan areas, where most hazardous waste facilities are located. Using the most recent census data, this current appraisal will answer the following questions:

1. What is the current extent of racial and socioeconomic disparities in the location of the nation's commercial hazardous waste facilities?

*For an explanation of distance-based methods, see Chapter 3 of *Toxic Wastes and Race and Twenty* ("Racial and Socioeconomic Disparities in the Distribution of Environmental Hazards: Assessing the Evidence Twenty Years after Toxic Wastes and Race") by Paul Mokai.[29]

2. Did disparities increase during the 1990s?
3. Are disparities greater for host neighborhoods with clustered facilities?
4. How are racial and socioeconomic disparities distributed in different regions of the country?
5. How important is race in predicting facility location in comparison to socioeconomic status and other nonracial factors?

To answer the first question, we will examine percentages of people of color as a whole and specific racial and ethnic groups living in neighborhoods and communities with commercial hazardous waste facilities. The neighborhood socioeconomic characteristics will be similarly compared to areas without facilities using indicators such as poverty rates, incomes and housing values.

Toxic Wastes and Race Revisited, the 1994 update of the original United Church of Christ (UCC) report, *Toxic Wastes and Race in the United States*, showed that racial and socioeconomic disparities associated with the location of the nation's hazardous waste facilities increased from 1980 to 1993.[3,4] The second question above asks whether this trend continued throughout the 1990s.

Both of the previous UCC reports found that people of color were concentrated in the most environmentally hazardous communities as measured by the number of commercial hazardous waste facilities and amounts of hazardous wastes handled. To answer the third question, a similar analysis is conducted in this current update, which examines neighborhoods where multiple facilities are clustered, i.e., where facilities are so close to each other that their respective neighborhood boundaries overlap.

The fourth question examines the extent to which racial and socioeconomic disparities are confined to particular regions of the country and if disparities are substantially greater in certain regions compared to others. Following the example of the previous UCC reports, this article examines racial and socioeconomic disparities for states and metropolitan areas. This allows us to detect environmental justice "hot spots," i.e., areas with high concentrations of hazardous wastes and large racial or socioeconomic disparities.

The final question asks whether the racial characteristics of neighborhoods independently predict the location of the nation's commercial hazardous waste facilities, separate from poverty levels and other socioeconomic characteristics. The preponderance of environmental inequality studies have found that race is an independent predictor of the location of polluting industrial facilities.[5,6] Indeed, the 1987 UCC report was the first study to find race to be an independent predictor of the location of the nation's commercial hazardous waste facilities. It also found race to be a much stronger predictor than socioeconomic status. Sorting out whether racial factors are associated with facility location regardless of socioeconomic status can be accomplished with multivariate statistical tests. It can thereby be determined if the significance of race noted in *Toxic Wastes and Race in the United States* persists 20 years later.

Hazardous Waste Management in the United States

In 2001, industry generated more than 41 million tons of hazardous wastes in the United States.[7] Some of these wastes are shipped out of state and even out of the country. Because of their toxicity, hazardous wastes are regulated by the U.S. Environmental Protection Agency (EPA) and state environmental agencies. Under the Resource Conservation and Recovery Act of 1976 (RCRA), hazardous wastes must be managed by specially designed facilities referred to as treatment, storage and disposal facilities. Companies operating such facilities must obtain permits from state and sometimes federal environmental agencies and conform to local land use regulations.

As the recent explosion of stored hazardous wastes in Danvers, Massachusetts, illustrates, even when operated according to accepted specifications, hazardous waste facilities can adversely impact nearby residents.[8] The city of East Palo Alto is home to another poorly operated facility, Romic Environmental Technologies.[9] Institutional discrimination in the form of lax governmental enforcement has contributed to numerous problems with chemical leaks, accidents and explosions at the plant. Indeed, hazardous wastes are well known to pose serious risks to health, property and quality of life. Because of these ordinary and extraordinary risks, public opposition to siting of these facilities is nearly universal, particularly regarding high-profile facilities such as incinerators and landfills. As a result, new facility sitings have tended to follow the path of least political resistance.[10,11] Although in recent decades communities of color have begun to mount their own resistance, their limited scientific, technical and legal resources have historically made such communities vulnerable to facility sitings.[12-14]

Data and Analysis

Several databases were used to identify currently operating commercial hazardous waste facilities in the U.S.: EPA's Biennial Report System (BRS); EPA's Resource Conservation and Recovery Information System (RCRIS); and the Environmental Services Directory (ESD), a private industry listing.[15-18] The EPA's Envirofacts Data Warehouse also was used to cross-reference information and obtain the most recent data for facilities, for example, if a facility recently received a new operating permit and therefore was not included in the aforementioned databases.[19] A facility was included if it met all the following criteria: (1) it was a private, nongovernmental business, (2) designated in 1999 as a hazardous waste Treatment, Storage and Disposal Facility (TSDF) under the Resource Conservation and Recovery Act (RCRA), and (3) operated as a commercial facility in 1999, i.e., received off-site wastes from another entity for pay. Geographic Information Systems (GIS) were used to precisely map facility locations. The current operating status and locations[20] were verified by contacting the companies or in some cases regulatory agencies.

In all, 413 facilities were identified. These represented all the commercial hazardous waste facilities operating in the U.S. in 1999. By using 2000 Census data, collected by the U.S. Census Bureau in 1999, it was possible to determine the racial and socioeconomic characteristics of neighborhoods containing these facilities that corresponded to *the same time the facilities were known to be in operation.*[20]

The areal apportionment method[1,2] was used to estimate the racial and socioeconomic characteristics of circular host neighborhoods of 1, 3, and 5 kilometer radius around the 413 facilities.[29] Because the results were very consistent regardless of the radius, only findings pertaining to the 3-kilometer radius are reported below to streamline the presentation. This radius, approximately 1.8 miles, corresponds to the distance within which empirical studies have noted adverse health, property value and quality of life impacts associated with hazardous waste sites, including hazardous waste facilities.[11, 21-26]

This radius is in line with those used in other environmental justice studies employing distance-based methods.[1,2] The circumscribed area is also about the size of the heavily polluted Greenpoint/Williamsburg neighborhood in Brooklyn.[27] The City of Vernon, located near heavily polluted areas of East Los Angeles, is also similar in size. Vernon has several commercial hazardous waste facilities and numerous polluting industrial facilities.[28]

Unless otherwise indicated, findings reported are aggregate values for all host neighborhoods (i.e., neighborhoods within 3 kilometers of a facility), not averages of each host neighborhood and the census tracts comprising them. This means that populations were summed for all neighborhoods to compute people of color percentages. For example, to compute people of color percentages for all host neighborhoods, the total number of people of color within 3 kilometers of any hazardous waste facility was divided by the total population within the same circular host neighborhoods. Similar procedures were used to compute poverty rates, mean households incomes and mean property values. The resulting values represent the overall racial and socioeconomic characteristics of the defined impacted areas. (See the Methods Appendix from Chapter 4 of *Toxic Wastes and Race at Twenty*.)[29]

Assessing Racial and Socioeconomic Disparities

To assess racial and socioeconomic disparities, the characteristics of the neighborhoods of 3-kilometer radius containing a commercial hazardous waste facility ("host neighborhoods") are compared to the characteristics of areas that lie beyond 3 kilometers ("non-host areas"). For the national-level analysis, non-host areas include all areas in the U.S. that lie beyond 3 kilometers of a facility. Likewise, for the state-level analysis, non-host areas in each state include all areas that lie beyond 3 kilometers of a facility (additional information is provided below regarding the metropolitan area analyses).

If people of color percentages are higher in host neighborhoods than in the non-host comparison areas, then a racial disparity is therefore said to exist. Likewise, socioeconomic disparities exist if poverty rates are higher, or mean household incomes and housing values are lower, in host neighborhoods than in the non-host areas. These disparities are consistent with an environmental justice claim.

Disparities in percentages of specific people of color groups were examined, including percentages of African Americans, Hispanics or Latinos, Asians/ Pacific Islanders and American Indians/Alaskan Natives. It should be noted that the U.S. Census Bureau defines Hispanic as an ethnic, not a racial category. Hispanics can belong to any of the recognized races, including the white category. Race, in fact, is a socially constructed notion.[30] Hispanics, or Latinos as they generally self-identify, suffer from similar forms of racial and institutional discrimination as other people of color.[31] Thus, for convenience, Hispanic or Latino disparities also will be referred to as racial disparities.

Two approaches are used to assess the magnitude of racial and socioeconomic disparities: (1) differences in values (percentages of people of color, poverty rates, mean household income, mean housing values, etc.) between host neighborhoods and non-host areas; and (2) ratios of host neighborhood values to non-host area values. For example, if Hispanic or Latino percentages were 30% and 10%, respectively, then differences would be 30% minus 10%, or 20%, and the ratio would be 30% divided by 10%, or 3.

Tests also were done to determine if these disparities were statistically significant (i.e., were not likely to be merely the result of random chance) and to assess the importance of race in predicting facility locations. A statistically significant disparity is defined as one where there is less than a 5% chance (1 in 20) that the disparity is due to random chance as determined by t-tests and logistic regressions. (See Methods Appendix.)[29]

Findings

More than nine million people (9,222,000) are estimated to live within 3 kilometers (1.8 miles) of the nation's 413 commercial hazardous waste facilities. This represents 3.3% of the U.S. population (281,422,000). More than 5.1 million people of color, including 2.5 million Hispanics or Latinos, 1.8 million African Americans, 616,000 Asians/Pacific Islanders, and 62,000 Native Americans, live in neighborhoods with one or more commercial hazardous waste facility.

Host neighborhoods are densely populated, with more than 870 persons per square kilometer (2,300 per mi^2), compared to 30 persons per square kilometer (77 per mi^2) in non-host areas. Not surprisingly, 343 facilities (83%) are located in metropolitan areas. Additional findings presented below begin with a look at racial and socioeconomic disparities for the nation as a whole, an assessment of changes from 1990 to 2000 and an analysis of disparities in neighborhoods with clustered facilities (i.e., host neighborhoods where the facilities are so close together that the 3-kilometer areas around them overlap). These findings are followed by similar analyses for the 10 EPA regions, states and metropolitan areas. This chapter concludes with an analysis of the importance of race in predicting facility locations.

National Disparities

Table 11-1 compares the racial and socioeconomic characteristics of the 3-kilometer circular host neighborhoods of the nation's 413 commercial hazardous waste facilities to the same characteristics of non-host areas. Data from the 1990 and 2000 Census are shown. For 2000, host neighborhoods with commercial hazardous waste facilities are 56% people of color whereas non-host areas are 30% people of color.* In other words, percentages of people of color as a whole are 1.9 times greater in host neighborhoods than in non-host areas. Similarly, percentages of African Americans, Hispanics and Asians/Pacific Islanders in host neighborhoods are 1.7, 2.3, and 1.8 times greater in host neighborhoods than non-host areas (20% vs. 12%, 27% vs. 12%, and 6.7% vs. 3.6%, respectively). However, percentages of American Indians/Alaskan Natives (hereafter referred to as Native Americans) in host neighborhoods and non-host areas are very small and roughly equal (0.7% vs. 0.9%).

Table 11-1 also reveals significant socioeconomic disparities. Poverty rates in the host neighborhoods are 1.5 times greater than those in non-host areas (18% vs. 12%), and mean annual household incomes in host neighborhoods are 15% lower ($48,234 vs. $56,912). Mean owner-occupied housing values are also disproportionately low in neighborhoods with hazardous waste facilities. These data reveal depressed economic conditions in host neighborhoods of the nation's hazardous waste facilities. Education and employment disparities also can be noted in Table 11-1. The percentage of persons 25 years and over with a four-year college degree are much lower in host neighborhoods than in non-host areas (18% vs. 25%, respectively). Similar disparities exist for the percentage of persons employed in professional "white collar" occupations, while percentages employed in "blue collar" occupations are disproportionately high in host neighborhoods. The above racial and socioeconomic disparities are statistically significant at the 0.001 level, which means that there is less than a 0.1% (1 in 1000) chance that the differences are merely the result of random chance.

---

*Note that 147 of the 413 host neighborhoods (36%) have a majority of people of color.

TABLE 11-1 Racial and Socioeconmic Disparities between Host Neighborhoods and Non-Host Areas for the Nation's 413 Commercial Hazardous Waste Facilities (1990 and 2000)

| | 2000 | | | | 1990 | | | |
	Host	Non-Host	Diff.	Ratio	Host	Non-Host	Diff.	Ratio
Population								
Total Pop. (1000s)	9,222	272,200	−262,979	0.03	8,673	240,037	−231,364	0.04
Population Density	870	29.7	840	29.0	820	25.1	790	27.3
Race/Ethnicity								
% People of Color	55.9%	30.0%	25.9%	1.86	46.2%	23.4%	22.8%	1.97
% African American	20.0%	11.9%	8.0%	1.67	20.4%	11.7%	8.7%	1.74
% Hispanic or Latino	27.0%	12.0%	15.0%	2.25	20.7%	8.4%	12.3%	2.47
% Asian/Pacific Islander	6.7%	3.6%	3.0%	1.83	5.3%	2.8%	2.5%	1.88
% Native American	0.7%	0.9%	−0.2%	0.77	0.6%	0.8%	−0.3%	0.68
Socioeconomics								
Poverty Rate	18.3%	12.2%	6.1%	1.50	18.5%	12.9%	5.6%	1.43
Mean Household Income	$48,234	$56,912	−$8,678	0.85	$33,115	$38,639	−$5,524	0.86
Mean Owner-Occpd. Housing Value	$159,536	$159,538	−$24,025	0.85	$101,774	$111,954	−$10,180	0.91
% with 4-Year College Degree	18.5%	24.6%	−6.1%	0.75	15.4%	20.5%	−5.1%	0.75
% Professional "White Collar" Occp.	28.0%	33.8%	−5.8%	0.83	21.8%	26.6%	−4.8%	0.82
% Employed in "Blue Collar" Occupations	27.7%	24.0%	3.7%	1.15	30.0%	26.1%	3.9%	1.15

NOTES: Data computed using areal apportionment method. Differences and ratios are between host neighborhood and non-host area values. Differences may not precisely correspond to other values due to rounding off. Population density is in persons per square kilometer (rounded off). Mean housing values pertain to owner-occupied housing units. Percent employed in "white collar" and "blue collar" occupations are not directly comparable between 1990 and 2000, because of changes in Census Bureau definitions.

243

Changes During the 1990s

Table 11-1 shows that racial and socioeconomic disparities also existed in 1990. The 1990 and 2000 data allow us to consider whether disparities increased in magnitude during the 1990s. People of color percentages in host neighborhoods increased from 46% to 56%, whereas percentages in non-host areas increased from 23% to 30%. Thus, the overall difference in people of color percentages between host neighborhoods and non-host areas increased from 23% to 26% during the 1990s. However, the ratio of the percentages between host neighborhoods and non-host areas decreased slightly from 1.97 to 1.86. Similar trends can be noted for racial subgroups and with respect to poverty, income and housing value indicators of neighborhood socioeconomic status. The education and employment measures show no change during the 1990s.*

Neighborhoods with Clustered Facilities

Figure 11-1 shows that people of color percentages in neighborhoods with clustered facilities (i.e., multiple facilities), nonclustered facilities (i.e., a single facility) and no facility.** Neighborhoods with clustered facilities have higher percentages of people of color than those with non-clustered facilities (69% vs. 51%). Likewise, neighborhoods with clustered facilities have disproportionately high poverty rates. These differences are statistically significant at a 0.001 level.

In addition, percentages of African Americans and Hispanics in the neighborhoods with clustered facilities are significantly higher than neighborhoods with non-clustered facilities (29% vs. 16% and 33% vs. 25%, respectively). Although Asians/Pacific Islanders are disproportionately located in all host neighborhoods (see Table 11-1), they are found in lower percentages in the neighborhoods with clustered facilities than in non-clustered facility neighborhoods (4.3% vs. 7.8%).

Native American percentages are very small and nearly equal (0.7%) in clustered and non-clustered facility host neighborhoods (see Figure 11-1).While there may be individual cases with striking disparities in Native Amer-

---

*To streamline the presentation, education and employment variables are omitted from subsequent tables, except for the table showing the results of the multivariate analysis, which examines the role of race and various indicators of socioeconomic status in accounting for the location of hazardous waste in the U.S. Poverty rates, mean household income and mean housing values are nevertheless shown in the following analyses of clustered facilities, states, EPA regions and metropolitan areas.

**A total of 49 clustered facility neighborhoods (42 with two facilities, five with three facilities, one with four facilities and one with six facilities) and 304 non-clustered facility neighborhoods were delineated. Thus, clustered facility neighborhoods and non-clustered facility neighborhoods contain 109 and 304 facilities, respectively. Most analyses reported, however, involve the combined clustered and nonclustered facility neighborhoods.

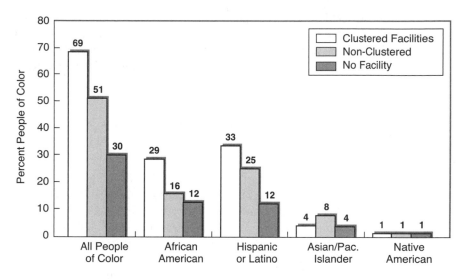

Figure 11-1. People of Color Percentages in Neighborhoods with Clustered Facilities, Non-Clustered Facilities and No Facility

ican percentages, they would be masked in this national level study. A definitive analysis of environmental injustices facing Native Americans is beyond the scope of this study. Environmental injustices in Indian Country have been well-documented, and Native Americans have been an important group in the struggle for environmental justice.* Indeed, 13 facilities analyzed in this study are located on Indian reservations, including a controversial facility on the Gila River Indian Community reservation in Arizona.[9] However, because of their small numbers relative to the other groups in this particular analysis, they are not included in subsequent tables.

Poverty rates in the neighborhoods with clustered facilities are high compared to non-clustered facility neighborhoods: 22% vs. 17%. Mean household incomes are 10% lower in neighborhoods with clustered facilities ($44,600 vs. $49,600), and mean housing values are 14% lower ($121,200 vs. $141,000).

All racial and socioeconomic disparities between neighborhoods with clustered and nonclustered facility host neighborhoods are statistically significant at the 0.01 level. Although measuring the concentration of hazardous waste activity in a slightly different way, these findings are similar to those of the previous UCC reports, which found that zip code areas with higher levels of hazardous

---

*The are several excellent accounts of the indigenous environmental movement[35-37] and studies of abandoned hazardous wastes and other toxic threats, such as nuclear, military and mining wastes impacting Native Americans, Alaskan Natives and Native Hawaiians.[38-40]

waste activity also had relatively higher percentages of people of color and higher poverty rates.* People of color and the poor thus continue to be particularly vulnerable to the various negative impacts of hazardous waste facilities. Moreover, the present findings show that this is the case for African Americans, Hispanics and Asians/Pacific Islanders.

EPA Regional Disparities

Racial and socioeconomic disparities were assessed for all 10 EPA regions, each comprising between 2 and 8 contiguous states (see Figure 11-2). Table 11-2 shows that regions with the greatest number of facilities include: Region 5, Great Lakes states (85 or 21%); Region 4, the southeast (67 or 16%); Region 6, south central states (61 or 15%); and Region 9, the West (55 or 13%). The fewest facilities are found in: Region 1, the Northeast (23 or 6%); Region 8, the mountain west (15 or 4%); and Region 10, the Pacific Northwest (8 or 2%).

EPA regional offices provide direct oversight of state environmental programs, which in turn monitor and enforce the operation of existing hazardous waste facilities and issue permits for the siting of new ones. This EPA regional analysis allows us to see how geographically widespread the racial and socioeconomic disparities noted above are. We also can identify regions with pervasive and severe racial disparities, regions where regulatory intervention may be needed to ensure environmental justice.

Table 11-2 shows that racial disparities for people of color as a whole exist in 9 out of 10 EPA regions (all except Region 3). These disparities are statistically significant at the 0.001 level. Disparities in people of color percentages between host neighborhoods and non-host areas are greatest in: Region 1 (36% vs. 15%), Region 4 (54% vs. 30%), Region 5 (53% vs. 19%), Region 6 (63% vs. 42%) and Region 9 (80% vs. 49%).**

---

*Similar analyses also were conducted of 3 kilometer host neighborhoods of hazardous waste landfills and incinerators compared to host neighborhoods of all other commercial hazardous waste facilities. For this comparison, facilities were classified according to their Standard Industrial Codes (SIC) and North American Industry Classification System (NAIC), hierarchical coding systems that classify all economic activity in various industry sectors. These codes were obtained from Envirofacts. Thus, people of color percentages were examined for host neighborhoods of 120 commercial hazardous waste facilities with an SIC code of 4953 ("Refuse Systems") and NAIC code of 592211 ("Hazardous Waste Treatment and Disposal"). The results very closely parallel those presented and therefore are not reported, but may be requested from the author.

**In Region 5, 28 of 85 (33%) of host neighborhoods are majority people of color (i.e., people of color percentages are greater than 50%). The number of majority people of color in host neighborhoods in Regions 1, 4, 6 and 9, respectively: 3 of 23 (13%), 28 of 65 (43%), 28 of 61 (46%) and 43 of 55 (73%).

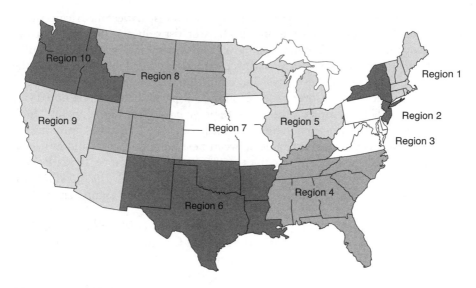

Figure 11-2. EPA Regions

Table 11-2 People of Color Percentage for Host Neighborhoods and Non-Host Areas by EPA Region

	Number of Facilities	Host Neighborhoods	Non-Host Areas	Difference	Ratio
U.S. Total	413	55.9%	30.0%	25.9%	1.86
Region 1	23	36.3%	15.0%	21.3%	2.43
Region 2	32	51.5%	36.0%	15.6%	1.43
Region 3	35	23.2%	24.5%	−1.33%	0.95
Region 4	67	54.3%	30.4%	23.8%	1.78
Region 5	85	52.6%	18.8%	33.8%	2.80
Region 6	61	62.7%	41.8%	20.9%	1.50
Region 7	32	29.1%	13.4%	15.7%	2.17
Region 8	15	31.2%	18.2%	13.0%	1.72
Region 9	55	80.5%	49.4%	31.1%	1.63
Region 10	8	38.9%	19.1%	19.9%	2.04

NOTES: Data computed using 2000 Census data and areal apportionment method. Differences may not precisely correspond to other values due to rounding errors.

Seven EPA regions have statistically significant disparities in African American percentages, seven EPA regions also have statistically significant disparities in Hispanic or Latino percentages, and six EPA regions have statistically significant disparities in percentages of Asians/Pacific Islanders. Table 11-3 shows the descriptive statistics for these racial and ethnic groups for each EPA region.

Geographically widespread socioeconomic disparities also can be noted (see Table 11-4). For example, nine EPA regions have disproportionately high poverty rates and disproportionately low mean household incomes and housing values. Differences in poverty rates between host neighborhoods and non-host areas are greatest for Region 1 (16% vs. 8.7%), Region 2 (19% vs. 12%), Region 5 (19% vs. 9.6%), Region 7 (15% vs. 10%), Region 8 (15% vs. 10%) and Region 9 (21% vs. 13%). Socioeconomic disparities are statistically significant in 9 of the 10 EPA regions, all but Region 9.

Disproportionately high percentages of people of color are found in 7 of the 9 regions with neighborhoods with clustered facilities. Differences between clustered and non-clustered facility host neighborhoods are greatest in Region 5 (62% vs. 46%), Region 7 (59% vs. 25%), Region 8 (55% vs. 26%) and Region 9 (89% vs. 75%). Regions 1, 3 and 4 also have large disparities between clustered and non-clustered facility neighborhoods.[29]

In sum, racial disparities in the location of the nation's commercial hazardous waste facilities exist in all EPA regions. For Hispanics, African Americans, and Asians/Pacific Islanders, statistically significant disparities exist in the majority or vast majority of EPA regions. Moreover, the pattern of people of color being especially concentrated in areas where facilities are clustered is also geographically widespread throughout the country.

State Disparities

Given the widespread geographic distribution of racial and socioeconomic disparities associated with the location of hazardous waste facilities among EPA regions, one could expect such disparities to be distributed widely among states as well. EPA regional offices and their environmental justice programs provide guidance to and oversight of state environmental programs (such as RCRA, Clean Air Act and Clean Water Act). States also are beginning to develop environmental justice and enhanced enforcement programs of their own to reduce risks to environmentally overburdened communities.[32] Thus, it is helpful to identify states where racial and socioeconomic disparities are the greatest. It is in these states where more stringent regulatory action may be warranted.

Alaska, Delaware, Hawaii, New Hampshire, Montana, Wyoming, and the District of Columbia did not have licensed and operating commercial hazardous waste facilities in 1999. Forty of the remaining 44 states with facilities have disproportionately high percentages of people of color in circular host neighborhoods. The average of these 40 states' percentage of people of color in host neighborhoods is about two times greater than the average of non-host areas for

Table 11-3 Racial Disparities Between Host Neighborhoods and Non-Host Areas by EPA Region

EPA Region	Percent African American				Percent Hispanic or Latino/a				Percent Asian/Pacific Islander			
	Host	Non-Host	Diff.	Ratio	Host	Non-Host	Diff.	Ratio	Host	Non-Host	Diff.	Ratio
Region 1	9.6%	4.8%	4.8%	2.00	19.5%	5.5%	13.9%	3.52	4.9%	2.6%	2.4%	1.91
Region 2	16.0%	15.0%	1.0%	1.07	23.3%	14.0%	9.3%	1.66	9.7%	5.4%	4.3%	1.81
Region 3	15.1%	16.6%	-1.5%	0.91	4.7%	3.7%	1.0%	1.26	2.0%	2.7%	-0.7%	0.75
Region 4	37.0%	20.4%	16.6%	1.82	13.7%	7.2%	6.5%	1.91	2.2%	1.4%	0.8%	1.59
Region 5	35.8%	10.1%	25.7%	3.55	11.3%	5.0%	6.3%	2.27	3.2%	2.0%	1.2%	1.59
Region 6	20.4%	13.5%	6.9%	1.51	37.9%	23.1%	14.7%	1.64	2.5%	2.1%	0.4%	1.17
Region 7	16.1%	6.7%	9.4%	2.40	8.9%	3.6%	5.3%	2.50	1.7%	1.3%	0.4%	1.30
Region 8	1.9%	2.0%	-0.1%	0.95	22.9%	10.5%	12.4%	2.19	3.1%	1.7%	1.4%	1.80
Region 9	11.8%	5.6%	6.2%	2.10	54.1%	28.7%	25.3%	1.88	12.3%	10.8%	1.5%	1.14
Region 10	6.6%	2.3%	4.2%	2.84	10.1%	7.5%	2.6%	1.35	17.1%	4.2%	12.9%	4.07

NOTES: Differences and ratios are between host neighborhood and non-host areas. Differences may not precisely correspond to other values due to rounding off.

TABLE 11-4 Socioeconomic Disparities Between Host Neighborhoods and Non-Host Areas by EPA Region

EPA Region	Poverty Rates				Mean Household Income				Mean Housing Value			
	Host	Non-Host	Diff.	Ratio	Host	Non-Host	Diff.	Ratio	Host	Non-Host	Diff.	Ratio
Region 1	15.7%	8.7%	7.0%	1.80	$48,368	$65,296	-16,928	0.74	$143,840	$202,102	-58,261	0.71
Region 2	19.4%	12.3%	7.1%	1.57	$50,793	$66,137	-15,344	0.77	$171,083	$202,579	-31,496	0.84
Region 3	12.6%	10.7%	1.9%	1.18	$47,493	$57,479	-9,986	0.83	$97,971	$139,278	-41,307	0.70
Region 4	15.7%	13.7%	2.0%	1.15	$45,811	$50,931	-5,120	0.90	$97,673	$118,962	-21,288	0.82
Region 5	19.4%	9.6%	9.7%	2.01	$44,933	$56,955	-12,022	0.79	$103,812	$137,470	-33,658	0.76
Region 6	18.8%	16.0%	2.8%	1.18	$45,072	$50,616	-5,545	0.89	$83,602	$101,518	-17,916	0.82
Region 7	15.0%	10.4%	4.7%	1.45	$44,084	$50,308	-6,224	0.88	$84,028	$106,808	-22,780	0.79
Region 8	14.8%	10.3%	4.4%	1.43	$40,801	$55,413	-14,612	0.74	$105,286	$163,390	-58,104	0.64
Region 9	20.7%	13.5%	7.2%	1.54	$52,947	$64,146	-11,199	0.83	$218,576	$246,673	-28,096	0.89
Region 10	10.9%	11.0%	-0.1%	0.99	$55,599	$55,889	-290	0.99	$180,716	$179,522	1,193	1.01

NOTES: Differences and ratios are between host neighborhood and non-host areas. Differences may not precisely correspond to other values due to rounding off.

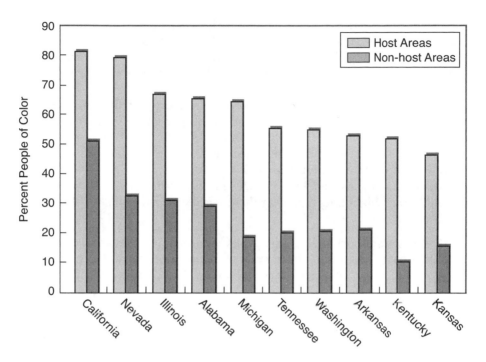

Figure 11-3.   States with the 10 Largest Differences in People of Color Percentages between Host Neighborhoods and Non-Host Areas

those states (44% vs. 23%).* Host neighborhoods in 19 states are majority people of color.

Figure 11-3 shows states with the 10 largest differences in people of color percentages between host neighborhoods and non-host areas. These states are shown in order (left to right) by the largest percentages of people of color living in the host neighborhoods. For both California and Nevada, these percentages are about 80%. For three additional states, people of color make up a two-thirds or more majority in these neighborhoods. In descending order by the size of the differences between host and non-host areas, these states are: Michigan (66% vs. 19%), Nevada (79% vs. 33%), Kentucky (51% vs. 10%), Illinois (68% vs. 31%), Alabama (66%vs. 31%), Tennessee (54% vs. 20%), Washington (53% vs. 20%), Kansas (47% vs. 16%), Arkansas (52% vs. 21%) and California (81% vs. 51%). Differences in these percentages range from a high of 47% for Michigan to 30% for California.

---

*States without racial disparities include North Dakota, Nebraska, New Mexico, and Idaho.

Numerous other states have large disparities in people of color percentages. Many of these have majority people of color host neighborhoods, including Arizona, Florida, Georgia, Louisiana, New Jersey, New York, North Carolina, and Texas. People of color disparities are statistically significant for 32 states, including all the aforementioned states.

Host neighborhoods in an overwhelming majority of the 44 states with commercial hazardous waste facilities have disproportionately high percentages of Hispanics (35 states), African Americans (38 states), and Asians/Pacific Islanders (27 states). Among these states, the average disparity between host neighborhoods and non-host areas is 17% vs. 9.0% for Hispanics, 24% vs. 11% for African Americans, and 4.5% vs. 2.2% for Asians/Pacific Islanders.*

Additional highlights regarding these racial disparities include the following findings[29]

- Host neighborhoods in Arizona, California, and Nevada are majority Hispanic or Latino. Other states with very large disparities in Hispanic or Latino percentages include Colorado, Connecticut, Florida, Illinois, Kansas, and Utah. Differences in these percentages between host neighborhoods and non-host areas range from a high of 32% for Nevada to 13% for Kansas.
- Host neighborhoods in Alabama and Michigan are majority African American. Other states with very large disparities in African American percentages: Arkansas, Illinois, Kentucky, Nevada, North Carolina, Ohio, Tennessee, and Wisconsin. Differences in percentages between host neighborhoods and non-host areas range from 46% (Michigan) to 19% (Nevada). Twenty-eight other states have African American disparities.
- The state of Washington has the largest disparity in the percentage of Asians/Pacific Islanders (26% vs. 5.6%). Other states with Asian/Pacific Islander disparities: California, Massachusetts, Minnesota, New York, Oregon, Rhode Island, and Utah.

Thirty-five states have socioeconomic disparities as indicated by poverty rates. For these states, the average poverty rate in host neighborhoods is 18% compared to 12% in non-host areas. States with very large poverty rate disparities include Arizona, Connecticut, Michigan, Minnesota, Nevada, and Ohio. In these states, poverty rates in host neighborhoods are more than two times greater than those in non-host areas. Poverty rate disparities are statistically significant for a majority of states with commercial hazardous waste facilities (23 out of 44).

---

*Disparities in Hispanic percentages are statistically significant for 21 states. Disparities in African American and Asian/Pacific Islander percentages are statistically significant for 25 and 11 states, respectively.

This analysis shows that statistically significant racial and socioeconomic disparities in the location of commercial hazardous waste facilities are very prevalent among the states and thus throughout the country. This reinforces the findings for the EPA regions and should allow more focused and effective attention to be devoted to regional environmental injustices. This might include additional research, since few published environmental justice studies have been conducted for many of these states where environmental justice claims could be made on the basis of these findings. This analysis of the states also shows that racial disparities are more prevalent and extensive than socioeconomic disparities, suggesting that race has more to do with the current distribution of the nation's hazardous waste facilities than poverty. The question of the relative importance of race and socioeconomic status is systematically examined below.

Metropolitan Area Disparities

The statewide disparities may in part reflect the fact that most commercial hazardous waste facilities are located in large cities where people of color are generally found in relatively high percentages. Various scholars have suggested examining host neighborhoods in metropolitan areas by themselves to avoid possible confounding effects of counting rural areas, which have relatively low percentages of people of color, among the non-host areas.[33,34] Such a comparison is more conservative in that the likelihood of finding disparities is reduced.

Metropolitan Areas (MAs) are prescribed by the Office of Budget and Management (OMB) to gather statistics and allocate resources to various federal programs. They are not political jurisdictions like incorporated towns, cities and counties. A single metropolitan area may encompass several counties and cities, which in turn may be located in adjoining states.

In 2000, 149 of the nation's 331 metropolitan areas (45%) contained 343 of the nation's 413 commercial hazardous waste facilities (87%). More than 9 million people reside in host neighborhoods of facilities located in metropolitan areas. This represents 98% of the total population living in host neighborhoods of all 413 facilities.

Table 11-5 compares the racial and socioeconomic characteristics of the metropolitan host neighborhoods to the characteristics of non-host areas. In this comparison, non-host areas include areas in all 331 U.S. MAs that lie beyond the 3-kilometer circular host neighborhoods. (See the Methods Appendix note 9 for further details.)[29]

In metropolitan areas, people of color percentages in host neighborhoods are significantly greater than those in non-host areas (57% vs. 33%). Likewise, the nation's metropolitan areas show disparities in percentages of African Americans, Hispanics and Asians/Pacific Islanders, 20% vs. 13%, 27% vs. 14% and 6.8% vs. 4.4%, respectively. Table 11-5 also shows socioeconomic disparities between host neighborhoods and non-host areas, for example, in poverty rates (18% vs. 12%). Mean household incomes and housing values in host neighborhoods are

TABLE 11-5   Racial and Socioeconomic Disparities Between Host Neighborhoods and
Non-Host Areas of Commercial Hazardous Waste Facilities in
Metropolitan Areas

	Host Neighborhoods	Non-Host Areas	Difference	Ratio
Population				
Total Population (1000s)	9,035	216,920	−207,885	0.04
Population Density	1,040	120	920	8.67
Race/Ethnicity				
% People of Color	56.6%	33.1%	23.5%	1.71
% African American	20.1%	12.8%	7.3%	1.57
% Hispanic or Latino/a	27.4%	13.7%	13.8%	2.01
% Asian/Pacific Islander	6.8%	4.4%	2.4%	1.56
Socioeconomics				
Poverty Rate	18.3%	11.6%	6.8%	1.59
Mean Household Income	$48,391	$60,438	−$12,048	0.80
Mean Housing Value	$136,880	$173,738	−$36,858	0.79

NOTES: Differences and ratios are between host neighborhood and non-host area percentages.
Differences may not precisely match other values due to rounding off. Population density is
persons per square kilometer (rounded off). Mean housing values pertain to owner-occupied
housing units.

about 20% lower than those in non-host areas ($48,400 vs. $60,000 and
$136,900 vs. $173,700, respectively). These racial and socioeconomic disparities
are statistically significant at the 0.001 level.

One hundred and five of the 149 MAs with facilities (70%) have host neighborhoods with disproportionately high percentages of people of color, and 46 of
these MAs (31%) have majority people of color host neighborhoods. These
MAs are widely distributed across the country. Metropolitan areas with large
disparities in Hispanic or Latino percentages are also located in all regions,
whereas MAs with large disparities in African American percentages are located
primarily in the South and Midwest. Thirteen metropolitan areas have large
disparities (host-non-host area differences of 3% or more) in Asian/Pacific Islander percentages. These also are distributed throughout the country. (See Ap-
pendices 4.8–4.9.)[29]

Table 11-6 on the opposite page shows the 10 metropolitan areas with the
largest number of people of color living in neighborhoods with hazardous
waste facilities. Host neighborhoods in these 10 metropolitan areas have a
total of 3.12 million people of color, which represents 60% of the total population of people of color in all host neighborhoods in the country (5.16 million). Six metropolitan areas account for half of all people of color living in
close proximity to all of the nation's commercial hazardous waste facilities
(Los Angeles, New York, Detroit, Chicago, Oakland, and Orange County,

TABLE 11-6   The 10 Metropolitan Areas with the Largest Number of People of Color
Living in Hazardous Waste Facility Neighborhoods

Metropolitan Area	Number of Facilities/ Host Neighborhoods	People of Color in Host Neighborhoods	People of Color per Host Neighborhood	% People of Color in Host Neighborhoods
Los Angeles	17	1,115,412	65,612	90.9%
New York	3	451,746	150,582	61.0%
Detroit	12	315,975	26,331	69.3%
Chicago	9	294,437	32,715	71.6%
Oakland	6	219,978	36,663	76.0%
Orange County (CA)	3	176,368	58,789	69.8%
Houston	10	165,729	16,573	78.6%
Newark	4	143,540	35,885	66.8%
San Jose	2	132,720	66,360	77.1%
Minneapolis—St. Paul	9	101,455	11,273	35.3%
TOTAL	75	3,117,360		

CA). Los Angeles alone accounts for 21% of the people of color in host neighborhoods nationally.

In sum, there is no doubt that significant racial disparities exist within the nation's metropolitan areas, which contain 4 out of every 5 commercial hazardous waste facilities. Racial disparities exist in a large majority of metropolitan areas that have facilities (105 out of 141), and these metropolitan areas are widely distributed throughout the country. The magnitude of these disparities is often quite substantial. Moreover, these disparities are not confined to a single racial group but can be found among African Americans, Hispanics, and Asians/Pacific Islanders. The significant disparities found when separately examining the nation's metropolitan areas as a whole, as well as individual metropolitan areas, demonstrate the robustness of the findings and underscore those of the EPA regional and state analyses.

The Race Factor

Toxic Wastes and Race in the United States found race to be more important than socioeconomic status in predicting the location of the nation's commercial hazardous waste facilities. Thus, it is appropriate to ask whether racial disparities reported above in the current distribution of hazardous wastes are a function of neighborhood socioeconomic characteristics. Because race is often highly correlated with socioeconomic status, it is difficult to tell if race plays an independent role in accounting for facility locations without conducting statistical tests (i.e., multivariate analyses) to isolate the effect of race alone.

To determine the independent effect of race, socioeconomic factors believed to be associated with race must be statistically controlled. A number of income, occupation, employment and education variables were selected to serve as indicators of neighborhood socioeconomic characteristics. Table 11-7 shows the results of the multivariate analysis with the race and socioeconomic variables separately grouped. All race variables (percentages of Hispanics, African Americans, and Asians/Pacific Islanders) are highly significant independent predictors of the facility locations (at the 0.000 level). The positive coefficient (B) indicates that the higher the people of color percentages, the more likely a census tract is to be within 3 kilometers of a commercial hazardous waste facility. Among the indicators of socioeconomic status, mean income and percent employed in blue collar occupations are significant predictors (at the 0.000 level). These variables are therefore independently associated with hazardous waste facility locations. Mean housing value is statistically significant, but in an unexpected direction (i.e., it has a positive coefficient).

Some socioeconomic variables are not statistically significant. For example, the percentage employed in management and professional (i.e., white collar) occupations is not a significant predictor. Likewise, the percentage of persons with a college degree does not quite achieve the threshold needed to be considered statistically significant, though it is trending that way. It also has a positive coefficient, which is in the unexpected direction. The results show that race contin-

TABLE 11-7   Multivariate Analysis Comparing Independent Effect of Race on Facility Location (Logistic Regression)

	Coefficient (B)	Est. Odds Ratio (Exp(B))	Significance Level
Race/Ethnicity			
% Hispanic or Latino	2.222	9.226	0.000
% African American	1.752	5.768	0.000
% Asian/Pacific Islander	3.583	35.964	0.000
Socioeconomic Status Indicators			
Mean Household Income ($1000s)	−0.011	0.989	0.000
Mean Housing Value ($1000s)	0.001	1.001	0.002
% with 4-Year College Degree	0.769	2.158	0.058
% Employed in Professional "White Collar" Occupations	−0.695	0.499	0.167
% Employed in "Blue Collar" Occupations	2.427	11.321	0.000
Constant	−4.453	0.012	0.000
−2 Log Likelihood	16977.135		
Model $X2$ (df=8)	1683.086		0.000

NOTES: Analysis uses 2000 Census tract data and 50% areal containment method with a 3-kilometer circular radius.

ues to be a significant and robust predictor of commercial hazardous waste facility locations when socioeconomic and other nonracial factors are taken into account. A separate analysis of metropolitan areas alone produces similar results.[29]

Conclusions

Twenty years after the release of *Toxic Wastes and Race in the United States*, significant racial and socioeconomic disparities persist in the distribution of the nation's commercial hazardous waste facilities. Although the current assessment uses newer methods to ensure that only nearby populations are counted, the conclusions are very much the same as they were in 1987. People of color and persons of low socioeconomic status are still disproportionately impacted and are particularly concentrated in neighborhoods and communities with the greatest number of facilities. Indeed, a watershed moment has occurred in the last decade. People of color now comprise a majority in neighborhoods with commercial hazardous waste facilities, and much larger (over two-thirds) majorities can be found in neighborhoods with clustered facilities.

This current appraisal also reveals that racial disparities are also widespread throughout the country—whether one examines EPA regions, states or metropolitan areas, where the lion's share of facilities is located. Moreover, race continues to be a stronger predictor of facility locations than other factors often considered to be associated with race.

Significant racial and socioeconomic disparities exist today despite the considerable societal attention to the problem. These findings raise serious questions about the ability of current policies and institutions to adequately protect people of color and the poor from toxic threats. In 1994, in their introduction to *Toxic Wastes and Race Revisited*, John Rosenthall of the NAACP and Charles Lee of the UCC Commission for Racial Justice remarked about "the continuing need for vigilance and action to ensure people of color are no longer disproportionately exposed to health and environmental risks."[2] These words are still relevant over a decade later. It remains clear that much more concerted attention is needed to address these persistent disproportionate environmental burdens on this twentieth anniversary of *Toxic Wastes and Race in the United States*.

References

1. Mohai P, Saha R. Reassessing Racial and Socioeconomic Disparities in Environmental Justice Research. *Demography* 2007; 43(2): 383–399.
2. Mohai P, Saha R. Racial Inequality in the Distribution of Hazardous Waste: A National-Level Reassessment. *Soc Problems* 2007; 54(3): 343–370.
3. Commission for Racial Justice. *Toxic wastes and race in the United States: A national report on the racial and socioeconomic characteristics of communities with hazardous waste sites.* New York: United Church of Christ; 1987.

4. Goldman B, Fitton L. *Toxic Wastes and Race Revisited: An Update of the 1987 Report on the Racial and Socioeconomic Characteristics of Communities with Hazardous Waste Sites.* Washington, D.C.: Center for Policy Alternatives; 1994.

5. Mohai P, Bryant B. Environmental racism: Reviewing the evidence. In Bryant B, Mohai P (Eds.), *Race and the incidence of environmental hazards: A time for discourse* (163–176). Boulder, CO: Westview Press; 1992.

6. Ringquist EJ. Assessing evidence of environmental inequalities: A meta-analysis. *J Pol Anal Man* 2005; 24(2), 223–247.

7. U.S. Environmental Protection Agency. *National biennial RCRA hazardous waste report: Based on 2001 data.* Washington DC: Office of Solid Waste & Emergency Response, EPA 530R03007. 2003. Available at www.epa.gov/epaoswer/hazwaste/data/biennialreport/index.htm.

8. Daley B. Oversight gap cited on waste at Danvers site. *Boston Globe* (Nov. 29). 2006. Retrieved from http://www.boston.com/news/local/articles/2006/11/29/oversight_gap_cited_on_waste_at_danvers_site/.

9. Jayadev R. Silicon Valley's dirty secret. *Metro Silicon Valley* (Jan. 3-9). 2007. Retrieved from http://www.metroactive.com/metro/01.03.07/environmental-racism-0701.html.

10. Bullard R, Wright B. Blacks and the environment. *Humboldt J Soc Rel* 1987; 14(1/2):165–184.

11. Saha R, Mohai P. Historical context and hazardous waste facility siting: Understanding temporal trends in Michigan. *Soc Problems* 2005; 52(4):618–648.

12. Bullard R. Solid waste sites and the black Houston community. *Soc Inq* 1983; 53:273–288.

13. Bullard R. *Dumping in Dixie: Race, Class and Environmental Quality.* Boulder, CO: Westview Press; 1990.

14. Taylor DE. Mobilizing for environmental justice in communities of color: An emerging profile of people of color environmental groups. In Aley J, Burch WR, Canover B, and Fields D (Eds.), *Ecosystem management: Adaptive strategies for natural resource organizations in the 21st century* (32–67). Philadelphia: Taylor & Francis; 1988.

15. U.S. Environmental Protection Agency. *National biennial reporting system.* Washington, D.C.: Office of Solid Waste and Emergency Response. 2001. Available at ftp://ftp.epa.gov/rcrainfodata/brfiles/.

16. U.S. Environmental Protection Agency. *Biennial report module introduction* Washington, D.C.: Office of Solid Waste and Emergency Response. 2001. Available at http://www.epa.gov/epaoswer/hazwaste/data/brs99/brshelp.pdf.

17. U.S. Bureau of the Census. LandView III (RCRIS and other computer files on CDROM). Washington, D.C.: U.S. EPA and U.S. Department of Commerce, Bureau of the Census. 1993.

18. Environmental Information Ltd. *Environmental services directory.* (Online paid subscription service and database). Edina, MN: Environmental Information Ltd. 2001/2002. Available at http://www.envirobiz.com/newSearch/EnvSerDir.asp.

19. U.S. Environmental Protection Agency. *Envirofacts data warehouse.* (Data accessed online through technical user platform from approximately March 2001 to June 2002.) 2001/2002. See http://www.epa.gov/enviro/html/technical.html.

20. Rhodes EL. The challenge of environmental justice measurement and assessment. *Pol Man Rev* 2002; 2(1):86–110.

21. Baibergenova A, Kudyakov R, Zdeb M, Carpenter DO. Low birth weight and residential proximity to PCB-contaminated waste sites. *Environ Health Perspect* 2003; 111(10):1352–1357.

22. Dolk H, Vrijeid M, Armstrong B, Abramsky L, Bianchi F, et al. Risk of congenital anomalies near hazardous waste landfill sites in Europe: The EUROHAZCON study. *Lancet* 1998; 352:423–427.

23. Fielder HMP, Poon-King CM, Palmer SR, Moss N, Coleman G. Assessment of impact on health of residents living near the Nant-y-Gwyddon landfill site: Retrospective analysis. *BMJ* 2000; 320:19–22.

24. Gerschwind SA, Stolwijk J, Bracken M, Fitzgerald E, Stark A, et al. Risk of congenital malformations associated with proximity to hazardous waste sites. *Am J Epidemiol* 1992; 135:1197–1207.

25. Nelson AC, Genereux M, Genereux J. Price effects and landfills on house values. *Land Econ* 1992; 68(4):359–365.

26. Edelstein MR. *Contaminated communities: Coping with residential toxic exposure* (2d ed.). Cambridge, MA: Westview Press; 2004.

27. Corburn J. *Street Science: Community Knowledge and Environmental Health Justice.* Cambridge, MA: MIT Press; 2005.

28. Pulido L, Sidawi S, Vos RO. An archaeology of environmental racism in Los Angeles. *Urban Geogr* 1996; 17(5):419–439.

29. Bullard R, Mohai R, Saha R, Wright B. *Toxic Wastes and Race at Twenty 1987–2007: Grassroots Struggles to Dismantle Environmental Racism in the United States.* Cleveland, OH: United Church of Christ Justice & Witness Ministries; 2007.

30. Jacobson M. *Whiteness of a Different Color: European Immigrants and the Alchemy of Race.* Cambridge, MA: Harvard University Press; 1998

31. Cole L, Foster S. *From the Ground Up: Environmental Racism and the Rise of the Environmental Justice Movement.* New York: New York University Press; 2001.

32. Targ N. The states' comprehensive approach to environmental justice. In Pellow D, Brulle R (Eds.), *Power, justice and the environment: A critical appraisal of the environmental justice movement* (171–184). Cambridge, MA: MIT Press; 2005.

33. Anderton D, Anderson A, Oakes JM, Fraser MR. Environmental equity: The demographics of dumping. *Demography* 1994; 31(2):229–248.

34. Mohai P. The demographics of dumping revisited: Examining the impact of alternate methodologies in environmental justice research. *VA Environ Law J* 1994; 14:615–653.

35. Clark B. The indigenous environmental movement in the United States. *Org Environ* 2002; 15(4):410–442.
36. LaDuke W. *All our relations: Native struggles for land and life.* Cambridge, MA: South End Press; 1999.
37. Weaver J. *Defending mother Earth: American Indian perspectives on environmental justice.* Maryknoll, NJ: Orbis Books; 1995.
38. Blackford MG. Environmental justice, native rights, tourism, and opposition to military control: The case of Kaho'olawe. *J Am Hist* 2004; 91(2): 544–571.
39. Grinde D, Johansen B. *Ecocide of Native America: Environmental destruction of Indian lands and peoples.* Santa Fe, NM: Clear Light; 1995.
40. Hooks G, Smith C. The treadmill of destruction: National sacrifice areas and Native Americans. *Am Soc Rev* 2004; 69:558–575.

Urban Horticulture in the Contemporary United States: Personal and Community Benefits

H. Patricia Hynes and Genevieve Howe

Introduction

Horticulture, the science and art of growing plants for consumption and happiness, for the health of communities, and for the integration of nature into human civilization,[1] has always been practiced in cities. In our ancestors' transition from nomadic to settled existence, their market gardens and farms gave birth to trading centers and cities; and cities became the incubators of insight, experiment, technique and exchange of ideas that advanced urban horticulture and that were disseminated to farmers in the hinterlands.[2] For thousands of years, built and cultivated environments coexisted: Homes, cottage industries, markets, public buildings, and sacred spaces were interspersed with kitchen gardens, farms, and common grazing land for animals. Not until the Industrial Revolution were dooryard and market gardens, orchards, and town commons usurped by brick, mortar, and asphalt. Banishing nature was "not the inevitable way to build cities, but instead a bad mutation brought on by nineteenth and twentieth century land greed."[3]

Horticulture, after being eliminated from nineteenth century factory neighborhoods, was then deliberately restored in selected urban open spaces, outside factory neighborhoods, as an antidote to the monotony, noise, congestion, and poor ventilation of industrial workplaces and the tenement dwellings of immigrants and the working class. City parks tranquilize and yet enliven, Frederick Law Olmsted, the designer of New York City's Central Park, observed about the capacity of trees, meadows, ponds, and wildlife to assuage the stresses of surrounding urban life. Jane Jacobs wryly observed, in her commentary on the downward spiral of many city parks into derelict and dangerous places, that parks need people no less than people need parks.[4]

Cities of the rapidly urbanizing twenty-first century, however, may need local community gardens* and nearby green spaces as much as they needed the grand central parks in the late nineteenth century—for the give-and-take of working in gardens attaches gardeners to a particular place through physical and social engagement. Community gardens create and sustain relationships between city dwellers and the soil, and can engender an ethic of urban environmentalism that neither grand central parks nor wilderness—which release and free us from the industrial city—can do. As the studies reviewed in this article strongly suggest, nature in cities that is cultivated or simply *nearby* enough to view and easily visit fosters personal well being and community benefits, such as more social interaction and sense of neighborhood, less crime, community food security, recovery from mental fatigue and increased life satisfaction.

Half the world's six billion people live in cities; and, according to United Nations estimates, almost two out of three people will be living in urban areas by 2030.[5] Thus, most people's experience, knowledge, and valuing of nature in the twenty-first century, their environmental literacy and claims to natural assets will be shaped and bounded by the natural, social, and built environments of urban settlements. A community garden might be seen as a minor, merely local, and cosmetic experience of nature that could be more authentically sought in wild and remote places. Yet, gardens, with their "middle ground between the wilderness and the lawn," may "suggest the lineaments of a new [urban] environmental ethic . . . and help us out in all those situations where the wilderness ethic is silent or unhelpful,"[6] and where the experience of wilderness is unaffordable, remote, or inaccessible.

Modern Community Garden Movement

Community gardens and small farms in U.S. cities are not altogether new. However, their purposes today—not short-term welfare during periods of recession, nor philanthropic charity to uplift "the masses," nor patriotic war relief, all of which catalyzed earlier urban horticulture movements—are new.[7] Their goals include teaching inner-city children ecological literacy and diverting them from the streets; cleaning up overgrown neighborhood eyesores and pushing out drug dealing, that, like weeds, overtakes neglected vacant lots; growing and preserving food from seed to shelf; restoring nature to the industrial and post-industrial city using heirloom plants and bird and butterfly gardens; and bringing the farming

---

*The majority of urban community gardens are created on vacant land that may be as small as a building lot and as large as a city block, and are gardened in individual plots by an organized group of people from the surrounding neighborhood. Common areas within the gardens may be sites for social, cultural, and artistic events. Unlike earlier periods, the modern community garden movement is initiated and driven by local communities with the financial and organizational assistance of government, foundations, and non-profit organizations.

tradition of the rural South to northern industrial cities. These are but a handful of the reasons that urban gardeners have given when asked why they garden.[8]

At its core, the community garden movement in the early twenty-first century is about rebuilding a spirit of local community tied to a place and restoring nature and food growing in the inner city. Some community gardens are linked to public housing projects, churches and social agencies; still others employ people who are incarcerated or recently released from jail. Most are neighborhood-based efforts, with multiple plots on once vacant land in which gardeners grow a mix of "food for the body and flowers for the soul."* Even where the legacy of philanthropy lingers, it has lost the odor of reform charity—of the "haves" uplifting the "have-nots"—that characterized earlier garden movements in cities.

Post–World War II Trends

With the exception of some creative garden projects promoted by public housing authorities in the 1950s and 60s for the purposes of beautification and tenant pride, the tradition of urban growing was abandoned in the United States after World War II, when the focus of residential and commercial growth became the new suburbs. Older center cities were left to decline and wither as the middle and upper middle classes and financial institutions quit old urban neighborhoods and pushed the edges of metropolitan growth into peri-urban and once-rural areas. Poor and minority populations became starkly concentrated in economically devastated urban slums and ghettos; and public policy and market forces have mainly failed to pierce the web of social, political, and economic forces that have racialized and feminized poverty.**,† Metropolitan areas in the

---

*Interview with B. Cozart, former director of the Greening of Harlem, June 1992 by H. Patricia Hynes for *A Patch of Eden: America's Inner-City Gardens*.

**Demographer Douglas Massey[11] argues that, with the worldwide phenomenon of urbanization, most of the world's poor will be clustered and segregated in poor neighborhoods of cities; the affluent will also be more segregated; and income inequality will continue the dramatic rise it began in the 1970s. Factors include stagnant incomes in the global economy and "racial and ethnic exclusion" which exacerbate growing class segregation. Inequality in the United States, as measured by the GINI index for family income, rose 14% between 1973 and 1991. In 1970, 56% of America's poor lived in central cities or suburbs. By the early 1990s, that concentration had risen to 72%, with the highest portion of the increase occurring in central cities.

†The extremes of racial and class segregation in the United States have changed minimally since the 1964 Civil Rights Act and the 1968 Fair Housing Act. Of all groups, Blacks faced the highest rates of residential segregation according to indices calculated for 1980.[12] In 18 major northern cities, poor Blacks had an average segregation index of 85.8, while the index for affluent Blacks was 83.2. In 12 major southern cities, the segregation index for poor Blacks was 74.4, while for affluent Blacks, it was 72.8.

United States sprawled* with middle and upper middle class migration to suburbs while center cities lost people, businesses, and buildings and devolved, in
many places, into vast, vacant, contaminated wastelands and neighborhoods of
isolated and segregated poverty.

An inadvertent, but predictable result of disinvestment in American center
cities in the latter part of the twentieth century was the emergence of vacant
lots, a blight that metastasized and spread like a cancer through neighborhoods.** Abandoned lots that had once accommodated houses, businesses,
parks, and industries became local eyesores and the site of waste dumping and
criminal activity. Between 1960 and 1990, about 30% of residential buildings in
Harlem, New York became derelict and uninhabitable. Chicago, Illinois, has
70,000 vacant lots; 18% of once-productive industrial land is vacant. The population of center city Philadelphia, the oldest industrial U.S. city, was 2.2 million
after World War II; today it is 1.6 million and shrinking. Philadelphia has more
than 30,000 vacant lots and 21,000 abandoned houses.[8,15–16]

The beginnings of the modern community gardening, urban agriculture,
and food security movements in these same neighborhoods were quiet, local, and
disparate—a group of progressive landscape architects in one city, an activist
politician in another, a director of a horticulture society in another, and, in many
cities, community organizers and residents disgusted with trash dumping and the
lack of safe greenspace. A low-key urban movement, with tributaries in the
peace, environmental, women's, civil rights, and "back-to-the-city" movements
of the late 1960s and early 70s as well as the environmental justice movement of
the 1980s and 90s, eyed vacant land and saw the possibility of community and
school gardens and, more recently, urban agriculture[†] and farmers' markets.

Today, some 30 years after the first community gardens were organized, we
do not have a complete census of urban gardens, their organizations and their
evolving activity—such is the movement's variable, local, and non-statistically-
inclined nature. However, we do have some survey data, informed estimates,
and in-depth case studies about the growth and diversity of the many efforts to

---

*Lopez and Hynes[11] designed a new method for measuring sprawl by analyzing popula-
tion density according to Census tracts. They established a sprawl index where 0 indicates
that the entire metropolitan area is high-density and has the least sprawl and 100, that the entire city is low-density and has the most sprawl. Between 1990 and 2000, sprawl had increased
in almost two-thirds of the 330 metropolitan areas analyzed.

**A number of studies have documented the "synergism of plagues" in abandoned and
vacant neighborhoods, including higher risk of HI2002,[12] higher prevalence of death from
heat stress,[13] and higher rates of substance abuse.[14]

†Urban agriculture is a small but growing phenomenon within urban core areas that includes vegetable, fruit, flower and fish growing, as well as animal husbandry for purposes of
personal consumption, job creation, and market sale.[17] Other purposes may include checking
sprawl, efficient use of vacant land, increasing urban food security, job training for youth,
reuse of urban waste, creating greenspace, and contributing to a sense of community.[10]

revive horticulture and agriculture for the purposes of community development and community food security in U.S. cities.

The American Community Gardening Association (ACGA) estimates that municipal governments and non-profit organizations operate gardening programs in about 250 cities and towns, although ACGA staff have said privately that the number could be twice as large (pers. commun., 1995). In its 1994 survey, the National Gardening Association found that 6.7 million households, which are not currently engaged in gardening, would be interested in community gardening if there were a plot nearby.[18]

The most recent survey of community gardens, in which ACGA polled residents of 38 cities across the United States, revealed some interesting issues and trends. First, despite a lack of security in land ownership (only 5.3% of the 6020 community gardens surveyed are securely owned or placed in trust), *more gardens are being created in these cities than are being lost* to economic development or lack of interest. Second, the primary reported use of community gardens is the neighborhood garden in which the land is divided into numerous plots cultivated for vegetables, flowers, and fruits by individuals and households. Other potential uses and kinds of community gardens, such as ones in public housing, senior housing, and schools, were reported in much smaller numbers. The survey also revealed the small but increasing use of community gardens as job training sites for youth and as market gardens from which plants and products made from plants would be sold, often in local farmers' markets.[19]

The lines of distinction between large community gardens, market gardens, and urban agriculture can be quite porous: Some community gardens may have a market component; some market gardens and urban farms enjoy the social benefits of community gardens. The recent rise of market gardens and agriculture in center cities of the United States coincides with the renaissance of urban farmers' markets. Urban horticulture in the United States—which loosely encompasses community gardens, market gardens, small farms and farmers' markets—is taking a noteworthy and admirable trajectory, one that is fluent with larger issues of community development and community food security.

Community Food Security

Urban farmers' markets flourished in the early twentieth century but then disappeared mid-century as downtown districts declined and suburban shopping malls proliferated. Concurrently, processed foods replaced fresh foods in the national diet with the growth of the convenience and fast food industries.* In

---

*Potatoes are a prime example of the change in food consumption and food growing. In 1950, 6% of potatoes purchased by Americans were in the form of processed food. By 1983, MacDonald's was the largest purchaser of potatoes and 60% of potatoes purchased by Americans were processed as chips, fries, etc.[20]

1977, the United States Department of Agriculture (USDA) initiated a significant urban gardening program to assist low-income people in cities to grow and preserve vegetables, primarily for nutrition and food security. At its zenith in 1989, almost 200,000 gardeners, of whom 64% were minorities, were producing vegetables on 800 acres of "farmland" in 23 major cities. For every dollar invested by the USDA, gardeners grew an estimated US$6 worth of food.[21]

In 1993, the government of the United States (US) inexplicably ceased funding this low-budget, highly successful program. Some non-profit organizations, already dedicated to community gardens, stepped in to provide services abandoned by the USDA urban gardening program. In 1994, a new coalition of environmental, community development and food system activists lobbied quickly, aggressively and successfully for funding under the aegis of *community food security*.* The subsequent U.S. Community Food Security Act has provided a new infusion of federal funding into certain inner cities for food growing and marketing through farmers' markets, nutrition education, and links between peri-urban growers and low-income families and urban schools. Farmers' markets, with their capacity to support local small farmers and provide fresh, unprocessed food to urban communities abandoned by supermarket chain stores are a particularly important ingredient of community food security.

Farmers' markets are now enjoying a revival, thanks to recent federal and state investment and community food policy activism. By the late 1990s, 2,500 farmers' markets were established in 50 states, earning small and organic farmers US $1 billion annually.[20] Community food security, in practice, generates alternative strategies for the dual crises of food supply (a lack of local markets for small farmers) and food consumption (hunger, malnutrition, and a dearth of supermarkets in inner cities). The self-defined goal of community food security is to achieve a safe, affordable, nutritious, and culturally acceptable food supply for all (particularly low-income) people, as much as possible from local sources. Food security analysts have undertaken innovative studies of food scarcity, price inflation, and inaccessibility in urban and inner-city neighborhoods. These include: surveys to expose the scarcity of supermarkets and food stores, surveys to uncover price inflation, and studies demonstrating insufficient urban public transportation service to larger, cheaper supermarkets.[22]

The findings of these studies have shaped and driven numerous food security projects. School food service staff and teachers have joined with farmers to

---

*The concept of community food security arose within international development in the 1970s and 1980s, as pressure on developing countries mounted to adopt the now-dominant industrial model of U.S. agriculture, that is to mechanize and organize for export-oriented agriculture. In the United States, community food security emerged during the 1980s and 1990s, a period of growing disparity between rich and poor, of small farm bankruptcy and loss, and of reliance on emergency food from soup kitchens and food pantries in numbers and rates not seen since the Great Depression.[20]

supply locally-grown produce to students. Supermarket price monitoring programs have been established. Some inner-city community organizations now work with nearby rural farms to make nutritious, lower-cost produce available through food coops and community-supported agriculture. Farmers' markets have been set up in inner-city neighborhoods where low-income residents can buy wholesome, locally-grown food with government vouchers. And, food-related transportation strategies have been created for low-income, transit dependent communities.[22]

In the opinion of many food policy activists, a new structure of local food growing and marketing has the potential to challenge and begin to redress the injustices of industrial agriculture, a vertically-integrated multinational system that has commodified food and subsumed food security to profit. Above all, the food security movement is grounded in a philosophy of social justice, which helps assure that community food security and its companion, urban community gardens, are not merely *ad-hoc* opportunistic programs, which, like the world war victory gardens, are dismissed once "the war" is over.*

Personal and Community Benefits of Urban Horticulture and Nearby Greenspace

The majority of urban community gardens are located on undeveloped public land to which gardeners have no title and no long-term security,[19] a great vulnerability for the movement. New York City is the most egregious example of a municipal landowner that pits "rent-free" community gardens against potential affordable housing and tax-paying retail development; the city has attempted to develop almost 20% of the 700 sites currently used for community gardens.

Community gardens, and more recently urban agriculture, cannot compete with market-based land uses, such as housing and retail, if they are evaluated solely by their tax generating and other economic potential. We need, therefore, to demonstrate and document the health, education, and social welfare benefits of community gardens, urban agriculture, and access to nearby greenspace for city dwellers in order to assess and validate their full value as natural assets that contribute to social, human, and financial well-being.**

---

*The community food security movement has consciously politicized urban horticulture, emerging as a local force in the face of the globalized food system; while the political potential of community gardens is more implicit and emerges at times of threat or crisis, such as their takeover and elimination by New York City for more profitable land uses.

**Any potential health liabilities of growing vegetables in the city, such as food contamination by lead in soil, must also be examined and remediated to maximize the benefits of urban horticulture on lead in urban soil.[23]

Nutrition and Cost Savings

US government studies have revealed that groceries in urban markets cost 3% to 37% more than the same goods in large suburban supermarkets.[24] Moreover, the inflation of food prices in urban stores and the lack of transportation from center cities to cheaper suburban stores aggravate malnutrition, poor diets, and related chronic health conditions among the urban poor.[25,26] Using 1990 census tract and population density data in 221 neighborhoods of four states, Morland et al. found that White neighborhoods had four times as many supermarkets as Black neighborhoods and that the wealthiest neighborhoods had larger numbers of supermarkets compared to the poorest neighborhoods.[26] Further, the poorest neighborhoods had three times as many bars and taverns as the wealthiest. Disparity in local access to nutritious, affordable foods and transportation access to larger supermarkets with greater varieties of healthy, food choices at lower costs led the authors to conclude, "the choices people make about what to eat are limited by the food available to them."[27]

A population-based study of 144 community gardeners in Philadelphia and 67 non-gardening controls evaluated the nutrition and economic benefits of community gardens. Researchers found that gardeners ate vegetables significantly more than comparable non-gardeners and consumed significantly fewer sweet foods and drinks and milk products. The mean value of vegetables grown in 1987 (the year studied) by gardeners was US$160±178, with a range of US$2 to US$1134.[28] Further, gardeners participated in community projects and shared produce with friends, family and food pantries more significantly than did the non-gardening controls.

The most systematic assessment of the value of food grown in community gardens was conducted by the USDA during 1977 to 1993, the period in which the agency promoted urban food growing among low-income communities in 23 cities. As cited earlier, urban gardeners grew, preserved, and consumed an estimated US $6 worth of produce for every US$1 invested by the government.[21] Thus, inner city community gardens can be a significant source of low-cost, nutritious food for communities threatened by food insecurity due to factors of poverty, inadequate public transit, and abandonment by supermarkets.

Emotional, Social, and Cognitive Effects

In a set of open-ended questions, community gardeners in Philadelphia were asked to list the reasons they gardened and to identify the single most important reason. Their responses were: recreation (21%), mental health (19%), physical health and exercise (17%), produce quality and nutrition (14%), spiritual reasons (10%), cost and convenience (7%), self expression/self fulfillment (7%), and other (5%).[28] Waliczek et al.[29] conducted a national survey of community gardeners using a set of quality of life questions based on Maslow's hierarchy of human needs model: physiological, safety, social, esteem, and self-actualization.

The majority of gardeners reported that gardens meet all of these needs, with African-American and Hispanic gardeners reporting statistically significant higher responses than Whites and Asians on most of the questions.[29] In a similar survey, American-born and immigrant gardeners in eight San Jose, California community gardens reported comparable personal and social benefits.[30]

The findings of the aforementioned studies resonate with the growing body of literature over the past 25 years that documents the beneficial effects of nature on human well-being and has provided theories concerning the role of nature in human restoration. Trees, grass, and flower gardens, by their presence and by their visibility, have been found to increase people's general life satisfaction in urban settings, reduce irritability and mental fatigue, restore calm,[31] and regenerate the capacity for directed attention.[32] Stephen Kaplan[33] theorized that the experience of nature restores people by giving them a feeling of release or escape from the quotidian life and by eliciting fascination within a natural setting that feels whole, adequate, and compatible.

Most people–plant interaction studies, however, have dichotomized city from nature, in comparing human response to remote nature scenes and urban built environment scenes. Honeyman[34] is one of a handful of researchers to test the restorative value of nature scenes in urban environments. She found that scenes of the urban built environment with vegetation produce more mental restoration than those without vegetation and that vegetated urban scenes had more positive psychological impact than nature only scenes. In studying the effect of nature near-at-hand in gardening, it was found that gardening elicits fascination in gardeners and "plays a role in people's lives not unlike that played by the more dramatic, more distant, and less frequent encounters with nature."[35] Residents in multiple-family housing reported that the most important factors in their neighborhood satisfaction were nearby trees, well-landscaped grounds, and places to go walking. Opportunities to garden and the view of nearby gardens were much more significant than large open spaces to a sense of community. National surveys have also found that easy access to nature is the strongest predictor of residents' satisfaction with their local neighborhood.[36]

A recent series of studies in Chicago public housing, one of the starkest of urban built environments, have found consistent results regarding the positive social and behavioral benefits of greenspace. In comparing residents' use of outdoor space, researchers found that greater numbers of people gathered in spaces with trees than in those without. Thus, trees created greater opportunities for social life and social cohesion.[37] A study among senior public housing residents found that greater access to common greenspace is positively associated with neighborhood social ties and a sense of community.[38]

Effects on Children

In an observational study of inner-city children playing outdoors, researchers found that children in highly vegetated spaces played more (by a factor of two) than children in non-vegetated areas, and that they played more creatively and interacted more with adults.[39] Wells[40] undertook a longitudinal study of low-income children who moved from poor housing with little vegetation into "Habitat for Humanity" housing with more vegetation to assess the cognitive benefits of the increased presence of nearby nature. She found that children had a significant increase in "directed attention capacity" (DAC), as measured in tests of concentration, after moving to a more vegetated environment and that the variance in their DAC attributable to change in vegetation was greater than that attributable to the change in housing.[40]

Physiological Effects

Others have used physiological testing to corroborate self-reported emotional states when viewing natural scenes. The simple act of gazing at a plant can lower blood pressure and muscle tension and can reduce stress, fear, and anger.[41] Merely viewing pictures of nature consistently and significantly held the viewers' attention and interest and induced higher alpha intensity (associated with relaxed feelings while awake) than did pictures of the urban built environment.[42] The same researcher found that post-operative patients with a window view of deciduous trees recovered more quickly, had better progress evaluations, and requested fewer analgesics that a matched set of patients with a view of a brown brick wall.[43] These findings complement those that have found that workers with views of nature, such as trees and flowers, reported fewer ailments and more job satisfaction than those without an outside view or with a view of the built environment.[44] Likewise, others have documented that prison inmates with a view of nature reported fewer stress symptoms and less sickness than those with views of prison yards, walls, and buildings.[45]

Reduction in Crime

Dense vegetation in urban areas has been associated with criminal activity as well as with fear of crime.[46] A study of the relationship between crime and non-dense vegetation in Chicago public housing has found that vegetation that preserves view and visibility (e.g., trees and low shrubbery) has a role in reducing crime. Comparing end-of-year reports on property and violent crime in buildings with and without vegetation, researchers found that buildings with a high level of greenery had 52% fewer crimes than those with no landscaping and those with medium levels had 42% fewer crimes.[47] Green spaces, *where vegetation does not block people's view*, may support residents spending more time outdoors in common spaces, which in turn fosters a culture of care for one's community and an informal surveillance that deters criminals. Drawing from studies linking mental stress and crime, the researchers concluded that nearby nature mitigates mental stress and mental fatigue, thereby reducing the emotional, psychological, and cognitive "precursors" to violent behavior. Related re-

Exercise

A more recently assessed benefit of community gardening—and one that most directly impacts public health—is the physical exercise of gardening. Regular physical activity, that is an estimated 30 minutes three to five times per week, has been found to reduce significantly the risk of dying of coronary heart disease and the risk of chronic diseases, including diabetes, high cholesterol, and high blood pressure, as well as age-associated declines in musculo-skeletal function.[49-50] Gardening is considered comparable to moderate walking, bicycling at <10 mph and water aerobics[51] and is increasingly promoted, like walking, for reducing the risk of chronic diseases from overweight and sedentary lifestyles. This benefit is particularly salient given the recent findings by the U.S. Centers for Disease Control and Prevention (CDC) on the epidemic in overweight and obesity in the United States and a similar trend worldwide. In 1999, an estimated 61% of US adults were either overweight or obese, an increase of approximately 5% from the 1988-94 federal study.[52]* The prevalence of overweight children has doubled since 1980 and tripled since 1960.[53] Both adult and child trends in overweight are attributed, in large part, to higher carbohydrate intake (while energy intake has remained fairly constant), sedentary lifestyle, and physical inactivity around routine daily tasks.[54]**

---

*This data was collected on the National Health and Nutrition Examination Survey (NHANES). While the federal NHANES study data is standardized and validated by physical examinations, the 1999 sample size is smaller than previous NHANES studies, such as the 1988–1994 study. Additional data will be sought to confirm the findings.

**The potential decline in recreational opportunities, particularly in poor communities, must also be investigated.

search on community gardens in upstate New York found that community gardens in *low* income minority communities were four times more likely to lead to organizing around community issues, including crime prevention and improved neighborhood services, than *non-low* income community gardens.[48]

CONCLUSION

Urban community gardens and the newer urban agriculture appear to be rooted in a more enduring substrate than the cycles of recession and war that generated urban food growing over the past 100 years, and they fulfill many more social purposes. Community gardens re-create a sense of "place" for those dispossessed of place by slum clearance and ghettos and for immigrants arriving from agrarian cultures. Offering physical, existential, and community support, they become *places that matter*.[55] Gardening and urban agriculture offer a source of nutrition in neighborhoods abandoned by supermarkets and a sorely needed regimen of exercise to reduce the risk of chronic diseases from overweight and inactivity. Nearby greenspace, including trees and open space play areas, increases social cohesion through attracting adults and children into common greenspace areas where they socialize, build a sense of neighborhood, and carry out an informal surveillance that creates greater security and deters crime.

If a mere view of nature—whether in a photograph or through a window—is balm for patients, students, workers, and inmates of prisons, how much more restorative is the sight, smell, sound, and touch of nature nearby in community gardens, urban farms, small sitting parks, tot lots, and even farmers' markets?

References

1. Relf D. *Human Issues in Horticulture*. 1992. www.hort.vt.edu/human/hihart .htm.
2. Jacobs J. *The Economy of Cities*. Random House, New York. 1969.
3. Warner SB. *To Dwell is To Garden*. Northeastern University Press, Boston. 1987.
4. Jacobs J. *The Death and Life of Great American Cities*. Vintage, New York. 1961.
5. Worldwatch Institute. *Worldwatch Paper 143*. September 1998.
6. Pollan M. Afterword: The Garden's Prospects in America. p.265. In: Punch W.(ed.), *Keeping Eden*. Little, Brown, Boston. 1992.
7. Bassett TJ. Reaping on the margins: A century of community gardening in America. *Landscape*. 1981; 25(2):1–8.
8. Hynes HP. *A Patch of Eden: America's Inner-City Gardens*. Chelsea Green, White River Junction, VT. 1996.
9. Massey DS. The age of extremes: concentrated affluence and poverty in the twenty-first century. *Demography*. 1996; 33(4):395–412.
10. Massey DS, Denton NA. *American Apartheid: Segregation and the Making of the Underclass*. Harvard University Press, Cambridge, MA. 1993.
11. Lopez, R, Hynes HP. Sprawl in the 1990s: Measurement, distribution and trends. *Urban Affairs Review*. 2006; 38(3):325–355.
12. Wallace R. A synergism of plagues: "Planned shrinkage," contagious housing destruction, and AIDS in the Bronx. *Environ Res*. 1988; 47:1–33.
13. di Leonardo M. Murder by public policy. *The Nation*. 2002; 9:31–35.
14. Fullilove M,. Fullilove III R. Place Matters. pp.77–91. In: R. Hofrichter (ed.), *Reclaiming the Environmental Debate: The Politics of Health in a Toxic Culture*. MIT Press, Cambridge, MA. 2000.

15. Gowda V. Whose garden is it? *Governing.* 2002; March:40–41.
16. Smit J. 1999. The Urban Agriculture Network: Activity Report. www .cityfarmer.org/TUAN.html. 1999.
17. Kaufman J, Bailkey M. Farming inside cities: Urban agriculture in the United States. Working Paper. Lincoln Institute of Land Policy. 2000.
18. American Community Gardening Association, Monograph on the 1994 National Gardening Association Survey. 100 North 20th St., 5th Floor, Philadelphia, PA 19103. 1995.
19. American Community Gardening Association, 1998. National Community Gardening Survey: 1996. 100 North 20th St., 5th Floor, Philadelphia, PA 19103.
20. Gottlieb R. *Environmentalism Unbound: Exploring New Pathways for Change.* MIT Press, Cambridge, MA. 2002.
21. United States Department of Agriculture Extension Service Urban Gardening Program FY 1989 Report. Washington, D.C. 1989.
22. Community Food Security Coalition. P.O. Box 209, Venice, CA 90294. www.foodsecurity.org. 2002.
23. Litt J, Hynes HP, Carroll P, Maxfield R, McLaine P, Kawccke C. Lead safe yards: A program for improving health in urban neighborhoods. *Journal of Urban Technology,* August 2002; 9(2):71–93.
24. U.S. House Select Committee on Hunger. *Food security in the United States. Committee Report.* U.S. Government Printing Office, Washington, D.C. October. 1990.
25. U.S. House Select Committee on Hunger. *Obtaining food: shopping constraints of the poor.* Committee Report. U.S. Government Printing Office, Washington, D.C. December. 1987.
26. U.S. House Select Committee on Hunger. *Urban grocery gap.* Committee Report. U.S. Government Printing Office, Washington, D.C. October 1992.
27. Morland K, Wing S, Roux AD, Poole C. Neighborhood characteristics associated with the location of food stores and food service places. *Am J Prev Med.* 2002; 22(1):29.
28. Blair D, Giesecke CC. Sherman S. A dietary, social and economic evaluation of the Philadelphia urban gardening project. *J Nutr Ed.* 1991; 23:161–167.
29. Waliczek TM, Mattson RH, Zajicek JM. Benefits of community gardening on quality-of-life issues. *J Environ Hort.* 1996; 14:204–209.
30. Lee S. Community gardening benefits as perceived among American-born and immigrant gardeners in San Jose, California. Unpublished paper. Environmental Science Department, University of California, Berkeley. 2001.
31. Kaplan R, Kaplan S. Restorative experience: The healing power of nearby nature. pp. 238–244. In: Francis M, Hoster RT (eds.), *The Meaning of Gardens.* MIT Press, Cambridge, MA. 1990.

32. Tennessen CM, Cimprich BE. Views to nature: Effects on attention. *J Environ Psychol.* 1995; 15(1):77–85.
33. Kaplan S. The restorative environment: nature and human experience. Proc. *The Role of Horticulture in Human Well-Being and Social Development: A National Symposium.* Arlington, Virginia. 19–21 April 1990. 134–142.
34. Honeyman M. Vegetation and stress: A comparison study of varying amounts of vegetation in countryside and urban scenes. pp.143–145. In: *The Role of Horticulture in Human Well-Being and Social Development: A National Symposium.* Timber Press, Portland, OR. 1992.
35. Kaplan R. Some psychological benefits of gardening. *Environ Behav.* 1973; 5(2):145–162.
36. Fried M. Resident attachment: Sources of residential and community satisfaction. *J Soc Issues.* 1982; 38:107–120.
37. Levine Coley R, Kuo FE, Sullivan WC. Where does the community grow? The social context created by nature in urban public housing. *Environ Behav.* 1997; 29(4):468–494.
38. Kweon BS, Sullivan WC, Wiley A. Green common spaces and the social integration of inner-city older adults. *Environ Behav;* 1998. 30(6):832–858.
39. Taylor AF, Wiley A, Kuo FE, Sullivan WC. Growing up in the inner city: green spaces as places to grow. *Environ Behav.* 1998; 30(1):3–27.
40. Wells N. At home with nature: Effects of "greenness" on children's cognitive functioning. *Environ Behav.* 2000; 32(6):775–795.
41. Ulrich RS, Parsons R. Influences of passive experiences with plants on individual well being and health. Proc. *The Role of Horticulture in Human Well-Being and Social Development: A National Symposium.* Timber Press, Portland, OR. 1992. pp. 93–105.
42. Ulrich RS. Natural versus urban scenes: Some psychophysiological effects. *Environ Behav.* 1981; 13(5):523–556.
43. Ulrich RS. View through a window may influence recovery from surgery. *Science.* 1984; 224:420–421.
44. Kaplan S, Talbot JF, Kaplan R. Coping with daily hassles: the impact of nearby nature on the work environment. Project Report. USDA Forest Service, North Central Forest Experiment Station, Urban Forestry Unit Cooperative Agreement 1988. 23-85-08.
45. Moore EO. A prison environment's effect on health care service demands. *Journal of Environ Syst.* 1981; 11:17–34.
46. Talbot J, Kaplan R. Needs and fears: The response to trees and nature in the inner city. *J Arboriculture.* 1984; 10:222–228.
47. Kuo F, Sullivan W. Environment and crime in the inner city: Does vegetation reduce crime? *Environ Behav.* 2001; 33(3):343–367.
48. Armstrong D. A survey of community gardens in upstate New York: Implications for health promotion and community development. *Health and Place.* 2000; 6:319–327.

49. Chakravarthy MV, Joyner MJ, Booth FW. An obligation for primary care physicians to prescribe physical activity to sedentary patients to reduce the risk of chronic health conditions. *Mayo Clin Proceed.* 2002; 77:165–173.
50. Galloway MT, Jokl P. Aging successfully: the importance of physical activity in maintaining health and function. *J Am Acad Orthop Surg*; 2000. 8(1): 37–44.
51. Relf D. Gardening really is good exercise. Virginia Polytechnical Institute. www.ext.vt.edu/departments/envirohort/articles/misc/exercise.html. 1996.
52. Centers for Disease Control and Prevention Prevalence of Overweight and Obesity Among Adults: United States, 1999. www.cdc.gov/nchs/products/pubs/pubd/hestats/obese/obse99.htm. 1999.
53. Centers for Disease Control and Prevention. Prevalence of Overweight Among Children and Adolescents: United States, 1999. www.cdc.gov/nchs/products/pubs/pubd/hestats/overwght99.htm. 1999.
54. Blair SN, Nichaman MZ. The public health problem of increasing prevalence of obesity and what should be done about it. *Mayo Clin Proceed.* 2002; 77:109–113.
55. Fullilove MT, Fullilove III, R. Place matters. pp. 77–91. In: Hofrichter R (ed.) Reclaiming the Environmental Debate: The Politics of Health in a Toxic Culture. MIT Press, Cambridge, MA. 2000.

ARTICLE 13

Cities: The Vital Core

Joel Rogers

On a cold day in February, just a couple of weeks after George W. Bush began his second term, I sat down with a dozen men and women from across the country to talk about what government could do to clean up the environment, provide workers with a living wage and fight discrimination. This was not some gripe session to coincide with the opening of another dismal four years of federal policy-making; the people who had gathered at a conference center on the shore of Lake Michigan were mayors who have the power—and the desire—to create a progressive alternative to the constant claim that government cannot be a force for good. And, as the enthusiasm that characterized the February gathering to forge a "New Cities" coalition of progressive mayors illustrated, they are not going to let the conservative interregnum at the federal level prevent them from leading the way in the cities, which remain the engines of American economic and social advancement.

Unfortunately, most Americans, even most American progressives, do not always think of cities when they consider where the antidotes to the right-wing politics of the moment are being developed—let alone where the models for the next progressive era are taking shape. In most nations, cities are a big deal—the mayor of Mexico City is likely to be his country's next president. But in America, cities are the neglected stepchildren, exploited and abused when not simply ignored. Often they are portrayed as rank collections of pathology, modern Gomorrahs deserving destruction, and often enough they get it, with the aid of racist and destructive policies. American indifference to the death of our cities regularly astounds foreign visitors: After wandering the desolate streets of Detroit on a tour of America, French intellectual Bernard-Henri Lévy pondered the "mystery of these modern ruins" and wondered whether, instead of sharing Europe's love of cities, America finds the concept of such love "perhaps foreign to it."

It is time for progressives to reconsider and realign our views on cities—the most productive and most sustainable centers of our economy, the most vital and generous centers of our culture and, potentially, the most democratic and forward-looking of our many units of government. It is time to recognize that properly organized and empowered metropolitan governments—which link cities and suburbs in pursuit of goals that cannot be achieved separately—may hold the key to rebuilding an American economy of broadly shared prosperity. And it is time, above all, to understand that these perspectives are not unduly optimistic; indeed, they are the sentiments being expressed by the mayors and City Council members who have come to refer to themselves as "new urbanists," and who are beginning to coalesce in the burgeoning New Cities and Cities for Progress movements.

Cities matter to America, and they matter especially to progressives, for three basic reasons.

The first is that, notwithstanding population loss and disinvestment, most of our population and economy is still located in our urban centers. Even narrowly defined by their central city limits, cities account for about 25 percent of the total US population. Add their adjacent suburbs to mark out what you might call the "metro core," and you get a majority of the population. Add the suburbs connected to this core and each other—what the Census describes as "metropolitan statistical areas"(MSAs)—and you get upwards of 80 percent. And since metropolitan areas are on average richer and more productive than nonmetro ones, their share of the economy is even greater than their share of the population. The metro core contains more than half the population but about two-thirds of the national economy; the broader MSAs account for close to 90 percent of the economy. Worth emphasizing is that, within metropolitan areas, the economic interdependence of suburbs to one another and the central city is high. They share common infrastructure and largely common labor and product markets. About 80 percent of the economic value these regions produce is consumed within them. Our national economy is largely and simply their aggregate. If you want to do anything about the American national economy, particularly anything constructive, it follows that you must do it with cities.

The second reason is that cities contain the natural base of progressive politics. The metro core is where the black and brown and white working class live; where union members are most densely congregated; where the middle- and upper-class liberals are; where most of our lead education and research institutions are located; where most innovation, new commerce, art and pop entertainment starts; where the associated "creative class" and "cultural workers" generally reside; and where gays, single professional women and young people with brains and attitude don't feel like freaks. Their combined presence is felt in city culture. Cities are more cosmopolitan than the rest of the country, more committed to science and reason, more skeptical of business and military bullies, more interested in new things and much more diverse and tolerant. Years of federal and state budget cuts, the bias of education-funding formulas that favor the schools of newly developed suburbs over those of aging urban cores, poor planning, racial divisions and trade policies that have shuttered once booming factories and sent service industries offshore, have made it harder for cities to function. But, at a fundamental level, cities remain home to dynamic, liberal, solution-oriented populations who, when they come together, as they did behind the candidacy of Antonio Villaraigosa to elect him mayor of Los Angeles, can use democratic structures to chart a future that reflects their shared progressive values.

In the imperfect measure provided by major party voting, this is clear enough. Behind the famous red/blue map of 2004 Electoral College results, and the pundit hokum about that map's reflecting a great cultural divide, the actual electorate appears in varying shades of purple, with a moderate opinion structure not much different from that of a generation ago. But within this purple haze of our politics, a deep blue urban archipelago of voting does stand out. Stretching across the country, it marks the islands of city life. On those islands the current generation of urban leaders is doing many new and good things— remarkable things, really—with an energy and practical intelligence and openness to experiment that should embarrass our national politicians. Far from being collections of pathology, cities are a prime source of new solutions to social problems. Indeed, well-run cities pretty much are the solution to most of those problems. Consider, for instance, the decisions of dozens of cities to abide by the Kyoto Protocol: While Washington fights the future, cities embrace it. When the mayors of the New Cities initiative gather in Chicago this month (June 2005), they will not be debating whether global warming is real; they will be developing strategies to make their communities models of energy efficiency.

This brings us to the third and most important reason progressives should pay attention to cities. The sheer size and weight of metro regions make them a point of leverage in the national economy. Businesses today can make money in two broad ways: They can compete essentially on price alone to produce lowest-common-denominator commodity goods (the "low road"), or they can compete on innovation, performance and distinctiveness, for which customers are willing to pay a premium (the "high road"). The low road is associated with downward wages, rising inequality and insecurity, poisonous labor relations, environmental damage, rootless businesses and a shattered tax base for public goods—basically, what we've seen increasingly in America during the past thirty years. The high road, in contrast, is associated with higher wages, greater shared prosperity, respect for workers, environmental sustainability, more rooted businesses and stable communities, more capable and resourced public authorities. To compete in the twenty-first century, America has to get on the high road. Unfortunately, the Bush Administration, with its rigid free-trade orthodoxy and refusal to invest in innovation, is not taking it, and neither are most of the states, which vie with one an other in a desperate race-to-the-bottom competition for the few factories that are still being built on the American mainland.

Cities are well positioned to follow the high road. Think Seattle. Think Silicon Valley. Cities and regions can do a great deal to choose the route they take to the economic future. Those choices are made easier when the federal and state governments are supportive. But even on their own, or in cooperation with one another, cities can provide an infrastructure of education and training systems, research institutions, advanced physical infrastructure, systems to promote cross-firm learning, information systems to measure accurately the value of social and natural assets and the costs of their renewal, systems of social insurance (such as healthcare) to improve the efficiency of labor markets, and a bottom line "social wage" independent of particular employment.

These public goods and conventions don't move around. You build them somewhere, and they stay there. And when they are well developed, companies begin to depend on them. These relationships give communities—and interest groups within them, such as trade unions—greater bargaining power. The synergy that is created when cities develop their social infrastructure does not just help create and keep jobs. By massively reducing waste in the economy, it can also massively reduce private consumption costs and increase real disposable incomes. Almost 60 percent of average household income is now spent on housing, transportation, utility bills, and healthcare; savings of 40–50 percent in all these areas could now be achieved through better organization, yielding a 25–30 percent permanent increase in workers' disposable income. And through their effects, workers in high-road communities are made more secure, more truly equal in enjoying the gift that membership in those communities provides and more willing to do constructive things to preserve and improve these communities. High-road cities thus accept the efficiency of markets but supplement that efficiency with the productivity of democracy.

Are cities going to create their own single-payer healthcare systems? Not in the short term. But especially where state governments are cooperative, they can create structures that lower healthcare costs while expanding access. And they can do even more in other areas. It is, for instance, much easier and economical to develop mass transit where there are lots of potential riders. The cost of a street light or sewer connector is no greater on a crowded street than on a nearly empty one, but more people get the benefits and the costs are more broadly spread.

These are not utopian calculations. They work because American cities inherit vast assets from their past—built infrastructure, residential and commercial stock, diverse human capital—which are a lot cheaper to fix or improve than build anew. They already have the preponderance of our most advanced companies, and they are overrepresented in the more knowledge-intensive economy we need to expand in the future. They already have a much larger share of their workers in this "new economy" than other regions (about 60 percent, as compared with 46 percent in the suburbs, and a tiny and rapidly dwindling share in rural areas), which is a big reason why the downtowns of many cities, even in the current anemic recovery, are booming. Knowledge industries require information exchange, and cities facilitate that through density, the all-time promoter of chat.

This is where the new-urbanist mayors come into the equation. Particularly in booming college towns such as Palo Alto, Madison, Ann Arbor, and Boulder, local officials have emerged as critical players in the sort of high-road economic development that is creating jobs without many of the challenges—pollution, heavy infrastructure demands—that once were associated with attracting and expanding industries.

But this is not just a college-town equation. Cities in general benefit from broad demographic and cultural trends: a growth in immigration, with cities and their inner suburbs the first destination of most new arrivals; a post-boomer boom of empty-nesters who are attracted to low-maintenance condo life, shorter commutes and more cultural amenities than suburbs offer; a growing population of elderly, eager to preserve their independence and seeking access to quality healthcare and personal services; an increase in the number of "non traditional" lifestyles and living arrangements, attracting everyone from single professional women without children to those raising kids on their own, same-sex couples with children and without, and people just deferring marriage or too busy with careers to bother thinking about mating—most of whom find the diversity, tolerance, and crowded anonymity of cities more welcoming than suburban or rural life. As a result, cities have begun to reverse past trends of population loss; in the past decade, cities as distinct as Atlanta, Chicago, Denver, and Memphis have experienced population growth, often for the first time in decades.

Such signs of life make the prospects for building a brighter future seem more realistic than at any time in recent years. What stands in the way is, as ever, politics: a federal budget that essentially sends the message "Bush to Cities: Drop Dead"; state policies that promote sprawl; regional politics that pit natural allies—central cities and older suburbs—against each other. But a growing number of young and innovative officials are finding ways to reduce the frustrations by working together and by borrowing ideas from one another and from some of the brightest thinkers on the planet.

The mayors I have worked with display an optimism and enthusiasm I have not seen enough of among progressives in recent years. It's infectious. We cannot abandon our struggles at the federal and state levels. But we need to turn more of our attention to the hometown fights that are far more winnable than distant battles in Washington. We always say we're for grassroots politics. Well, the grassroots are growing in our cities.

Afterword

In this article first published in *The Nation*, Joel Rogers argues for the centrality of cities to the future and their potential for economic and social development. Cities matter to the United States for three basic reasons. First, the majority of the population and the economy of the country are located within cities and their adjacent suburbs or "metro cores"; together they can form the natural base of progressive politics. Second, cities are where cultural workers, community organizers and the "creative" class live. Far from being collections of pathology, cities are a prime source of new solutions to social problems. Third, cities are positioned to take "the high road" rather than join the race "to the bottom," by developing their social infrastructure, reducing waste in the economy, reducing private consumption costs, and increasing real disposable incomes. High-road cities thus accept the efficiency of the markets but supplement with the productivity of democracy.

Article Credits

Section I: The Social Environment

Chapter 1: *The Age of Extremes: Concentrated Affluence and Poverty in the Twenty-First Century, Douglas S. Massey*

From Douglas Massey. The Age of Extremes: Concentrated Affluence and Poverty in the Twenty-First Century. *Demography*. Vol. 33, No. 4, Nov. 1996, pp. 395–412. Reprinted with permission from the Population Association of America.

Chapter 2: *Health Inequities in the United States: Prospects and Solutions, Dennis Raphael*

From Dennis Raphael. Health Inequities in the United States: Prospects and Solutions. *Journal of Public Health Policy*. Vol. 21, No. 4, 2000, pp. 394–427. Reprinted with permission of author.

Chapter 3: *To Mitigate, Resist, or Undo: Addressing Structural Influences on the Health of Urban Populations, Arline T. Geronimus, ScD*

From Arline T. Geronimus. To Mitigate, Resist, or Undo: Addressing Structural Influences on the Health of Urban Populations. *American Journal of Public Health*. Vol. 90, No. 6, June 2000, pp. 867–872. Reprinted with permission from the American Public Health Association.

Chapter 4: *Neighborhoods and Violent Crime: A Multilevel Study of Collective Efficacy, Robert J. Sampson, Stephen W. Raudenbush, Felton Earls*

From Robert J. Sampson, Stephen W. Raudenbush, and Felton Earls. Neighborhoods and Violent Crime: A Multilevel Study of Collective Efficacy. *SCIENCE*. Vol. 277, No. 5328, August 15, 1997, pp. 918–924. Reprinted with permission from AAAS.

Section II: The Built Environment

Chapter 5: Housing and Health: Time Again for Public Health Action,
James Krieger, MD, MPH, and Donna L. Higgins, PhD

From. James Krieger and Donna Higgins. Housing and Health: Time Again
for Public Health Action. *American Journal of Public Health*. Vol. 92, No. 5,
May 2002, pp. 758–768. Reprinted with permission from the American Public
Health Association.

Chapter 6: Indoor Environments and Health: Moving Into
the 21st Century, Jonathan M. Samet, MD, MS,
and John D. Spengler, PhD

From Jonathan M. Samet and John D. Spengler. Indoor Environments and
Health: Moving Into the 21st Century. *American Journal of Public Health*. Vol.
93, No. 9, September 2003, pp.1489–1493. Reprinted with permission from the
American Public Health Association.

Chapter 7: Urban Sprawl and Public Health, Howard Frumkin

From Howard Frumkin. Urban Sprawl and Public Health. *Public Health Reports*.
Vol. 117, May–June 2002, 201–217. Reprinted with permission from the Association of Schools of Public Health.

Chapter 8: Obesity, Physical Activity, and the Urban Environment:
Public Health Research Needs, Russell P. Lopez,
and H. Patricia Hynes

From Russell Lopez and H. Patricia Hynes. Obesity, Physical Activity, and the
Urban Environment: Public Health Research Needs. *Environmental Health: A
Global Access Science Source*, Vol. 5, No. 25, September 18, 2006.

Section III: The Physical Environment

Chapter 9: Health, Wealth, and Air Pollution: Advancing Theory
and Methods, Marie S. O'Neill, Michael Jerrett,
Ichiro Kawachi, Jonathan I. Levy, Aaron J. Cohen,
Nelson Gouveia, Paul Wilkinson, Tony Fletcher,
Luis Cifuentes, and Joel Schwartz

From Marie S. O'Neill, Michael Jerrett, Ichiro Kawachi, Jonathan I. Levy, Aaron
J. Cohen, Nelson Gouveia, Paul Wilkinson, Tony Fletcher, Luis Cifuentes, and

Joel Schwartz, with input from the participants of the Workshop on Air Pollution and Socioeconomic Conditions. Health, Wealth, and Air Pollution: Advancing Theory and Methods. *Environmental Health Perspectives.* Vol. 111, No. 16, December 2003, pp.1861–1870. Reprinted with permission from *Environmental Health Perspectives.*

Chapter 10: Examining Urban Brownfields Through the Public Health, Jill S. Litt, Nga L. Tran, and Thomas A. Burke

From Jill S. Litt , Nga L. Tran, and Thomas A. Burke. Examining Urban Brownfields Through the Public Health "Macroscope." *Environmental Health Perspectives.* Vol. 110, Supplement 2, April 2002, pp. 183–193. Reprinted with permission from *Environmental Health Perspectives.*

Chapter 11: A Current Appraisal of Toxic Wastes and Race in the United States—2007, Robin Saha

From Robin Saha. *Toxic Wastes and Race at Twenty 1987–2007: A Report Prepared for the United Church of Christ Justice & Witness Ministries.* Chapter 4, A Current Appraisal of Toxic Wastes and Race in the Untied States—2007. Copyright © March 2007. United Church of Christ. All rights reserved. Used by permission.

Chapter 12: Urban Horticulture in the Contemporary United States: Personal and Community Benefits, H. Patricia Hynes and Genevieve Howe

From H. P. Hynes and G. Howe. Urban Horticulture In the Contemporary United States: Personal And Community Benefits. *Acta Hort.* 2004. (ISHS) 643:171–181. http://www.actahort.org/books/643/643_21.htm. Reprinted with permission from ISHS.

Chapter 13: Cities: The Vital Core, Joel Rogers

From Joel Rogers. Cities: The Vital Core. *The Nation.* June 20, 2005. pp. 20–22. Reprinted with permission from the June 20, 2005 issue of *The Nation* magazine.

Index

outcomes, health, air pollution and, 195
outdoor spaces, and physical activity, 175.
    See also greenspace
overweight
    disease associated with, 146
    disparities in, 170
    in minority populations, 154
    prevalence of, 146, 271
    and suburbs, 170
ozone
    exposure to, 197
    formation of, 142, 149
    and prevalence of asthma, 200
    and respiratory symptoms, 143

P

P* isolation index, 9
Pan American Health Organization's
    environmental health plan, 57
parenting, 44
parking facilities, and physical activity, 176
parks
    New York Central Park, 187, 261
    renovation of, 175
pedestrian fatalities, among minority groups,
    154
pedestrians, injuries and fatalities of, 145
people-plant interaction studies, 269
Personal Responsibility and Work
    Opportunity Reconciliation Act
    (PRWORA) (1996), 69, 70
pest infestations, in substandard housing,
    102–103
PHDCN. See Project on Human
    Development in Chicago
    Neighborhoods
Philadelphia, 144, 145, 264
Phoenix, 144, 145
phthalates, in built environment, 135
physical activity
    and built environment, 180
    disparities in, 170
    gardening, 271
    and income inequality, 177
    of inner-city residents, 171, 172, 173
    and suburbs, 170
    and urban sprawl, 146
plasticizers, in brownfields study, 229
playgrounds, renovation of, 175
politics
    and housing issues, 117
    and housing policy, 109–110
    progressive, 282

pollutants
    distribution of air, 196
    physiochemical behavior of, 197
    primary and secondary, 194
pollutants, indoor, 130, 198
    asbestos, 132
    biological agents, 133
    from cooking and heating, 133
    involuntary smoking, 131, 132
    nitrogen dioxide, 133
    radon, 132
pollution. *See also* air pollution; water
        pollution
    indoors, 99–100
    and poverty, 191–192
    residential indoor air, 131
polybrominated diphenyl esters, in built
        environment, 135
polychlorinated biphenyls (PCBs), in built
        environment, 135
polycyclic aromatic hydrocarbons, and water
        pollution, 148
polyvinyl chloride flooring, and chronic
        disease, 103
the poor
    access to education of, 23
    class isolation among, 9
    decreased mobility of, 12
    exposure of violence to, 27–28
    and tax cuts, 53
    as topic of study, 29
    and urban health, xvii
Portland, 144, 145
postindustrial era, 17–18
    access to education in, 23
    consumer markets in, 18
poverty
    of African Americans, 69
    in brownfields study, 224, 226
    and collective efficacy, 92
    concentrated, 12
    and crime, 79
    and education of children, 28
    effects on health of, 39–40, 66
    geographically concentrated, 26
    and industrial revolution, 6
    invisibility of, xviii
    and location of hazardous waste facilities,
        252
    measuring, 83
    in metropolitan areas, 10, 11–12
    in Mexico, 16
    policies to reduce, 54
    political ecology of, 22–23